DISPLACEMENT AND REHABILITATION IN NEPAL

DISPLACEMENT AND REHABILITATION IN NEPAL

Law, Policy and Practice

By

DR. ANANDA MOHAN BHATTARAI

ANMOL PUBLICATIONS PVT. LTD.

NEW DELHI - 110 002 (INDIA)

ANMOL PUBLICATIONS PVT. LTD.
4374/4B, Ansari Road, Daryaganj
New Delhi - 110 002

Displacement and Rehabilitation in Nepal: Law, Policy and Practice

First Edition, 2001

ISBN 81-261-0959-9

Author's address
Shantinagar, Baneswar-34
Kathmandu
PO Box 7044, Nepal
Email: anandmb@enet.com.np

PRINTED IN INDIA

Published by J.L. Kumar for Anmol Publications Pvt. Ltd., New Delhi - 110 002 and Printed at Mehra Offset Press, Delhi.

Dedicated to
The Project Affected Persons,
The Victims of Unaccounted State Power

CONTENTS

FOREWORD

It was a matter of great interest and pleasure for me to go through the doctoral research work carried out by Dr. Ananda Mohan Bhattarai in one of the highly debatable issues of involuntary displacement on account of 'development projects'. The author has made an attempt to look at the issue of displacement in the broader framework of development conceived by the Constitution of Nepal and various existing as well as emerging international and regional norms on human rights and environment.

As has been pointed out by the author, the Constitution of Nepal shuns the paternalistic approach to development and looks at it within the framework of rights. Under this, various developmental issues like food, nutrition, health care, housing, clean and healthy environment, protection of heritage sites etc. that are essential for a dignified life, are looked as constitutive rights fitting into the broader sweep of the right to life. This approach of the Constitution of Nepal, to my mind, discards the need based concept of development and opens up a dialogic space for a consultative and participatory process. It thereby resonates to the definition of development advanced by the UN Declaration on Right to Development which takes development as a comprehensive social, economic and political process requiring active and meaningful participation in the decision making and benefit sharing. This process does not decenter the state but makes it more accountable to people's developmental aspirations. In other words, this process puts people before the project, weaves development around people and allows imposition of restriction on livelihood rights only when overriding public interest, not achievable by other means, requires so. While imposing restriction the state needs to prove convincingly that the proposed venture has real public use or benefit, as in such cases, presumption always lies in favor of rights.

Another noteworthy aspect of our Constitution is that it proposes to establish a just order striving to ensure economic, social and political justice. A just order is an order of reason. The bottom line for state activities under such an order is that it needs to do justice not only to the beneficiaries of development but also to those who bear the brunt of it. What in essence is required by the Constitution is that development activities do not result in concentration of wealth within a small cross-section at the livelihood cost of millions.

While examining the issue of project induced displacement the author at the very outset argues that the Constitution guarantees no fewer rights to project affected persons(PAPs) than it does to others. To substantiate this further, the author proceeds to examine and analyze various rights enumerated in the Constitution in the light of the jurisprudential premise of rights. After making a detailed analysis of the rights that come to the fore in the context of displacement, he argues that under the Constitution of Nepal the PAPs do possess a right not to be arbitrarily displaced. This seems logical especially in the light of the recognition of rights in the burgeoning constitutional and human rights literature, and also in the light of immense human, social and environmental cost that displacement brings. When such a right is fully entrenched, imposition of restriction becomes possible only when the restriction meets both substantive and procedural requirements. In other words, the restriction should be within the permissible grounds justifying the same, respond to a pressing public or social need, pursue legitimate aim and be appropriate to the aim. Secondly, imposition of restriction is possible only when it is imposed by law or is under the authority of law, and not by executive fiat. Such a law no doubt should be a valid law and not a mere nomenclature.

The juxtaposition of constitutional and international norms with the existing normative and institutional framework of Nepal for project identification, acquisition of property and resettlement of PAPs is another important part of the present work. Here, the author examines the South Asian legal regime on land acquisition where he dexterously draws the parallelism that prevails in our thinking process. The laws examined by the author bear similar weaknesses and suffer from the same malaise of over reliance on executive wisdom. I agree with the author that there is a lack of sufficient judicial agility and alertness to curb executive indiscretion in the exercise of sovereign power of eminent domain. However, it would not be wholly correct to state that the judiciary has adopted a policy of total hands off with regard to curbing the abuse of executive power. In a number of cases the courts of Nepal and India, for instance, have quashed the government decisions on acquisition for not serving public purpose or vaguely stating public purpose. Where Courts have found that there is a colourable exercise of sovereign power they have not hesitated to stamp it out.

Most of the problems that have affected PAPs adversely have cropped up due to the lack of correct approach to displacement, resettlement and rehabilitation and due to a legal vacuum that exists in most of the countries. Even where displacement results as legal consequence the issue of resettlement and rehabilitation is left to executive mercy. It is my considered view that the author has done a commendable job by presenting an outline of the policy and law on displacement, resettlement and rehabilitation. While I congratulate the author for his seminal contribution, I have only one fear in my mind that the legislative solution which he is advancing may judicialise the whole developmental process and ultimately harm those whose interest it intends to protect, as people belonging to the lower bracket of the socio-economic ladder have chances of remaining at the receiving end of judicial adventure. But all the same I should not hesitate to put on record here that the minor snag which might appear in adopting the solution advanced by the author can be avoided through judicial pragmatism. I have no hesitation in recommending the book to the academics, activists, students and other interested people of South Asia.

Keshav Prasad Upadhyaya
Chief Justice
Supreme Court of Nepal

ACKNOWLEDGEMENTS

The present work is a substantially based on findings of doctoral research work carried out at National Law School of India for the degree of Doctor in Jurisprudential Science during 1998-2000. A number of people have supported in varied ways and helped me to carry out and complete this otherwise arduous task. In retrospect, I am beholden with gratitude to all of them.

At the outset I would like to place on record my sincere thanks to Dr. N.L. Mitra, Professor of Law and Director of National Law School of India University, Bangalore, for calling me back to NLSIU and offering me an opportunity to pursue J.S.D. studies, arranging financial support and guiding and supervising the work. This work has benefited in a great deal from his jurisprudential thoughts, incisive comments and critical estimations.

I also place on record my sincere thanks and appreciation to Rt Hon'ble Sri Om Bhakta Shrestha, Chief Justice (retd.), Nepal for sparing me from the judicial responsibility and granting study leave.

I am thankful to Dr. M.V. Nadkarni, Professor and Vice-Chancellor, Gulbarga University, Karnataka for his guidance and comments on the draft of this work. Dr. Sitaramam Kakarla, Asst. Professor, NLSIU, was kind enough to provide guidance from the day one of this work all through up to the final stage. I extend my sincere thanks to Dr. Ram.

Prof. T. Devidas has been the guiding light and continuing source of inspiration throughout the research period. He was kind enough to go through the draft and give his comment both on content and language. I am obliged to him.

I am also indebted to Prof A. Jaygovind, Prof V. Vijay Kumar, Prof G. Ajappa, Prof Babu Matthew, Dr Ravi Ghorane and several other members of the Faculty of NLSIU with whom I had interacted on several occasions and benefited from their ideas.

Thanks are also due to several other persons. My friend Prof Surya Subedi, School of Law, University of Hull, England was constantly in touch through e-mail in the progress of this work. I owe to him for his ideas on the position of Nepal vis-à-vis international legal regime.

I am also thankful to Prof Ben Boer of Sidney University, Prof. Nicholas Robinson, Pace Law School, USA, Dr Mohan Gopal, Regional Legal Counsel, World Bank, Mr Paneer Sylvam, World Bank, Delhi, Mr Walter Fernandes, ISI, Delhi, for their insights and support during the progress of this work.

My friends at NLSIU, Mr Mohd Sawad (Maldives), Mr T.S.K. Hameratne (Sri Lanka), Mr Raza (Bangladesh), Mr Chhoining Dorjee (Bhutan) and friends from Nepal, Mr Kedar Paudyal, Mr Saroj Shrestha and Mr Hari Phuyal, Mr Achyut Bista, Mr Kulratna Bhurtyal, Mr Madhav Paudel and Mr Diwakar Chapagain were instrumental in supplying important documents and information. Mr Rakesh Kumar, a brilliant LL.M. scholar at NLSIU, whom I was fortunate to mingle with during my stay at Bangalore, was helpful to me both intellectually and logistically. Despite his busy academic schedule, he took pain to go through each and every page of my work and gave comment on several aspects of the work. My sister Anu K., an LL.M. scholar at NLSIU, quite unmindful of her several academic works and an approaching marriage, proofread several chapters. Mr Antony Dias and Ms. Rooma Chakravarty, doctoral colleagues, Mr Srihari Phanikumar, Mr Ashutosh Mishra, LL.M scholars, and Mr Navaras Chaulagain also went through various part of the work and gave their comments. I am thankful to all of them.

My friend Mr Bibhu Prasad Tripathy was always with me in good times and bad times to inspire me to surmount several hardships that came across during the study.

My brother judge Mr Yagya Prasad Basyal provided logistic support and made my stay comfortable during my field study at the Royal Suklaphanta Wildlife Reserve. I got the support of Mr Laxman Karki, Mr Govinda Bhandari who introduced me to the respondents in carrying out the work at the Pokhara Airport Project. I express my sincere thanks to them. Sincere thanks are also due to all interviewees—the displaced and affected persons of both the projects who by their willing co-operation made my task so easy.

I express my thanks to my mother and other family members for their moral support. Thanks are also due to my wife Pushpa, who had to shoulder single handedly all the responsibility of running the household while I was away for studies, and to my kids Samhita and Samir, to whom I could not provide filial attention and care.

Last, but not the least I would like to extend my sincere thanks to Rt. Hon'ble Sri Keshav Prasad Upadhyaya, the Chief Justice of Nepal, for inscribing a foreword for the book and Anmol Publications Pvt. Ltd., New Delhi for taking initative for publication.

Ananda Mohan Bhattarai

TABLE OF CASES

a) Nepal

Baburam Paudel v HMG/Cabinet Secretariat NKP 1994 (2051) 143

Balakrishna Neupane v Parliament Secretariat, NKP 1993 (2050) 450

Balakrishna Neupane v PM Girija Prasad Koirala, 1:11 *S.Ct Bulletin* 11992 (2049)

Balakrishna Neupane v. Ministry of Water Resource, NKP 1997 (2053) 210

Bedkrishna Shrestha v Department of Industries, Commerce, Food and Civil Supplies NKP 1959(2016) p. 234

Ganesh Bahadur Shrestha v Office of the Regional Police Unit, NKP 1994 (2051) p 388

Gopal Sivakoti v Ministry of Finance, NKP 1994 *(2051)256*

Iman Singh Gurung v HMG/ Council of Ministers, NKP 1992(2049) p. 710, 725

Jagannath Das Baisnav v District Office, Dhanusha NK.P 1987(2044) p.1211

Krishna Bahadur Gurung v HMG/Cabinet Secretariat, NKP 1995(2052) p. 227

Krishna Bahadur Kunwar v Special Police Department, NKP 1994(2051) p. 550

Leaders Inc v Godavari Marble Industries 4 S.Ct. Bulletin 1 Feb, 1997(Magh 16-29, 2052)

Nanda Kumari Rawal v Ministry of Industry, NKP 2051(1994) p. 180

Netraraj Upadhyaya v HMG/Dept. of Industry, NKP 1968(2025) p. 308

Prakash Mani Sharma v HMG/Cabinet Secretariat NKP 1998(2054) p 312

Private and Boarding School Organization v HMG , NKP 1994(2051) p.609

Purna Chaitanya Brahmachari v HMG/Cabinet Secretariat, NKP, 2044 (1987) p.1076

Ram Kishore Prasad v HMG/Ministry of Food and Agriculture [Writ no 1177 of the yr. 1971(2028) judgment dated July 26,1971 (2028/3/10/4 BS)

Rishikesh Shah v HMG/Ministry of Finance NKP 1994 (2051) p 302

Siddhi Bahadur Shrestha v Royal Nepal Martial Court, NKP 1994 (2051) p. 634

Sita Bista v Ministry of Home NK.P 2051 (1995) p 852

Sumitra Devi Marwadi v HMG/Ministry of Industry and Commerce (writ no 742 of the year 1973(2030) - unpublished judgment dated Aug 26,1975(2032/5/10 BS)

Surya P.S. Dhungel v Godavari Marbles, NKP (Golden Jubilee Issue) 1995 (2052) p.169

Yogi Naraharinath v Prime Minister 5 S.Ct Bulletin 5, Aug. 1998 (Bhadra 1-15, 2053)

Yagyamurti Banjade v Bagmati Special Court, NKP 1970(2027) p.57

b. India

A.D. M. Jabalpur v Shivakant Shukla (1976) 2 SCC 521

Aflatoon v Lt Gov. Delhi (1975)4 SCC 28

Arnold Rodricks v State of Maharastra AIR 1966 SC 1788

Arya Krishnan Shivaghal v Union of India (1996) 10 SCC 72

Babu Baskya Thakur v State of Bombay AIR 1960 SC 1203

Baldev Singh Dhillon v Union of India 1998 AIHC 1

Benwasi Seva Ashram v State of UP AIR 1992 SC 920

Budhan Chaudhary v State of Bihar AIR 1955 SC 191

Chaitram Verma v L. Acq. Officer, Raipur AIR 1994 MP 74

Charanjit Lal v Union of India AIR 1951 SC 41

Chemile Sing v State of UP (1996)2SCC 549

Dahanu Taluka E. P. Group v Bombay Suburban Electricity Supply Co. AIR 1991 SC 910

E.P. Royappa v State of Tamilnadu AIR 1974 SC 555,583-84

Franjee Petit v Secretary of State 42 IA 44

Gadadhar Ghosh v State of West Bengal AIR 1963 Cal 565

Gandhi Grah Nirman Sahakari Samiti v State of Raj AIR 1994 SC 2329

Goa Foundation v Konkan Railway AIR 1992 Bombay 471

Golakh Nath v State of Punjab AIR 1967 SC 1643

Gramin Seva Samstha v State of MP 1986 (supp) SCC 578

Gramophone Company of India v Birendra Bahadur Pandey, AIR 1984 SC 667

Gurudas Shah v First Land Acquisition Officer of Calcutta AIR 1957 Cal 495

Habib Ahmad v State of U.P AIR 1965 All. 349

Hambai Framjee v Secretary of State for India AIR 1914 PC 20

Hannovara Taluka Parisara v State of Karnataka dated 2/11/1990 (writ no 8170 of 1988 Karnataka HC)

Jaga Ram v State of Haryana AIR 1971 SC1033

Jai Narayan v UOI (1996) 1 SCC 9

Jiwani Kumar Paraki v First Land Acquisition Collector (1984)4 SCC 612

Jolly George Varghese v Bank of Cochin AIR 1980 SC 470

Julubhai Nanbhai Khachar v State of Gujarat 1995 Supp(1)SCC 596

Kamalnath v Union of India (1997)1 SCC 388

Kanayalal Maneklal Chinai v State of Gujarat (1969) 3 SCC 456

Kaijan Jalasay Yojana Sangarsh Samiti v State of Gujarat AIR 1987SC 352

Karnataka STDC v Karnataka STATE (1986)4 SCC 421,430

Keshavananda Bharati v State of Kerala (1973)4 SCC 225

Lachhman Das v Municipal Committee, Jalalabad (1969)1SCC 653; AIR 1969 SC 1126

Laxmi Kant Pandey v Union of India AIR 1987 SC 232

Life Insurance Corporation of India v Consumer Education and Research Centre (1995)5 SCC 482

Lindsley V Natural Carbonic Gas Co 220 US 61(1911)M.C. Mehta v Tamilnadu (1996) 6 SCC 756

M.C. Mehta v Kamalnath(1997)1 SCC 38

Madhya Pradesh Housing Board v Mohd Shafi (1992)2 SCC 168

Maganbhai Patel v Union of India, AIR 1969SC 783,792

Maneka Gandhi v Union of India AIR 1978 SC 597

Mithu v State of Punjab (1983) 2 SCC 277, AIR 1983 SC 473

New Riveria Housing Society v Special Land Acquisition Officer (1996)1 SCC 731

Nilabati Behra v State of Orissa (1993) 2 SCC 746; AIR 1993 SC 2366

P.G. Gupta v State of Gujarat 1995 supp(2) SCC 182

P. Vejravelu Mudaliar v Special Dy Collector for Land Acquisition AIR 1965 SC16

Pandit Jhandu Lal v State of Punjab AIR 1961 SC 343

People's Union for Civil Liberties v Union of India, JT 1997(2) SC 311

Peoples' Union for Civil Liberties v Union of India (1997)1 5CC 301

PUDR v Union of India AIR 1982 SC 1473

R. C. Cooper v Union of India AIR 1970 SC 564(1970) 1 SCC 248

R.K. Agrawala v State of West Bengal AIR 1965 SC 995

R.L. Arora v State of U.P. AIR 1958 All. 872

Raja Anand Brahma Shah v State of Punjab AIR 1967SC 1081

Ram Chand v Union of India (1994) 1 SCC 44

Ram Jawaya Kapur v State of Punjab (1955) 2 SCR 255

Ram Narayan Singh v State of Bihar AIR 1978 Pat. 136

Ranikrishna Dalmia v J. S.R. Tendolkar AIR 1958 SC 538

Ratni Devi v Chief Commissioner (1975) 4 SCC 467

Rural Litigation Entitlement Kendra v State of UP, AIR 1985SC 539, AIR 1985SC 652

S. Jagannath v Union of India (1997)2 SCC 87

S. Sivaprakasa Mudaliar v State of Madras AIR 1964 Mad 115

S.S Darshan v State of Karnataka (1996)7SCC 302 AIR 1996 SC 671

Sachindra Mohan Nandy v State of West Bengal AIR 1963, Cal 373, 380

Sagir Ahmad v State of UP AIR 1954 SC 728

Samatha v State of AP (1997)65CC 47

Sami Motor v Shankaraswami Mutt AIR 1963 SC 864

Shah & Co v State of Maharashtra AIR SC 1877

Somawanti v State of Punjab AIR 1963 SC SC 151

Somawanti v State of Punjab AIR 1963SC 151

Srivinisa Cooperative House v Madam Gurumurthy Sastry (1994) 45CC 675

State of Bihar v Kameswar Prasad Singh AIR 1952 SC 252

State of Bombay v R.S. Nanji AIR 1956 SC 294, 297

State of Gujarat v Musamigau Imam Haider AIR 1977 SC 594

State of Gujarat v Shantilal Mangaldas AIR 1969 SC 634

State of Karnataka v Narasimhamurthy (1995) 5 SCC 524

State of Karnataka v Ranganatha Reddy (1977) 4 SCC 471

State of MP v Ranjijirao Shinde AIR 1968 SC 1053

State of T.N. v L Krishnan (1996) 1 5CC 250

State of Tamilnadu v L Knishnan AIR 1996 SC 497

State of WB v Subodh Gopal Bose AIR 1954 SC 92

State of West Bengal v Union of India, AIR 1963 SC 1241

State of Karnataka v Narusimhamurthy (1995)5 SCC 524

Subash Kuniar v State of Bihar, AIR 1991 SC 420

Tilak Ram Wada v State of Punjab AIR 1956 Punj. 83

Tractoroexport, Moscow v M/s Tarapore & Co. (1969) 3 5CC 562

Union of India v Metal Corporation AIR 1967 SC 637

UP Avas E. V. Nigam v Friends Coop Housing Society Ltd 1995 Supp(3)SCC 456

UP Avas Evam Vikash Nigam v. Friends Coop Housing Society 1995 supp(3) SCC 456

Vellore Citizens Forum v Union of India AIR 1996 SC 2715, (1996) 5 SCC 647

Visakha v State of Rajasthan AIR 1997 SC 3011

Visakha v State of Rajasthan JT 1997 (7) SC 384; AIR 1997 SC 3011

West Bengal v Bela Banerjee AIR 1954 SC 170

c. Bangladesh

Mohiuddin Farooque v Bangladesh 48 DLR 1996

d. Pakistan

General Secretary, West Pakistan Salt Miners Labour Union Khwra Khelum v Director,

Industries and Mineral Development, Punjab, 196 SC MR 206 1(Pakistan)

e. Phillipine

Juan Antonio et at (minors) v Secretary, Department of Environment and National Resources 33ILM173(1994)

f. The US

Adams v Housing Authority of Daytona Beach (Fla) 60 So2d 663

Alpin v Clinton County (Iowa) 129 NW 2d 726

Armstong v US 364 US40, 49 (1960)

Belovsky v Redevelopment Authority, 357 **Pa**329, 54 A 2d. 277, 172 ALR 953

Birmingam v Brown 241 Ala 203, 2 So 2d 305

Blackwell Lumber Co v Empire Mill Cp 28 **Idaho** 556, 115 p. 680

Boom Co v Patterson, 98 US 403,406 (1878)

Browneller v Natural Gas Pipeline Co 233 **Iowa** 686, 8 NW 2d 474,

Charlotte v Heath 226 NC 750, 40 **SE** 2d 600, 169 ALR 569)

Charlottee v Heath 226 NC 750, 405 SE 2d 600, 169 ALR 569

Cincinnati v Vester (CA 6) 33 F2d 242, 68 ALR 831, affd 281 US 439, 74 L ed 950, 50 S. Ct. 360

Citing Blamtpm v Fagerstrom, 249 A1a485, 31 So 2d 330 172 ALR 128

Connecticut v Calvert, 87 Conn 421, 88 A 633

Ccx v Revelle 125 Md 579,94 ALR 203

Delaware L & W.R. Co v Morrison 276 US 182).

Dohany v Rogers 281 US 362, 74Led 904, 50 S.Ct 299, 684 ALR 434

Dolan v City of Tigard 114 S.Ct 2309, 2319 (1994)

Fallsburg Power and Mfg Co v Alaxender, 101 Va 98 43 SE 194

Gaylord v Sanitary Dist. 204 **Iu** 576, 68 NE 522

Georgia v Chattanooga 264 US 472, 68 L ed 796, 44 S. Ct. 369

Hawaii Hous. Auth. V Midkiff 467 US 229 (1984)

International News Service v The Associated Press 248 U.S. 215 (1918)

Jacobs v US 290 Us 13, 78 Led 142, 54 S.Ct 26, 96 ALR 1

Khol v United States 91 US 367,376 (1876)

King County v Seattle Cedar Lumber Mfg Co 94 Wash 84,162 p 27

Minnesota Canal & Power Co. v Kooching Co. 47 Minn. 429,107 NW 404

Mt Vernon Berry Cotton Dock cc v Albama Interstate Power Co 240 US 80, 60 L ed 507, 36 S.Ct 234;

Nicholas v Central Virginia Power Cc, 143 Va 405,130 SE 764, 44 ALR 727

Nichols v Central Virginia Power Co. 143 **Va** 405, 130 SE 764, 44 ALR 727

Nollan v California Coastal Commission 483 US 825 (1987)

Penn Central Transportation Cd. v New York City 438 US 104, 124 (1978)

Riden v Philadelphia B & W. R. Co 182 Md 336, 35 A 2d 99

Ridge Co v Los Angeles County 262 US 700 67 Led 1186,43 S.Ct 689

Rogers v Toccoa Power cc 161 GA 524, 131 SE 51744 ALR 534

Schulmanv People 10 NY 249, 176NE2d817,219NYS2d241

Smith v City Board of Education, 272, **Ala 227,130** So 2d 29

Southern Bell Tell Co v Newwingham (Mo app) 386, SW 2d 663

Strickley v Highland Boy Gold Mm Cc, 200 US 527, 50 Led 581, 26 S.Ct 301

United States v Jones, 109 US 513,518 (1883)

United States v Miller 317 US 369 87 Led 366, 63 5. Ct 276, ALR 55

Vetter v Broadhurst 100 Neb 356, 160 NW 109, 9 ALR 578

Weaver v Pennsylvania -Ohio Power Co (CA 6 Ohio) 10 F2d 579

West v Chesapeake and P Tel Co 295 US 662 74 Led 1640, 55 S.Ct 894

Western U Teleg. Co v Lousiville and N.R. cc 270 Iii 399, 110 NE 583

Illinois Central Railroad v People of the Illinois 146 US 387 (1892)

National Audubon Society v Superior Court of Alpine Country 33 Cal 3d 419

g. European Court

X v UK and Ireland (1982) Appl 9829/82 (Unpublished) and Simon-Herald v Austria (1971) 14 YB 351

X v UK and Ireland (1982) App! 9829/82 (Unpublished) and Simon-Herald v Austria (1971) 14 YB 351

h. ICJ

Barcelona Traction, Light and Power Co II phase judgement, ICJ Repol4s 1970 P3, 37-3 8 ii Britain and Other Jurisdictions

Attorney General of Canada v Attorney General of Ontario 1937 PC 326,

Byane v Ireland (1972) Irish Report 241

In Buvot v Barbuit [(1737) Cas. T. Talbot.2811

Minister of Immigration and Electric Affairs v Toeh 69 AUST.LR 630 (1995)

Philipson v Imperial Airways Ltd (1939) AC 332

Post Office v Estuary Radio Ltd. (1968) 2 QB 740

Quin v Ryan (1965) Irish Report 70

Salomon v Commission of Customs and Excise (1967)2 QB 144

Simpson v Attorney General (1994) New Zealand Reports 667

Triquit v Bath [(1764)4 Burr. 1478, 1479]

Zoerhseh v Waldock (1964)1 WLR 675.

LIST OF STATUTES

a) Nepal

The Breton Woods Act, 1961

The Compensation Act, 1961

The Development Board Act, 1957

The Electricity Act, 1992

The Electricity Rule, 1995

The Environmental Protection Act, 1997

The Environment Protection Rules, 1997

The Extradition Act, 1988

The Foreign Investment and Technology Transfer Act, 1992

The Forest Act, 1961

The Forest Act, 1993

The Highways (Construction) Act, 1961

The Immovable Property Requisition Act, 1955

The Irrigation Act, 1962

The Kathmandu Valley Development Authority Act, 1988

The Land Act, 1964

Land Acquisition Act of Nepal, 1977

The Land Revenue Act, 1977

The Land Survey Act, 1961

The Local Self Government Act, 1999

The MULUKI AIN (The Old Civil Code of Nepal)

The MULUKI SAWAL (Law in operation during Rana Regime in Nepal)

The Nepal Treaty Act, 1990

The Petroleum Act, 1983

The Plant Protection Act, 1977

The Public Roads Act, 1974

The Public Roads Act, 1979

The Right of the Child Act, 1990

The Rapti Doon Development Area Act, 1967

Regional Development Projects (Execution) Act, 1955

The Soil Conservation Act, 1977

The Solid Waste (Management and Resource Mobilization) Act, 1987

The Summary Procedure Act, 1997

The Tikapur Development Board Rules, 1971

The Town Development Committee Act, 1962

The Town Development Act, 1984

The Water Resource Act, 1992

The Water Resource Rule, 1995

b) India

The Bengal Regulation Act, 1824

Bombay Building Act, 1839

The Draft Land Acquisition (Amendment) Bill, 1998

Government of India Act, 1935

The Karnataka Resettlement of Project Displaced Persons Act, 1987

Land Acquisition Act, 1852

The Land Acquisition Act 1894 (India, Pakistan and Bangladesh)

The Madras Building Act, 1852

The Madhya Pradesh Pariyojana ki Karan Visthapit Vyakti Punarsthapan Adhiniyam, 1985 (The MP Project Displaced People Resettlement Act

The Maharastra Project Affected People Rehabilitation Act, 1989

Water Dispute Act, 1956

c) Sri Lanka

The Land Acquisition Act, 1950

d) Maldives

The General Laws (statute no 4J/68-1 1/1 1/1968), Maldives

The Law Relating the Transfer of *Wakf* Property in Male to Other Islands and Abolition of Wakf Property in Male (statute no 2J/70 - 12/4/1970)

e) Bhutan

LAND CODE, Bhutan

f) China

Land Administration Law 1986 (amendment 1988)

Regulation on the Acquisition of Land for State Construction Projects, 1982

Reservoir Resettlement Law and Regulation, 1981

The Law of Land Management, 1987

The Regulation for Land Requisition, Compensation and Resettlement Provision for Large and Medium sized Water Conservancy and Hydro power Projects issued by the State Council Degree no 74 PRC May 1991

The Reservoir Resettlement Design Requirement, 1985 (Issued by the Ministry of Water Resources)

GAZETTE NOTIFICATIONS

1. Nepal Gazette March 18, 1976 (Vol. 25 No 48 Chaitra 2, 2032 BS)
2. Nepal Gazette Jan. 3, 1982 (Vol. 31 add not 56. Paush 17, 2038 BS).
3. Nepal Gazette, Jan. 4 1982 (Vol. 31 add no 57 Paush 18,2038 BS)
4. Nepal Gazette Apr. 2 1, 1982 (Vol. 32 add.no 1, Baishak 5, 2039 BS);
5. Nepal Gazette, Aug. 1, 1983 (Vol. 33 Add no 13.(e) Shrawan 15, 2040 BS)
6. Nepal Gazette Jan. 6, 1988 (Vol. 37 No 37, Paus 20, 2044 BS)
7. Nepal Gazette, Apr. 19, 1990 (Vol. 40 add not 2(A) Baisakh 3, 2047 BS)
8. Nepal Gazettee May 25, 1994 (Vol. 43 no 5 Jestha 9295 1 BS)

LIST OF TABLES

LIST OF FIGURES & MAPS

LIST OF MAPS

ABBREVIATIONS

ACRP	:	Acquisition Compensation and Rehabilitation Package
AIR	:	All India Reporter
AJIL	:	American Journal of International Law
AM JUR	:	American Jurisprudence
ARC	:	Acquisition Resettlement Committee
Art	:	Article
BS	:	Bikram Samvat (the Official Calendar of Nepal)
CA	:	Compensation Act 1962/Nepal
CBSN	:	Central Bureau of Statistics/Nepal
CDO	:	Chief District Officer/Nepal
CFC	:	Compensation Fixing Committee/Nepal
Ch	:	Chapter
CPR	:	Common Property Resources Development
DNPW	:	Department of National Parks and Wildlife/Nepal
DOS	:	Department of Statistics/Nepal
DPs	:	Displaced Persons
EA	:	Environmental Assessment
EDC	:	Electricity Development Committee
EGAT	:	Electricity Generating Authority of Thailand
EIA	:	Environmental Impact Assessment

EP	:	Environmental Protection
EPA	:	Environmental Protection Act
EPW	:	Economic and Political Weekly
GOI	:	Government of India
HH	:	Household
HMG	:	His Majesty's Government/Nepal
IBRD	:	International Bank for Reconstruction and Development
ICCPR	:	International Covenant on Civil and Political Rights
ICESCR	:	International Covenant on Economic Social and Cultural Rights
ICOLD	:	International Commission on Large Dams
IEE	:	Initial Environmental Impact Examination
IFC	:	International Finance Corporation
IPRA	:	Immovable Property Requisition Act 1955/Nepal
IUCN	:	International Union for Conservation of Nature
Kar Act	:	Karnataka Resettlement of Project Displaced Persons Act 1987
LAA	:	Land Acquisition Act
LRMP	:	Land Resource Mapping Project/Nepal
Mah Act	:	Maharashtra Project Affected People Rehabilitation Act1984
MIGA	:	Multilateral Investment Guarantee Arrangement
MP Act	:	Madhya Pradesh Project Displaced Persons Resettlement Act, 1987
MRD	:	Ministry of Rural Development/India
MWR	:	Ministry of Water Resource/Nepal

NBA	:	Narmada Bachaoo Andoolan/India
NDC	:	National Development Council/Nepal
NEA	:	Nepal Electricity Authority
NORAD	:	Norwegian Agency for Development
NPC	:	National Planning Commission/Nepal
NTEC	:	Nam Theun Electricity Consortium
OD	:	Operational Directives/ World Bank
OECD	:	Organization for Economic Cooperation and
OED	:	Operation and Evaluation Department/World Bank
PAFs	:	Project Affected Families
PAPs	:	Project Affected Persons
PIMC	:	Planning, Implementation and Monitoring Committee
R	:	Rule
RBNP	:	Royal Bardia National Park/Nepal
RCNP	:	Royal Chitwan National Park/Nepal
RED	:	Regional Environmental Division/World Bank
RNP	:	Rara National Park/Nepal
RSWR	:	Royal Suklaphanta Wildlife Reserve/Nepal
S	:	Section
S.Ct	:	Supreme Court
SAARC	:	South Asian Association for Regional Cooperation
SC	:	Supreme Court
SCC	:	Supreme Court Cases
SLC	:	School Leaving Certificate

SMEC	:	Snowy Mountain Engineering Consultants/ Australia
SPAF	:	Seriously Project Affected Families
Ss	:	Sections
TM	:	Task Manager/World Bank
UDHR	:	Universal Declaration on Human Rights
UN	:	United Nations
UNDRD	:	United Nations Declaration on Right to Development
VDC	:	Village Development Committee
WB	:	World Bank
WECS	:	Water and Energy Commission Secretariat/Nepal

1

INTRODUCTION

Displacement is generally characterised as the movement of people from one place to another owing to different reasons. Where the movement is self induced, as it happens often in case of migration, it is termed as voluntary displacement, but where it is induced by some extraneous forces, it is termed as involuntary displacement. In the former case, displacement results from the willingness of people to move as part of their natural drive for economic opportunities and better life, and is generally influenced by push and pull factors. In the latter, whether nature induced or human induced, the push factor generally comes to the fore.[1] Whereas displacements caused by the natural disasters like earthquake, flood, landslide are generally taken as examples of nature induced displacement, war, internal strife, mass ethnic cleansing, population transfer, construction of infrastructure and other projects[2] are considered as causative factors for human induced displacement. In all forms of human induced displacement, the removal of persons from their homes or land is directly or indirectly attributable to the state.

While the involvement of the state and presence of force are common factors in all forms of human induced displacement, the reason, level of involvement, or intervention in each category of displacement generally vary. For instance, in project induced displacements the specific government decisions are responsible for forced eviction. Virtually in all instances, forced evictions are planned, formulated and often announced prior to being carried out. Such decisions are often included in the government development plans or other policies as well. In other words, development projects causing displacement are seen to fit into ideology and larger social goods of the nation. But one may not find this in other forms of displacements, as in the case of war or internal strife when people often flee their homes for personal safety and security due to failure of the state to intervene in time. This, of course, would not relieve the state of its responsibility. Still, in several instances, forced eviction does not result from conscious government decision.

Secondly, in project induced displacement, forced eviction occurs rather as a byproduct of the decision of the government to undertake a project like construction of dams, highways, industrial estates, ports, forestry, natural resource management projects, and so on. In such cases, though the displacement is permanent, it is not a primary objective by itself.[3] But this may not be so in other forms of human induced displacements such as ethnic cleansing. In case of war, ethnic strife and sometimes in nature induced displacement also, people return to their original habitat once the trauma is over.

Finally, in project induced displacement the state generally attempts to justify its actions by taking recourse to sovereign power. Expressions like "public purpose" or "national interest" or "common good" are invoked to justify land acquisition and consequential displacement of people. The validation of state action is generally clothed in some remnant of law or policy prescriptions, which may also provide compensation in some forms. Attempts are also made to bring such laws and policies in conformity with the Constitution of the state. However, in other forms of displacements neither the sovereign power is invoked nor is it accepted as a valid excuse for eviction of people.

A few other terms like relocation, resettlement and rehabilitation are also used hand in hand with displacement. The term "relocation" generally implies finding a new habitat for the displaced and other project affected families. Semantically the term "resettlement'" does not imply anything other than translocation of the displaced persons (henceforth DPs) or the project affected persons (henceforth PAPs). The term "rehabilitation" is generally used to encompass the restoration of asset and earning capacity, and reconstruction of the pattern of socio-economic life of PAPs, at least to the pre-move level.[4]

The question of resettlement and rehabilitation is linked with displacement. In the absence of any occurrence of displacement, the issues of resettlement and rehabilitation do not arise. However, as displacement, resettlement and rehabilitation are inter-linked in any project decision, it becomes imperative to look into all the three issues while undertaking a study on displacement.

As the present study is confined to the issue of the project induced displacement and issues related there to, reference to other forms of human induced displacements is incidental and of only analogical value.

1.1 Understanding Displacement

1.1.1 The General Scenario of Displacement

Project induced displacement is not a new phenomenon. It started with industrialization. World over, people were uprooted from their natural habitats, dwellings and surroundings making places for the projects. But, the pace of displacement surged in this century mainly due to high dam and similar other displacing projects.[5] The newly liberated states of post World War II era adopted the same model of development pursued by developed countries and thus looked upon projects of gigantic size as the only alternative left for them to catch up with developed countries. Therefore, construction of large projects was linked with national pride, or a mission for nation building.[6] In this zeal for development, the human and social aspects were either ignored or neglected. Displacement of people was considered as one bottleneck in the execution of the project. Several countries either handled the issue in a policy or legal vacuum or relied on obsolete laws, which at best partially addressed the issue of acquisition and compensation. These laws were not linked to displacement, or the resettlement and rehabilitation of the people who were uprooted from their habitat.

Of late, project induced displacement, mainly because of the magnitude and impact on human and social environment, has become one of the hotly debated issues the world over.[7] According to an estimate of the World Bank, every year about four million people are displaced by approximately 300 large dams (above 15m high) that on an average enter construction phase annually.[8] In addition, six million people are displaced by urban development and transportation projects that get commissioned each year. Thus, a total of 10 million people each year or at least 90 to 100 million people over a decade are displaced as a result of infrastructure programmes like dams, urban transportation projects, etc.[9] This is quite a huge number, even higher than the annual exodus and absolute number of refugees.[10] Though the steep graph of dams induced displacement has flattened to some extent in recent times, it is only indicative of a shift in the nature of displacing projects. In many countries of Asia and Africa dams are still the major culprits for displacement of people.[11]

1.1.2 *Effect of Displacement*

Though apparently displacement looks like an issue related to the expropriation of assets to allow the project, in reality it is not just an expropriation or a simple transfer of property in exchange of compensation. It is a process of unravelling of the existing patterns of social organization, a social crisis and some times a political one as well.

A series of events follow once the declaration of the project is made. The process of displacement generally begins with the survey of land, physical possession, determination and payment of compensation, the actual movement of people and finally the resettlement of persons in a new location. Though these events that generally operate in succession, they hardly maintain a time and space order. Some times the time gap between the first notification and the resettlement takes decades causing immense socio-economic and psychological trauma.[12] Displacement adversely affects every community but its effect on women, children, tribals and other weaker sections are far more serious.[13] Sociologists and anthropologists have analysed the stress dimension involved in the process of displacement and have termed that at different phases DPs pass through different socio- economic, physical and psychological stress.[14] Michael Cernea maintains that DPs not only face the socio-economic stress but also the risk of impoverishment. He has identified eight such risks that DPs face due to displacement.[15] As these risks are of general nature and relevant and applicable in any context, albeit with varying intensities, a little elaboration is made here.

A) Landlessness

As displacement occurs on account of physical dispossession of land by the acquiring authority, landlessness is the most prominent risk.

Where the government sticks to the cash compensation policy and land for land is not adopted as a policy measure for resettlement, PAPs need to find land by themselves.[16] In such a situation it is very unlikely that they will be able to purchase the same quantum of land at the same price. Due to an array of factors like the time gap in physical possession and payment of compensation, increase in land prices, inflation, use of money for consumption purposes etc, PAPs generally end up in purchase of land smaller in size and lower in quality. Sometimes, they become unable to purchase any land at all. Where PAPs hold small parcels, most often the compensation will be too meagre to enable them to invest the amount in purchasing land or other productive assets. Due to scarcity of land, even where resettlement package is handed down by the government, PAPs are generally offered not the same area of land that they lose. Landlessness results not only in physical expropriation, it removes the foundation upon which people's productive systems, commercial activities and livelihood are constructed. With the loss of land PAPs lose both natural and man made capital. [17]

B) Joblessness

Around four-fifths of the people in Nepal are employed in the agriculture sector.[18] Agriculture is still the main provider of employment in most of the countries of south Asia. The loss of agricultural land, therefore, means the loss of job as well. The loss of land not only deprives the land owning class of their job, but also affects small businessmen, agricultural labourers, village artisans and other wage earners.[19] As the absorptive power of agriculture, compared to business and industry sectors is high, the adverse effect to be felt by its loss also turns out to be massive.

Besides the loss of job due to the loss of land, PAPs some times lose jobs in the non-agriculture sector by the closure of local enterprises, shops, etc. When the new resettlement site happens to be at a greater distance from the original habitat or the urban centre it becomes difficult for PAPs to continue with the job. Though the construction work in the project area may create a boom, such a boom is only temporary. Mining or some labour intensive operations no doubt have the potentiality of absorbing people but their potentials are mostly overestimated.

C) Homelessness

The term "homelessness" needs to be understood both in its semantic and symbolic sense. In the former sense, homelessness results from the state's acquisition of the dwellings. This, in most of the cases, is a temporary phenomenon and ends with the construction of another house by the displaced family. But even here the threat of homelessness exists. Though the prevailing laws on acquisition provide for compensation for the loss of dwellings, it is generally assessed at historical value and not at the replacement cost. The sufficiency or insufficiency of the amount for constructing a house is never a consideration required by the law.[20] This makes the displaced person very vulnerable. The non-availability of construction materials and the use of money for other purposes compel DPs in constructing less spacious and low quality houses. Sometimes violent destruction of the house also makes DPs to shift to temporary shades and tents, where they spend years and ultimately end up as homeless destitutes.

Homelessness in a broader sense also means the loss of social relationship, cultural space and identity and kinship, that traumatise DPs. With segregation, the displaced persons lose their sense of identity, which they had consciously or unconsciously established with their original landscape and human environment.

D) Marginalization

Marginalization occurs when families lose economic power and slide on a path downwardly mobile.[21] Irrespective of the size of acquisition, or that of holdings, every displacing project has the effect of marginalization.

In many instances the process of marginalization begins even before the physical occupation of property. Once the project is declared banks and other financial institutions stop taking the property as collateral security. Along with this the government stops investment in the infrastructure sector in the area. Repair of the public services, schools etc also gets neglected. The value of land in the adjoining areas also shoots up. This makes the chances of regaining the earning power dim. Where resettlement plans are not well planned, productivity of the land and the carrying capacity of the natural resources around the resettlement site are not studied and off farm opportunities are not explored and exploited, resettled families often cannot get earning capacity fully restored.[22] This leads to marginalization.

The non-availability of civic amenities and other public infrastructures like schools, service centres etc. and lack of institutional support also adversely affect PAPs. Still at a deeper psychological level, marginalization results in the acceptance by PAPs that they can never regain their previous status and wealth.

E) Loss of Health

The loss of health results from psychological stress,[23] non-availability of physical and sanitary facilities, outbreak of diseases and food scarcity. The risk begins with a psychological trauma, which is caused by the prospective loss of habitation and the fear of an unknown destination. When the physical movement and construction work begin, due to poor sanitary conditions and non-availability of safe drinking water, parasitic and vector born diseases cause several health problems.[24] The loss of health also results from the change in the environment of the project site. The discharge of effluents from industries, slush and other wastes from mines, unsafe water supply, poor sewerage and water logging in the field due to poor drainage system mostly affect infants, children and the elderly.

F) Food Insecurity

Displacement generally results in food shortage. Keeping in mind the uncertainty of food availability PAPs begin to consume less and try to save food. This results in undernourishment. Undernourishment is both a symptom and a result of an inadequate resettlement. Even if people are resettled, the building of food production capacity at the relocation site takes time. Food insecurity also results due to low productivity of the land as well as due to the reduced size of the newly purchased sites.[25] Therefore, where transitional food support system does not exist, food scarcity becomes rampant.

G) Loss of Common Property Resources (CPR)

The CPR provide sustenance to both the landed and the landless class in the form of food, fuel, fodder, water, pastures for cattle etc. In rural and tribal areas the dependence on CPR generally remains very high.[26] But when the property is acquired the loss of CPR is hardly accounted and paid for. While its effect on the landless and magrinalised section is much more severe the loss of these resources dislocates the life of the whole community.

H) Unravelling of the Social Fabric

Displacement tears apart the social fabric. People are compelled to leave their places, their relations and most of the location specific things. Even where arrangements are made for resettlement, people face a lot of other problems like unsuitable climate, hostile host population, a very weak production system, the lack of informal social network and the lack of mutual help among people.[27] Group resettlement mitigates the pain to some extent. But where resettlement is not properly done various manifestations of social dis-articulation like loosening of kinship ties, growing alienation, weakening of control in inter-personal behaviour and lower cohesion in family structure, decrease in social participation and in group action etc., result.[28] Research studies have also found non-integration or incompatibility with the host population among the resettlers.[29]

1.1.3 The General Approaches to Displacement, Resettlement and Rehabilitation

The review of literature on the subject enables one to trace out three predominant approaches to the issue of displacement:

- The traditional approach,
- The people centred approach, and
- The right and/or entitlement approach.

1.1.3.1 *The traditional approach*

Governments, bureaucracy and technical experts follow the traditional approach mostly in the Third World Countries.[30] The predominant characteristics of this approach are reliance on obsolete laws and policies, indifference to the suffering of PAPs as well as to any research findings which shed light on their suffering.[31] A tendency to de-link development, displacement, resettlement and rehabilitation and to look at each of them in isolation, presence of a culture of secrecy and non-consultation with and non-participation of the people in the development decisions are other characteristics of this approach.

This approach takes displacement as a problem of development and DPs as impediments to progress.[32] The executive branch of the government is vested with the power to take development decisions. Though the executive power is exercised *de jure* by the representatives of the people, development decisions are *de facto* taken by bureaucracy basing on the technical soundness of the project and a parochial cost-benefit analysis. Due to the usual proclivity to maximize the benefit and minimise the cost, technical experts generally err on the side of large projects, with little or no care for the human, social and environmental cost aspects. Reports are prepared in complete secrecy. They are hardly brought even for enlightened public discussion or debate. The participation of the affected persons and prospective beneficiaries is almost unknown to technical experts. As detailed engineering nuances and technical data are beyond the comprehension of non-experts, technical reports receive more weight over other views and are relied on by decision makers, courts and even by general public.

Even where the political leadership takes decisions, over reliance is placed on intransigent bureaucracy and obsolete laws. The wisdom of the executive or the existence of "public purpose" is hardly questioned in a court of law. The general tendency of the judiciary to keep its hands off on the question of "public purpose" delimits the area of maneuverability to the question of compensation only.

Once the project decisions are taken, the acquisition of property begins. Rights are individuated, and compensations are paid accordingly. The overall criterion in the payment of compensation is the individual ownership and not use or occupation. The loss of private land is often equated with the loss of income and avenues of livelihood. The loss of common property resources is not accounted for. The traditional approach looks at displacement in isolation and resettlement as a favour extended by the government and not as a right of the people corresponding to a basic duty of the state. In case of acquisition of property, cash compensation determined in official wisdom, bereft of empirical realities, is the norm. Resettlement, as a rule, does not exist in the wisdom of the officialdom. Resettlement operations, if at all undertaken, are generally taken in a policy-vacuum. Even where some paper work is done, it is hardly brought into implementation. Restoration of earning capacity of the PAPs is never taken as a goal.

1.1.3.2 People Centered Approach

Sociologists, anthropologists and grass-root social activists are the pioneers of this approach.[33] This approach takes displacement as a human and social problem and not only as a problem of development. The proponents of this approach reject lopsided view on development—a development that benefits a cross section of people at the cost of others. They advocate a holistic approach to displacement, resettlement and rehabilitation.[34] Though they do not question the power of "eminent domain" of the state as such, they argue that displacement should be for genuine public purpose only suiting the developmental need and environmental concerns and also conforming to the concept of sustainable development. The avoidance and minimization of displacement is their primary concern. Wherever it is unavoidable they argue that displacement should be taken as an opportunity for development. Restoration of the earning capacity, according to them, should be a minimum objective of the resettlement programme. The proponent of this view *inter alia* argue for a) carrying out a household survey of the earning capacity and resource use pattern, b) payment of compensation for property acquired at replacement value, c) detailed working out of resettlement plan with participation of the affected persons or their representatives, d) preservation of cultural values, e) special protection to women, the weaker sections including indigenous and tribal people, f) sufficient allocation of budget, g) institutional accountability etc. Their main emphasis is on the formulation of a resettlement policy. Though some of them also argue for legal reform, they are not firm on it.

1.1.3.3 The Right and/or Entitlement Approach

The proponents of this view take displacement as a human rights problem. Development according to them is not a need-based concept but rather a right based concept.[35] They consider arbitrary displacement of people of their home, and property as a breach of human rights. According to them where development decisions affect basic rights of an individual, for instance, the right to life (living and livelihood included), health and environment, the imperative on the planners is to respect these rights by looking into alternatives. Where overriding national interest makes certain amount of restriction on the rights of a person unavoidable, the basic duty cast on the state would be to design plans to mitigate the adverse impact, restore the livelihood and earning capacity of the person affected.[36] The proponents of this view question the power of the executive to take development decisions in breach of the rights of the affected persons. Some of them also argue for jettisoning the executive role on development and vesting it with the legislature.[37] According to them, a human notion of resettlement must go beyond cash compensation, beyond even land for land and must extend to compensate all opportunity cost of uprooting from habitat, i.e., complex social, religious, cultural and material way of life.[38] Though they subscribe to most of the views of sociologists and anthropologists, they appear less inclined to rely on resettlement and rehabilitation policy as a bulwark to check executive tyranny. According to them only a robust legal regime can effectively check the executive abuse, and accord respect to individual rights.[39] It is to their main disquiet that in many countries the national legal framework takes resettlement issues only as a subset of property and expropriation law.[40] The use of existing legal tools of the domestic as well as international legal regime, and creation of new norms which would compel the state to take affirmative actions to correct the past ills and prevent the future abuse is the concern of these scholars. They also emphasise the need of a comprehensive legal framework to deal with development induced resettlement.[41]

1.2 The Project Induced Displacement Scenario in Nepal

Though there exists no consolidated list of affected people

officially recognised, displacement of people on account of acquisition of property has been a regular feature of infrastructure development process in Nepal. People were displaced by construction of roads, irrigation schemes, hydropower projects, airport, national parks and wildlife reserves.[42] In comparative terms, national parks and wildlife reserves and water resource projects have displaced more people than other types of projects in Nepal.

When the process of establishing national parks and wildlife reserves began in all earnest in 1970s, Nepal adopted the Yellowstone model. Under this model national parks are considered as areas of wilderness secluded from human habitation. Therefore, the model prescribes for relocation of people from areas declared for the parks.[43] The first park set up under this model was the Royal Chitwan National Park (henceforth RCNP). Following this, two other parks viz., the Royal Bardia National Park (henceforth RBNP) and the Rara National Park (henceforth RNP) were established in the same decade. While, there exists no record of resettlement in the RCNP, the RBNP is reported to have displaced 120 families from two villages. The displacees were given land for land they lost and resettled in the outskirts of the Park.[44]

The establishment of National Park around the Rara Lake caused displacement of 331 families spread in two villages viz., Rara and Chhapru. These people were airlifted to Nepalgunj and resettled in Motipur in Bardia district. A land for land package was developed for the purpose. However, the resettlers soon left the given land complaining of poor soil quality for cultivation and lack of irrigation, and moved to Chisapani and Gobhar, north of Kohalpur on their own accord.[45]

The land for land package was adopted in the resettlement of the displaced persons of the Koshi Tappu Wildlife Reserve[46] and the Royal Suklaphanta Wildlife Reserve also.[47] The process of establishing and extending the existing parks is also taking place in Nepal.[48]

The displacement of substantial number of people due to construction of hydropower project in Nepal began in 1960s with the construction of Trishuli hydropower project.[49] About 174 ha. of cultivated land was acquired for the Kulekhani project, the first reservoir project of Nepal, leading to displacement of 937 families and seriously affecting 1200 families.[50] Though a feeble effort for land settlement was made mainly under the pressure of the World Bank, it was later discarded and the PAPs were given cash compensation determined by local authorities. As such, in water resource projects cash compensation, by and large, has been the norm. In Marsyangdi Hydro Project, even after pressure from the displaced community no effort was made to provide land in lieu of compensation, irrespective of the fact that a provision of the Land Acquisitions Act, 1977 gives the government a discretion to provide land as compensation.[51]

In Nepal generally at the planning and design stage of the water resource projects land for land packages are recommended but such recommendations are invariably ignored at the implementation stage.[52]

In comparative terms, Nepal is yet to see large-scale displacement due to dams. However, given the huge hydropower potential[53] of the country, the displacement due to water resource projects is likely to shoot up in the years to come. So far at least 114 projects having the potential to generate 45,610 MW of economically feasible power have been identified in Nepal. Most of these projects are located in the mid-hills.[54] Among these two high dam projects—Mahakali (Pancheswar)[55] and West Seti[56] projects are already in the process of execution. Another very large project, which for quite some time has been on the high burner of government agenda in Nepal, is the 10,400 MW Karnali Chishapani Project.

If constructed, the 320 sq. km size reservoir will displace 78,000 people (60,000 in 1989) spread in 24 Village Development Committees (henceforth VDCs) of four districts.[57] Besides these projects, there are at least seven other high dam projects which are at different level of studies. If implemented, these projects will displace around 152 thousand people in Nepal.[58]

In comparative terms, Nepal is yet to witness mass displacement of people due to infrastructure and other development projects. But it in no way makes the issue of displacement a less important subject for research. In the first place violation of rights is independent of the magnitude. Secondly, irrespective of the magnitude of the project, the severity of impact is by and large similarly felt in every kind of displacement caused by any project big or small. And, finally, *ad hoc*, inconsistent and conflicting project specific policies are more problematic from the point of equity and justice.[59]

The over reliance on an unaccountable bureaucracy, technical experts' opinion, and obsolete laws, non-involvement of PAPs at any stage from project planning to project implementation are the attributes of the Nepali decision making process. The decentralised and participatory development process, which has recently been introduced in Nepal, is yet to inhabit or have an impact on the centralised planning process.[60] The techno-bureaucratic approach obviously emphasises on the economic and technical aspects of the project. The human, environmental and other social costs,[61] as a rule, are not internalised and included in the cost benefit analysis of the project.[62] Without any questioning, these are taken as unavoidable and unaccounted costs of development. This faulty presupposition neglects the legal and moral basis of arguments that call for imaginative solutions of the problem.This is distinctly witnessed in the non-inclusion of the resettlement and rehabilitation package in the project design. Wherever resettlement policy guidelines are delineated in the feasibility reports, they are not based on the socio-economic need or environmental conditions of the particular project area but are guided by extraneous considerations like the conditionalities of the funding agencies. Neither the cost involved in the resettlement is worked out nor is it included in the project design.[63] Where the pressure from the international financial institutions already exists or the government foresees such a possibility, project specific land acquisition and resettlement guidelines are issued,[64] but neither the guidelines are published in the official Gazette nor is any thought given about their legal validity.

Another interesting feature of the feasibility reports is that where the report visualises the need for resettlement programmes, emphasis is generally on finding sites in forest areas of Terai.[65] The EIA study is the weakest part of these reports. Neither the EIA studies of the project area are carried out properly, nor is the EIA of the resettlement site thought to be necessary.

Given the prioritization of the hydropower sector and emphasis on high dams, while the magnitude of displacement is likely to increase in the years to come, the authorities appear to be blind to the outcome of research on displacement at home[66] and elsewhere.[67] So far no national policy or law has been formulated to make resettlement and rehabilitation mandatory. The biased techno-eco approach does not appear to be prepared to consider displacement as a challenge to development and help PAPs to turn it into an opportunity for development. Even where displacement is inevitable, PAPs are never considered as partners in development and involved in resettlement planning or implementation.

Certain facts like the ruggedness local topography of Nepal,[68] the subsistence economy, heavy dependence of people on agriculture,[69] and low per-capita land availability, the skewed distribution of land[70] and low productivity are naturally very important considerations for any project decision in nepal.[71] A majority of peoples in Nepal live in the mountain areas.[72] As most of these areas are food deficit,[73] people in these areas rely on narrow valleys, relatively flatter lands at lower elevation and river stripes for food supply. Besides, mountain areas are supported by the food production in Terai, which physically covers only 14.3 per cent of the total territory. If any large project comes up in the Terai land or the valleys and other low lying areas in the mountains, this besides affecting the life of those directly depending on the acquired land, also affects a wider cross-section depending on the food supply from land to be condemned. Therefore the protection of cultivable land in a country like Nepal deserves careful consideration.

Although, the resettlement of landless hill people and victims of natural calamities to the lands in Terai was actively pursued for almost three decades since it was first unveiled in 1950s, PAPs were never considered as eligible for resettlement under the mandate accorded to the Nepal Resettlement Company (estd. 1963) or the Resettlement Department (estd. 1968).[74] In a nutshell, the absence of law, policy guidelines and institutional mechanisms, the prevalence of a techno-economic approach to development, blindness to research studies, violation of the basic rights of the people have pervaded the project induced displacement, resettlement and rehabilitation scenario in Nepal.

1.4 The Objective of the Study

The present study attempts to examine the problem of project induced displacement from a legal perspective. This perspective requires one to look into the legal norms developed at both the domestic and international legal regime. By way of analogy it also requires one to look into the norms developed in other countries to address similar problems.

The primary objective here is to analyze the issues from the point of view of the rights of PAPs. The attempt is to examine the rights of the PAPs by juxtaposing them with the rights of other individuals and the collectivities to enjoy the fruits of development. It is also to juxtapose them with the duty of the state to undertake appropriate development programmes in order to fulfil its primary objective of securing for the people of Nepal "social, political and economic justice".[75]

The Constitution of Nepal envisages the establishment of a just order, which regulates behaviour of men in a way satisfactory to all men, so that all men find their happiness in it. A just system is a system of reason and just even to those who are adversely affected. Respect to life, liberty, equality, property etc is the salient feature of such a system.[76] In case of violation of rights, access to an independent judiciary for finding remedy is also guaranteed by the Constitution.[77] The basis of governance is the popular will of the people. Transformation of the rule of law into a living reality is the constitutional promise.[78]

The guarantee of freedom of opinion and expression and the right to demand and receive information on any matter of public importance[79] and the duty cast on the state to establish a participatory and decentralised government promoting and protecting human rights, undoubtedly envisage a democratic decision making process. Under this process consultation with affected persons and collectivities, invitation and solicitation of enlightened public opinion, conducting of expert opinion and public hearing on possible social and environmental impact becomes a pre-requisite of developmental decisions. Such a process does not de-center the state but makes it more responsible and responsive without acknowledging it as a sole judge to peoples' developmental aspirations.[80] The democratic and participatory approach also requires the state to take a broad perspective and abandon the paternalistic attitude to development and look at people (including PAPs) not as objects but subjects of development.[81] It also requires the synchronization of the concept of "public purpose" or "public interest" for that matter, with the objectives of development as enshrined in the Constitution.[82] It enables one to put a good defense against arbitrary use of the power of eminent domain, and challenge the legitimacy of the exercise of the state power to the extent their objectives are at variance with the constitutional imperatives or interfere with the rights guaranteed under the Constitution.

The promise of the Constitution 'to promote and protect human rights'[83] brings internationally recognized human rights norms closer to the constitutional framework and allows one to peruse the realm of human rights through the constitutional prism. Besides, the legislative process of ratification of Treaty[84] the provision of the Nepal Treaties Act, 1991[85] and accession of Nepal to the Optional Protocol I and II[86] have made the application of international law in domestic jurisdiction possible. The gravitation of the human person to the central arena of the discourse on international human rights and environmental law leaves a positive note for the formulation of people centered development approach.[87] Though in a strictly legal sense, the provisions of the soft law may not possess the same legal force, nevertheless, they help in giving effect to the existing provisions of domestic law and thereby impose moral obligations on the state to formulate "appropriate development policies."[88] While the international human rights and environmental law might have general influence on the policy formulations, the ILO Convention 169 lays down rules for the protection of indigenous and tribal people. Therefore, in the context of complementarity of the domestic and international legal regime, and the evolving norms thereunder, the nature and extent of state obligations also need to be examined.

The major concern in the present work is to examine the prevailing policy and legal regime and to analyze the gaps between (a) the constitutional promise and the legal response, and (b) the constitutional promise and institutional response to the issue of displacement. The institutional response and impact of displacement is examined by carrying out empirical study of two projects of Nepal viz, the Royal Suklaphanta Wildlife Reserve Project and the Pokhara Airport Project and the purpose is also to examine whether the prevailing regime is sensitive enough to respect the rights of the displaced and other project affected persons.

The study is intended to provide a better understanding of the rights/entitlements of the PAPs under domestic and international legal regimes. It will also help to understand a few other issues relating to PAPs, especially their right to participate in and direct the process of development, evolve strategies, which will avoid or minimize the adverse effect of displacement, which have hitherto remained unanswered. The study is also intended to help to evolve a humane approach to development by enriching knowledge in this particular area of study. This in turn could bridge the gap between the constitutional aspirations and the prevailing practices in Nepal.

REFERENCES

1. Roli Astha, *Involuntary Resettlement: Survey of International Experience,* 31(24) ECONOMIC AND POLITICAL WEEKLY (henceforth EPW) 1468 (1996) (Citing Gunnenheim and Cernea 1993).
2. The Indian Draft National Policy on Resettlement and Rehabilitation defines Projects to include every activity, public, semi-public or private, which result in acquisition of land or displacement or disturbs the habitat and way of life of people. See GOI/MRD, *Draft National Policy on Resettlement and Rehabiiitation, 1998* (in the file of Ministry of Rural Development) para 3.1.5.
3. However, one variant of displacement which occurred in South Africa during the apartheid regime resulting in forced eviction

and resettlement of people was the product of a conscious government move. To remove black spots from white settlements was manifestly the primary motive. *See* Harriet Nguhene, *The Politics of Land Restitution in South Africa;* Charles De Wet, *Moving Away from Apartheid: Resettlement in a Changing South Africa,* (Papers presented to the Conference on Development Induced Displacement and Improverishment, Weldam College, Oxford, Jan. 3-7, 1995).

4. The expression "resettlement and rehabilitation" (henceforth RR) is understood in India in a much refined form. According to Indian social scientists resettlement does not result automatically afterrehabilitation. Rehabilitation according to them includes not only the rehabilitation of household but also of communities as well by engrafting them to a new place and nurturing them to ensure steady and balanced growth. *See* Walter Fernandes et al., *DISPLACEMENT AND REHABILITATION: AN ESTIMATE OF EXTENT AND PROSPECTS* in DEVELOPMENT DISPLACEMENT AND REHABILITATION 62-88 (Walter Fernandes and E.G. Thukral eds.), (Delhi, Indian Social Institute, 1989).
5. For instance, 85 per cent of the 40,000 large dams obstructing rivers all over he world were built in the last 60 years. *See* Himansu Thakkar, Book Review, 478 SEMINAR 0 73 (1999) (reviewing PATRICK MCCULLEY, SILENCED RIVERS: THE ECOLOGY AND POLITICS OF LARGE DAMS (Hyderabad, Orient Longman, 1998).
6. Pundit Nehru is often mistakenly referred to as one praising large projects especially large dams, for his comparison of dams with "secular temple of India," though he in explicit terms warned against the disease of gigantism. *See* BRAFORD MORSE AND THOMAS BERGER, STANDARD SAROVAR: REPORT OF THE INDEPENDENT REVIEW COMMISSION 1 (Ottawa, Resource Futures International, 1992) (henceforth MORSE COMMISSION REPORT). For Nehru's views on disease of gigantism, *see* his speech made at 29th Annual Meeting of the Central Board of Irrigation on 17th Nov. 1958 quoted in Narmada Bachao Andolan v Union of India (Writ on 319 of 1994) (written submission made by Counsel of the petitioner Mr. Prasant Bhushan in the Supreme Court on Jan., 1999 in the file of the Supreme Court at 1-2).
7. Michael Cernea, *Public Policy Responses to Development Induced Displacement*, 31(24) EPW 1515(1996) (arguing that the issue of involuntary displacement was brought to focus by sociologists

and anthropologist in 1980s the debate has been broadened by growing media attention, by the invovlement of NGO activists growing political resistance and active opposition developed in several countries by displaced people).

8. This categorisation is based on the definition of large dams given by the International Commission on Large Dams (ICOLD). According to it a large dam is the one which measure 15 meters or more from the foundation to crest—taller than a four-story building. *See* PATRICK McCULLEY, SILENCED RIVERS ECOLOGY AND POLITICS OF LARGE DAMS 3-4 (London, Zed Books, 1996).
9. MICHAEL CERNEA, HYDROPOWER DAMS AND SOCIAL IMPACTS; A SOCIOLOGICAL PERSPECTIVE.6 (Washington DC, World Bank, 1997).
10. The Norwegian Refugee study Center gives the figure of refugee as 20 to 22 million refugees. *See* http://www.nrc.no/global idp survey.htm assessed on Sept. 1, 1999.
11. Whereas till the decade of 1970s dams were considered as major causes for displacement, a shift in this was felt in the following decade. And in the present decade urban development, mining (particularly the open cast mining), transport, forest and other projects have caused more displacement than dams. *See* MICHAEL CERNEA, *supra* note 9; *See also* PATRICK MCCULLEY, *supra* note 8.
12. The Sardar Sarovar Project in India is a fit case in point where the land for the Kavadia colony was acquired in 1961 but the "oustees" are still struggling for resettlement. *See* MORSE COMMISSION REPORT, *supra* note 6, at 350.
13. *See generally* Enakshy G. Thukral, *Development, Displacement and Rehabilitation: Locating Gender,* 31(24) EPW 1500-1503 (1996) (arguing that women suffer more because of bias in ownership laws, loss of common property resources and due to lack of support during transition period); *see also* Mathew Areeparamil, *Displacement Due to Mining in Jharkhand, id.* 1544-1528; Nita Mishra, *Tribal Resistance in the Chhechhari Valley, id.* 1539-1940; Smitu Kothari, *Whose Nation, Displaced as Victim of Development, id.*, 1476, 1478.
14. One of such study is of Robert Chambers. He analysed the land settlement as a three-phase process. T. Scudder and E. Colson made a further distinction of the process into four stages: recruitment, transition, adaptation, and incorporation. But recent studies have cast a doubt on the validity of extending the four-stage framework. For a brief discussion of these models, *See*

MICHAEL CERNEA, AFRICAN INVOLUNTARY POPULATION RESETTLEMENT IN A GLOBAL CONTEXT 10 (Washington DC, World Bank, 1997.

15. *See* Michael Cernea, *The Risk and Reconstruction Model for Resettling Displaced Populations*, (Keynote address presented at the International Conference on Reconstructing Livelihoods: Towards New Approaches to Resettlement, September 9-13, 1996, University of Oxford, RSP, Oxford) (arguing that if the risks are addressed with a suitable policy framework on a one to one basis the risks can be reversed). *See also* Michael Cernea, *Understanding and Preventing Impoverishment-Reflections on the State of Knowledge* in UNDERSTANDING IMPOVERISHMENT: THE CONSEQUENCES OF DEVELOPMENT INDUCED DISPLACEMENT 3 (Christopher McDowell ed) (Oxford Berghann Books, 1996); Ranjit Dwivedi, *Displacement, Risk and Resistance: Local Perceptions and Actions in the Sardar Sarovar*, 30 DEVELOPMENT AND CHANGE 14, 45 (1999)

16. Though Land Acquisition Acts of several sought Asian Countries have provisions for providing land in lieu of cash compensation, they do not cast a mandatory duty on the government. *See* the Land Acquisition Act of Nepal, 1977, S. 14; *see* also the Land Acquisition Act, 1894 (a common Act of India, Pakistan and Bangladesh), S. 31 (3).

17. MICHAEL CERNEA, EIGHT MAIN RISKS: IMPOVERISHMENT AND SOCIAL JUSTICE IN RESETTLEMENT 10 (Envt. Dept, The World Bank, 1996). (giving the example Kiambre Hydro Project where studies showed that farmer's average land holding, yield per hactare as well as family income decreased considerably).

18. NSAC, NEPAL HUMAN DEVELOPMENT REPORT *1998* ii (Kathmandu, Nepal South Asia Centre, 1998).

19. The landless lose their jobs in three ways: a) they lose access to land owned by others and leased or share cropped; b) job opportunities primarily in urban areas; and c) foregone assets under common property regime. *See* Astha Roli, *supra* note 1, at 1470 (citing World Bank 1994).

20. The law does not even require the full payment of compensation before asking the owner to vacate the house. *See* Land Acquisition Act of Nepal, 1977, S. 12(2).

21. MICHAEL CERNEA, *supra* note 17, at 14.

22. *Id.* (citing examples of Kulekhani Project in Nepal and Kotmale Project in Sri Lanka)

23. The mental stress is caused by loss of the place generally

termed as "cultural bereavement" and unusual level of sorrow, unresolved anger and bitterness leading to varied neuro-psychiatric illness. *See generally* Byron J. Good, *Mental Health Consequences of Displacement and Resettlement,* 31 (24) EPW 1504-1508 (1996).

24. Besides Malaria, Schistosomiasis (caused by flat worm called schistosome found in water), Cirrhosis of liver, Diarrhoea, Filariasis, Ochocerciasis (river blindness wide spread Central and South American river basin), other location specific diseases (e.g. sleeping sickness caused by Tetse Fly found among Tonga Tribesmen resettled as a result of Kariba Dam in Togo, Malaria among the resettlers of Mahawali dam in Sri Lanka) are in found resettlement sites *See generally* EDWARD GOLDSMITH AND NICHOLAS HILDYARD, 1 THE SOCIAL AND ENVIRONMENTAL EFFECTS OF LARGE DAMS 86-89 (France/UK European Ecological Action. Group (ECORPA), 1984). In India Malaria due to defective and untidy irrigation were detected as early as 1938 and nicknamed as "engineers made malaria." *See* MORSE COMMISSION REPORT, *supra* note 6, at 323.

25. See Balgovind Baboo, *Big Dams and the Tribals: The Case of Hirakund Dam Oustees in Orissa,* SOCIAL ACTION 289, 299 (1991).

26. MICHAEL CERNEA, *supra* note 17, at 17 (citing a study conducted by Debra Sequeira, in semi arid regions of India where it was found that 91-1000% of firewood, 68-89% of domestic fuel, 69-80% of grazing needs of the poor households were supplied by lands under common property resource regime).

27. *See* S. Parasuraman, *Development Projects Displacement and Outcomes for Displaced: Two Case Studies,* 31 (24) EPW 1529-31 (1996) (reporting social dis-articulation among the DPs of Upper Krishna Project in India).

28. MICHAEL CERNEA, *supra* note 17, at 14 (citing studies conducted by P.K. Nayak on Rongali Dam in Orissa, India).

29. Balgovind Baboo, *supra* note 25, at 299.

30. *See generally* MICHAEL CERNEA, AFRICAN INVOLUNTARY POPULATION RESETTLEMENT IN A GLOBAL CONTEXT 21-22 (Washington DC, World Bank, 1997).

31. Michael Cernea, *supra* note 7, at 1518.

32. For instance, proponent of this view in India often validate their action by referring to Nehru who while laying down foundation of Hirakund dam in Orissa India in 1950s said; "If you have to suffer, you should suffer in the interest of the

country." *See* Smitu Kothari, *supra* note 13, at 1473 (quoting Government of India) (arguing further that planners and administrators invariably capitalise and manipulate the relatively weaker socio-economic and political position of most of the people facing displacement).

33. This approach now also finds expression in the World Bank policies on involuntary resettlement, EIA studies and on indigenous people *See* OD 4.30, OD 4.20 etc. of the World Bank at http://www.world bank.org/inv.res.htm accessed on Sept. 2, 1999; *see also* Smitu Kothari, *supra* note 13, at 1480 (outlining the basis for policy formulation).

34. *See generally* Walter Fernandes et al., *supra* note 4; *see also* Michael Cernea, *supra* note 7; Michael Cernea, *supra* note 9; Smitu Kothari, *supra* note 13.

35. Neera Chandhoke, *Why People should have Rights,* 29(4) EPW 2697-2700 (1994); *see also* Niraja Gopal Jayal, *Displaced Persons and Discourse of Rights,* 33 (5) EPW PE 30-36. (1998) Both the authors reject the idea of putting project over people, the culture of benbefiting a section of people at the livelihood cost of others and essentially question the bonafidy of the exercise of the power of eminent domain. Apparently this view seems to be more anthropocentric but it is submitted that to the extent the Constitution of Nepal supports a co-existential view with regard to environment to that extent the approach embraces eco-centricism. *See generally* Catherine Redgwell, *Life, The Universe and Everything: A Critique of Anthropocentric Rights* in HUMAN RIGHT APPROACHES TO ENVIRONMENTAL PROTECTION 71-88 (Alan Byole and M Anderson eds.) (Oxford, Clarendon Press, 1996); *see also* Bill Devall, *The Deep Ecology Movement* in KEY CONCEPT IN CRITICAL THEORY ECOLOGY 125-139 (Carolyn Merchant ed.) (Jaipur, Rawat Publications, 1996); Arne Naces, *Deep Ecology* in *id.* at 120-124; George Sessions, *Ecocentricism and Anthropocentric Detour id.* at 140-151.

36. Upendra Baxi, *Notes on Constitutional and Legal Aspects of Displacement and Rehabilitation in* DEVELOPMENT DISPLACEMENT AND REHABILITATION 168 (Walter Fernandes and Enakshi Ganguley Thukral eds.) (New Delhi, Indian Social Institute 1989).

37. *Id.*

37. *Id.*

39. Usha Ramahathan, *Displacement and the Law,* 31 (24) EPW 1486-1491 (1996).

40. Ibrahim F. Shihata, *Involuntary Resettlement in World Bank Financed Projects* in THE WORLD BANK IN A CHANGING WORLD 181 (Netherlands, Martinus Nijhoff Publishers, 1991).
41. Chhatrapati Singh, *Rehabilitation and the Right to Property* in *supra* note 36, at 91, 98 (arguing for a frontal attack on discriminatory land and forest laws on the basis of Art 13, 14 and 19 of the Indian Constitution). *See also* Upendra Baxi *id.* at 167 (arguing for the use of Art 21 of the Indian Constitution to remedy the evils of displacement).
42. Ajaya Dixit, *Water Projects in Nepal; Lessons From Displacement and Rehabilitation,* 4(1) WATER NEPAL 74, 79 (1994).
43. SANJAY K. NEPAL AND KARLE WEBER, STRUGGLE FOR EXISTENCE: PARK PEOPLE CONFLICT IN THE ROYAL CHITWAN NATIONAL PARK, NEPAL 1-2 (Bangkok, Asian Institute of Technology, 1993). At present Nepal has eight national parks, five reserves and two conservation areas covering 20, 058 sq. km i.e. around 14% of the total area of the country. *See* DOS, STATISTICAL SURVEY OF NEPAL 1995 (Kathmandu, Department of Statistics, 1995).
44. B.N. UPRETY, ROYAL BARDIA NATIONAL PARK 29 (Kathmandu, HMGN/NPC/IUCN, 1994) Beyond this also there is no information about the norm developed and criteria adopted and support provided to the displaces.
45. However, the government extended support to the resettlers in the new area as well, *see* Harka Gurung, *Review of Policy and Experiences of Project Related Resettlement in Nepal,* 1(4) WATER NEPAL 4 (1989).
46. Established in 1977 through a Royal Order, an area of 3092 bigah (i.e., 2061.43 ha) of cultivated land was acquired for the project resulting in the displacement of 1287 families (including 370 landless). Initiative to resettle these people in Mahendranagar of Sunsari district began in 1980s. However, due to various problems resettlement of displaced people is yet to be complete. Based on personal communication with the Warden of the Reserve on March 29, 1999 *see also The Displaces of Koshi Tappu and Koshi Bank Decide to Go for Agitation,* KANTIPUR DAILY Aug. 1, 1999 at 3.
47. Before initiation of extension programme in 1982 at least three village settlements viz., Bamla, Baskola and Kilikich were removed from the area of the RSWR. The DPS were resettled around Mahendranagar. The process of removal of another 17 settlements in falling in five villages viz., Rauteli Bichawa

Pipladi, Jhalari, Dekhatbhuli, and Daiji began after the extension programme was announced in 1982. This is discussed in Chapter 6.2 of this work.

48. Recently the government has cleared some 500 ha to relocate families from two villages in the area of RCNP, based on personal communication with Mr. Tikaram Dhakal, The District Forest Officer of Chitwan on January 12th, 1998.

49. However, no record of the extent of displacement or number of DPS is available.

50. Jagdish Pokharel, Large Scale Resource Development Projects and Problems of Dispalcement, Compensation and Resettlement 25-35 (1989) (unpublished M.Sc. dissertation, University of Hawaii).

51. Harka Gurung, *supra* note 45, at 5 (The 69 MW Marshyangdi project affected 222 households).

52. In the past in both Kulekhani and Marsyangdi projects and presently in Kaligandaki project [(201MW) project which is under construction in Nepal], despite recommendation at the planning stage, land for land package was not adopted.

53. The hydropower potential of Nepal is said to be 83,000 MW while the present use is only 0.3 per cent. *See generally* HMGN/NPC, THE NINTH PLAN (1999-2003) 66, 458-482 (Nepali text) (Kathmandu, National Planning Commission, 1999).

54. Ajay Dixit, *supra* note 42, at 75 (citing Water and Energy Commission of Nepal, 1994).

55. Mahakali (Pancheswar) is a 315m high 6480 MW multipurpose high dam project — a joint venture of Nepal and India proposed over Mahakali, a border river. A treaty has been already signed with India for the construction of this project and detail project report (DPR) is under preparation. If constructed the project will submerge 65 major and minor settlements of 14 VDCs in two districts on the Nepal side alone. Besides, 1316 households 11,466 people and 12,000 livestock and at least 94 structures including 20 schools, 3 health posts 9 irrigation facilities etc. are to submerge in the 116 sq. km. reservoir. *See* HMGN/MWR/EDC, PANCHESWAR MULTIPURPOSE DETAILED PROJECT REPORT, ch 9.3 (1995) report available at the WECS, Kathmandu), (henceforth PANCHESWAR REPORT).

56. The West Seti Project (750 MW) is being developed by the Snowy Mountain Engineering Consultants (SMEC) of Australia as a private venture for exporting electricity to India. The proposed project has a 185m tall concrete tam and will affect

2834 ha of cultivated land and some 1620 people. *See HMG/ SMEC Talk for Power Export Near Conclusion*, The KATHMANDU POST, Apr. 22, 1977 at 1; *See* also HMGN/MWR/NEA, WEST SETI HYDRO ELECTRICITY PROJECT, DETAIL STUDY FINAL REPORT (prepared by SOGREAH/SUGLER, Feb.1991, report available at the WECS, Kathmandu).

57. *See* HMGN/MWR, KARNALI CHISHAPANI MULTIPURPOSE PROJECT FEASIBILITY STUDY MAIN REPORT ch. 28 (henceforth KARNALI REPORT) (prepared by Himalayan Power Consultants 1989 report available at WECS, Kathmandu). Among the 24 VDCs to be submerged 3 fall in Kailali, 15 in Surkhet, 4 in Doti and 2 in Achham Though the population to be displaced was recorded to be 60,000 in 1989, with an annual growth rate of 3 per cent recorded in that area, the present estimate has been made. In Aug 1997, the government of Nepal invited Enron, an American, Power Company, with a view to issue a survey license. But as the political debate got heated up in Nepal, the government could not issue the same. *See generally* Dipak Gyawali and Ajaya Dixit, *Mahakali Impasse and Post 1999 Indo-Nepal Water Conflict*, 34(9) EPW 553-564 (1999).

58. They are Sapta Koshi (3600 MW), Kali Gandaki-2 (660 MW), Burhi Gandaki (600 MW), Sapta Gandaki (225 MW), Naumure (Rapti) 466 MW), Bagmati (180 MW), Kankai (60 MW). *See* Ajaya Dixit, *supra* note 42, at 77.

59. For instance, whereas in park projects, the government of Nepal formulated land of land package, the same was not followed in the water resource projects. Even where land for land policy was adopted the norm in all the projects was not uniform. For instance, in the resettlement of PAPs of the RNP air lifting of people, belonging and other materials, provision for timber for construction and monetary aid, food aid, provision for tube-well and school was made but the same was not uniformly followed in Koshi Tappu, or Suklaphanta and for the resettlement of the PAPs of the RNP. In Marsyangdi Project, compensation for fruit trees was paid but the same was not aid in Kulekhani. *See* Harka Gurung, *supra* note 45, at 4. The information on Koshi Tappu and Suklaphanta was collected by the author himself.

60. Nepal has enacted and introduced a Local Self-Government Act, 1998. This Act provides autonomy to the institutions of local self-government in formulating, implementation, monitoring and evaluation of development project. *See* Mukti Rijal, *Local Self Government Bill* (Statute Review), 27 ESSAYS ON CONSTITUTIONAL LAW 67-74 (1198).

61. Social costs are defined as project costs that are left to accrue to the society outside the project, as opposed t the project's direct internal cost (labour materials, equipment and so forth). But social costs are fully project costs in that they would not accrue without the project. Social or external cost include (but not limited to) all that is lost by the forcibly displaced, for instance, land, house, trees, crops, jobs, productive time, cultural assets, CPR, shrines, place of prayer, burial grounds, access to social service etc. Environment Costs refer to the loss caused to local environment by the project, experienced by a wider community. *See* Michael Cernea, *Why Economic Analysis is Essential to Resettlement*, 34(31) EPW 2149,2154 (1999).

62. Internalisation of externalised cost basically means a) compensations to the displaces at replacement cost, plus b) investment for facilitating recovery and accelerated take off for those uprooted and regeneration and revival of environment. The feasibility study report do not include these costs. *See generally*, NEA, TAMUR MEWA PROJECT, (Detail Feasibility Study Report prepared by Canadian International Water and Energy Consultants (CIWEC), 1997, report available in WECS, Kathmandu). *See also* NEA, RAHUGHAT HYDROPOWER PROJECT (Detail Feasibility Study Report prepared by Water Resource Consult/Time Consult/Mashina Consulting Associates, 1998, report available at WECS, Kathmandu).

63. *See id.; see also* KARNALI REPORT, *supra* note 57; PANCHESWAR REPORT, *supra* notes 55; *See also* HMGN/NEA/UNDP/UN DEPARTMENT FOR TECHNICAL COOPERATION, KALI GANDAKI HYDRO POWER PROJECT, (Detail Feasibility Study Final Report, prepared by Norwegian Power Consultant, Oslo, 1962, report available at WECS, Kathmandu).

64. Such Guidelines, in the past, were issued for Arun III Access Road Project in 1989, for Arun III project in 1992, and for Nepal Multi-model Trade and Transit Facilitation Project in 1993. (In these projects funding by the World Bank was expected.) The Guidelines are heavily drawn from the policy of the WB.

65. *See* PANCHESWAR REPORT, *supra* note 55; KARNALI REPORT, *supra* note 57. The Karnali Report goes to the extent of recommending the de-notification of some portion of the Royal Bardia National Park.

66. At least two studies have already appeared on the impact of displacement on the PAPs of Kulekhani Project. These studies have shed light on the flaws in the policy adopted on displacement

and the execution of the project. *See Jagadish Pokharel supra* note 50; *See also* MARIE BJONSS, SOCIO ECONOMIC ANALYSIS OF THE EFFECTS FROM KULEKHANI HYDRO ELECTRICITY PROJECT, NEPAL, 33 (Department of Geography, University of Oslo, 1983).

67. Now a rich body of knowledge exists on the ways and means of preventing impoverishment. *See generally* Michael Cernea, *Understanding and Preventing Impoverishment from Displacement: Reflection on the State of Knowledge,* 8(3) JOURNAL OF REFUGEE STUDIES 245-262 (1995).

68. In Middle and High Mountain area only 9% of the land has less than 5 degree of slopping where as 30% of the land is inclined between 5 degree to 30 degree, and the remaining 53 per cent is slopped more than 30 degree. *See* HMGN/LRMP, LAND UTILISATION REPORT Appendices 4 to 10. (Kathmandu, Land Resource Project 1986), *See also* SAARC, REGIONAL STUDY ON THE CAUSES AND CONSEQUENCES OF NATURAL DISASTERS AND THE PROTECTION AND PRESERVATION OF ENVIRONMENT 4 (Kathmandu, SAARC Secretariat, 1992); Balkumar K.C., *Physiolography of Nepal,* in NEPAL, PERSPECTIVES ON CONTINUITY AND CHANGE 08 (Kathmandu, Tribuvan University, 1989).

69. Of the 19 million people around 90 per cent live in rural landscape. Agriculture is the main occupation of these people. Agriculture accounts about 40 per cent of the GDP and 80 per cent of the employment. Crop production, livestock and forest contribute 60 per cent and 10 per cent of the agricultural output respectively. The annual population growth is 2.08 per cent. While nearly four fifth of the population depends upon agriculture for its primary source of earning, nearly four fifth of all works force employed in he agriculture sector. While agriculture GDP grew annually by only 2.3 per cent during the last two decade but the per capita GDP did not increase at all during he period. NPC, THE EIGHTH PLAN REPORT (1992-1997) 624 (Kathmandu, National planning Commission, 1992); *see also* WB, TRENDS IN DEVELOPING ECONOMIES 36-64 (Washington DC, World Bank, 1994); *see also* http://www.world bank.org/html/extdr/offrep/sas/no2.htnt accessed on Sept. 1, 1999.

70. Only 17% (?) of the land in Nepal is arable. The rest is mountainous. Over 50% of the households own only 66% of total cultivated land and about 10% of the households are landless. A survey conducted in 1984-85 showed that the top

10% of the population received 28% of income, whereas the bottom 40% accounted for only 18%, *see* MAHABUB UL HAQ, HUMAN DEVELOPMENT REPORT IN SOUTH ASIA 47-50 (Karachi, Oxford Univ. Press, 1997).

71. While Nepal has the highest density of mountain population, the per capita land availability is only 0.13 ha which is less than that of China and India for similar regions. *See* Ananda M. Bhattarai, Participatory Forest Management in the Mountain 13 (1995) (unpublished. L.L.M. dissertation, National Law School of India University, Bangalore) (citing Jayanta Bandyopadhyay). The ratio of population per sq km is 600 which is one of the highest in the world. Around 69 per cent of the holdings are less than one ha in size. Among them 44 per cent of the holdings are of less than 0.5 ha size. For more information on this, *see* http://www.worldbank.org/html/extdr/offrep/sas/no2.htm accessed on Sept. 1, 1999.

72. Whereas, 46.62% of the people live in the narrow flat agricultural belt on the southern part stretching from the east in the west, 53.3% live in the mountain. *See* NPC EIGHTH PLAN, *supra* note 69.

73. GERARD J. GILL, MOUNTAINS THE GRANARY 4. (Kathmandu, Winrock International 1996).

74. Harka Gurung, *supra* note 45, at 3; Ajaya Dixit, *supra* note 42 at 76-78.

75. THE CONSTITUTION OF NEPAL 1990 (henceforth NEP. CONST.), Preamble.

76. *Id.*, Art 11 to 22

77. *Id.*, Art 23.

78. *Id.*

79. *Id.*, Art 12 (2) (a) and Art 16.

80. Upendra Baxi, *The Development of Right to Development* in HUMAN RIGHT IN. CHANGING WORLD 4 (E.S. Venkataramaiah ed.) (New Delhi, International Law Association Regional Branch, India, 1988).

81. This perspective is now provided in the UN Declaration on Right to Development 1986. It defines right to development as "a comprehensive economic, social, cultural and political process, which aims at the constant improvement of the well-being of he entire population and all individuals on the basis of their active, free and meaningful participation in development and in their fair distribution of benefits resulting therefrom" (Preamble).

82. The displacement of people results in the context of development decisions. It is therefore necessary to examine the broad objective criteria underlined in the Constitution, beside the constitutional imperatives discussed above. A few objectives enshrined in the Constitution and relevant for our purpose are: promotion of conditions of welfare; establishment of a just system in all aspects of national life including social, economic and political life; protection of the life, property and liberty of people; prevention of concentration of available resources and means of the country within a limited section of society; making arrangements for equitable distribution of economic gains on the basis of social justice; prevention of economic exploitation of any class or individual; elimination of all types of economic and social inequalities; maintenance of conditions suitable to the enjoyment of fruits of democracy through wider participation of people in the governance of the country by way of decentralisation; promotion of human rights; equitable distribution of investment of economic resources for balanced regional development; mobilisation of natural resources and heritage of the country in a manner which might be useful and beneficial to the interest of the nation; priority to the protection of environment and also the prevention of its further damage due to physical development activities; and interests of women, children and other weaker sections and promotion of their interest through special provisions. NEP. CONST., Art 25, 26.
83. *Id.*, Preamble
84. *Id.*, Art. 126
85. S. 9 of the Act gives primacy to international law over domestic law. An elaborate discussion on this is made in chapter 4.2.
86. Nepal acceded to the Optional Protocol 1 on May 14, 1991 and Optional Protocol II on Sept. 26, 1997, See Optional Protocol I to International Covenant on Civil and Political Rights, UNGA Res. 2200 A (XXI) 21 *Session Supp.* no. 16 at U.N. Doc. A 6316 (16 Dec. 1966) Optional Protocol II, G.A. Res 44/128 reprinted in 29 ILM 1464
87. *See for e.g.*, Art 2(1) of the UN Declaration on Right to Development, G.A. Res. 41/128, 4 December 1986 (henceforth UNDRD) provides "The human person is the central subject of development and should be active participant and beneficiary of the right to development." Similarly the UN Declaration on Environment and Development, U.N. Doc. A.CONF. 15/25 Vol. 1 (14 June 1992 Principle I states "Human beings are at the centre of concerns for sustainable Development."
88. This expression is used in UNDRD, *id* Art 2(3).

2

THE RIGHTS OF THE PROJECT AFFECTED PERSONS UNDER THE DOMESTIC LEGAL REGIME

2.1 Introduction

The Constitution of Nepal guarantees no fewer rights to PAPs than it does to others.[1] They are capable of enjoying the same rights, privileges, immunities etc. with regard to life, liberty and property both as individuals and as members of the society. They can assail any law and practices as well as any other actions of the state which are discriminatory in nature or effect.[2] They can also question the morality of state actions, which go against the declared Directive Principles and Policies of the State,[3] though the forum for raising such questions may not always be the court.

The projects causing displacement affect several rights of the PAPs. The Right to life, liberty, freedom of movement, residence, property often come into direct confrontation with state action, which causes displacement. What is the ambit of the rights that get affected by state action and what is the scope of the state action which affects these rights? This is the focus of inquiry in this Chapter. In the first part, after presenting a brief note on the constitutional premise of right, a detailed discussion has been made on the jurisprudential and constitutional aspect of the right to property. A few aspects of state power like the "police power", the "power of taxation", and more importantly the power of "eminent domain"[4] has been presented with specific reference to the experience of other countries more particularly India and the US. Attempt has also been made to throw light on the power of the state to acquire, requisition and encumber property and its duty to pay compensation. In the second part, the scope and ambit of a few other rights relevant in the context of displacement has been examined. Towards the end a general discussion has been made on the constitutional imperative in the context of displacement.

2.2 The Constitutional Premise of Rights

The term 'right' in the Constitution of Nepal is used in a broad generic sense to include claims, powers, privileges, immunities, and the process of empowerment. For instance, while "right" against preventive detention or "rights" relating to criminal justice are immunities, the five freedoms mentioned in Art 12(2) are liberties. Similarly, right of the press or right to privacy are liberties, immunities, privileges etc. depending on the situation and circumstances.

The very purpose of incorporating rights in the Constitution is to impose restrictions on the power of the majority. The declaration of rights compels every creature of the Constitution to revolve within its axis and forbids it from entering the defined orbit of the other without the permission of law. To the extent rights are declared and entrenched, the power of the majority to interfere with personal rights under the utilitarian garb of general welfare is limited.[5] It implicitly means that so long as the rights are exercised within the permissible limits, there is no need for the state to worry whether or not such exercise serves the general welfare of the community.[6]

The incorporation of rights in the Constitution is also a

departure from the orthodox British notion of right. Under this notion, rights and freedoms are considered to be residual. The residual notion of rights is expressed in the form of an often-quoted phrase, which states; "freedom remains after legal restraints are subtracted." According to Halsbury, the concept of liberty is stashed in two generally accepted principles, (a) the subject may say or do what he pleases, provided he does not transgress the substantive law or infringe the legal right of others; and (b) public authorities (including the Crown) may do nothing but what they are authorised to do by some rule of common law (including the royal prerogative or statute)[7] This notion is no longer considered valid today. Once such rights are entrenched and their limits explicitly drawn, neither are the rights taken as residual nor is the majority empowered to put further constraints on rights through legislative enactment. Similarly, the notion of limited power of public authorities outlined in the second principle by Halsbury, has also been given a go bye. Under a liberal constitutional order the executive is generally considered to have residuary power of action to the extent such an exercise does not encroach upon personal rights or interfere with the power of a co-ordinate branch.[8]

While discussing about the premise of rights it is also necessary to look at them as casting a positive duty on the state for protecting and respecting rights. The state is required to protect rights against all possible threats, as invasions are possible not only by the state but also by persons as well.[9] Depending on the nature, extent and source of threats, protection of rights needs to be extended through executive order, legislative enactment as well as judicial pronouncement. In a democratic constitutional order, the recourse to judicial remedy is generally made available also as a fundamental right.[10] While citizens/persons may exercise the right of judicial recourse, duty is also cast on the state to respect some other rights encapsulated in the form of Directive Principles and

State Policies in Part IV of the Constitution through legislative enactment. Such enactment of course should not interfere with the rights in Part III of the same. Recent constitutional trend in this regard is geared towards engrafting the provisions of Part IV while interpreting rights guaranteed under Part III.[11]

Ideologically, the rights guaranteed under Part III of the Constitution are heavily drawn from the instruments on human rights, viz., the Universal Declaration on Human Rights 1948, (henceforth UDHR), the International Covenant on Civil and Political Rights 1966 (henceforth ICCPR), and the International Covenant on Economic Social and Cultural Rights 1966(henceforth ICESCR). The guarantee of human rights to every citizen of Nepal is the preambular promise of the Constitution of Nepal. The use and enjoyment of human right is possible only in a society governed not by men but by the rule of law. As the promise of the Constitution is to transform the rule of law into a living reality,[12] the natural assumption with regard to role of the State in the context of present constitutional premise is that the interest and concerns of the weaker and more vulnerable sections are to be taken care of, and protected against the assault of discriminatory and exploitative practices.

2.3 Right to Property under the Constitution of Nepal

The introduction of right to property in the Constitution of Nepal in 1990 heralds a new era in the revival of this right in the South Asian setting. Perhaps no other right in South Asia has invited so much debate than this right has both in the course of enactment and its interpretation.[13] In the context of the acquisition of the property as well as in other context also courts often make several pronouncements having theoretical and jurisprudential implications on the right to property.[13a] Courts often refer to concepts like "eminent domain" and "police power" to justify state actions sometimes with less concern about the applicability of the concept in a particular fact situation. This kind of position is writ-large in the Nepali case laws.[14] Therefore, before examining the ambit and scope of the right to property under Constitution of Nepal, an attempt has been made to briefly dwell upon the structural, theoretical, and historical analysis of property and the right to property. After this, the scope and ambit of this right is examined, keeping in mind the present socio-economic scenario of the country and the need to protect this right. An attempt has also been made to draw inferences which may be useful in testing the *vires* of present laws of Nepal on land acquisition vis-a-vis the constitutional recognition accorded to the right to property.

2.3.1 *Property as a Concept*

In common parlance, a property is a thing. But it would be too naive an expression to rely on for any practical purpose. To a lawman 'property' is a legal concept because, for its existence, legal recognition is required. It is only under a legal order that a concept like 'property' can come into being.[15] However, some authors argue that for the existence of the institution of property, existence of an organic social order is more important, because, according to them, social norms may exist even outside legal order.[16] Though, the existence of "property" in the form of a physical object may pre-date a legal order, for its existence in the form of a relation "between a person(s) and an object" or "between a person(s) and an object in relation to a person(s)", the existence of a legal order is a condition precedent.

Over time the concept of property has undergone a tremendous change. For a hunter or a food gatherer the concept of property in its rudimentary form might have been limited to a few implements and instruments or to his prey also at the most. But gradually as the society entered into agricultural and pastoral practices, the concept of property widened to include land and chattel. With the emergence of industrial society the concept of property transcended the physicality and began to connote some economic interests and rights like trade mark, copy right, industrial design etc. [17] One can see that with the expansion of the concept of property over time the rationale for owning it also got changed and the economic value or interest took over other interests like subsistence and other intrinsic and aesthetic values

It has often been a practice to employ Hohfeldian correlatives and opposites for understanding a right to property. According to this analysis the person(s), in relation to an object at hand will have certain power, claim/right, privilege and immunity against a person(s) having disability, no right, duties and liabilities respectively.[18] If applied to property, these incidents generally, but not always, result in the right/claim to possess, use, manage, and receive income; the liberty to consume or destroy; the immunity from expropriation, the duty not to use harmfully and liability for execution to satisfy a court judgement etc. If a person has with him all of these incidents or most of them, with respect to a thing, then it can be said that he/she owns it. [19] The subject of these incidents is generally called the owner. But it would be a mistake to equate property right with ownership alone. By virtue of having some incidents enumerated above a person may have a proprietary right over an object still he may not have ownership on that object. The examples to illustrate this are easement, bailment, and right to till a land by the tenant etc where persons other than the owner exercise certain advantages.

Another connected issue with regard to property right relates to the body right. The issue has generated a lot of debate in recent times. Patenting of human gene is one of them and may be a matter of a separate study. The question related to the present discussion is does a person own his body in the same manner he owns his labour (both physical and mental), car or a house? Do all the incidents of property right enumerated above apply to a person's right over his body? It is obvious that human body as an object does not certainly meet many qualifications that a property as a physical object meets. For instance, unlike property a person cannot be transferred, consumed or destroyed. But he can sell his labour, sue for and enjoy the fruit of the same. Whereas human beings enjoy a certain degree of autonomy, "property" on its own does not enjoy such autonomy. Yet, body right as a property right has been hotly contested. Some philosophers and jurists go even to the extent of taking the view that a person owns his body in the same manner that he owns his labour.[20] The current view on the issue is that though ownership of human body by human being himself is not accepted, a limited property right on body is increasingly getting recognised. Those body rights, which protect the choice to transfer, are considered property rights and the rest as personal rights.[21] Some body rights like right to donate an organ upon death, right to publicity, right to sell semen, right to sell the skill or ability to work as it happens with football contract in some European countries can be taken a few examples of property rights.[22]

2.3.2 *Property Right as a Bundle of Rights*

With the change in the concept of property over time, as the holistic definition of the right to property became difficult, jurists and judges have attempted only an *ad hoc* definition of property.[23] Nevertheless, a few definitions appear more comprehensive than others. One can see a relative comprehensiveness in the definition advanced by justice Hidayatullah. He said:

> The right to property can be referred to mean a *bundle of rights* (interest or thing) with direct or indirect regard to any *external object* (i.e. than person himself) which is *material*

> *or quasi-material* (i.e. a protected process) and which the then and there organization of society permits to be either private or public, which is connected by the legal concept of *occupying, possessing*. The right is enforced *by excluding entry or interference* by a person not legally entitled[24]

The exposition given by Justice Hidyatullah covers almost all the components that make a property right except body right. Theoretically property right, as has been rightly pointed out by him, is considered to be a bundle of rights. But as to what consists in this "bundle"; how many fragments are required to be present in the bundle in order to constitute full ownership; are these constitutive fragments independent of each other or are they connected, and form a hierarchical order; these are some of the questions on which there is no unanimity among jurists.[25]

The right to property is taken as a "bundle of right" in English law. It looks at ownership by breaking it up into fragments and reads it as collection of fragments.[26] But the Roman law takes ownership as an overarching concept, which includes all the constituent rights that can, to some extent, be split up.[27] This split surfaces in the course of alienation. In different legal systems, one may notice the presence of some components and the absence of a few others. For instance, the right to exclusion may not be that firm in a society that recognises communal property right. Similarly, in a communist legal system the right to exclude and right to alienate may not appear very concrete whereas the right to exclude is the kernel of a private property right system.[28] Therefore, it is submitted that though some constitutive rights that give rise to ownership, like right to possess, or privilege to exclude others, may appear more prominent than some other constituent rights, while determining the ambit and scope of the right to property and deprivation of the same in "public interest" under a legal order, all the constituent rights should be taken into consideration.

2.3.3. Property as a Social Institution

For the reason that property fulfils various needs of man in society, it is to be considered a social institution.[29] It springs from social conditions and needs. Not only the economic but also the aesthetic and sentimental values are also attached to the institution of property. These values are expressed in the form of satisfaction—either enjoyed individually or communally. In fact, the idea of property is linked to the personality of the individual.[30] Therefore, it is submitted that to confine property exclusively to any economic aspect of the human situation and to ignore the subjective elements involved in it is subject to fallacy.

The desire for property perhaps resulted from a desire to secure subsistence and survival. Besides human being, the instinct of survival is found in animals and insects as well. The protection of food, off-springs and peers is found even in animals and insects.[31] The common interest in subsistence is supposed to have created a social order. Social order recognised the occupation and the use of property but at the same time forbade causing harm to others. It is beyond doubt that the first right over a property enjoyed by man is the right to occupy and possess. So long as the resources were not scarce, and the people did not permanently settle in one place, the right to exclusion perhaps did not get much prominence. Where communal practice of cultivation was more prominent, it is probable that people did not attach so much importance to the right of ownership. Perhaps similar was the condition of right to exclusion. The fact that the concept of ownership is historically of late origin[32] sufficiently indicates that this concept was used either to protect or prevent the greed of the powerful forces. Even when property was occupied and owned by individuals, chieftains claimed the superior right of ownership in the form of eminent domain. Perhaps this residuary right is still claimed by the state in various forms including the acquisition, requisition or expropriation, escheat of land and other property resources or the right over common property resources.

2.4. Historical Development of the Right to property as Constitutional Right

No doubt, the concept of right to property is a product of written Constitutions; the protection to property against invasion was a major concern in all societies which recognised these rights. Whenever the property was physically taken away, payment of compensation was the norm, though in such cases reliance used to be placed on the political processes to take care of such incidents.[33] In such a scenario when the property rights were left to the wisdom of the political leaders, the possibility of discrimination, excessive invasion, non-action etc on the part of the state was not ruled out. The evolution of the legal regime against the state invasion to property right owes this apparent tension between the state action and the general expectation of society.

While the Fifth Amendment to the U.S. Constitution accorded the protection to private property strongly for the first time, several fundamental documents, charters, and constitutions contained provisions relating to property rights even before the Fifth Amendment was brought into existence. While a few states recognised the right to property as a substantive right a few others accorded procedural protections[34]

In England the provisions relating to property rights can be traced back to Art 39 of the Great Magna Carta, which stated:

> "No freeman shall be dispossessed ... except by the legal judgement of his peers or by the law of the land"

The above stated provision of Magna Carta could lay down conditions only for procedural regularity owing, perhaps to the concept of the supreme and absolute authority of the state over private property which was supposed to be exercised by the Parliament.[35] However, under the British legal system property was protected against arbitrary taking, and also in case of expropriation, the owner was granted a right to claim compensation.[36]

The property right clause in the Fifth Amendment of the U.S. Constitution heralds a new era in the property right discourse. With this provision a strong foundation against physical invasion to property was laid down.[37] The limits to the power of eminent domain were enshrined in the Constitution whereby, the state could take property only (a) for public use, and (b) after just compensation is paid or secured. However, after the Fifth Amendment, it was believed for a long time that the constitutional protection was available only against physical invasion and not against other forms of interference.

With *Pennsylvania Coal*[38] case, a new phase began in the US where the protection to property right transcended the limit of physicality. In this case, which involved a challenge to Pennsylvania's Kholer Act, which barred coal companies from removing coal when such removal caused subsidence resulting in consequential loss, the court held that it amounted to taking. Writing for the Majority Holmes J. observed; "The general rule at least is that while property may be regulated to a certain extent, if regulation *goes too* far it will be recognised as taking".[39]

The ruling transcended the criterion of physical seizure of property. The general meaning that one can derive from this ruling is that the exercise of property rights had certain implied limitations. Limitations to the use and enjoyment of this right could be imposed, for instance, by the exercise of police power, which may lead to diminution of values. But so long as the diminution is only incidental, and not substantial, the government should be allowed to go ahead with its programme without paying compensation for the diminished values. But if the loss of value in property is too substantial the state should pay compensation.[40]

The ruling in *Pennsylvania coal*, no doubt, made a seminal contribution for the development of the concept of regulatory taking in the US, but it is not free from problems. In years subsequent to the *Pennsylvania case* the American courts took quite divergent views to decide the question as to how far is "too far" though the courts have tried to solve the problem by developing standards.[41] Despite difficulties in determining the threshold level, regulatory taking is compensable in the US and the benchmark set by the *Pennsylvania* ruling still holds good.

So far as the constitutional protection to the property right in South Asia is concerned, the countries of the region are at different stages of development. While Bhutan does not have a written Constitution, the Sri Lankan Constitution is silent on the question of property right. In case of other South Asian countries, namely, Nepal, India, Bangladesh, Pakistan and Maldives, the provisions relating to right to property are couched in varied languages. Different parameters are laid down with regard to use and enjoyment, and limits to the exercise of this right. However, despite variations, one common feature which emerges is that, except in case of Nepal, physical invasion, either permanent or temporary, is taken as a necessary precondition to constitute the taking of property. In *Solapur Spinning Mills*,[42] the Indian Supreme Court tried to evolve a principle very close to both "the concept of encumbrance" of the Constitution of Nepal and the concept of "regulatory taking" as laid down by the US courts. In that case, the Indian Supreme Court held that a person could be said to have been deprived of the property if it withheld the property from the possession and enjoyment of the owner, or "seriously impaired its use and enjoyment by him or materially reduced the value". In the Case Mahajan J. observed; "The correct approach in such cases would be this: what in substance is the loss or injury caused to the owner and not what manner or method has been adopted by the state in taking the property."[43] However, the court added, in such taking the deprivation had to be substantial in which case the form of deprivation was unessential[44]

The principle laid down in *Sholapur Spinning Mills* was superseded by the Fourth constitutional amendment, which barred the courts from taking cognisance of cases where the state neither acquired nor requisitioned the property.[45] When Right to Property was purportedly repealed as fundamental right in 1979 this provision was also repealed.[46] Though there is a possibility of resurgence of the ruling advanced by the court in *Sholapur spinning Mills,* this has not happened so far in India.

2.5. The Right to Property under the Constitution of Nepal

The right to property is recognised as a fundamental right under the Constitution of Nepal. All citizens of Nepal are guaranteed the right to acquire, own, sell and otherwise dispose of property.[47] Besides the rights enshrined in Art 17(1), there are other provisions, which have a bearing on the right to property. They are:

- The right of the press against closure and seizure,[48]
- The right of the religious denomination to manage and protect its religious place and trust,[49]
- The right of the community to operate school,[50]
- The right of a person to maintain the privacy of his house, property, document, information etc.[51]

The constitutional guarantee accorded to property right

appears to be in consonance with basic norms and practice of a liberal constitutional order. One of the very fundamental tenets of this order is the guarantee to freedom of contract, as is permissible within the overall framework. The Constitution of Nepal guarantees that freedom. The Constitution also respects the sanctity of property and allows the market to operate in the distribution of economic goods in line with its promise to "promote welfare on the basis of the principles of an open society."[52] However, it should be noted that Constitution does not accept the right to property as an absolute right. This right is to be enjoyed "subject to existing laws."[53] However, the limitation to private property can be imposed only through legislative measures. No executive fiat can put restraints or encumbrance on private property.

The Supreme Court of Nepal has tried to interpret Art 17(1) in a few cases. One such case was the *Private and Boarding School* case.[54] This involved the *vires* of S 120(1) of the Education Rules, 1991 that interfered with the right of the private school to hold property after such school ceased to operate. The Supreme Court took the view that as the parent Act (i.e. the Education Act 1990) did not empower the state to declare the property held by such school a public property in case the school closed down or ceased to operate, the same could not be done by the executive by framing the Rule. Thus the Court held that, as the Rule 120(1) of the Education Rules 1991 attempted to change the nature of the property and usurp it forcefully, it was *ultra vires* Article 17 of the Constitution. In *Rishikesh Shah,*[55] the Supreme Court went on to observe that even where existing statutory provisions entitled the government to interfere with property rights, any attempt to interfere with such rights had to be made in accordance with legitimate procedures. In the instant case, the Court held that confiscation of the books written by the petitioner and keeping them under the control of government without initiation of necessary proceedings amounted to a violation of fundamental right to property.

The ruling advanced by the Supreme Court of Nepal in the two cases discussed here and also a few others[56] lead us to infer that restriction or encumbrance on property can be created only through legislative action and not by executive decision. Secondly, such a law should possess all the characters of a valid law, meaning thereby that it should be just, fair and reasonable and not arbitrary, fanciful or confiscatory. Perhaps the exercise of police power by the state to regulate a citizen's property or the protection of public health, morals and comfort, or the power of taxation, should meet the conditions laid down by Art 17 and other provisions of the Constitution.

2.5.1. *The Sanctity of Right to Property v Intervention by the State*

The sanctity of right to property is considered a hallmark of a democratic society and a salient feature of liberal constitutions. Protection of property right was one major agenda in the march towards liberalism and constitutional order expressed either in the Great Magna Carta or the American War of Independence. With the emergence of *Laissez faire* economy it was felt that the state had no business to invade private property right of a person to benefit another. A strand of thought even advocated a very minimal role for the state in the affair of the citizens.[57] However, this view could not attain much currency, as the utilitarian concept of the greatest happiness of the greatest number, with necessary modification, remained the dominant ideology of governance under the welfare state. It is perhaps the reason why the right to property was never considered an absolute right. Intervention of the state was considered just for a multitude of functions like attainment of distributive justice by levelling up of the weaker section through direct distribution of economic goods, protection of public morals, health and comfort, and overall development of the country. Therefore, the quest for a proper balance between property right and the intervention of the state under the garb of police power or the concept of eminent domain or the power of taxation has been a perennial quest of jurists and judges in the liberal constitutional settings. It is submitted that as the constitutional postulates of Nepal are not totally new creations bereft of history and ideology, the Constitution is no exception so far as the quest for a proper balance is concerned.

2.5.2. *Scope of Intervention by the State*

Another aspect of the right to property is the scope of interference, which is stipulated in Art 17(2) and 17(3) of the Constitution of Nepal. Put simply Art 17(2) and (3) empower the State to deprive a person of his property right subject to the conditions and parameters laid down therein. A plain meaning of these two clauses appears to be as follows.

- The state can acquire, requisition or create encumbrances on the property of a person (not only citizens) only in public interest.
- In case of such acquisition, requisition or creation of encumbrance, the State is required to pay compensation.
- Law should prescribe the basis of and procedure for giving compensation for any property thus acquired, requisitioned or encumbered by the state in public interest.

The first requisite for acquisition, requisition or creation of encumbrances on the property of a person by the State is that it should be in "public interest." On a cursory reading the expression "public interest" seems to be a wider expression than "public use"[58] or "public purpose."[59] For example, certain cross-section of the public may have general interest in certain governmental activities like construction of hotel to generate foreign revenue or some export business even though such activity may be of no public use or benefit. It is submitted that such a broad interpretation of the term "public interest" would be repugnant to the very concept of constitutional guarantee to property right. Therefore, it should be understood in a restrictive sense to imply "public use" or "public object"[60]

The state intervention to property right appears in various forms, like the exercise of the power of eminent domain, police power or the power of taxation. There seems to be a lot of confusion as to under which garb the state acquires the property in normal or emergency situations.[61] Therefore, an attempt has been made here to present the distinction between these powers of the state.

2.5.2.1 Power of Eminent Domain v. Police Power

Both police power and the power of eminent domain are exercised by the state to interfere with property right. But they are exercised to serve different purposes. Whereas under the police power, the state tries to curb the use of property against public health, morality or comfort, the power of eminent domain is supposed to be exercised for a public purpose—for public benefit or use. Under the police power, right to property is impaired not because the property may become useful or necessary to public, or because some advantage can be gained by disregarding the right, but because its free exercise is believed to be detrimental to public interests. It may be said that the state takes property by eminent domain because it is useful to the public, and under the police power because it is harmful. The former recognises a right to compensation, while the latter on principle does not.[62]

2.5.2.2 Power of Eminent Domain v Power of Taxation

The power of eminent domain also needs to be distinguished from the power of taxation. While the power of eminent domain and taxation both originate in the political necessity and rest substantially on the same foundation, there are material distinctions between them. The payment of compensation is the preconditio · for the exercise of the power of eminent domain no such *quid pro quo* exists in the exercise of the power of taxation. The amount paid towards tax is considered a contribution and a public duty whereas the same cannot be said to be true in case of acquisition of property. The incidence of exercise of the police power and the power of taxation leave uniform impact among the subjects, while the effect of the exercise of the power of eminent domain is selective. In the latter the impact remains concentrated in certain pockets.[63]

However, American courts have traced the nexus between the power of eminent domain and taxation. The U.S. Supreme Court in *Cole v La Grange* [64] tried to establish this nexus. The court observed; "the general grant of legislative power in the Constitution of a state does not enable the legislature, in exercise either of the right of eminent domain, or of the right of taxation, to take private property ... for any but a public object"[65]

2.5.2.3 Public Interest and the Power of Eminent Domain

Among the three conditions set out by the Constitution of Nepal for imposition of restriction to the right to property, the first one is "public interest."[66] Couched in a negative prescription, the Constitution clearly stipulates that the property cannot be acquired, requisitioned or encumbered except in "public interest".[67] But what then is "public interest"? What is the rationale behind giving the state the power to acquire, requisition and encumber property? Is the action of the state under the garb of "public interest" is judicially reviewable? Who is the best judge to decide the matter? Can any state action, in the name of public interest, be justified if it deprives people of their basic human rights? These are some of the questions, which require to be addressed here.

The power to acquire property for public interest is considered to be an inherent power vested in a sovereign state. It is often said that this power does not emerge from the

Constitution but is independent of it[68] and is equated with what American lawyers call the power of "eminent domain." This expression has got a very deceptive connotation in the courts of the Third World. There are instances where this expression has been used to justify the power of the state to acquire property as it is an unlimited power. Therefore, a brief discussion on the nature, scope and limits of the power of eminent domain will facilitate the current understanding of the expression. While doing so a brief look on the US and Indian practice will not be out of place here.

The expression "eminent domain" is generally defined as the power of a nation or a sovereign state to take or to authorise the taking of private property for public use without the owner's consent, conditioned upon the payment of just compensation.[69] The expression "eminent domain" was first used in 1625 by Hugo Grotius[70] in the continent and was later adopted and popularised in the United States.[71] In England and Canada the term "expropriation" is used to denote a similar power of the State.[72]

The power of the eminent domain is considered as an attribute of sovereignty—inherent in a state. This power is supposed to be the one springing from political necessity and not depending for its existence on a specific grant in the Constitution.[73] It exists in a sovereign state even without any recognition thereof in the Constitution.[74] As the power of eminent domain is considered an inalienable power of the state, no Legislature can bind itself or its successor by any resolution to alienate or contract for non-exercise of this power.[75]

Connected to the power of eminent domain is the Grotian theory of the absolute and original ownerships of the state, wherein all individual ownerships are supposed to have resulted from the sovereign grant, and therefore, subject to extinguishment by an exertion of the original ownership. Hugo Grotius said:

> The property of subjects is so far under the eminent control of the state, that the state or the sovereign who represents it, can use that property, or destroy it, or alienate it, not only in cases of extreme necessity, which sometimes allow individuals the liberty of infringing upon the property of others, but on all occasions, where the public good is concerned, to which the original framers of society intended that private interests should give way.[76]

The notion of this power as enunciated by Grotious was adopted by several American states for quite some time. But later this view was rejected for being a regressive theory of slavish Hobbesian vintage legitimising the concept of absolute monarchy.[77] It is now generally understood that the power of eminent domain is not a property right or an exercise by the state of its right of ultimate ownership but a power, as stated earlier, springing from public necessity.[78]

The right of eminent domain encompasses property of every kind and character, whether real or personal, tangible or intangible, including all property or rights of the owner within the jurisdiction of the sovereignty authorising such exercise.[79] The power of eminent domain extends to personal property in general. It also extends to incorporeal rights like contracts, corporate stock, and franchise, easements, patent rights and chooses in action. But except in war, under ordinary conditions it doesn't seem to encompass the expropriation of money. In other words direct expropriation of money is not done under eminent domain.[80]

Under a controlling Constitution, the power of eminent domain is exercised subject to the limits set by the Constitution. Where the Constitution is wholly silent on the subject, the power of eminent domain lies entirely with the legislature. Under such conditions, until the legislature takes initiative this power remains dormant.[81] But once authority is given to exercise the power of eminent domain, the matter ceases to be wholly legislative. The executive authorities may then decide on the need and the extent of the exercise of eminent domain. But a few questions like the alleged violation of constitutional right and compensation are generally considered justiciable questions.[82]

2.5.2.4 *The Power of Eminent Domain: The US Experience*

Under the US Constitutional system, the State's power of eminent domain is limited chiefly by two considerations: [83]

- that property shall not be taken for public use without just compensation, and
- that no person shall be deprived of his life liberty or property without due process of law.

According to the first rule of the eminent domain, as enshrined in the US Constitution, private property can be taken only for "public use".[84] Apparently the concept of "public use" looks simple, but it has appeared to be the most problematic part of the taking clause of the US Constitution in relation to the power of eminent domain. As the expression has not been defined in precise terms, most often the controversy arises with regard to its meaning. Courts have interpreted "public use" to connote two things entirely different namely, "public employment" and "public advantage."[85]

One strand of ruling holds that "public use" means use by the public, i.e., public employment. According to this view, there must be a right on the part of the public, or a portion of it, or some public or quasi-public agency on behalf of the public, to use the property after it is condemned.[86] The use of the property condemned should be as a matter of right and not favour.[87] If the term "public use," as the proponents of this view argue, is used to mean "public benefit or advantage," it may open up an indefinite field, as almost every business enterprise may indirectly benefit public to some extent.[88]

The second strand of ruling holds the view that "public use" means public advantage, convenience, benefit etc. In other words, it means the use for, not necessarily by, the public. According to this view, anything, which tends to enlarge the resources, increase the industrial energies and promote the productive power of any considerable number of the inhabitants or a section, or which leads to the prosperity of the whole community constitutes a "public use". According to this view, "use by the public" as a test for "public use" is inadequate because, under this criterion, eminent domain might be employed to secure sites for hotels and theatres where people have a right to access.[89]

However, courts have accepted neither of these opposing stands without qualification. The US Supreme Court has emphasised for a great caution in the employment of this term. It recognised the inadequacy of the "use by the general public" as a universal test, as one may come across a situation where the very foundation of public welfare cannot be laid without requiring concessions from individuals.[90]

Going by the catena of cases on "public use" one finds that, for a long time, the American courts advanced a restricted view of the term "public use" to mean "use by the public" But with expansion of the functions of the government a concomitant expansion in the interpretation of concept of public use occurred. Now the predominant view in the US is that the expression "public use" means "use for, not necessarily by, the public." If the acquisition is beneficial to a considerable number and is warranted by public necessity it will be considered as "public use."[91] Nevertheless, at academic level the debate on "public use" or "public purpose" is yet to die down.[92]

The generally considered view in the US today is that the public nature of a project that needs to be looked into and not the numerical strength of those to be served. For any state action to constitute taking for a public use it is enough if the people of a particular locality receive benefit, if the action is guided by public necessity and the power is exercised for common benefit in contradistinction to "individual benefit".[93]

Another approach developed by the American courts is the approach of "incidental use". By employing this approach the courts have held that the exercise of eminent domain for a public use, which is primary and paramount, will not be defeated by the fact that incidentally a private use or benefit has resulted or is likely to result which by itself would not have warranted the exercise of the power.[94] The controlling question is whether the paramount reason for the taking of the property is in "public interest" and the benefit to private interests are merely incidental or is this the other way round.[95] Incidental benefit accruing to public is not sufficient to make the purpose of an enterprise a public one. Where the private purpose or benefit too clearly dominates the public use, the power of eminent domain cannot be exercised.[96]

Another interesting American experience on public private dichotomy is that where there is a combined purpose or use—partly public and partly private—and the two uses or purposes cannot be separated, eminent domain cannot be exercised.[97] Similarly, where a statute authorises a single taking to the necessities of the public and private use, it is considered unconstitutional.[98] However, when a private benefit and public use are blended and the undertaking is capable of furthering a public use, it is in general the US judicial practice to regard the private benefit as merely incidental.[99] Besides, attempts have been made to mitigate the rigour of this through both legislative and judicial process. A few of such examples, which can be of interest for our purpose, are illustrated here.

- Many states have adopted constitutional provisions or amendments to limit the exercise of the power of eminent domain in favour of the individual owner of property. The most important of these are the requirement of compensation when property is damaged and of jury trial, provisions which go to making the necessity for taking as a justiciable question.[100]

- As a rule of construction, it has been laid down that a constitutional provision allowing the exercise of the power of eminent domain should be liberally construed in favour of the private property owners.[101]
- As the exercise of the power of eminent domain is in derogation of the rights of the citizen, statutes conferring the power of eminent domain are to be strictly construed against the one exercising the power and in favour of the land owner. Such statutes are not to be extended or abrogated by inference or by implication or by judicial construction. The exercise of this power has to be limited to the express terms or clear implication of the statute in which the grant is contained.[102]
- So long as the use is public, the courts are not concerned with the wisdom of a law that delegates the power to condemn, but where there is clear abuse of power or a colourable exercise or fraud on the Constitution, courts intervene.[103]

2.5.2.5 The Doctrine of Public Purpose: The Indian Experience

The doctrine of "public purpose" is the basis for making invasion to private property in India. It principally means that private property can be acquired for public purpose, and for such acquisition the state has to pay compensation. Despite the foundational article i.e. Art 31 of the original Constitution being repealed in 1979, the Constitution guarantees a right to property. The implicit recognition to the doctrine of public purpose now is accorded in Art 300 A of the Indian Constitution.

In *Julubhai Nanbhai Khachar*, the Indian Supreme Court observed that the expression "deprived of his property" used in Art 300 A comprehends the power of the state to acquire property for public purpose.[104] But what does the term "public purpose" imply? Is the state competent to acquire property only for public purpose? Is this power accompanied with a duty not to acquire property for private purpose? Is there a tension between the constitutional mandate and the prevalent practice? These issues will briefly be discussed here in the light of the constitutional provisions and judicial decisions. But before touching upon the scope and meaning of the doctrine of public purpose, a brief recount of the historical perspective will be worthwhile here.

The provision on the right to property was one of the hotly debated provisions in the Constituent Assembly. Perhaps no other article took so much time and patience of members as this article did.[105] It was mainly because of the importance attached by the framers to social transformation and empowerment of the downtrodden. To achieve these objectives under a liberal democratic legal and social order was a daunting task demanding courage and vision as well as legal acumen and scholarship. It is because the desired transformation or reform had to be achieved without impairing the basic individual freedoms and rights. Therefore, as put by Nehru, the Framers tried to forge a compromise between the two approaches viz., individual right to property and the interest of the community in that property.[106] The framers tried to safeguard individuals' right to property by making it inviolable save by authority of law. At the same time they tried to protect community interest in property by drawing a distinction between petty holdings and the big ones, and allowing the state to regulate big holdings. Insulation of the land reforms laws from the possible attack by the courts was one such strategy which was reinforced later by the 21st amendment to the Constitution in 1967.

While the Assembly discussed threadbare the question of compensation, very little was discussed on the scope of the term "public purpose." It may be partly because the term was a legacy of the British legislation consistently used in the Land Acquisition Act of 1894[107], its predecessor Acts[108] and the Government of India Act 1935.[109] All these Acts used the expression "public purpose". Besides, a body of case law already existed on the use of the expression "public purpose".[110] Therefore, in the Constituent Assembly when a few amendment drafts were moved using the term "public use" instead of "public purpose"[111] it was opposed. This was, of course, not because of any love for the expression "public purpose" against the expression "public use" but because the latter had, as it was feared, a chance of affecting the acquisition made in pursuance of some social objectives, such as the abolition of *zamindari* and other land reform measures.[112] Finally, when the final draft emerged from the Constituent Assembly it followed the beaten track by adopting the expression "public purpose" rejecting the expression "public use."

Despite the efforts in the Assembly, the concept of public purpose could not come over as an overarching doctrine, or a touchstone for any state invasion on property rights. It was mainly for two reasons. First, the Constitution did not affect the provisions of any existing laws. Second, it allowed the legislature to enact laws for evacuee property without caring for the provisions of 31(2)[113]

Like its counterpart expression "public use" in the US, the expression "public purpose" in India is also considered equally elusive. Though there exists a Privy Council decision attempting to determine the ambit of "public purpose", it was not further concretised in post-independent India.[114] So far Indian courts have avoided taking a definite stand with regard to the meaning of the term as well as its applicability and justiciability. Taking almost a unanimous view the Indian courts have said that the expression "public purpose" is an elastic concept changing with time, facts and prevailing conditions.[115] The Indian Courts have taken the view that since the concept of public purpose changes with the growth and development of the state and its political philosophy a live constitutional jurisprudence must be able to adjust it to the changing concept of public purpose.[116] Partly for ideological reasons but largely due to the common law heritage, courts have taken a very broad view of the expression "public purpose." According to Das J., whatever furthers the general interest of the community as opposed to the particular interest of the individual is a public purpose. [117] Courts have even taken public purpose to be synonymous with governmental purpose.[118]

Going by the huge body of case law evolved on this particular point one comes across a wide range of considerations being taken into account to determine the purpose of the projects. For instance, where cost of the acquisition has been borne out of the public fund;[119] where lands have been acquired for rehabilitation of the displaced persons;[120] or for residential and industrial sites;[121] or for memorial[122] all of these have been considered as public purpose. Similarly acquisition of land for rehabilitation of slum dwellers,[123] for the construction of railway siding,[124] and a few other dubious purposes like the acquisition for housing board,[125] or private hospital,[126] or a privately run technological park[127] have also been considered as public purposes. Thus, the broad spectrum of case laws enumerated here suggest a sweepingly broad ambit for "public purpose" in India.

A connected issue on the point in India is the acquisition of land for companies. While the Constitution prescribes for the acquisition of property for "public purpose" the Land Acquisition Act, 1894 provided for acquisition of land for companies (not necessarily a public purpose).[128] After the promulgation of the Constitution of India, the Act was saved by virtue of being an existing law.[129] Therefore, on the question whether an acquisition for company should meet the criteria laid down by the Constitution one comes across by and large three streams of thoughts prevailing in India.

- Decisions justifying acquisition by offering a very generic meaning or a harmonious construction to the expression "public purpose";[130]
- Decisions skipping the question by stating that the government is the best judge to decide whether such acquisition serves public purpose or not;[131] and
- Decisions justifying acquisition by stating that acquisition (for companies)need not be for public purpose.[132]

Of late, however, Indian courts have adopted a more cautious approach and devised tools to curb executive freedom to invade private property. One of such tools, though employed very rarely, is the "vagueness of purpose". In *Mohd Safi*[133] where a notification under S. 4 of the Land Acquisition Act was published for acquisition of an area of 2.29 ha of land for the construction of Housing Board, and where only a word "residential" was mentioned in the detail of public purpose, the Supreme Court struck down the notification and proceedings. Speaking for the court Justice A.S Anand (as he then was) observed; "the public purpose which has been mentioned as residential is hopelessly vague and conveys no idea about the purpose of acquisition".[134] Though the ruling in *Mohd Shafi* appears to be progressive, it would, however, be a mistake to take the case as a trend setter because in several other cases, despite the purpose stated being equally vague, the courts have declined to strike down the government decisions.[135] A sum up by Justice Syed Jafer Imam in *State of Bombay v R.S. Nanji(s)*, by and large, states the position of

Indian Courts on the issue of justiciability of "public purpose"[136] as follows:

Prima facie the government is the best judge as to whether 'public purpose' is served by issuing a requisition order but it is not the sole judge. The courts have the jurisdiction and it is their duty to determine the matter whenever a requisition order is or is not for a public purpose.[137]

2.5.3 *Acquisition, Requisition and Creation of Encumbrance on Property and Compensation*

For the first time the Constitution of Nepal has used the terms "acquisition", "requisition" and "creation of encumbrance" in the context of compensation. Acquisition and requisition are two different concepts. While in the former the title of the property passes to the acquiring authority, in the latter it remains with the owner and only the possession passes to the authority requisitioning such property. In requisition, possession of the property is taken for a limited period where as in acquisition, the property permanently passes on to the acquiring authority.[138]

The expression "creation of encumbrance" generally means the creation of interest in the property in favour of the state. As a matter of fact, encumbrance can be permanent as well as temporary in nature, which may put burden on the person having right over the property thus encumbered. For example, requiring the owner to restrict the use of land to a certain kind of cultivation is an action of putting encumbrance.[139] Such action may impose additional burden to the property owner. He may also lose economic value in the property. In each of these three state actions viz., acquisition, requisition or creation of encumbrance, the method of calculating compensation needs to be different. However, one commonality in terms of state action, in all the three incidents is that the state can acquire, requisition, or create encumbrance only in public interest.

The question of compensation has been addressed by the Constitution of Nepal in a little circuitous manner. The Constitution does not straight away mention that the state shall not acquire, requisition or encumber property without paying compensation. It only states that "the basis of compensation and the procedure for giving compensation ... shall be prescribed by law."[140] What does this imply? Is the state bound to pay just compensation or can it acquire, requisition or encumber property paying anything other than what can be called as just compensation? These questions need to be examined here.

Even though the Constitution of Nepal does not specifically mention whether or not acquisition of property without compensation is proscribed in Nepal, a combined reading of Art 17(1)(2) and (3) makes it amply clear that no property can be acquired, requisitioned or encumbered without paying compensation.

In general parlance, compensation means anything given to make things equal in value. Anything given as an equivalent to recover the loss is compensation.[141] Applied to Art 17 of the Constitution, it means any measure which brings a person, who suffered loss due to acquisition or requisition or creation of encumbrance on the property by the state, at least, to a situation of *status quo ante*. This ideally being the minima that can be attributed to the term "compensation", to what extent can the *status quo ante* be ensured while interfering with the property right of a person, is a vexing question.

The idea of compensation appears to be based on the notion that the government must not disturb the distribution of wealth that people have earned in their private dealings with one another. Whenever it takes something from individuals it must give them equivalent compensation.[142]

The Constitution of Nepal has not used any adjectives to

qualify the term "compensation", nor has it stated that, in terms of value, it can be any thing less than the value, which can make amends for the loss or damage. Given that the term compensation itself means just and equitable compensation, it is unlikely that any law that is enacted by the Parliament which fixes the basis and procedure of compensation can derogate from the protection accorded to the right to property by the Constitution. However, before forming any concrete opinion about the meaning and scope of the term "compensation" it will be worthwhile to have a perusal of the concept of "just compensation" employed in the US and the debate on the issue in India.

2.5.3.1 *The Concept of Compensation: The US and Indian Experience*

The concept of just compensation in the US springs from the Fifth Amendment to the Constitution. It is now settled rule of law in the US that private property cannot be taken in any way for public use without compensation being made[143] or secured.[144] Almost all the state Constitutions have followed the dictate of the Fifth Amendment, and even where this provision is not applicable the taking of private property without compensation being paid is considered as a derogation from the due process of law.[145]

In contrast to the US, the Constitution of India does not approve of the idea of just compensation, as it was understood in the former. Though some drafts introduced in the Constituent Assembly provided for using the term "just compensation", it was ultimately rejected.[146] The idea of the framers was not to do away with the concept of 'just compensation', for they understood quite well that the term 'compensation' itself was sufficient to mean just compensation. It was rather to adopt a cautious approach, whereby the big holdings would be paid a reasonable amount against what they would loose but not just compensation.[147] Notwithstanding their wish, however, the question of compensation in the context of Art 31 became a subject matter of tension between the executive and the judiciary in the post-constitutional era.

Dwelling upon the provision of Art 31(2) the Indian Supreme Court in *Bela Banerjee* [148] took the view that though the legislature was given discretionary power of laying down the principles which would govern the determination of the amount, such principles must ensure that what was determined as payable was compensation, i.e. a just equivalent of what the owner has been deprived of. The free play of legislative judgement in evolving principle was possible when such principles ensured "full indemnification of the expropriated owner". The court observed, " whether the principles take into account all the elements which make up the true value of the property expropriated and exclude matters which are to be neglected is a justiciable issue to be adjudicated by the court."[149]

The Parliament attempted to scuttle the effect of the ruling in *Bela Banerjee* through the Fourth Amendment, which made the question of adequate compensation non-justiciable.[150] However, this did not prevent the Indian Supreme Court from looking into the question of compensation. In *Vejravelu*[151] the Supreme Court pointed out that even after the amendment, the provision for compensation or laying down of the principles for determining compensation was a necessary condition for making of a law relating to acquisition or requisition, as according to it, the amendment had only prevented the court from questioning the law on the ground that the compensation provided was inadequate. That, however, did not prevent it from striking down a law as a fraud on the Constitution if the principles for determining compensation were irrelevant to the value of the property at or about the time of acquisition or if the law provided for illusory compensation.[152] Thus, with *Vejravelu* one witnesses the partial revival of the ruling given by the Court in *Bela Banerjee*.

Though the Indian Supreme Court in *Shantilal Mangaldas*[153] deviated a bit from the stand it had taken in *Vejravelu*, it corrected itself in *R.C. Cooper*[154] by following *Vejravelu* again. It held that the bank nationalization law was liable to be struck down as it failed to provide the expropriated banks compensation determined according to relevant principle. The reasoning advanced in *R. C. Cooper* was that the principle specified by law for determining compensation was beyond the pale of challenge only if it was relevant for the determination of compensation.[155]

The difference of opinion between the executive and the judiciary on the question of compensation took another turn after *R.C. Cooper*. By the Twenty Fifth Amendment the Parliament dropped the word "compensation" from clause (2) of Art 31 in order to avoid judicial review of compensation as just compensation.[156] However, even after the 25th Amendment the justiciability of Art 31(2) was not given up by the judiciary. The Supreme Court in *Keshavananda Bharati*[157] considered the validity of the amendment, and a majority took the view that the amount fixed by law can be questioned in a court, if the amount so fixed is illusory or if the principles specified are irrelevant or a fraud on power.[158]

After *Keshavananda Bharati* the legislative response to the judicial pronouncement came in the form of the 42nd Amendment to the Constitution which repealed Art 19(1) (f) and Art 31 of the Constitution. With this, the controversy surrounding these Articles died out but not the fundamentality of the right to property and several issues connected with it including the scope and limit of public purpose and compensation. The partial insertion of Art 31 in Art 300A, to the claims of academic lawyers in India has made the right to property more fundamental than before.[159] They also claim that the revival of *Bela Banerjee* dictum has become more imminent, though on this new dimension of the right, the law is yet to evolve in India.

2.5.3.2 Resonance of the Indian and US Experience

One clear message that one can derive from the US and the Indian experience on the question of compensation is that courts in both the countries were guided by the same approach, i.e., full exoneration to the property right holder in case of state expropriation of the property.[160] Whereas the US practice on the issue seems to be more streamlined and stabilised the same cannot be said about India where tension still persists with regard to the governing principles for the payment of compensation.[161]

Going by the provisions of the Constitution of Nepal on compensation, they seem to be closer to the relevant clauses of Art 31 of the Constitution of India as it originally was. Art 31 required the expropriating law either to fix the amount of the compensation or specify the principles on which, and the manner in which, the compensation could be determined. The Constitution requires the law to lay down "the basis and procedure for giving compensation." The provision of the Constitution of Nepal however, differs from its Indian counterpart in the sense that it makes no distinction between smallholdings and big holdings. Therefore, the Constitution demands a uniform criterion for compensation irrespective of the type, size and nature of holding. Even a cursory reading of the provision of the Constitution of Nepal will enable one to infer that the call of the Constitution is for just compensation —the full exoneration of the expropriated property right holder.

2.5.4 Creation of Encumbrance and Regulatory Taking

Protection against creation of encumbrance without the

authority of law is another aspect of the right to property under the Constitution of Nepal. In general parlance "encumbrance" refers to the creation of a burden. Going by the lexical meaning of the term, "encumbrance" is any right or interest in land which may subsist in another to the diminution of its value ... a claim, lien, charge or liability, attached to and binding on real property. For example, a mortgage, judgement lien, mechanic's lien, lease, security are called encumbrances.[162] The state, by exercising this power, may impose on the property owner a positive duty or a burden to meet certain demand or bear certain costs. Taken from this standpoint, one finds a very close nexus between the power of eminent domain and the police power in the context of encumbrance.[163]

While the Constitution provides the power to the state to create encumbrance on a property, it also casts a duty; (a) to exercise this power public interest and (b) to pay compensation for the exercise this power. The Constitution also gives immunity to the state when the above conditions are met.

The creation of encumbrance is possible without physically invading the property. When such incidence is possible, it would offer scope for claiming compensation in cases where the property owner has incurred economic loss not because the property was acquired, requisitioned or encumbered but because the action of the state resulted in substantial economic loss to him. It also seems to be plausible to argue that when the state is willing to take the obligation to pay compensation for the burden it imposed on account of its conscious decision to create encumbrance, it should also be ready to pay compensation in case substantial loss is caused to the holder of property which is not acquired, requisitioned or encumbered. This takes us very close to a situation what is termed as "regulatory taking" by American lawyers.[164]

The history of the property right demonstrates certain patterns. While in the first phase the protection to property was left to the political wisdom, in the second phase the protection to property was available only against physical invasion. Protection against diminution of economic value signifies the third phase of state protection. This means that while in the first phase chances of non-compensatory taking were more, they were reduced in the second phase. However, during this phase full indemnification was beyond the realm of certainty. During this phase the concept of just compensation was made a rule and attempts were made to ensure justiciability in a few jurisdictions. Where the concept of just compensation was still under debate, and justiciability under suspicion, the courts by taking liberal stands tried to provide compensation which was just equivalent of what the expropriated owner lost, wherever the constitutional framework permitted. The expansion of the concept of taking in the third phase to include regulatory taking further concretised the right to property but this theory is yet to get full recognition at least in the South Asian region. It is submitted that the Constitution of Nepal has opened up that possibility.

2.5.5. *Common Property Rights and the Constitutional Protection*

The predominant notion today considers common property rights beyond the realm of constitutional protection. But such a notion, it is submitted, is riddled with fallacy. It was mentioned earlier that in the "bundle of rights" relating to property, all the sticks are not necessarily overlapping or co-terminus. The use right is one such right. In the case of common property the use right is exercised collectively and the right of exclusion is exercised only against those who do not belong to the community or the family. In some tenure the property is registered but not in others. The Hindu joint family system and India and Nepal are some examples of collective exercise of use rights.[165] In the Himalayan highland owing to the nature of the topography, pasture lands are used and managed collectively.[166] The *Kipat* tenure in some parts of eastern, central and western Nepal is one such tenure under which the property of a particular locality is registered in the name of the clan head, and not in the name of the family head.[167] These tenure systems are either still recognised or were recognised for a long time in the past before the onset of individualist concept of property. The detour towards the individuated system of property holding system in Nepal is rather recent.

The Constitution of Nepal no where mentions that the protection it extends is only to private property, for it would be erroneous to hold that view. Under the prevailing legal system, there are several practices where use rights on property are exercised collectively and benefits are shared. The community forest system of Nepal is one of them. The harvest arising from the management of the community forest belongs to the community collectively.[168]

The property right recognised by the Constitution of Nepal is, subject to law. In other words it is subject to reasonable restrictions. But the law imposing restrictions on this right should be a valid law and not just a nomenclature.[169] When the law makes unreasonable discrimination between persons or impairs the guarantee of a fundamental right,[170] or arbitrarily deprives one of his right to life or does not take into consideration the existing social practices or, norms rooted in the notion of survival, or does not possess the minimum moral content, then, it is submitted that the authority of such a law can always be questioned under the present constitutional framework of Nepal. This apart, a defective law can very much be amended or repealed or even declared *ultra vires*. Therefore, it is very much plausible to argue that the

Constitution of Nepal extends protection to every form of property and proprietary interest. But how are these constitutional guarantees translated into action, and whether or not the present laws relating to the acquisition of property respect this constitutional mandate will be the query of the next chapter.

2.6. Other Rights

The other rights, which generally come to fore in the context of acquisition of property for development projects are right to equality, right to life and personal liberty, and right to information and right to privacy.

2.6.1. *Right to Equality*

The Constitution of Nepal guarantees to Nepali citizens "equality before law" and "the equal protection of law".[171] In fact the expressions "equality before law" and "equal protection of laws" are two different concepts. While the former implies the absence of privileges in favour of any one in the operation of law—an attribute of the English doctrine of the rule of law, the latter is an assurance about treating like case alike, refrain of which can be found in the Fourteenth Amendment of the US Constitution.[172]

The basic objective of the equality clause is to treat citizens equally as far as possible. So long as the specific characteristics or situation do not demand separate treatment, equality is the rule. When persons in same situations are discriminated against in the application of laws, the guarantee of the right to equality becomes operative.[173] In *Balakrishna Neupane*,[174] the Supreme Court of Nepal pointed out that Art 11(1) of the Constitution, which guarantees the right to equality, envisages equal application of laws between equals, and that neither the equal application of laws between unequals nor the unequal application of laws between equals is justifiable.

The equality clause demands an impartial and even handed dealing in state action, and a sense of equanimity in the legislative enactment. However, it does not rule out the possibility of unequal treatment altogether. Theoretically, where equal treatment is not possible on account of the possibility of a resultant inequality, reasonable classification is allowed.[175] For a long time, class actions and legislation purporting to protect specific groups were tried to be justified under the doctrine of classification. However, it was soon realised that classification has the tendency of mortifying equality. Judges and jurists now are unanimous in their view that, through imperceptible extension, a theory of classification may subvert equality. They hold the view that over-classification has a tendency to generate inequality.[176] One method to check this deviation and ensure equality is to add vitality to the equality clause by expanding its amplitude and to do away with the doctrinaire method. Courts in recent times have attempted to ensure equality by striking at arbitrariness of executive actions and legislative enactment lock stock and barrel, as according to them, arbitrariness and equality are antithetic to each other. Where an Act is arbitrary, the necessary implication is that it is unequal—both according to political logic and constitutional law- and violates Art 11 of the Constitution.[177] Now the courts are more inclined to look at justness, fairness and reasonableness of the state action or enactment and where it is found not to be so, such actions or enactment are knocked down.[178]

The second method to curb inequality is the principle of integration. According to this principle, while determining whether or not the impugned state action or legislative enactment meets the test of equality, one is required to look at other articles of the Constitutions as well. In case such state actions and enactment are found to be violating other rights and freedoms, for instance right to personal liberty under Art 12(1) and freedoms guaranteed under Art 12(2) or right to property under Art 17, such actions or enactment even though not impermissible under Art II(i) in *stricto sensu* are considered to be discriminatory, and hence violative of the equality clause.[179] Though the Supreme Court of Nepal has not yet adopted the integrative principle, given the constitutional framework under which it is working, which accords increasing regard to human rights, the adoption of such principle seems imminent.

The integrative principle, in reality unfolds the chances of importing the due process clause while interpreting the equality clause. Such an importation has one clear advantage so far as the case of PAPs are concerned. That is, if one can establish that the state action or legislative enactment is deficient and denies the due process of law, it can be considered discriminatory as well. Thus, as one can see, the principle of integration and fairness seem to have better promise for PAPs than the traditional doctrine of classification. Once these principles are entrenched in the equality clause, such state actions, which are discriminatory in content or in effect, are also likely to be struck down.

2.6.2. *Right to Life and Personal Liberty*

Though the Constitution of Nepal does not use the expression "right to life" given the democratic temper of the Constitution according highest possible respect to basic human rights, it can be said that protection to right to life is subsumed in Art 12(1) of the Constitution. A combined reading of Art 12(1), other articles of Part III including the preamble of the Constitution, along with section 12 of the Civil Rights Act 1955 also supports this view.[180]

Theoretically, by guaranteeing the right to life to person, the Constitution imposes on the state limitations generated by the following duties; first, a duty to refrain from acts or omissions which directly endanger life; second, a duty to take reasonable steps in order to prevent the deprivation of life by other persons;[181] and finally, a duty to create conditions which allow a person to live a life with dignity— and not a mere animal or vegetable existence.

A life with human dignity, no doubt, requires the fulfilment of basic necessities like adequate nutrition, clothing, shelter, educational facilities, and means of expression. The state is under an obligation to fulfil these necessities under Part IV of the Constitution. Some of these rights like the right to a healthy environment[182] and right to protect a cultural and religious site (heritage)[183] have already been engrafted as rights emanating from right to life. If the present trend of the courts in giving expansive interpretation to rights is any indication, there is a likelihood of other rights also being engrafted upon the right to life. With regard to the restrictions, the Supreme Court of Nepal has held that when depriving a person of his life or liberty both substantive and procedural requirements of law must be duly observed, with maximum care and presence of mind.[184] It is noteworthy that the court considered the due process of law as a precondition for imposing restriction on personal liberty right from the fifties.[185]

In the context of displacement, where property is acquired without an alternative for livelihood being provided, the life of the PAPs begins to degenerate compelling them to live in sub-human condition. Such a situation is no doubt a deprivation of the basic necessities, amenities and condition of life. However, despite undertaking a liberal attitude in the interpretation of rights the Supreme Court of Nepal is yet to thrash out corrective measures that could allay the grievances of the PAPs.[186]

2.6.3. *Freedom of Movement, Residence, Trade, Occupation etc.*

The freedom of movement and residence are two different

rights guaranteed by the Constitution of Nepal but, they are closely connected. In the same vein they are also equally connected with the freedom to trade and occupation as without freedom of movement or residence carrying out of trade and occupation becomes impossible. Arguably freedom of movement within its ambit includes the freedom not to move or freedom to stay in the place of choice. Where a citizen is forcibly evicted, the freedom of movement probably includes a right to return to the original habitat. Like the freedom of movement, the right to freedom of residence also carries with it both positive as well as negative connotations. Similar interpretation can be given with regard to the right to freedom of trade and occupation. As displacement affects all these rights it is submitted that the limit of the state power in imposing restriction on these rights also needs to be examined.

2.6.4 Right to Information and Right to Privacy

Other two very important rights that need to be discussed in the context of the rights of the PAPs are the right to information and the right to privacy. For the first time, these two rights have been explicitly guaranteed as fundamental rights to citizens of Nepal.[187]

In a democratic constitutional order, the government is supposed to be open and accountable to people. The affairs of the state are considered a matter of concern of the citizen. The democratic government requires a minimum amount of transparency in state action and inform people about its activities. Only when transparency is assured, the government may expect informed consent and willing co-operation of the people in its activities. Where the right to information is not guaranteed by law, citizens have to rely on the will, whim and fancies of the authorities for information even on issues vitally important for their livelihood.

With the incorporation of the right to information as a

fundamental right, the Constitution has made open government a rule, and secrecy the exception. Where the exigencies require secrecy, the state can maintain it only by law and not by executive fiat. The implicit presumption on the matter is that the government documents are public unless legal provision states otherwise. A right to access to such document is established when the person proves that the information sought is of public importance. Except this, the citizen seeking such information need not establish any *standi* for the same.[188]

Though the Right to Information Act is yet to come into existence in Nepal, and the pre-constitutional Confidentiality of Documents Act 1982 is still in place, the Supreme Court on several occasions was seized on the issues relating to the right to information and passed some path breaking rulings. A few of such rulings, which are very much relevant for our purpose, are the *Tanakpur* [189] case and the *Arun III*[190] case. The first case involved a treaty with India relating to the construction of afflux bond and allied matters in Tanakpur barrage over Mahakali—a border river between India and Nepal. In this case the court declared (per BN Upadhyaya CJ) that the natural resources of the country are the national wealth of Nepal and common property of all the citizens of the country. As every citizen has a meaningful relation with the economic development, environmental protection, the court observed, it cannot be called improper if a citizen shows his curiosity about how or what type of treaty or agreement or understanding has been reached with a foreign country by his government regarding the exploitation of such resources. As the country as a whole is entitled to profits and liable to bear losses from favourable or adverse impacts of such projects, the court held, every citizen has a right to seek information from the government under Art 16 of the Constitution.

Similarly, in *Arun III*, which involved the construction of a dam for hydropower from Arun river—a tributary of river

Koshi in eastern Nepal—the Supreme Court held that, as the matter relating to the construction of a medium sized hydropower project with collaboration of the World Bank was a topic of public concern, every citizen had a right to demand and receive information under Art 16 of the Constitution. Feeling that, the absence of an appropriate legal framework on the subject may have adverse effect on the exercise of the right to information, the court in the instant case issued guidelines for effective exercise of the right.[191] In yet another case, which involved the right to seek information about an Action Plan for the use of water resources between Nepal and India, the Supreme Court held that, since the Action Plan contained nothing which required to be kept secret, it should be published.[192]

Under Art 16 of the Constitution, every citizen is vested with a right to seek information from the state as well as person—both natural and legal. Looked from this angle, not only the state but also every corporate entity is under an obligation to provide information on matters of public importance. Though the expression "public importance" is not defined, any activity either run by the state or a person, which has a likelihood of affecting the public can plausibly be considered a matter of public importance. Similarly, information relating to development projects, which has a likelihood of affecting the life of the people, either direct by acquisition of their property or by its impact on the local environment, is undoubtedly a matter of public importance. In such cases, the state as well the executing authority is under an obligation to provide information to every citizen who has a meaningful relation to the project initiatives.

Another right, which needs to be juxtaposed with the right to information, is the right to privacy. Whereas the former guarantees the citizen a right to demand and receive information on any matter of public importance, the latter allows the person (not only citizen) a right to privacy of his property, information etc. The latter, no doubt, is a personal right and is considered inviolable. However, as both the rights, viz., the right to information and right to privacy, can be regulated by law, which, of course, needs to be a valid law, the state can play a very meaningful role in drawing a balance between the competing public and private rights and interests. Given that the Constitution espouses a democratic and transparent government, it can be argued that, if the activities of a person affect the rights of other persons guaranteed by the Constitution, the veil of privacy should be lifted and the right of the affected person to demand and receive information on matters concerning him should get precedence over the right to privacy.

2.7. Constitutional Imperatives in the Context of Displacement

This exercise began with the proposition that the rights of the PAPs are no less guaranteed under the Constitution of Nepal than in case of others. What does this imply in the context of displacement is the focus of inquiry here.

In the first place the constitutional framework requires the juxtaposition of displacement in the context of right to life (right to living and livelihood included). The emergence of integrative approach to fundamental rights enables one to link various other rights like, right to choose residence, right to trade, right to occupation, right to religion and culture, right to information, right to education etc as a corollary extension of the right to life. Therefore, the bottom line for any state action is that it should not result in deprivation of right to life. Given that people eke out a living under an socio-economic and cultural environment, and that forced displacement adversely affects means of life and living, it is plausible to argue that the PAPs do possess the right not to be arbitrarily displaced and deprived of environment under which they have made their living possible.

What amounts to an arbitrary deprivation of the right to life is the second important question. This needs to be looked at from two angles, viz., the substantive conditions and the procedural requirements. It is a fact that rights are not guaranteed under the Constitution in absolute terms. In fact such absolute framework of rights is not possible in any democratic order. The Constitution empowers the state to impose certain amount of restrictions for greater public benefits under the parameters laid down by itself. This means that such restrictions should be based on the permissible grounds justifying the same, respond to a pressing public or social need, pursue legitimate aims and should be proportionate to the aims. The point can be further elucidated with reference to the right to property. The Constitution of Nepal empowers the state to impose restrictions on the right to property in "public interest" by paying "compensation". Here, "public interest" and the "payment of compensation" should be considered as minimum permissible substantive conditions which broadly subsums the conditions mentioned above. That such a restriction should be imposed only by law would be the procedural requirement. Any state action, which imposes restriction other than for public interest and without the payment of compensation or which imposes restrictions not through law but by executive fiat, is undoubtedly arbitrary, and hence beyond the constitutional ambit.

The issue of "public interest" is a very thorny one and more so in the context of displacement. The power of the state to acquire, requisition or encumber property is often linked with the power of eminent domain. It has been made clear that the power of eminent domain is not an absolute power. The very characteristic of a democratic Constitution presupposes that the power of eminent domain is limited by the parameters laid down in the Constitution. It was also clarified that, unlike the general supposition, the power of eminent domain is not a proprietary right of the state emerging from the traditional Grotian notion of original ownership of the state. It is rather a power springing from public necessity. The very fact that acquisition or requisition of property is possible only by paying compensation rejects the absolute authority of the state over proprietary rights.

The concept of "public interest" is of course not a uni-dimensional concept. On what constitutes "public interests" and what amounts to a private interest, multitude of opinions and views exist. The difference of opinion between economist and lawyers is also not less striking. Whereas any decision of the state, which results in general welfare of the community or a section thereof, or which results in capital accumulation through revenue generating or export promoting schemes, may be looked upon by economists as sufficiently serving "public interest," such a broad sweep may not be acceptable to lawyers. Though no fixed definition of public interest or other cognate expressions like "public purpose" or "public use" has been attempted by courts so far, certain yardsticks, and assumptions have been developed to curb the abuse of power in other countries. A discussion on these yardsticks and assumptions has been made earlier while looking at the US and Indian experience. The legal perspectives require the question of "public interest" to be linked with the constitutional parameters laid down in the Constitution, more specifically, the parameters laid down in Part III and Part IV of the Constitution. Any state action, which is at variance with the rights guaranteed under Part III or the parameters of development laid down in Part IV, may be argued to be not in "public interest". The Constitution rejects the view, which judges the state action only in terms of aggregate economic benefits. So does the legal view. Any paternalistic state action, which goes blatantly against the principles of economic and social justice enshrined in the Constitution, cannot be termed a decision serving "public interest."

Another substantive condition laid down by the Constitution is that state intervention on property is possible only on payment of compensation. As stated earlier, though the Constitution does address this question in a circuitous manner, the basic presumption underlined is the full exoneration of the expropriated owner—a just and full compensation. Principally, the constitutional premise requires the determination and payment of compensation in such a manner, which ensures restitution of the proprietary rights, interests and entitlements at least to the pre-move level. This in the first place, requires a clear understanding of the earning pattern of prospective displacees and other PAPs. As the idea of compensation for the loss of property stipulated in the Constitution of Nepal is not limited to individual/personal property, to limit it to ownership would be a travesty of justice to the holder and user of property. In fact such a view also goes against the juristic concept of property. Property is not only limited to economic interests but also encompasses subsistence and other aesthetic values as well.The fuel, fodder, usufructs are not only economic interests but also means of subsistence. The loss of these interests affects the PAPs. Because in Nepal as the law secures several interests on property on the basis of communal use, the individuated concept of compensation goes against the notion of property.[193] Besides, as the idea of compensation in the context of displacement is linked with the livelihood of the people, it essentially means the restoration of the livelihood of the PAPs if the project decision results in deprivation of livelihood, irrespective of the type and nature of property that a person holds. As the Constitution embraces a broader principle on the question of compensation which goes beyond the physical loss of property it seems very much plausible to contend that the Constitution favours the payment of compensation for the loss of common property resources as well as other substantial losses, which occur to the holder even when property is not physically condemned. In other words, the loss, which can be construed as regulatory taking, is compensable. It is submitted that the Constitutional framework of Nepal opens up that possibility.

Displacement is not only a problem of acquisition of property and payment of compensation for the same. Though a liberal interpretation of right to property to encompass proprietary interest solves a host of problems, there is a need for the right to property to be interpreted in conjunction with other rights as well. The examination of Art 17(2) in a broader constitutional scheme may secure for individual the fullest protection of his basic rights.

With regard to the procedural requirement, it should be noted that the Constitution allows the derogation from the right only where it is permitted by the Constitution itself. No executive fiat is a permissible ground for making invasion into the rights of the PAPs. When such a law is enacted it should lay down conditions under which not only a claim for the restoration of the loss of property is possible but the legality of state action under the concept of "public interest" can also be reviewed through democratic means such as people's participation in the decision making stage itself. This would ensure that the people most likely to be affected will have an effective say in policy making. Besides, the democratic means of scrutiny of public interest includes the judicial scrutiny as well. In fact justiciability of public interest and justifiability of the state action are necessary preconditions for democratic governance. For a law to be just, fair and reasonable, it should encourage democratic participation. Secondly, Art 17(3) of the Constitution of Nepal requires that the law relating to acquisition, requisition or creation of encumbrance should lay down the basis and the procedure for compensation, both of which are to be just fair and reasonable. In a democratic legal order, questioning and constant probing of the basis of and procedure followed for the determination of compensation should be considered a fundamental rights of the citizens.

The guarantee of right to life casts a duty on the state to refrain from acts or omissions, which directly or indirectly endanger life, and to take reasonable steps to prevent deprivation of life by others. Besides, the duty to create conditions which allows fulfilment of basic necessities like adequate nutrition, clothing, shelter, education etc. requires the state to look into displacement resettlement and rehabilitation holistically and not at each one of them in isolation. This is perhaps the minimum that the state is required to keep in mind while formulating legal framework on displacement under the permissible constitutional limits. Whether the existing legal regime meets these basic requirements underlined by the Constitution is the subject of inquiry in the next chapter.

REFERENCES

1. *See e.g.* NEP. CONST. Art 11 (Right to equality); Art 12(1) (Right to Personal Liberty); Art 12(2)[(a) Freedom of opinion and expression; (b) freedom to assemble peaceably and without arms; (c) freedom to form unions and associations; (d) freedom of residence; (e) freedom to practice any profession, or to carry on any occupation, industry or trade]; Art 16 (Right to information); Art 17 (Right to Property); Art 18 (Cultural and Educational Right); Art 19 (Right to religion); Art 20 (Right against exploitation); Art 22 (Right to Privacy).
2. *Id.* Art 23 and Art.88.
3. They include: promotion of condition of welfare, establishment of a just system in all aspects of national life, protection of the life, property and liberty of people, preventing the available resources and means of the country from being concentrated within a limited section of society, making arrangement for the equitable distribution of economic gains on the basis of social justice, establishing justice and morality in governance by eliminating all types of economic and social inequalities, maintaining conditions suitable to the enjoyment of the fruits

of democracy through wider participation of people in governance, *see Id.* Art 25.

4 Literally it means "the power to take private property for public use by the state,...authorized to exercise functions of public characters." *See* BLACKS'S LAW DICTIONARY 470(5th ed St Paul Minn, West Publishing Co., 1979).

5. *See generally* RONALD DWORKIN, TAKING RIGHTS SERIOUSLY, 184,194-196 (Cambridge MA, Harvard Univ. Press, 1977).

6. This view also finds support in Mill, who said; "The only purpose for which power can rightfully be exercised over any member of a civilised community against his will is to prevent harm to others. His good either physical or moral is not a sufficient warrant. He cannot rightfully be compelled to do or forebear because it would be better for him to do so, because it would make him happy or because in the opinion of others, to do so would be wise or even right."*See* J.S.MILL,ON LIBERTY AND REPRESENTATIVE GOVERNMENT 8 (London, Blackswell, 1948).

7. HALSBURY LAWS OF ENGLAND 540 (para 828)(4th ed London, Butterworth, 1974).

8. Ram Jawaya Kapur v State of Punjab (1955) 2 SCR 255, 235; *see also* H.M.SEERVAI,1 CONSTITUTIONAL LAW OF INDIA 356(4th ed Bombay, N.M. Tripathy 1991)(1967).

9. PUDR v Union of India AIR 1982 SC 1473,1490 (holding that State is under an obligation to ensure the enjoyment of fundamental rights).

10. NEP. CONST. Art 23; *See also* THE CONSTITUTION OF INDIA (henceforth IND. CONST.) Art 32, 226.

11. Prakash Mani Sharma v HMG/Cabinet Secretariat NKP 1998(2054) p 312, 320 (holding that the Directive Principles are not vacuous jargons, the court can issue necessary instruction if they are found to be overlooked).

12. NEP. CONST. Preamble

13. For instance, in India the right to property enshrined under Article 19(1)(f) and Article 31 of the original Constitution was amended several times and finally removed from Part III of the Constitution by the 44th Amendment 1979 and introduced as constitutional Right in Art 300A. However, Indian Jurists and Constitutional experts are of the view that with the amendment this right has become more fundamental than any other fundamental rights. *See generally* A.M.BHATTACHARJEE,

EQUALITY, LIBERTY AND PROPERTY UNDER THE CONSTITUTION OF INDIA 133-147 (Calcutta, Eastern Law House 1997); *see also* P.K. Tripathy, *Right of Property After 44th Amendment—Better Protected than Before,* AIR 1980 Journal 49-52; S.P. Sathe, *Right to Property After the 44th Amendment: Reflections on Prof. P.K. Tripathy's Observations, id.* 97-100. Detailed provisions regarding the Right to Property in the Constitution of Pakistan speak in volume that the framers had in their mind a fear about over-expansion of this right, *see for e.g.* (THE CONSTITUTION OF PAKISTAN (henceforth PAK. CONST.) Art 23,24,253. In Bangladesh the same apprehension about the ambit of this right has been expressed in Art 42(2) itself. It states "...no such law [i.e. the law relating to acquisition, nationalization or requisition] shall be called in question in any court on the ground that any provision in respect of such compensation is not adequate." It is only in the Constitution of Maldives that the expression "just compensation" is used. *See* THE CONSTITUTION OF MALDIVES (henceforth MALD CONST) Art 23(2).

13a. Recently in Mithilesh Kumar Singh V. the prime Minister [(Writ No. 2531 of the year 1966) unpublished judgment dated June 6, 1999] the court went to the extent of denying fundamental character to Art. 17 of the CONST (Per Laxman Aryal j.) This judgement gives rise to several complications which will be discussed separately.

14. Nanda Kumari Rawal v Ministry of Industry, NKP 2051(1994) p 180,189; *See also* Sita Bista v Ministry of Home NKP 2051 (1995) p 852.

15. Bentham and Justice Holmes are the people who take this view as Bentham put it: "Property and law are born together and die together. Before laws were made there was no property; take away laws and property ceases to exist." JEREMY BENTHAM, THEORY OF LEGISLATION 69 (R. Hildreth trans.Bombay, N.M. Tripathy 1986)(1876); *see also* International News Service v The Associated Press 248 U.S. 215 (1918).

16. R.S. BHALLA, THE INSTITUTION OF PROPERTY 40,74(Lucknow, Eastern Book Company, 1984); *see also* M HIDAYATULLAH, RIGHT TO PROPERTY AND THE INDIAN CONSTITUTION 12 (New Delhi/Calcutta, Arnold Heinemann/ Calcutta University 1983) (arguing that instinct and tradition of the community justify a person in claiming the rights, in supporting a person's claim over property).

17. *See generally*, Ernest Beaglehole, *Property* in 12 INTERNATIONAL

ENCYCLOPAEDIA OF THE SOCIAL SCIENCE 589-592 (David L. Sill ed. Macmillan & Co., 1968); *see also* Walton H. Hamilton & Irene Till, *Property*, 11 ENCYCLOPAEDIA OF THE SOCIAL SCIENCE 528-538 (Edwin R.A. Seligman ed. New York, Macmillian, 1933).

18. For a detail ed analysis of right *see* WESLEY N. HOHFELD, FUNDAMENTAL LEGAL CONCEPTIONS 35-64 (Walter Wheeler Cook ed., Green Wood Press, 1978).
19. A.M. Honore, *ownership* in 1 OXFORD ESSAYS IN JURISPRUDENCE 107-47 (AG. Guest ed., London, Clarendon Press, 1961); *see also* STEPHEN R MUNZER, A THEORY OF PROPERTY 19-27 (Cambridge, Cambridge University press, 1990).
20. *See* MUZNER, *id at* 58 (citing John Locke and Robert Nozick).
21. *Id.* at 49-50.
22. *Id.* at 57.
23. Such definitions are attempted in a plethora of cases; *see for e.g.* Sagir Ahamad v State of UP AIR 1954 SC 728; State of MP v Ranjijirao Shinde AIR 1968 SC 1053; State of WB v Subodh Gopal Bose AIR 1954 SC 92; Charanjit Lal v Union of India AIR 1951 SC 41; R. C. Cooper v Union of India AIR 1970 SC 564, Sami Motor v Shankaraswami Mutt AIR 1963 SC 864
24. *See* Golakh Nath v State of Punjab AIR 1967 SC 1643, 1709 (quoting Noyes)(Italics added).
25. BHALLA, *supra* note 16, at 7-13 (denying the separate existence constitutive rights); *see also* W FRIEDMANN, LAW IN A CHANGING SOCIETY 95 (2d, London, Sweet and Maxwell, 1972 (1959) (citing Art 544 of the French Civil Code which allows the trustee and to a certain extent the settlers to dispose property also allows the beneficiary to have a right to enjoy). He further argues that the concept of trust in common law has attained the common law mind to the division of property between parties. *See also* A.M. Honore, *supra* note 19, at 109 (Citing historic reason for fragmentation of property right he argues that in early middle age property in England could not plausibly be said to be 'owned' because the standard incidents were so divided between the lord and tenant that the position neither present a sufficient analogy with the paradigm case of owning a thing.).
26. BHALLA, *supra* note 16, at 9. Ownership is considered to comprise the right to possess, the right to use, the right to capital, the right to security, the right or incident of transmissibility

and absence of term, prohibition of harmful use, liability to exclusion and the incident of residuality. *See* A.M. Honore, *supra* note 19, at 113.

27. Thus *jus utendi, jus fruendi, and jus abutendi* under the Roman Law, are derivatives of ownership. Pound has further extrapolated these rights into *jus possidendi, jus utendi, jus fruendi, jus abutendi, jus disponendi, jus prohibendi. See* BHALLA, *supra* note 16, at 8.

28. Holmes said that property depends upon exclusion by law from interference see International News Service v The associated Press 248 U.S.215 (1918).

29. Baxi said; "The legal right of property is an aspect of the satisfaction of human needs". U.Baxi I*ntroduction* to K.K. MATHEW, DEMOCRACY, EQUALITY AND FREEDOM LXXVII (Lucknow, Eastern Book Co., 1979)

30. Hegel said; "Property is the embodiment of personality" *see* G.W.F HEGEL, PHILOSOPHY OF RIGHTS 45 (T.M. Knox trans. London , Oxford Univ. Press, 1971).

31. Earnest Beaglehole, *supra* note 17.

32. *See generally* M. HIDAYATULLAH, *supra* note 16, at 18-19,21.

33. Willian Michael Treanor, *The Original Understanding of the Taking Clause and the Political Process*, 95 COLUMBIA LAW REVIEW 782,785 (1995).

34. For instance, a provision of the Massachusetts Body of Liberties, adopted in 1641, imposed requirement for compensation, though it was limited to the seizure of personal property. Section 8 of the document stated; "No mans cattel of goods of what kinde soever shall be pressed or taken for any publique use or service, unless it be by warrant grounded upon some act of the generall court, nor without such reasonable proces and hire as the ordinarie rates of the countrie do afford. And if his cattle or goods shall perish or suffer damage in such service, the owner shall be sufficiently recompensed". Quoted in Willliam M. Treanor *id.* at 785. Similarly, the 1669 Fundamental Constitutions of Carolina, drafted by John Locke, though never fully implemented, provided compensation for the seizure of real property. Art 44 stated: "The damage the owner of such lands (on or through which any such things shall be made) shall receive thereby shall be valued and satisfaction made by such ways as the grand council shall appoint "*id.;* So far as the incorporation of the compensatory provision in the constitution is concerned, states like Vermont (1777), Massachusetts (1780), and Northwest (1787), contained such provisions. For instance,

Ch 1 art II of the Vermont Constitution(1777) stated "Whenever any particular mans property is taken for the use of the public owner ought to receive an equivalent in money" *id.* at 790; Similarly Part I art X of the Massachusetts Constitution (1780) stated; "whenever the public exigencies require that the property of any individual should be appropriated to public use, he shall receive a reasonable compensation therefor" quoted in *id.* Similarly Art 2 of the Northwest Ordinance (1787) passed by the continental congress provided: "[S]hould the public exigencies make it necessary, for the common preservation, to take any person's property, or to demand his particular services, full compensation shall be made for the same," quoted in *id.* While these are the substantive provisions requiring compensation, some other American states had provisions to protect personal and real property through procedural regularity. For instance, the 1683 New York Charter of Liberties and Privileges provided in similar terms to Magna Carta, the lawful judgement of peers and the authority of law as a precondition for the dispossession of property. It stated; "Noe freeman... be disseized of his freehold... But by the lawful judgment of his peers and by the law of his province" quoted in *id.* Several other American states like Pennsylvania, West New Jersey, Maryland etc also had provisions relating to procedural regularity. *See id.* at 787n 16.

35. Arthur Lenhoff, *Development of the Concept of Eminent Domain* 43 COLUMBIA LAW REVIEW 596,598 n 15 (1942).
36. Wiliam Blackstone argues that compensation was due when real property was taken , *see* William Trenor, *supra* note 33 at, 786 n 15 (citing Blackstone)
37. *Id.*at 791.
38. Pennsylvania Coal Co.v Mahon 260 US 393 (1922).
39. *Id.* at 415 (emphasis added).
40. *Id* at 413.
41. Penn Central Transportation Co. v New York City 438 US 104, 124 (1978) (evolving the balancing test for the first time the court observed that the court should look into the character of governmental action, the extent of interference with investment backed expectations and the economic impact of the governmental action on the property owner); *see also* Nollan v California Coastal Commission 483 US 825 (1987). See also Tyler E. Chapman, *To Save and Not Save: The Historic Preservation Implications of the Property Right Movement*, 77 BOSTON UNIVERSITY LAW REVIEW 112, 115(1997) (arguing that

regulatory taking pose more difficult theoretical and conceptual problems, as a consequence, there is no clearly established standard for determining what constitutes a regulatory taking and that the law in this regard is unsettled due to decades of inconsistent pronouncements in taking decisions);*Cf.* Dolan v City of Tigard 114 S.Ct 2309, 2319 (1994) (discussing a number of state court's taking standards and holding that the "reasonable relationship" test adopted by a majority of the state courts is closer to federal constitutional standard than other standards). This apart, efforts are being made at the state and federal level in the US to draw a threshold level above which diminution of value becomes compensable (for e.g. the Property Right Act of 1995 [S 204(a)(2)(D)] proposed at 33% Wiskinson Bill at 20%.

42. AIR 1954SC 119. In this case, by an ordinance, the Indian government had taken away the power of management and administration, but had not, however, acquired or requisitioned the property, which was challenged as being violative of the right under Art. 31of the Constitution.

43. *Id* at 129 (Mahajan J. in this case with approval referred the Pennsylvania Coal case as well).

44. *Id* at 238 (per Bose J.).

45. *See* IND. CONST. Art 31 (2-A) (introduced by the Fourth Amendment 1955).

46. *See* IND. CONST. (25TH AMENDMENT) ACT, 1979).

47. "*Right to Property: (1)* All citizens shall, subject to the existing laws, have the right to acquire, own, sell, and otherwise dispose of, property.

    (2) The State shall not, except in the public interest, requisition, acquire or create any encumbrance on the property of any citizen.

    (3) The basis of compensation and procedure for giving compensation for any property requisitioned, acquired or encumbered by the State in the public interest, shall be as prescribed by law", *see* NEP. CONST. Art 17.

48. *Id.* Art 13(2).

49. *Id.* Art 19(2).

50. *Id.* Art 18(2).

51. *Id.* Art 22.

52. *Id.* Art 25(1).

53. One may disagree with the use of the expression "existing

laws" as it gives one an impression that it refers to only those laws which are already in existence at the time of the promulgation of the Constitution, and not to the law that Parliament may subsequently enact. However, the fact that the power to limit property right springs from the sovereign exercise of power, the interpretation of the expression 'existing laws" should include both existing as well as the laws to be enacted subsequently by Parliament and be construed as "prevailing law."

54. Private and Boarding School Organization v HMG, NKP 1994(2051) p.609.
55. Rishikesh Shah v HMG/Ministry of Finance NKP 1994 (2051) p. 302.
56. Siddhi Bahadur Shrestha v Royal Nepal Martial Court, NKP994 (2051) p. 634;Krishna Bahadur Kunwar v Special Police Department, NKP 1994(2051) p 550; Ganesh Bahadur Shrestha v Office of the Regional Police Unit, NKP 194 (2051) p 388.
57. ROBERT NOZICK, ANARCHY, STATE AND UTOPIA 149 (Oxford, Basil Blackwell 1974) (arguing that minimal state is the most extensive sstate that can be justified, any state more extensive violates peoples'rights).
58. THE CONSTITUTION OF THE USA (henceforth U.S. CONST. amend V.
59. IND. CONST. Art 31 (original).
60. American courts have distinguished between a use which is public and an interest which is public, and have said that where there is simply a public interest, as distinguished from public use, the power of eminent domain can not be exercised. *See e.g.* Minnesota Canal & Power Co. v Kooching Co. 47 Minn. 429,107 NW 404; Nicholas v Central Virginia Power Co , 143 Va 405,130 SE 764, 44 ALR 727.
61. In several instances this confusion has surfaced in the Nepalese case laws. The latest of the series is Nanda Kumari Rawal v HMG/Ministry of Industry NKP 1993(2050) p 180, 194 (in the context of acquisition of land, referring to police power, eminent domain, public purpose as tools of the state in a muddled manner).
62. *See* AIR 1968 SC 394 In this case, the Indian Supreme Court (per Sachwat J) observed; "The police and eminent domain powers are essentially distinct. Under the police power, many restrictions may be imposed and the property may even be destroyed without compensation being given whereas under the power of eminent domain the property may be appropriated to public

use on payment of compensation only. In the exercise of police power the state may pass regulations designed to ensure public health, public morals, public safety and also public convenience or general prosperity. In the exercise of its power of eminent domain the State may take any property from the owner and may appropriate for public purpose" *id* at 399.

63. RAMACHANDRAN'S LAW OF ACQUISITION AND COMPENSATION 3 (8th ed C. Mathur ed Lucknow, Eastern Book Co.1996) (1960).
64. 113 US 1(1885). La Grange involved a case where a municipality had pledged some of its future tax revenues to support a private commercial venture.
65. *Id.* at 6; *see also* John A. Humbrach, *Constitutional Limits on the Power to Take Private Property: Public Purpose and Public Use,* 66 ORGEON LAW REVIEW 547, 561-62 (1984).
66. NEP. CONST. Art 17(2).
67. *Id.*
68. State of West Bengal v Union of India, AIR 1963 SC 1241, (per Sinha J) (observing further that the state gets this power independent of the constitution, and that the power may be exercised in respect of all property in the state for effective enforcement of the authority of the Union against private property or property of the state. *Id* at 1258.
69. 26 AM JUR 2D *eminent domain* (para 1)638 (1966).
70. *Id,* one author even contends that the concept has Biblical vintage. *See for e.g.* William B. Sroebuck, *A General Theory of Eminent Domain* 47 WASHINGTON LAW REVIEW 553, 555 (1972).
71. State of Bihar v Kameswar Prasad Singh AIR 1952 SC 252, (per Mahajan J).
72. 26AM JUR 2D *eminent domain* (para 2)638 (1966).
73. Boom Co v Patterson, 98 US 403,406 (1878); United States v Jones, 109 US 513,518 (1883); Khol v United States 91 US 367,376 (1876).
74. Georgia v Chattanooga 264 US 472, 68 L ed 796, 44 S. Ct. 369.
75. 26 AM JUR 2D *eminent domain* (para 2) 639 (1966).
76. Buckner F Melton, Jr, *Eminent Domain, "Public Use" and the Conundrum of Original Intent,* 36 NATURAL RESOURCE JOURNAL 59, 70 (Winter1996)(quoting Hugo Grotious).
77. 26 AM JUR 2D *eminent domain* (para 2) 639 (1966) (quoting several US cases).

78. *Id.*
79. *Id.*
80. *Id.*
81. Blackwell Lumber Co v Empire Mill Cp 28 Idaho 556, 115 p. 680; Rogers v Toccoa Power co 161 GA 524, 131 SE 517 44 ALR 534.
82. 26 AM JUR 2D *eminent domain* (para 5) 644(1966).
83. U.S. CONST. amend V and XIV the relevant clauses are as follows:

    "No person shall... be deprived of life, liberty or property without due process of law; nor shall private property be taken for public use without just compensation...".

    U.S. CONST. amend V

    "... nor shall any state deprive any person of life, liberty or property, without due process of law; nor deny to any person within its jurisdiction the equal protection of laws." U.S. CONST. amend XIV.
84. Hawaii Hous. Auth. V Midkiff 467 US 229 (1984).
85. Mt Vernon Berry Cotton Dock co v Albama Interstate Power Co 240 US 80, 60 L ed 507, 36 S.Ct 234; *See also* Lawrence Berger, *The Public Use Requirement in Eminent Domain* OREGEON LAW REVIEW 203, 205 (1978); Buckner F. Melton Jr. *supra* note 76 at 59-85.
86. And where a person holds property appropriated by the right of eminent domain, such person should furnish the public use intended with this right of the user. The public also holds a right to secure expected benefit. 26 AM JUR 2D 673(1966) (citing Charlottee v Heath 226 NC 750, 405 SE 2d 600, 169 ALR 569; Vetter v Broadhurst 100 Neb 356, 160 NW 109, 9 ALR 578).
87. 26 AM JUR 2D *eminent domain* (para 29, 30)678 (1966).
88. 26 AM JUR 2D *eminent domain* (para 28) 675(1966).
89. *Id* at 673. However, the authorities cited in support of "public benefit" doctrine, taken as a group also support a somewhat more limited principle. The power is not sustained in all cases where a benefit to the general public is shown. In fact the question is partly one of degree of public benefit, but it is more of necessity for the development of the resources of a country or a state. *Id* at 677 (citing Connecticut v Calvert, 87 Conn 421, 88 A 633 (college conducted by a private corporation with discretion as to the admission of students as one not serving

public benefit); *See also* Riden v Philadelphia B & W. R. Co 182 Md 336, 35 A 2d 99).

90. Strickley v Highland Boy Gold Min Co, 200 US 527, 50 Led 581, 26 S.Ct 301.

91. SUKLA'S CONSTITUTION OF INDIA 253 (M.P. Singh ed 9th ed Lucknow, Eastern Book Co 1994)(1950) (citing Willis Constitutional Law 817).

92. *See* Michael W Treanor, *supra* note 33, at 877-887 (arguing for the adoption of the original intent); Buckner F. Melton, *supra* note 76, at 65-89.

93. 26AM JUR 2D *eminent domain* (para 31) 679(1966) (citing Charlotte v Heath 226 NC 750, 40 SE 2d 600, 169 ALR 569); Ridge Co v Los Angeles County 262 US 700 67 Led 1186, 43 S.Ct 689, Cox v Revelle 125 Md 579,94 ALR 203).

94. *See* John A Humbrach, *supra* note 65, at 596-98.

95. Weaver v Pennsylvania -Ohio Power Co (CA 6 Ohio) 10 F2d 579; Belovsky v Redevelopment Authority, 357 Pa329, 54 A 2d. 277, 172 ALR 953.

96. Adams v Housing Authority of Daytona Beach (Fla) 60 So2d 663.

97 Cincinnati v Vester (CA 6) 33 F2d 242, 68 ALR 831, affd 281 US 439, 74 L ed 950, 50 S. Ct. 360.

98. Gaylord v Sanitary Dist. 204 Iu 576, 68 NE 522.

99. Nichols v Central Virginia Power Co. 143 Va 405, 130 SE 764, 44 ALR 727; Fallsburg Power and Mfg Co v Alaxender, 101 Va 98 43 SE 194.

100. 26 AM JUR 2D *eminent domain* (para 7) 646(11966)(citing cases and state legislation).

101. King County v Seattle Cedar Lumber Mfg Co 94 Wash 84, 162 p. 27.

102. 26 AM JUR 2D *eminent domain* (para 18) 659(1966) (citing Blamtpm v Fagerstrom, 249 Ala485, 31 So 2d 330 172 ALR 128; Smith v City Board of Education, 272, Ala 227,130 So 2d 29; Birmingam v Brown 241 Ala 203, 2 So 2d 305; Southern Bell Tell Co v Newwingham (Mo app) 386, SW 2d 663; Schulman v People 10 NY 249, 176 NE 2d 817,219 NYS 2d 241; Browneller v Natural Gas Pipeline Co 233 Iowa 686, 8 NW 2d 474, Delaware L & W.R. Co v Morrison 276 US 182).

103. Western U Teleg.Co v Lousiville and N.R. co 270 Ill 399, 110 NE 583; Alpin v Clinton County (Iowa) 129 NW 2d 726.

104. Julubhai Nanbhai Khachar v State of Gujarat 1995Supp(1)SCC 596(per Ramaswami J).

105. *See generally* GRANVILLE AUSTIN, THE INDIAN CONSTITUTION: THE CORNERSTONE OF NATION 40-93 (New Delhi, Oxford Univ Press, 1991) (throwing light on the debates and proceeding in the CAD and its Sub-Committees).

106. *See* Nehru in 9CONSTITUENT ASSEMBLY DEBATES 1192(Delhi Lok Sabha Secretariat 1950); *See also* SHIVA RAO, 2 FRAMING INDIA'S CONSTITUTION 291(Delhi, Indian Institute of Public Administration, 1968).

107. *See* Land Acquisition Act, 1894 S. S 2.

108. *See for e.g.* The Bengal Regulation Act 1824, Bombay Building Act 1839, Th.e Madras Building Act 1852, Land Acquisition Act 1852 etc.

109. *See* the Government of India Act, 1935 S 299.

110. *See e.g.* Franjee Petit v Secretary of State , 42 IA 44.

111. *See e.g.* the resolution moved by B.N. Rau in 9 CONSTITUTIONAL ASSEMBLY DEBATES 1198.

112. This view was taken by Govind Ballav Pant. He proposed that the term "public use" can be replaced by "governmental purpose". *See* SHIVA RAO, *supra* note 106, at 284.

113. IND. CONST. Art 31(5) (original) which *inter alia* provided that the Art 32(2) will not affect (a) the provisions of any existing law, (b) in pursuance of any agreement entered between India and any other country with respect to evacuee property. Besides the tax laws and laws enacted for the promotion of public health or prevention of danger to life or property also escaped the requirement of Art 31(2).

114. *See* Hambai Framjee v Secretary of State for India AIR 1914 PC 20, 21The court in this case held (per Lord Denudin) that the phrase "public purpose" must include a purpose that is an object or aim in which the general interest of the community as opposed to the particular interests of individuals is directly and vitally concerned.

115. *See* State of Bombay v R.S. Nanji AIR 1956 SC 294, 297; *See also* Somawanti v State of Punjab AIR 1963 SC 151,161, 163; State of Bihar v Kameswar Prasad Singh AIR 1952 SC 252, 289-291.

116. Sachindra Mohan Nandy v State of West Bengal AIR 1963,Cal 373, 380; *see also* R.K. Agrawala v State of West Bengal AIR 1965 SC 995

117. State of Bihar v Kameswar Prasad Singh , AIR 1952 SC 252, 289-291; Somawanti v State of Punjab AIR1963SC 151,161,163 *cf* Franjee Petit v Secretary of State, 42 IA 44(Privy Council linking public purpose with the general interest of the community as opposed to the particular interest of the individuals).

118. State of Karnataka v Ranganatha Reddy (1977) 4 SCC 471,479, 481, 501, 505.

119. Pandit Jhandu Lal v State of Punjab Air 1961 SC 343, 347.

120. Lachhman Das v Municipal Committee, Jalalabad (1969) 1 SCC 653; AIR 1969 SC 1126, 1128 : Tilak Ram Wada v State of Punjab ART 1956 Punj. 83,84.

121. Arnold Rodricks v State of Maharastra AIR 1966 SC 1788, 1798.

122. Kanayalal Maneklal Chinai v State of Gujarat (1969) 3 SCC 456.

123. S. Sivaprakasa Mudaliar v State of Madras AIR 1964 Mad 115, 117.

124. Chaitram Verma v L Acq Officer, Raipur AIR 1994 MP 74,76.

125. State of Tamilnadu v L Krishnan AIR 1996 SC 497.

126. Ram Narayan Singh v State of Bihar AIR 1978 Pat. 136.

127. S.S. Darshan v State of Karnataka (1996) 7 SCC 302 ; AIR 1996 SC 671.

128. Land Acquisition Act 1894 S. 2.

129. IND. CONST. Art 31(5)(original).

130. Gurudas Shah v First Land Acquisition Officer of Calcutta AIR 1957 Cal 495 (holding that acquisition for a company could be made if it served public purpose and justifying the construction of housing for labour as public purpose); Babu Baskya Thakur v State of Bombay AIR 1960 SC 1203 (justifying construction of dwelling houses for workmen as public purpose). The courts followed this line of reasoning till the term "companies" was inserted in Land Acquisition Act in 1967.

131. Jaga Ram v State of Haryana AIR 1971 SC1033; Somawanti v State of Punjab AIR1963SC 151,161,163; Raja Anand Brahma Shah v State of Punjab AIR 1967SC 1081; State of Gujarat v Musamigau Imam Haider AIR 1977 SC 594 (holding that whether acquisition serves public interest or not is a sociol-economic question to be decided by the government. According to this view until and unless there is a collateral purpose or colourable exercise of power the courts should not go behind declaration). *See also* Gandhi Grah Nirman Sahakari Samiti v State of Raj AIR 1994 SC 2329, 2336 (holding that government's view takes

precedence); Gadadhar Ghosh v State of West Bengal AIR 1963 Cal 565,572 (holding govt the best judge); Habib Ahmad v State of U.P AIR 1965 All. 349, 344-45 (holding the govt as the sole judge).

132. R.L Arora v State of U.P.AIR 1958 All. 872 (invoking Art 31(5)(a) and Art 366 (10) of the Constitution which saved existing laws). However, in Srivinisa Cooperative House v Madam Gurumurthy Sastry (1994) 4SCC 675, which involved the acquisition of lands belonging to small farmers to a private house building society for chartered accountants, advocates, businessmen the Indian Supreme Court took a slightly different view. It held that though the acquisition under Ch VII [of LAA 1894] need not for public purpose, but all the same the purpose should be connected with public utility, it should be beneficial to general public and not to private persons.

133. Madhya Pradesh Housing Board v Mohd Shafi (1992) 2 SCC 168.

134. *Id.* at 177. Another case of similar line is Baldev Singh Dhillon v Union of India 1998 AIHC 42 where the Delhi High Court required the preparation of scheme before S. 4 and S6 notification of the Land Acquisition Act 1894 is issued. *See id* 76-78.

135. *See for e.g.* Arya Krishnan Shivaghal v Union of India (1996) 10 SCC 721; Aflatoon v Lt Gov. Delhi (1975) 4 SCC 285; Ratni Devi v Chief Commissioner (1975) 4 SCC 467; Ram Chand v Union of India (1994)1SCC 44; State of T.N. v L Krishnan (1996)1SCC 250; Jai Narayan v UOI (1996)1SCC 9.

136. AIR 1956 SC 294.

137. *Id* at 297.

138. Jiwani Kumar Paraki v First Land Acquisition Collector (1984) 4 SCC 612; Shah & Co v State of Maharastra AIR SC 1877.

139. *See* the Soil Conservation Act of Nepal 1977 S 3-5, 8, 10 and 11

140. NEP. CONST. Art 17(3).

141. A similar meaning of compensation is advanced by Indian courts. *See e.g.* R.C Cooper v Union of India (1970) 1 SCC 248; P.Vejravelu Mudaliar v Special Dy Collector for Land Acquisition AIR1965SC16; West Bengal v Bela Banerjee AIR 1954 SC 170 (holding compensation is just equivalent of what the owner has been deprived of).

142. JOHN H. GARVEY & ALEINKOFF, MODERN CONSTITUTIONAL THEORY: A READER 254 (2nd ed.StPaul Minn, West Publishing Co1991).

143. West v Chesapeake and P Tel Co 295 US 662 74 Led 1640, 55 S.Ct 894; 26AM JUR 2D *eminent domain* (para 150) 811 (1966).
144. Dohany v Rogers 281 US 362, 74Led 904, 50 S.Ct 299, 684 ALR 434; 26AM JUR 2D *eminent domain* (para 150) 811 (1966).
145. Jacobs v US 290 US 13, 78 Led142, 54 S.Ct 26, 96 ALR 1; 26AM JUR 2D *eminent domain* (para 150) 812(1966) (citing a plethora of cases). It is now also established that damages are to be assessed and compensation determined as of the time of taking, *See* United States v Miller 317 US 369 87 Led 366, 63 S. Ct 276, ALR 55; 26 AM JUR 2D *eminent domain* (para 150) 814(1966).
146. *See* SHIVA RAO, *supra* note 106, at 283, (the clause 27 draft report) *See also* Munsi's view *id* at 281; *See generally* T.K TOPE, CONSTITUTIONAL LAW OF INDIA 262, (Lucknow, Eastern Books, 1992)(1982); *see also* GRANVILLE AUSTIN, *supra* note 105, at 91.
147. The predicament of the framers is clearly reflected both in their suspicion about the possible court intervention and assertion that there should be no role for the court to play in determination of compensation *See generally* 9 CONSTITUENT ASSEMBLY DEBATE, *supra* note 106, at 1192-1311.
148. West Bengal v Bela Banerjee AIR 1954 SC 170.
149. *Id* at 172 (per Patanjali Shastri CJ). In other words the Supreme Court in Bela Banerjee laid down three points, viz., (a) the compensation under Art 31(2) shall be a "just equivalent of what the owner has been deprived of;" (b) the principles which the legislature can prescribe are only principles for ascertaining a "just equivalent" of what the owner has been deprived of or if the principles did not take into account all relevant elements or took into account irrelevant elements for arriving at the just equivalent, the question there to is a justiciable issue.
150. *See* IND. CONST. Art 31(2) (as amended by the Constitutional Fourth Amendment Act 1955).
151. P.Vejravelu Mudaliar v Special Dy. Collector for Land Acquisition AIR 1965 SC 1017; The ruling was followed in Union of India v Metal Corporation AIR 1967 SC 637.
152. *id* at 1022-1023 (per Subba Rao J).
153. State of Gujarat v Shantilal Mangaldas AIR 1969 SC 634.
154. R. C. Cooper v Union of India AIR 1970 SC564.
155. *Id* at 609 (per majority).
156. THE CONSTITUTION (25TH AMENDMENT) Act 1971. For the same reason the expression" or that the whole or any part of such amount is to be given otherwise than in cash".

157. Keshavananda Bharati v State of Kerala (1973) 4 SCC 225.
158. *Id* Per Sikri J. at 392,per Shelat and Grover JJ at 457, per Hedge and Mukherjea JJ at 497, per Jaganmohan J. at 463.
159. *See* P.K. Tripathy , S.P. Sathe and A.M. BHATTACHARJEE, *supra* note 13.
160. Armstong v US 364 US40, 49 (1960) (holding that the fundamental goal is "to bar the government from forcing some people alone to bear public burdens which in all fairness and justice should be born by the public as a whole").
161. This will be further discussed in the Chapter III.
162. BLACK'S LAW DICTIONARY 473 (5th ed, St Paul Minn, West Publishing Co, 1979).
163. Though creation of encumbrance by satisfying conditions laid down in the Constitution is possible in every type of property, but such power is more likely to be used in incorporeal property like, copy right, trademarks, patents, industrial design etc.
164. A general discussion on the concept of regulatory taking in the US is made in *supra* section 2.4.
165. *See* M.HIDAYATULLAH, *supra* note 16, at 27 (He states that co-proprietorship was always a feature of family law in India. He further maintains "so strong was this sentiment of coownership that a son born in the family (and in places a daughter) became a co-owner by the mere fact of birth).
166. *See* M C REGMI, LAND TENURE AND TAXATION IN NEPAL 40-41 (Kathmandu, Ratna Pustak Bhandar 1978)(writes that pasture land in some areas of Nepal, particularly in high altitude in the hill districts and Western Terai is sometimes found as a separate category of taxable land. Pasturel and has never been measured or graded. In the absence of measurement, taxes on pasture land are assessed on the basis of number of cattle grazed, the size of the pasture land estimated in a rough and ready fashion or in a number of graziers using it'. Similarly in some parts, tax was different for local and outsiders; the latter used to be required to be paid more. However taxes on pasture were not levied for grazing cows, bullocks etc).
167. M.C. REGMI, *id* at 29-30 writes that Kipat is essentially a form of communal tenure, prevalent among Limbus of Dhhankuta and Ilam in eastern Nepal and several sub-groups of Tamang in East No 1 and various other groups in Palpa, Achham and Dailekh... The land is held on a tribal, village, kindred or family basis, and individuals have definite rights in this land by virtue of the membership in the relevant social unit. Hence, title to

land has a communal character and it is usufructuary rather than absolute. A chief may be custodian of the land but he is not its owner. *See also id* at 575-587.

168. The Forest Act 1993 of Nepal S 25, 35, 36 43.

169 Rishikesh Shah v HMG/Ministry of Home NKP 1994(2051) p 302

170. R.C. Cooper v Union of India 1970 SC 564 (holding that a person may be deprived of his property of a statute only if it does not impair the fundamental right guaranteed to him (per Shah J. at 592).

171. NEP. CONST. Art 11(1) states; "All citizens shall be equal before Law. No person shall be denied the equal protection of laws."

172. SURYA P.S. DHUNGEL ET AL, COMMENTARY ON THE NEPALESE CONSTITUTION 102 (Kathmandu, Delf Publications, 1998).

173. Baburam Paudel v HMG/Cabinet Secretariat NKP 1994 (2051) 143, 164-65.

174. Balakrishna Neupane v Parliament Secretariat, NKP 1993 (2050) 450.

175. DHUNGEL ET AL, *supra* note 172, at 113-14 This doctrine allowed different treatment where the action or enactment; (a) is founded on an intelligible differentia which distinguishes persons or things grouped together in the class from others left out of it, and (b) has some rational relation to the objects sought to be achieved by law. The doctrine of classification was first enunciated by American courts [for e.g. Lindsley v Natural Carbonic Gas Co 220 US 61 (1911)]. Indian courts incorporated this doctrine right in 1950s (for e.g. Budhan Chaudhary v State of Bihar AIR 1955 SC 191; Ramkrishna Dalmia v J. S.R. Tendolkar AIR 1958 SC 538) as a necessary adjunct to Art 14 of the Constitution.

176. A.M. BHATTACHARJEE, *supra* note 13, at 39 (quoting a plethora of case laws and authors).

177. Iman Singh Gurung v HMG/Secretariat of the Council of Ministers,NKP 1992(2049) p.710,725. A strong resonance of this ruling is found in E.P. Royappa v State of Tamilnadu AIR 1974 SC 555,583-84 where the court enunciated the test of reasonableness to strike at arbitrariness.

178. Maneka Gandhi v Union of India AIR 1978 SC 597,624; Indian courts have struck down several state actions by declaring

them to be arbitrary. *See for e.g.* Mithu v State of Punjab (1983)2 SCC 277, AIR 1983SC 473 (striking down S 303 of I..P.C. for being discriminatory against the convicts who commit murder while they are in jail); Karnataka STDC v Karnataka STAT (1986)4 SCC 421,430 (invalidating clause iv of S63(7) of the Motor Vehicle Act 1939).

179. *See e.g.* Maneka Gandhi v Union of India AIR 1978 SC 597.

180. Further the fact that Nepal has acceded to International Covenant on Civil and Political Rights 1966(henceforth ICCPR) and the Optional Protocal I and Optional Protocol II, the right to life guaranteed in non-derogable form in ICCPR, Art 6 can be illustrated to support this view. [Under Art 4(2) of ICCPR art 6,7,8,(1)(2), 11,15,16, and 18 are non derogable).

181. Such inference can be drawn from the decisions of the European Court of Human Rights. *See e.g.* X v UK and Ireland (1982) Appl 9829/82 (Unpublished) and Simon-Herald v Austria (1971) 14 YB 351; *See also* DHUNGEL ET AL, *supra* note 172, at 123.

182. Leaders Inc v Godavari Marble Industries 4 S.Ct. Bulletin Feb. 1, 1997 (Magh 16-29, 2052).

183. Yogi Naraharinath v Prime Minister 5 S.Ct Bulletin Aug. 5, 1998 (Bhadra 1-15, 2053).

184. Yagyamurti Banjade v Bagmati Sepcial Court, NKP 1070(2027) p. 57.

185. Bedkrishna Shrestha v Department of Industries, Commerce, Food and Civil Supplies NKP 1959(2016) p. 234.

186. On this front even the Indian courts have not done much. A brief discussion on Indian case laws has been made at Ch 5.3.

187. NEP. CONST. Art 16 reads: "Every citizen shall have the right to demand and receive information on any matter of public importance.

Provided that nothing in this Article shall compel any person to provide information on any matter about which secrecy is to be maintained by law."

Similarly Art 22 reads: "Except as provided by law, the privacy of the person, house, property, document, correspondence or information of anyone is inviolable."

188. DHUNGEL ET AL, *supra* note 172, at 166.

189. Balakrishna Neupane v PM Girija Prasad Koirala, 1:11 S.Ct Bulletin 1 1992 (2049)(popularly known as the Tanakpur case).

190. Gopal Sivakoti v Ministry of Finance, NKP 1994 (2051) p.256 (popularly known as the Arun III case).

191. Gopal Sivakoti v Ministry of Finance NKP 1994 (2051) p.256.
192. Balakrishna Neupane v. Ministry of Water Resource, NKP 1997 (2053) p. 210.
193. The use pattern of the communal pastureland in the highland and community forestry are still recognised as property of the community.

3

THE NORMATIVE AND INSTITUTIONAL FRAMEWORK FOR PROJECT IDENTIFICATION, ACQUISITION OF PROPERTY AND REHABILITATION OF THE PROJECT AFFECTED PERSONS IN NEPAL

3.1 Introduction

The context in which the rights of the PAPs are being discussed requires one also to have a perusal of the issue of displacement vis-a-vis the overall development orientation of .the country. This orientation is generally expressed in various forms in the Constitution of Nepal. There is a tendency to consider decisions relating to the identification, selection and implementation of project as political decisions not because these decisions contain something inherently political, but because they are generally taken by the executive and implemented by the bureaucracy. Whether one takes project decisions as political decision or not does not, however, absolve the policy makers to be informed of the parameters and major considerations with regard to development laid down in the Constitution nor can they bypass the prevailing normative framework.

Modern constitutions no longer cherish the orthodox notion that they should remain unblemished of the political orientation and economic philosophy of the framers. On the contrary, the predominant belief today is that constitutions are not only political documents devising a mechanism or a contrivance to create a ruling class through ballot box, they are at the same time social documents. Therefore they need to be informed of the contemporary social reality and the aspiration of the people and the beacon path that the country needs to follow. In tune with the contemporary view the Constitution of Nepal carries with it certain values, visions and aspirations of the Nepali people. These values, visions and aspirations are interspersed in the preamble, the fundamental rights, the directive principles and other provisions of the Constitution. The most fundamental of them, which the Constitution promises as an objective goal, is "justice in all spheres of life."[1] Justice- political, economic and social—has been enshrined in the Constitution as one of the most cherished objectives. The Constitution tries to achieve this not only by guaranteeing the basic human rights, the rule of law, a transparent and accountable government, but also by laying down the principal developmental policies as well.[2] This, in broad terms, comprise, (a) the protection of the life, property and liberty of the people, (b) prevention of the concentration of available resources of the country within a limited section of society, (c) equitable distribution of economic gains to people on the basis of social justice, (d) prevention of economic exploitation of any class or individual, and (e) elimination of all types of economic and social inequalities.

In a society like Nepal, which has subsistence agrarian economy, mass illiteracy, rampant poverty and backwardness, chances of a limited section of society taking undesirable benefits are always more.[3] Therefore, while it is important to tap the limited resources of the country for overall development, it is also necessary to ensure that the benefits are not siphoned to limited area or people and such activities do not adversely affect the life of the people directly dependant on the resources. It also needs to ensure that such activities do not cause irreversible damage to the environment. Where anthropogenic activities lead to the destruction of life, livelihood, society, culture and the environment, it is the duty of the state to restore the same by forsaking reactive and the neutral role and using its pro-active discretion.

While the commitment made by Nepal to the international community, especially in relation to the protection of human rights and the environment[4] calls upon itself to undertake plans, strategies and courses of action for a people centered environmentally benign approach to development, the incorporation of these ideals in the instruments of instructions, namely the Directive Principle and Policies of the State, impose on it a duty to implement these principles and policies through law.[5] It is an irony that in the Third World situation most of the commitments made at the international fora are hardly actuated by domestic legislation and programme of actions. But it in no way can absolve the state from its duty to its people, nor will it be correct to say that legal and moral gaps provide sufficient justification for state non-action. It is in this light that an attempt has been made here to trace out the normative and institutional framework relating to project selection and implementation, the acquisition and requisition of property, the resettlement and rehabilitation of the PAPs. The purpose is to examine to what extent the present policy regime is responsive to the constitutional promise and aspiration of the people for development. Towards the end, a critical review of the normative and institutional framework has been made.

3.2 The Project Selection and Implementation: The Policy and Legal Perspective

The selection of development projects is the product of a

centralised planning process in Nepal—a process, which commenced in 1953. The Planning Commission of Nepal is a wing of the cabinet secretariat and is headed by the Prime Minister.[6] It takes guidance from the National Development Council (henceforth NDC) and inputs from the concerned ministries. Keeping in mind the guidance of the NDC and the plan priorities of the concerned ministries, the Planning Commission draws five-year development plans. The plan documents delineate the long term development objectives, strategies and plans and also touch upon some prioritised sectoral issues.[7] The design of the annual plans and the budget sanction for the implementation are basically considered to be the business of the concerned ministry. Interestingly, as no legal framework guides this planning process, the task of planning is left to the political wisdom.

The government is the sole authority to decide on the identification and feasibility of the central level projects in Nepal. It also identifies the implementing authority. Generally the projects are either implemented by government departments or are executed by parastatals—the semi-autonomous Development Boards/Authorities etc.[8] In some instances, brief enactment are also drawn for the execution of the projects.[9] However, after 1990 one may witness a paradigm shift in a multitude of forms in the selection, design and implementation of projects. Whereas during the pre 1990 Panchayat era private participation was limited only to the feasibility study of the development projects,[10] in the post 1990 scenario their participation in the implementation and operation has also become a reality[11]

3.2.1 The Local Self-Government Act 1999 and the Emergence of Participatory Development Process

Another significantly noteworthy development that has taken place in this decade is the introduction of the concept of participatory system of governance. The decentralization of power is one such strategy, which has a likelihood of ushering in greater participation of the people.[12] With the recent enactment of the integrated Local Self-Government Act, 1999 a bottom up approach of development has been initiated in Nepal. Now, the Institutions of Local Self Government, viz., the Village Development Committee, the Municipality and the District Development Committee are empowered to identify their development priorities, plan and design projects and implement them at the local level.[13] No doubt, this legislative effort has opened up a space for increased participation of the people, and thereby, reduced the chances of imposed and arbitrary decision on the part of the central government. However, it is too early to predict to what extent the attempt will usher in a truly people centered approach to development as contemplated by the Constitution. The paradigm shift witnessed is not only in the selection and implementation of the projects, but also in the process, major considerations and criteria for selection of the projects as well. The environmental aspect of the project is one such consideration. Now, growing environmental concerns have changed the traditional notions under which protection of the environment was considered a duty of the state.[14] Of course, this notion is still valid and is instrumental in evolving a few principles like the principle of public trust,[15] the precautionary principle and the inter generational equity in the management and use of natural resources.[16]

3.2.2 *The Judicial Assertion*

But coupled with the duty imposed upon the state to protect environment are the right considerations entrenched in the Constitution. Now courts have moved further and declared the right to a healthy environment as a fundamental right of the citizen. There are a couple of cases that may have an impact on the prevailing discourse on development and help us to evolve principles, and which in turn, may influence the normative framework on the subject. For instance, in

Godavari Marbles the Supreme Court of Nepal declared the right to a healthy environment as a fundamental right under Art 11(1) of the Constitution.[17] Similarly in *Yogi Narahari Nath,*[18] which involved the issue of the protection of a heritage site at Devaghat, precipitated by the allotment of a large parcel of land in the area to a Medical College, the Supreme Court, following the dictum in *Tanakpur case,*[19] observed that citizens have a meaningful relation to the protection of the environment and heritage. The Court said if the government takes any decision against the Directive Principles and the State Policies the court could intervene in the matter and pass the necessary order.[20] In yet another case, which involved the protection of a Tank—a heritage site- in the city of Kathmandu, the Supreme Court observed that the Directive Principles and Policies enshrined in Part IV of the Constitution are not vacuous jargons that could just be overlooked. The Court held that if the Principles and Policies are found being overlooked, it could issue necessary instructions.[21]

The expansive interpretation of rights by the court is, of course, not a specifically Nepali phenomenon. In fact, the Nepali Supreme Court has just reiterated the concern that courts in other jurisdictions have shown.[22] However, the basic point that needs to be stressed here is that all these judicial enunciation taken together, have sufficiently indicated that the new path to development is a people centered, environmentally benign and a path to sustainable development. This is yet to be embraced in project planning and execution.

3.2.3 The Legal Norms on Environmental Protection.

Besides the constitutional provisions and the judicial pronouncements mentioned above, another noteworthy development of recent times, which is very much relevant to our discussion, is the enactment of the Environmental Protection Act 1997.[23] Maintenance of clean and healthy environment, minimization of adverse effect of environmental degradation on human life, proper uses and management of natural resources for sustainable development are the set objectives of the Act. The Act has introduced the concept of Initial Environmental Examination (henceforth IEE) and the Environmental Impact Assessment (henceforth EIA).[24] Under the present legislative framework of Nepal, while the IEE and the EIA studies are to be carried out by the project proponents, the sponsoring government agency has to examine the assessment, have public consultation and issue the license by laying down conditions that need to be adopted by the proponent.[25] The Schedule to the Environment Protection Rules 1997 gives a list of projects requiring IEE and EIA. The projects requiring IEE are smaller in size than the ones requiring EIA.[26] For instance, while any water resource or drinking water supply project, which causes the displacement of up to 100 people, requires IEE studies, projects bigger than this in size require EIA studies. The necessary implication of the schedules would be that the projects left out by them do not require IEE or EIA studies.[27] If that were so, one may come across certain projects which cause change in the existing land use pattern, and still may not be covered by any entry of the schedule I or II. For instance, golf courses or race courses, stadium, camp sites for trekking parties, resort hotels, to mention a few, fall in neither of the schedules, and thus, may be interpreted as not requiring IEE or EIA studies.

The EPA also appears to be weak on the public hearing aspect of the IEE or the EIA study. The Act does not make public hearing with prior dissemination of information as a mandatory process. Soliciting of public opinion is only half hearted. The Act requires the Ministry to make arrangements for allowing the general public to make copies of the report at their own cost and render opinions and suggestions. The constitution of Expert Committee for reviewing the EIA report is also not mandatory.[28] Under the EP Rule, the proponent of the project is required only to send a copy of the report to the

Village Development Committee or the Municipality and the District Development Committee for opinion.[29] He/She is not required to meet and explain them the technical nuances of the report, clarify their doubts and solicit their informed consent. Any other person or institution willing to study the report is required to do so at its own cost within a prescribed period.[30] Neither at the stage of preparation of the report by the proponent nor, at the stage of examination by the concerned government agency, has the public hearing been made mandatory.[31] Once the proponent submits the report, the same is examined by the concerned agency or by the Ministry. Since at no stage an independent body examines the IEE or the EIA report,[32] there is a great likelihood of the IEE and the EIA studies remaining mere formalities. Though the Act empowers the government to issue guidelines, in the present scheme of the EP Act and the Rules such guidelines are likely to have only limited effect. The unnecessary bureaucratization of the Act has eclipsed some other welcome provisions of the EPA like the provisions relating to the conservation of heritage,[33] or the environment conservation trust, or promotion of voluntary compliance etc.[34]

Besides the EPA. a few other recent legislation also contain provisions relating to the environmental aspect of resource use. For instance, the Forest Act 1993 empowers the government to decline from giving assent to the use of forest for national priority projects if such activities are likely to cause significant adverse impact on the environment.[35] The Act requires the proponent to ensure that the proposed activity does not cause significant adverse impact on the environment. In case any damage is caused to any person by the assent of the government, the government is required to take proper measures to mitigate the hardship.[36]

Similarly, the Water Resource Act, 1991 and the Electricity Act 1991 also contain some provisions relating to the environmental aspect of the rescurce use. For instance, any proponent willing to conduct survey or utilization of the resource, needs to submit to the Ministry a detailed report consisting, *inter alia*, the environmental aspect of the project.[37] The environmental study should explore and examine the environmental, social and economic impacts that are likely to occur and state the measures that could be adopted to mitigate the same. Such report more specifically should state the possible adverse impact to the land holding and other [landless?] farmers, a detailed statement of the people required to be displaced and steps to be taken for their resettlement.[38] The Rules also provide that the Water Resource Committee should publish information on this aspect after necessary investigation.[39] Acts leading to land erosion, landslides, flood, pollution of water resources, and thereby, likely to cause significant adverse environmental impact are prohibited by law.[40]

Despite their inadequacies and shortcomings, the legal provisions and judicial enunciation, no doubt, have given rise to a new paradigm. The proponent of the development project needs to be informed of the legal requirement and satisfy them in letter and spirit. The non-satisfaction and non-fulfilment of these requirements under the present constitutional framework may be considered a violation of individual and collective rights or a breach of the public trust by the state. Therefore, there is a need for the policy makers, planners and proponents of development projects to take stock of the new legal imperative in the identification, and the selection of the project.

3.3 The Acquisition and Requisition of Property in Nepal: A Brief Overview

The practice of acquisition or requisition of property by the state did not result in a concomitant normative framework for a long time in Nepal. A bulk of legislation relating to the acquisition or requisition are not more than fifty years old, though one may also trace a few scattered provisions in the pre-1950 laws.[41] The first legislation that came into existence is the Regional Development Projects (Execution) Act 1955. This Act provided for the acquisition of land for development projects though the Act neither defined nor categorized such projects. The person whose land is acquired, except in cases where the land has been left fallow for two years preceding to the acquisition, was entitled to compensation[42] In the same year, another piece of legislation titled Immovable Property Requisition Act (henceforth IPRA) also came into existence. This Act provided for requisition of immovable property for "public purpose."[43]

The first comprehensive enactment for the acquisition of land in Nepal came into existence in 1961.[44] Another piece of legislation of the same period providing for the acquisition of land is the Forest Act, 1961.[45] This Act provided for acquisition of land or the dwelling place if it fell inside an area demarcated for national forest.[46] The following year, the Compensation Act was enacted. The Act empowered the government to acquire any type of property—movable, immovable, tangible, intangible etc—for public purpose by paying compensation in the form of stocks issued by the government.[47] Similarly the Irrigation Act,1962 empowered the state to dig canal for public purpose and provided for compensation to the affected persons for the loss of property.[48]

However, the same type of commitment for compensation was not shown by the Highways (Construction) Act 1961. Under this Act, a person was entitled to get compensation only when his dwelling or more than fifty per cent of his land was taken for the construction of the highway.[49] Other loses like taking away of mud, stone, or sand to be used for the construction or the repair of the highway were declared to be non-compensational.[50]

Besides, a host of other Acts, for instance, the Town Development Committee Act 1962, the Public Roads Act 1979, the Town Development Act 1984, the Solid Waste (Management and Resource Mobilization) Act 1987, the Kathmandu Valley Development Authority Act 1988, the Petroleum Act 1983, the Water Resource Act 1992 and the Electricity Act 1992[51] provide for acquisition of land pursuant to the provisions of the prevailing law viz. the Land Acquisition Act (henceforth LAA) 1977, or the Immovable Property Requisition Act (henceforth IPRA) 1955 and the Compensation Act,(henceforth CA) 1962. These three Acts along with the Forest Act 1993 are governing laws on acquisition or requisition of property in Nepal. Therefore, in what follows a brief discussion on the salient features of these Acts will be made.

3.3.1 Purpose of Acquisition or Requisition

The basic premise of acquisition or requisition delineated by the Constitution is "public interest." The CA 1962, the IPRA, 1955 empower the state to acquire or requisition property for public interest or purpose.[52] However, the LAA, 1977 does not limit strictly to "public purpose." It empowers the state to acquire land even for institutions.[53] While the expression "public purpose" or "public interest" is not defined in the former two Acts the LAA defines "public purpose" to mean functions undertaken in the interest or for the benefit or use of the general public, or function to be undertaken by the government. The expression also includes projects approved by the government, and projects undertaken by units of local self-government.

The expression "project approved by the government" which was introduced in the LAA for the first time in the Act in 1977 is a wide expression. Under the present legal regime, either for licensing or for environmental clearance, the proponent of the projects is required to take government's approval before such projects actually come into existence. It is submitted that if such an interpretation is accepted, any project under that pretext will have a chance to take state intervention in getting land and thereby put property right under jeopardy.

Besides the acquisition for public purpose the LAA also empowers the state to acquire land for institutions.[54] The term "institution" is defined to mean a company, development board or corporation established or formed according to the law in force.[55] It is submitted that this is again a departure from the Act of 1961, under which the state was empowered to acquire land for the corporations only for a limited purpose like construction of quarters for labour, staff or for providing some amenities to them. Apart from this, acquisition for the corporation was possible only when such acquisition served the general public.[56] Under this condition where the land was to be acquired, before any initiative was taken by the government, the corporation was required to sign a bond, laying down, *inter alia,* the conditions under which the general public would be entitled to enjoy the benefit. Such an undertaking would be published in the gazette and would hold as good as the law.[57] Now, as no such undertaking is required allowing the general public to use or enjoy the benefit,[58] projects having only incidental public purpose may also take advantage of the law.

Secondly, the term "institution" has been defined to include company. In the absence of a further definition or clarification as to what the term' company" means, the general definition given by the Company Act become applicable. This provision clearly provides an opening to business enterprises to take the intervention of the state and does not limit itself to the government companies as is often believed.[59] In a nutshell, the LAA provides a very blurred picture of "public purpose" and thereby assists legitimizing invasion on property right. It is under the opening provided by the LAA that the Water

Resource Act 1992 and the Electricity Act 1992 have already made a departure from the prevalent notion. These Acts empower the government to acquire land for any license holder.[60] Therefore, as the process of invasion has already commenced and lands are being acquired for private enterprises having objective to generate electricity either to be sold to the government or to export to other countries, a re-look on the framework of LAA is called for.

A connected problem with regard to the acquisition of land is that the law imposes no restriction with regard to the area of land that the state or the institution can acquire.[61] The decision relating to the size of the land is left to the wisdom of the acquiring authorities. Even in cases where the land acquired ultimately turns out to be surplus, under the present law it is still perfectly legal for the authorities to use it for other purposes. The right of the expropriated owner to regain such unused property is by and large left at the mercy of the authorities[62]

3.3.2 The Procedure of Acquisition, or Requisition

While the CA does not virtually lay down any procedure for the acquisition of property barring a notification in that regard,[63] the IPRA prescribes for two notifications. The first gives the owner or the user to show reason as to why the property should not be requisitioned.[64] The second notification is issued after giving a hearing to the objections. It is considered as a conclusive proof of the intention to requisition property. The decision is unassailable under the Act.[65] The LAA, 1977 prescribes more detailed procedures for acquisition of land. It prescribes three methods of acquisition, viz., acquisition by negotiation, acquisition in normal circumstances and the acquisition in special circumstances. Where the government adopts the first method, no procedure laid down in the Act needs to be followed.[66] Therefore, the procedure that is discussed here will be generally applicable to normal acquisition methods.

As per the prescribed procedure, if the government deems it necessary to acquire land for public purpose, or if an institution requests the government to acquire land by fulfilling the necessary conditions laid down by S 4 of the Act, the government initiates preliminary action by appointing an officer to begin the process of acquisition.[67] The officer so assigned or empowered is required to issue a notice for the information of the concerned persons. One copy of the notice has to be affixed at each of the following places:

- At the thoroughfare around the concerned land,
- At the appropriate Village or Town Development Committees, and
- The house or compound wall, if such house or compound wall is to be acquired.

After three days of the issue of the notice, the Designated Officer may begin his work. He is required to submit his report to the Local Officer[68] within fifteen days in which he needs to write about the suitability of the land for acquisition along with other necessary information. Once the report by the designated officer is submitted, the Local Officer is to issue the second notification, which should contain:

- The purpose for which the land is to be acquired,
- The description of land and other property to be acquired, and
- Its area and other necessary particulars[69]

The purpose of these notifications is to inform the person who is likely to be affected by the acquisition of property. But the law does not make it mandatory to deliver the notification to such person at his/her address. If the notification is affixed in government offices or the project office or the office of the Village Development Committee or the Municipality or thoroughfare the legal formality will be complete. The delivery of the notification to the concerned person has been left to the discretion of the Local Officer. Neither the law requires the notification to be gazetted nor to be published in the newspaper or notified by radio and/or television.[70] It is submitted that such provisions hardly meet the demand of the fundamental right to information as they have the chances of robbing the concerned person of his right to object to the acquisition or to protect his right otherwise.[71] The LAA does not provide an opportunity to raise objections to the project. But it only allows the PAPs to complain against inclusion of their land.[72] It is further submitted that the seven days time given by law for lodging complaint to the Chief District Officer (henceforth CDO) is also too short a period for taking any effective recourse.

After the complaint is lodged against acquisition of the property, the CDO is required to pronounce his decision ordinarily within fifteen days from the date of receipt of the complaint. This provision really does not help completing the proceedings in time because the law fails to fix time for several other things. For instance, the time for publishing the second notification after the Local Officer receives the report of the Designated Officer is not mentioned in the Act. Secondly, the permissible time within which the whole proceeding should be complete is also not mentioned in the Act.

The complaint against the acquisition or determination of compensation is heard by the CDO.[73] No provision permits judicial hearing. The basic purpose of limiting the hearing to administrative officer seems to be to err on the side of speedy disposal of the dispute, but it does not, however, rule out the possibility of an administrative bias.

The LAA also prescribes for acquisition of land in special circumstances.[74] When such an emergency situation arises, the government is empowered to issue order to the Local Officer upon which the latter is to issue a notice for the information of the concerned persons and occupy the land. From the date of such occupation, the ownership of the land devolves on the government.[75] The law, thereby, leaves the owner only with a right to claim compensation.[76] It is submitted that in spite of the exigency of the situation the provision does not fulfil the minimum formality that is required to make it a just and fair procedure. For instance, under the prevailing law the owner virtually gets no time to remove the crop, his house and belongings,[77] nor does he get any emergency relief on account of such sudden turn of event compelling him to face the hardship resulting from state action.

3.3.3 Compensation

Only those persons holding property under individual ownership and tenants having a dwelling on the cultivated plot constructed with the consent of the owner of the property are eligible for compensation.

The dominant mode of payment of compensation is monetary compensation. While the CA, 1962 provides for the payment of compensation in the form of stock,[78] the IPRA 1955 provides for cash compensation for the requisition of immovable property.[79] Under the LAA also the predominant mode of payment is cash compensation.[80] The allotment of land in exchange of land acquired is left to the discretion of the government.[81]

With regard to the procedure for determination of compensation, while the IPRA emphasizes on negotiation and arbitration,[82] the LAA provides for negotiation and unilateral determination of compensation, at the discretion of the government.[83] Under the LAA, a Committee of local officers, which includes a representative of the District Development Committee, is to determine compensation.[84] The representation of the PAPs in the Compensation Fixing Committee (henceforth CFC) is not envisaged by the Act.[85]

The legal considerations that the law calls the CFC to keep in mind while determining compensation are as follows:

- Whether the acquisition of land would deprive the person of his land partially or wholly,[86]
- Whether the land is being acquired for the government, institutions of local self-government, and institutions fully owned by the government, or is it being acquired for other institutions.[87]

The criteria delineated by the LAA are difficult to be justified because in all the cases the basic consideration should be the property lost and not the persons who lose it. In all cases, justice demands full restitution to the holder of the expropriated property. Any compensation less than this will obviously be violative of the right to property guaranteed by the Constitution.[88] The creation of differentia may be justifiable in providing additional benefits like resettlement and rehabilitation to those whom the payment of compensation alone would not help to restore their lost earning capacity and assets. The discrimination in the payment of compensation on the amount or percentage of the holding a person loses would, however, not be justified.

The LAA also prescribes different criteria for the determination of compensation for the government and for institutions other than the government.[89] Whereas in the former, the Compensation Fixation Committee needs to follow the government guidelines issued from time to time, the same is not necessary in the latter. Similarly, where the land is to be acquired for other institutions, the value of the crops, houses, walls, sheds, etc acquired along with the land would need to be determined, while no such valuation would be necessary if the land is to be acquired for the government or its parastatals. It is submitted that if the basic objective of determination of compensation is to restitute the expropriated holder of property, different criteria for valuation for different clients (i.e. the acquiring authorities) would hardly meet the objective sought to be achieved. They, thereby, also violate the right to equality guaranteed by the Constitution.[90]

On the whole the provisions relating to compensation as provided in the LAA appear deficient both from constitutional logic and the point of view of fairness and justice. The provisions do not take into account all the losses that the PAPs suffer on account of acquisition of property, nor do they offset the losses incurred due to defective tenurial laws. For instance, loss of common property resources, the loss of pasture, fodder, resources of the community forests, spring sources, recreation facilities, religious sites etc are not considered while determining compensation. Similarly, the loss of livelihood employment, and environment are also not measured.

The fact that authorities are empowered to occupy the land even before the payment of compensation really gives a high handedness to the government officials in the whole process. Once the second notification is issued the land legally devolves on the acquiring authorities after which they can use the land for the project purpose.[91] Further, the law does not make it mendatory for the payment of compensation in a single instalment. This allows the authorities to pay compensation in a single or multiple instalments and as and when the budget is sanctioned for the project. It is submitted that such a provision of law goes against all norms of fairness and justice because the deprivation is instantaneous and total but the restitution is in instalments.

3.4 The Judicial Response

A sizable body of case law has developed on the question of acquisition of property in Nepal.[92] Broadly the response of the court can be discussed under the following sub heads:

- On the question of purpose,
- On the question of procedure, and
- On the question of compensation.

3.4.1 *On the Vires of the Act*

The question of constitutionality of the Land Acquisition Act was brought to the Supreme Court on several occasions during the Panchayat era[93] and subsequently. During the Panchayat era as the Constitution did not offer explicit scope for judicial review, the plea mainly used to rest on a provision of the 1962 Constitution—a provision which provided that any legal restriction on the exercise of a fundamental right would be possible only when such restriction was imposed for "public purpose".[94] The Constitution, however, did not leave it wide open for the judiciary to review whether or not the Act in question served public purpose. It provided that if the impugned legislation in its preamble swore that it was enacted for any or all the purposes mentioned in sub-clause (a) to (j) of Art. 17(2), the Act would fall beyond the pale of judicial review. Interestingly, neither the Land Acquisition Act of 1961[95] nor its successor the 1977 Act contained any such expressions as required by the 1962 Constitution for immunity from judicial scrutiny.

In *Purna Chaitanya Brahmachari,*[96] where, *inter alia,* the issue of the *vires* of the LAA, 1977 was raised, the Supreme Court, in principle, agreed that the impugned Act in its preamble was required to mention any or all the objectives stated in Art 17(2) of the 1962 Constitution. It however, declined to strike down the Act by resorting to a very implausible logic. The Court observed that as the 1977 Act was only an amending and consolidating Act and its predecessor, the 1961 Act in its preamble mentioned that it was made for public benefit, the same purpose should be inferred in the 1977 Act.[97] In *Jaggannadash Baisnav* the court repeated the same logic.[98]

It is true that the Constitution barred the review of the Act if the Act stated any of the objectives mentioned in clause (a) to (j) of Art 17(2), of the 1962 Constitution. But nothing would have perhaps prevented the Court from testing the vires of the Act under Art 17(1) of the same.[99] However, prior to 1990, the Land Acquisition Act 1977 was reviewed neither under this clause nor any other provision of the Constitution including Art 15 which guaranteed right to property.[100]

The *vires* of the Land Acquisition Act, 1977 was examined from a different angle in *Nanda Kumari Rawal*.[101] In this case, the proceedings for acquisition of the property of the petitioner for a cement company had been initiated under the LAA 1961, but before the acquisition was completed, the Act was superceded by the Act of 1977. The main contention of the petitioner before the acquiring authorities was that the compensation determined was too low to enable her to find an alternative residence. When the plea was rejected she moved the Supreme Court, where she, *inter alia*, raised the constitutionality of the Act on the same old ground that it did not contain any of the clauses of Art 17(2) in its preamble, and therefore, the acquisition was violative of Art 11(2)(e) which recognised the freedom to acquire, use, sell or otherwise dispose of property" and Art 15 of the same.[102] Interestingly, while rejecting the contention of the petitioner, the Court in this case did not endorse the earlier rulings but employed Art 15 as the touchstone for imposing restrictions on the property rights. For this, the Court first drew a distinction between the rights guaranteed by Art 11(2)(e) and Art 15 of the 1962 Constitution. It observed that the right to use the property does not include the right against deprivation. Since the right to acquire, use and otherwise dispose of property under Art 11(2)(e) is not an independent provision but is subject to other provisions of Part III including Art 15, any law enacted within the ambit of Art 15 cannot be held as violative of Art 11(2)(e). The Court further observed that since an enactment under Art 15 was possible, provided that such an Act emanated from the valid exercise of legislative powers, it was not discriminatory in nature, and did not infringe upon other rights guaranteed by the Constitution. Where these conditions are fulfilled, adoption of special legislative measures prescribed by Art 17 and 55 was not necessary. The Court held that in the context of the LAA 1961 or 1977, by the reason that the enactment was possible under Art 15 of the 1962 Constitution, the provision of Art 11(2)(e) had no relevance, and these Acts cannot be declared *ultra vires* simply for not undergoing the special legislative procedure prescribed by Art 17 and 55 of the Constitution.[103]

Further the ruling of the Supreme Court of Nepal in *Nanda Kumari Rawal* can be summarised as follows:

- That the freedoms and rights guaranteed under Art 11(2)(e) and Art 15 are two different things;[104]
- That the expropriation or deprivation of property under Art 15 does not deprive a person a freedom under Art 11(2)(e);
- That ownership of a property does create a right to possession in the owner, but the vice versa is not true (i.e. the latter does not create the former); and
- That in an underdeveloped country like ours (i.e. Nepal), we should not encourage an unrestricted right to property based on narrow individualism.

It is submitted that the ruling of the Supreme Court of Nepal in *Nanda Kumari Rawal* rests on faulty jurisprudential premises. In the first place, property as an economic interest over an object consists in a bundle of rights.[105] The right to acquire, possess, own, sell or otherwise dispose of is nothing but an attribute of right to property. The act or omission, which affects any of the constitutive rights, affects the enjoyment of right to property. Therefore, to state that expropriation or deprivation of property under Art 15 does not deprive a person of freedom under 11(2)(e) is jurisprudentially implausible.[106] It is true that generally the ownership of a property does create a right to possess it, but it is not without qualifications. Instances of adverse possession, lien, bailment and tenancy under the Land Act 1964 of Nepal impose restriction on the right to possess the property even if the ownership is vested in the owner.

Secondly, as possession is the first step towards obtaining ownership, it is incorrect to argue that possession does not create ownership.[107] Whereas possession is a matter of fact, ownership is a legal artifact. The history of property law amply demonstrates that possession is always considered as a moral base for regularisation of proprietary rights, especially the land. It is submitted that the observation that possession does not create ownership, besides being jurisprudentially incorrect, holds regimental bias against peasants, tribals, occupants and minions belonging to the lower bracket of the socio economic ladder.

And finally, on the sermon of the Supreme Court that "an underdeveloped country like ours should not encourage unrestricted right to property based on narrow individualism" is also difficult to be accepted, for it is against the *raison d'etre* of the entrenchment of right to property in the present Constitution. It also lacks a proper understanding of the socio economic reality of the country. The question of unrestricted property right does not exist in the present Constitution at all. In fact no democratic Constitution tolerates unrestricted or absolute rights. In a country like Nepal which is based on agriculture, where 90 per cent of people are land, dependant and make their living by farming, where nearly 70 per cent of people hold land less than 1.00 ha in size per capita and where only around one per cent hold land more than 4 ha in size,[108] the protection accorded to right to property against arbitrary expropriation undoubtedly protects the interest of the proletariat than it serves the interest of propreitariat class. The fact that the case in point was a case of land acquisition, where the petitioner was seeking redressal for the loss of shelter itself goes against the assumption by the court.

Though not a very fit case, yet the question of constitutionality of the LAA was once again brought for review to the Supreme Court in *Sita Bista Chhetri.*[109] However, in this case the court took a casual view of the provisions of the Act and declined to strike down the law. The stand taken by the court in this case was that the LAA provided for acquisition of land for public purpose and that arrangement for compensation was made by the Act, it was not *ultra vires* the Constitution.[110] True, LAA provided for acquisition of land for public purpose, and also makes provision for compensation, but the Act also empowers the state to acquire land not only for public purpose. Secondly, so long as the amount paid does not fully restitute the expropriated property right holder it cannot be called compensation in the true sense of the term.[111] The court in the instant case neither made an in-depth study of the purposes for which land could be acquired, nor did it go into the detail arrangements and yardsticks developed for the payment of compensation. Similarly, the Court also did not see whether or not the provisions fully restitute the expropriated owner, nor did it juxtapose the procedure delineated by the Act against various rights guaranteed by the Constitution. Therefore, it is further submitted that in view of the new constitutional context, ironing out of the shortcoming and plugging the loopholes of the Act either through judicial or legislative initiative is necessary.

The benchmarks created by the new Constitution of 1990 for the protection of right to property and the limits imposed on the legislative power to encroach upon the right to property call for a look afresh on the prevailing expropriatory legislation of the Kingdom. Any law imposing restriction on the right to property should not pay only a lip service to Art 17, but such a law also needs to be in conformity with the letter and the spirit of the Part III and the Part IV of the Constitution. This is specially so in the context of the emerging liberalised economic paradigm where more openings are created for private enterprises in areas like harnessing of water resource, mining etc which were traditionally assigned for the state.

3.4.2 On the Purpose of Acquisition

The most problematic issue on any acquisition is perhaps the issue relating to the purpose of acquisition. The basic premise determined by the Constitution for any law relating to the acquisition or requisition of property is that it should be in "public interest."[112] While having a detailed discussion on the constitutional premise of right in the previous chapter[113] it was submitted that the expression "public interest" should be interpreted in such a manner that enterprises having only incidental public purpose do not get chance to make inroads and invade private property in the name of "public interest". This is of course a very daunting task as one may come across several legislative and executive measures, which may hover or even go beyond the basic premise. It is here that the role of the court becomes paramount. Unfortunately, the judicial approach in this regard in this subcontinent is not very encouraging. Courts have time and again declined to intervene in the matter arguably on the ground that in such matter the government is the best judge. However, a few cases illustrated here would present the correct enunciation on the subject. For instance, in *Netraraj Upadhyaya,*[114] which involved the acquisition of a vast parcel of land for cultivation of sugar cane for a private sugar factory, the issue before the court was whether or not the proposed acquisition could be called an acquisition for the "benefit of the general public" as required by the law.[115] The court observed that the expression "any construction work for benefit of general public"[116] meant that the thing so constructed should be of such a type which could be used by the public.[117] Before the initiation of the proceedings for acquisition, a written undertaking by the corporation laying down the terms and conditions for use by the public is mandatory. The court observed that it is necessary that the acquisition under 3(b) of the LAA 1961 should be for what can be directly used by the public.[118]

A corollary issue in the case was whether or not the government was competent to acquire land for "company" under the LAA. The court addressed this a little indirectly. It took the view that as the sugar factory was a private limited company registered under the Company Act, 1963 it was a person in the eyes of law. It was beyond doubt that the utilization of the produce from the sugar farm would benefit the company alone. Such an activity, therefore, cannot be considered as the one for the benefit of general public required by S 3(b) of the LAA 1961.[119] The court in the instant case quashed the decision of the government to acquire land for the sugar factory on the ground that the decision was beyond the authority of law.[120]

The ruling of the Supreme Court in *Netraraj Upadhyaya* is an excellent judicial response on the question of public purpose advancing the correct constitutional and jurisprudential exposition. It was a ruling against the exercise of state power of acquisition for a predominantly private and only incidentally public purpose. The production of sugar would, no doubt, have served the public to the extent any private enterprise would do, but it would in no case justify the state intervention for acquiring land for creating farms for the cultivation of sugar cane by the company which would be its private property. Members of the general public can have no right concurrently with the company's right to property in such land.[121] Even mere entry on the land without the permission the company would amount tresspass.

In *Sumitra Devi*,[122] which involved the acquisition of land for the construction of a pump for the Nepal Oil Corporation, the contention of the petitioner was that the invocation of section 3 of the LAA 1977 for acquiring land for a corporate body carrying out business activities with a profit motive was illegal. Here also the Supreme Court did not directly address the issue. Instead, it relied on the provisions of S. 3(b) and S. 7(3)(d)[123] and observed that as no bond was signed by the corporation before the proceeding for acquisition was undertaken, the proceeding for acquisition was bad in law.[124]

General notion about public purpose is that the general public should benefit from the acquisition. Instead of the general public, if, from any acquisition, only individuals take benefit, the purpose is not considered as public purpose. However, there are exceptions to this rule. For instance, acquisition for the resettlement of the victims of natural calamities like flood, land slide, earth quake or resettlement of the PAPs of the development projects are considered to serve public purpose even though in such cases the direct beneficiaries are individuals.[125] In at least two cases, the Supreme Court of Nepal rightly said that the acquisition of land for the resettlement of the victim of natural calamities is a public purpose[126] because it was the duty of the state to resettle them.

3.4.3 On the Procedure

In addressing the question of infringement of rights, the courts generally adopt two pronged strategies: the first, whether any substantive law allows such infringement, and second, in restricting or regulating the rights whether the prescribed procedure of law has been duly followed.

Generally the question of procedure is considered as vital as the substantive question of acquisition or requisition. The Supreme Court of Nepal on several occasions has struck down the decision of the government for not following the prescribed procedure.[127] The rulings reinforce the view that the court gives equal importance to procedural considerations as well.

3.4.4 On Compensation

This is perhaps a relatively undeveloped area of case law in Nepal. So far the adequacy or inadequacy of compensation has remained outside judicial scrutiny. There is no decision of the Supreme Court which has quashed the decision of the government for not paying just compensation, nor has the court as of now issued any guidelines for ensuring just equivalent compensation. The court has not even bothered to clarify the basic concept of compensation. It has by and large limited itself to see whether the prescribed procedure for determining compensation has been complied with or not. Flouting of the procedure has been frowned upon but the issue of adequacy or inadequacy of the compensation has been left to executive wisdom. It is only in a recent judgement that the Supreme Court ventured to look into the criteria adopted for determining compensation. In *Krishna Bahadur Gurung,* [128] the Court observed that it is not a good practice to fix the amount without having a look on the objective facts and circumstance. The CFC, the Court stressed, needs to state in writing the objective criteria adopted by it while fixing the amount.[129] Though the ruling of the court is still not clear on several aspects, its main concern seems to be to bring in objectivity into the compensation determination process. By "objective criteria," as one may surmise, the Court emphasised on the adoption of relevant criteria by leaving out the irrelevant criteria, which is vital from the point of view of justice and fairness. The importance of the ruling of the Court in *Krishna*

Bahadur[130] would seem to lie in the fact that, for the first time, the Court shook off the ritualistic approach and made an attempt to bring in the principle of equity and justice in the determination of compensation though it was still far off from declaring that "compensation" means just equivalent amount to restitute the expropriated holder. The court could have very much done it had taken judicial notice of the constitutional mandate.

3.5 Land Acquisition and Resettlement in Nepal: the Evolution of Norms

As stated earlier, the prevalent mode of payment of compensation for the acquisition or requisition of property in Nepal is the monetary compensation. The allotment of land in lieu of compensation has been left to discretion of the government.[131] The LAA does not touch upon the question of resettlement of the project affected people. However, one witnesses a primarily World Bank driven initiatives resulting in the emergence of project specific guidelines in Nepal during the 1980s.[132] These guidelines issued under section 16 and 27 of the LAA 1977 have made a clear departure from the till then prevalent view on land acquisition. Therefore, before presenting a critical analysis of the guidelines, it would be worthwhile examine the salient features of the same.

The overall objectives of the Guidelines, as one can cull out, seem to be to ensure that after the transition period is over the affected families are able to restore their income and livelihood. For this, the assistance is proposed to be extended to the affected families in the form of compensation, rehabilitation grants, employment, training etc.[133] For the purpose of offering assistance and benefits, the Guidelines have divided the affected persons into two groups, viz., the Project Affected Families (henceforth PAFs) and the Seriously Project Affected Families (henceforth SPAFs) mainly on the basis of the loss of income and loss of residence.[134]

The scope of the Guidelines has been kept wide to include people whose land has not been acquired but is damaged by the project activities. The Guidelines also include within their ambit regulatory taking. Secondly, the Guidelines include not only the owners of land but also the tenants, businessmen, and occupants of land who derive their main source of income from the land, house or house plot, and who due to acquisition for or the damage caused by the project are unable to regain the standard of living enjoyed prior to the implementation of the project. The Guidelines consider the loss of income and not the loss of land as a major factor in extending assistance to the PAFs and the SPAFs. [135]

The Guidelines consider the comparative market value as the guiding principles for the valuation of compensation. A study of the similar assets in the vicinity has been accepted as one method of ascertaining such value.[136]

As has been envisaged by the Guidelines, the overall responsibility of executing the compensation and rehabilitation package lies with the ARC.[137] The Project Manager finalises all arrangements required and provides the compensation and rehabilitation measures and executes the package under the supervision of the Acquisition and Rehabilitation Committee (henceforth ARC).[138] The Guidelines have made an attempt to link acquisition and rehabilitation package with the mainstream project activities.[139]

In case of PAFs the compensation package includes (a) compensation in cash for the assets acquired or damaged due to the project and (b) a rehabilitation grant to cover the suffering and hardship caused.[140] And in case of SPAFs, the package mainly contains the following:[141]

- A substitute assets of the equal productive potential to the assets acquired or damaged by the project,[142]
- A rehabilitation grant for the suffering and hardship

caused which would be based on the family size and other criteria to be determined by ARC,

- Employment for at least one member of the SPAFs, and
- Provision for training.

The major shortcomings of the Guidelines surface on the legality of the Guidelines themselves. Both the guidelines framed by the Ministry of Water Resources and the Ministry of Transport have so far not been published in the Gazette. The Guidelines are issued by the government in exercise of the power conferred to it by S. 16 and 27 of the Land Acquisition Act, but S. 16 implicitly empowers the government to issue guidelines only in case of acquisition for the government or institutions of local self government or institutions fully owned by the government.[143] In other instances, the CFC is not bound to follow the guidelines issued by the government. As one can see, the CFC under the Land Acquisition Act and the ARC under the Guidelines are entirely different bodies,[144] the Guidelines do not stipulate any measures by which their range of activities can be harmonised. And in what way the guidelines will be applicable to the CFC has also not been clarified.

Confusion has also been created by S. 4(g) of the Guidelines which envisages for an agreement between the Project Manager and the PAFs and SPAFs. It states that the agreement reached thereunder shall be binding on both the parties. If this provision is juxtaposed with the overall premise of the Land Acquisition Act, 1977 where the government, while acquiring land exercises its sovereign power, the concept of agreement stipulated in the Guidelines appears to be incongruent with it. The power given to the government under S. 27 of the Land Acquisition Act is not an abdication of the sovereign power which, in fact, no government can do. The whole purpose of S. 27 is to ensure justice to the affected families on the question of compensation. So long as the state does not abdicate its power to acquire, negotiation for price of the land will only help to attain the objective of law. But once such power is abdicated and only a contractual right is invoked by the state, then one has to recognise the right of the PAFs and SPAFs not to enter into contract. From this point of view, the Guidelines would seem to have created a legal anomaly on the question of acquisition and rehabilitation in Nepal.

As the Guidelines are project specific and depend on the will of the government, there is always a great likelihood of the government abdicating its responsibility of rehabilitation of the PAFs and SPAFs by not bringing out the guidelines altogether. Moreover, the project specific Guidelines are very particular in nature. In the absence of generality, they in effect, can generate discrimination against the PAFs and SPAFs in whose case the Guidelines are not issued, or even if issued, do not come into operation.

Apart from the general comments that surface on the face of the Guidelines, one also comes across a major deficiency on the functioning of the guidelines. First, though it sets time for the commencement of the acquisition, compensation and rehabilitation package (ACRP), it no where fixes the time limit for the completion thereof.[145] Secondly, the Guidelines does not seem very practicable with regard to providing substitute assets to SPAFs, as in large projects it is not physically possible for the Project Manager to assist the SPAFs to identify the land, negotiate the price etc. This means that the SPAF, which does not accept the government plan for substitute land, is practically left to fend by itself with no assistance forthcoming. Besides this, time given for identifying the substitute land is also short.

The Guidelines do not allow for the participation of the affected people in the design and execution of the RCAP package nor do they set any guidelines as to how the rehabilitation package should be designed and executed. It is also silent about several other aspects like the infrastructure development, environmental management, social security, health and education etc. which have a bearing on the right to life.

3.6 The Institutional Arrangement for Resettlement and Rehabilitation

In the absence of a normative framework, the issue of resettlement and rehabilitation of the PAFs is handled on an ad-hoc basis and the implementing authorities formulate project specific policies. While the activities of the CFC under the LAA are limited to determining and distributing compensation, the ARC under the Land Acquisition Guidelines deals with rehabilitation only in the project for which the Guidelines are issued. The Department of Resettlement under the Ministry of Housing and Physical Planning is not specifically entrusted with the obligation or resettling the PAFs.

3.7 A Critical Review of the Normative and Institutional Framework

As is seen from the discussion made here to fore, the major thrust of the Constitution with regard to development is to secure to the people justice in all spheres of life. Justice to the people can be ensured only when an environment is created which protects the basic rights, prevents the concentration of available resources within a limited section and ensures equitable distribution of economic and social benefits among all the people. The use of the state machinery for the aggrandizement of the economic interest of a small cross section at a vast human and environmental cost is disallowed by the Constitution.

People's participation in the identification, and selection of projects by devoluting powers on the institutions of local self government, and the introduction of environmental parameters, and a few judicial pronouncements have no doubt changed the traditional notion which used to take development as a prerogative of the executive. Now, it is rather considered as a right of the people and a trust reposed in the government to unveil a people centered environmentally benign development discourse. But as the legal framework relating to development is yet to be neatly drawn and people's rights to development are yet to be concretised, a great gap and mismatch still exists in Nepal between the constitutional promise and the legislative enactment especially in the context of displacement.

The major problem of the Land Acquisition Act is its non-relevance to the present day situation. In a situation where the per capita size of holding has receded to 0.15 ha[146] a law, which empowers the state to acquire "any amount of land in any place" still prevails. This law expands the power of the state to.acquire land not only for government purposes but for the purposes of the public sector undertakings and companies. Further the law empowers the state to acquire land for "institutions" which includes semi-autonomous development board, corporations and companies.

The law requires no prior appraisal of project by the government with regard to its purpose, need and its impact on the population and environment. Though the IEE and EIA requirements have attempted some sort of rationalization in the project selection process, in the absence of an independent body to examine the proposal and a commitment to public hearing, there is a likelihood of these requirements turning into mere legal formalities. The over-reliance on the bureaucracy is likely to scuttle the force of law and place the citizenry in helpless captivity with only a few formal sops of satisfactions indicated in the law.

Another major shortcoming of the laws on the acquisition of property is its non-linkage with the development process. There is not a single instance in Nepal where the project construction and rehabilitation works are considered as one single component of the project. Nor is there any example where the displaced and other affected families have been substantially better off on account of the amount paid to them by the project authorities. The major shortcoming of the law is that neither it pays the replacement value, nor does it take into account the loss that the PAF suffer. Its over-reliance on the record based ownership, affects the PAF variously. First, a large cross section, for instance, the landless agricultural labourers, the village artisans, and the tribals are made ineligible for compensation. And secondly, a lot of benefits which help to sustain life in the rural settings like the loss of common property resources, heritage, environment etc are not accounted for while calculating the compensation. Thus right to a quality of life under constitutional protection seems to be at a discount.

The non-linkage of displacement with resettlement further compounds the matter. Through the Land Acquisition Guidelines, the government has tried to bridge the gap, but in the absence of generality and publication these stipulations hardly meet the general requirement of a valid law. Besides the Guidelines still leave several questions unanswered. Any norm, which does not meet the constitutional benchmark of public interest and just compensation, can hardly be accepted as a just, fair and reasonable law.

The plight of the PAFs cannot be improved in the absence of a permanent institutional structure and a mechanism to forge horizontal coordination among the various branches of the government. This can be achieved only when a comprehensive legal framework, in tune with the constitutional aspiration and the international commitment is put in place. If done, this will check the reckless intervention of the state on the property right and the common property resources of the country. This would also respect the rights and aspirations of the affected population. A detail discussion on this is reserved for Chapter VII.

REFERENCES

1. NEP.CONST., Preamble
2. These policies include promotion of welfare on the basis of just system in all aspects of national life, protection of lives, property and liberty of people as chief objective. The economic objective includes the transformation of national economy into an independent and self reliant system, prevention of available resources from being concentrated within a limited section of society etc. *See id* Art 25
3. Of the 19 million people (1991 census) around 90 per cent live in rural areas. Agriculture is the main occupation of these people. Agriculture accounts 40 per cent of the GDP and 80 per cent of employment. Crop production, livestock and forest contribute 60 per cent 30 per cent and 10 per cent of the agricultural output respectively. The annual population growth of Nepal is 2.01%. *See* WB, TRENDS IN DEVELOPING ECONOMIES 36-64(Washington DC, The World Bank, 1994); *See also* NPC, THE EIGHTH PLAN REPORT 624(1992-1997), (Kathmandu, National Planning Commission, 1992); *See also* http://www.worldbank.org/html/extdr/offrep/sas/no2.htm accessed on Sept 1, 1999.
4. The list of the human rights and environmental conventions acceded or ratified by Nepal is given in annexure 3
5. NEP. CONST. Art 24(1) uses rather direct expression in imposing duty upon the state. It states that the principle and policies enshrined in Part IV "shall be implemented in stages through laws".*cf* the relevant clause of Art 37 of the IND.CONST. which states," ... it shall be the duty of the state to apply these principles in making law."
6 The government appoints the Vice-Chairman and the nine members including the ex-officio members and the member secretary.
7. *See.e.g.* the NPC, NINTH DEVELOPMENT PLAN REPORT (Kathmandu, National Planning Commission,1998)
8. These Boards/Authorities are constituted under the Development Board Act, 1957

9. *See e.g.* the Rapti Doon Development Area Act 1967; The Tikapur Development Board Rules, 1971

10. Though the legal space for private participation for implementation and management of projects like irrigation and hydropower projects under licence was created no such participation is seen in the country till 1990.

11. For instance, the Foreign Investment and Technology Transfer Act 1992, The Water Resource Act, 1992 and the Electricity Act, 1992 have opened up several areas for private participation. Similarly the Industrial Policy 1992 encourages private sector participation in the community and private forest development, generation and distribution of hydro-electricity and construction and management of nursing homes, hospital, power propelled railings, road, bridges, tunnels etc. The policy does not speak a word about displacement and resettlement. *See* HMGN, INDUSTRIAL POLICY 6 (Kathmandu, Ministry of Industry, 1992)

12. NEP. CONST. Art. 25(4) opens up the space for such a system of governance.

13. *See* the Local Self Government Act, 1999 Ss. 43-54, 111-124, 195-214. (The Act came into force on May 2, 1999).

14. NEP.CONST. Art 26(4) states: "The state shall give priority to the protection of the environment and also to the prevention of its further damage due to physical development activities by increasing the awareness of the general public about the environmental cleanliness, and the state shall also make arrangements for the special protection of the rare wildlife, the forests and the vegetation."

15. The concept of Public Trust as understood in traditional Roman and English law was limited to the duty of the state to protect certain interests like seashore, highways, running water, navigation and fishing for the benefit of the public has now been expanded in India and the US to protect freshwater, wetland, forest, tidal areas and other natural resources. *See* M.C. Mehta v Kamalnath (1997)1SCC 38; *See also* Illinois Central Railroad v People of the Illinois 146 US 387 (1892); National Audubon Society v Superior Court of Alpine Country (popularly known as Mono Lake case) 33 Cal 3d 419; In this case the Supreme Court of California said, "The Public Trust Doctrine is more than an affirmation of the state power to use pubic property for public purpose. It is an affirmation of the duty of the state to protect the people's common heritage of streams, lakes, marshland and tidelands, surrendering that right of

protection only in rare cases when the abandonment of that right is consistent with the purpose of the trust" as quoted in M.C Mehta *id* at 411. *See also* Joseph Sax, *Public Trust Doctrine in Natural Resource Law: Effective Judicial Interaction*, 68 MICHIGAN LAW REVIEW 473(1973) (arguing that the Public Trust doctrine need not be limited to traditional areas and can be extended to pollution, and resource exploitation etc).

16. *See for e.g.* Vellore Citizens Forum v Union of India (1996)5SCC 647 (holding that Precautionary Principle and Polluter Pays Principle are essential features of sustainable development); *See also* Juan Antonio et al (minors) v Secretary, Department of Environment and National Resources 33ILM173(1994) (upholding the right to intergenerational equity).
17. Surya PS. Dhungel v Godavari Marbles, NKP (Golden Jubilee Issue) 1995 (2052)p.169,186-187 The court in this case issued instructions to the government to bring out a comprehensive legislation for the protection of environment. see id 188
18. Yogi Narahari Nath v PM Girija Prasad Koirala NKP 1996(2053) p.39
19. Balakrishna Neupane v PM Girija Prasad Koirala (popularly known as the Tanakpur Case S.Ct Bulletin 1(11) 1992(2049) p 1
20. *See e.g.* Yogi Naraharinath v PM Girija Prasad Koirala NKP 1996(2053) p.39, 48-49. The court in this case struck down the decision of the government to allot land.
21. Prakash Mani Sharma v HMG/Cabinet Secretariat, NKP 1998(2054) p.312,320.On the question of implementing the Directive Principles the assertiveness of the court punctuates with the constitutional prescription.
22. *See e.g.* Subash Kumar v State of Bihar, AIR 1991 SC 420; Mohiuddin Farooque v Bangladesh 48 DLR 1996; General Secretary, West Pakistan Salt Miners Labout Union Khwra Khelum v Director, Industries and Mineral Development, Punjab, 196 SC MR 2061(Pakistan)
23. Environmental Protection Act Nepal, 1997, Preamble. (henceforth EPA)
24. EPA, Ss. 3 to 6
25. *See* NEA, RAUGHAT HYDRO-POWER PROJECT, The detailed Study Report 17 (prepared by Resource Consult/Time Consult/ Mashina Consulting Associates 1998); NEA, TAMUR-MEWA PROJECT, Detail Study Report 24 (prepared by Canada Int'l Water & Energy Consultancy, Kathmandu 1997,(both the reports in the library of the Water and Energy Commission, Kathmandu, Nepal)

26. The Environment Protection Rules, 1997, Sch 1 and 2 (henceforth EPR)
27. EPR, Rule 3 (The wording allows one to draw that inference).
28. EPA, Ss. 6(3) and (4)
29. EPR, Rule 8
30. *Id* Rules 9,10, 11(2). The confusion regarding the public access to the IEE and the EIA studies is that, whereas the Rule 8 does not require the proponent to open the document for public inspection, Rule 10 requires him to take into consideration the public opinion before preparing and submitting the report to the concerned authorities.
31. *See* EPA, S. 6(4) and (5) (providing that the concerned public may ventilate their views after having a perusal of the document when it is kept for public inspection).
32. *Id* S. 6(5)
33. EPA Ss. 9,10; EPR Rules 26 to 33
34. EPR Rules 39 to 44
35. Forest Act, 1993, S. 68
36. *Id.*
37. *See* The Water Resource Act, 1992 S. 8(1) and the Electricity Act, 1992 S. 4(1). These provisions should be read with the hydro-power Development Policy of the Government 1992, which states that the construction and operation of the hydro-electric project should be made in such a way that it would have minimum adverse effect on the environment.
38. *See* The Water Resource Rule, 1995 Rule 17(e); The Electricity Rule, 1995 Rule 12(f) & 13(g)
39. The Water Resource Rule,1996 Rule 19; the Electricity Rules, 1995 Rule 16
40. The Water Resource Act, 1991 S. 20; the Electricity Act, 1991 S. 24
41. *See generally* No 5, Chap. titled " Jagga Jamin Goswara (the Land Office), and no 40 of the chap"Sahu Ashaami"(of debtor and creditor), MULUKI AIN (The Old Civil Code of Nepal) and Ss 15&16 of the Chapt."Jagga Jamin ko" (Of Land), of the MULUKI SAWAL. As outlined by these provisions if the state intended to construct some projects it was empowered to take the land of the subjects in which case the state was bound to pay market value of the land or to give substitute land. If the subject had a dwelling on the land, then the compensation had

to be determined by *Chhevandel* (an office dealing with housing) or by Panchas depending on the place where the land was situated. In case of such acquisition, the subject was to be served a notice of seven days. The law also provided for the negotiation of the price of the land and if an agreement was reached there was no need to call Panchas.

42. *See* the Regional Development Projects (Execution) Act, 1955 S. 4. It provided that where the government decides to sell the land after developing it, people from whom the land was acquired without compensation being paid, shall have a peremptory right to purchase such land.

43. The Act lays down a procedure for requisition, restriction on requisition, release of the requisitioned land and the principles and methods for fixing compensation. A Rule was also framed under the Act in 1958.

44. The Rule under this Act was framed in 1969.

45 . This Act was repealed by the Act of 1993

46. The Forest Act 1961, Ss. 3 to 20

47. The Compensation Act, 1962 Ss 2(a), 3 to 7

48. *See* the Irrigation Act, 1962 Ss. 4 to7. However incidental loses, for instance, the loss caused due to flood or water logging, deterioration of the quality of soil, hindrance caused to passage, pasturage, or hardship caused due to labourers leaving the job are not compensable under the Act.

49. *See* the Highways (Construction) Act 1961, S 5(2). (This Act was repealed by the Public Roads Act ,1974).

50. *Id* Ss. 5 & 6

51. *See* the Act Town Development Committee Act,1962 S. 7; The Town Development Act, 1984 S.16; The Public Roads Act 1979, S.15; The Solid Waste (Management and Resource Mobilization) Act, 1987 S. 7(2); The Kathmandu Valley Development Authority Act 1988 S.11; The Petroleum Act, 1983 S. 17; The Water Resource Act, 1992 S. 16; The Electricity Act, 1992 S.33.

52. *See* the IPRA1955 S. 3 and the CA 1962 S.3. Further, under the IPRA, the state is not empowered to requisition certain places like the dwelling house of a person, religious place, school, hospital, public library, orphanage, Dharmashalas etc. *id* S 3(2)

53 *See* the LAA 1977 Ss. 3 and 4

54. *Id.* S.4

55. *Id.* S. 2(e)

56. The LAA 1961 S. 3(b) (though the term was used to include companies as well)
57. *Id* Ss. 7(3)(d), & 7(4)
58. *See* The LAA 1977 S. 4(2)(c)(requiring only the institution to state for which purpose the land is going to be used).
59. This kind of opening has already been created in case of hydropower projects in Nepal.
60. *See* The Water Resource Act, 1992 S. 16 and the Electricity Act, 1992 S. 33
61. The LAA 1977 Ss. 4 & 5 provides that the state can acquire any amount of land for public purpose or for the institution.
62. *Id* Ss. 33 & 34
63. The Act is silent even on this point. One may infer this from a reading of the Constitution.
64. The IPRA 1955, S. 3
65. *Id* Ss .3 & 4
66. The LAA 1977 S. 27
67. The officer may be a government officer of the rank not less than that of gazetted third class or the chief of the office for which the land is to be acquired. Upon request the government may also empower the officer of the acquiring institution to initiate the proceeding *See* LAA, 1977 Ss. 5(1)& 5(2).
68. The Local Officer is defined to mean an officer designated by the government, and where no such officer is designated, the Chief District Officer. *See* LAA, 1977 S. 2(C)
69. *Id.* S 9
70. Be it noted that S.7 of the LAA, 1961 provided for gazetting the notification. Though the present Act does not require the notification to be published in the Gazette, there is a practice to publish the second notification in the Gazette. *See* LAA, 1977 S.9
71. A detail discussion on right to information is made in supra Ch 2.6.3
72. The LAA, 1977, S. 11(1)
73. *Id.* S. 11
74. Where it is necessary to acquire land to maintain transport or communication facilities or to ensure safety of life and property against extensive damage or to protect any other property in the event of sudden diversion of the river, natural disaster or

any other extraordinary circumstances, the government is empowered to bypass the normal procedures laid down for acquisition. *See Id.* S. 25

75. *Id.*
76. *Id.* S. 25(6) provides; "Except in cases relating to the amount of compensation no complaint against the acquisition of land shall be entertained".
77. Under LAA 1894(India) even in case of emergency the Collector is required to give 48 hours to the occupant of the building to remove his movable property. S. 17(2)
78. The Compensation Act, 1962 S.4
79. IPRA 1955 S. 7 & 8
80. The LAA 1977 S. 13(1)
81. *Id* S. 14
82. The IPRA 1955 S. 8
83. *See* LAA 1977 Ss. 13, 14, 16, & 27 (But where the government goes for negotiation it need not follow the procedure provided in the Act).
84. The official members of the committee are the CDO, the Land Administrator or the Chief of the Revenue Office, the Project in-charge
85. The LAA, 1977 S. 13(2)
86. *Id.* S. 13(3) It states, notwithstanding anything contained in sub-section(1), the amount of compensation may be determined separately in case of persons whose land is wholly acquired and of those whose land is partially acquired.
87. *Id.* S. 16(1) &(2)
88. NEP. CONST. Art 17
89. LAA, 1977 S. 16(1) & (2)
90. NEP. CONST. Art 11(1). For a detail ed. discussion of this right in the context of displacement, *see supra* ch 2.6.1
91. *Id.* Ss. 12 and 22. It is only where the houses are actually been dwelled by the PAFs, the authorities are required to pay fifty per cent of the compensation before taking possession of the land.
92. As there is no case law on the Compensation Act 1962, and the IPRA, 1955, the discussion in this section will be limited to the LAA, 1977.

93. The period between 1960-1990 in Nepal under the direct rule of the King was popularly known as Panchayat era.
94. NEP. CONST. 1962 Art 17(1)
95. As it pre-dated the Constitution of 1962
96. Purna Chaitanya Brahmachari v HMG/Cabinet Secretariat, NKP 2044 (1987) p. 1076.
97. *Id.* at 1081-82 (per Hiranyaswar M. Pradhan J.) But it should be noted that the expression" public benefit" was inserted in LAA 1961 only by some Nepal Law Amendment, Repeal and Rearrangement Act in Apr 16, 1963).
98. Jagannath Das Baisnav v Section Officer, District Office, Dhanusha NKP 1987(2044) p.1211, 1218-19
99. NEP. CONST. 1962 Art. 17(1) stated; "Law may be enacted in public interest for restricting and regulating the exercise of the rights mentioned in this part"[i.e. Part III]
100. *Id* Art 15 stated; "No one will be deprived of property save according to law."
101. Nanda Kumari Rawal v HMG/Ministry of Industry NKP 1993 (2050) p. 180
102. NEP.CONST. 1962 Art 11(2) stated: "All citizens shall, subject to the other provisions mentioned in this part, have the following freedoms.

(e) Freedom to acquire, use, sell or otherwise dispose of property."

Art 15 *Right to Property:* No one will be deprived of property save by authority of law."

103. Nanda Kumari Rawal v HMG/Ministry of Industry NKP 1993 (2050) p.180
104. NEP. CONST. Art 11(2)(e) Guarantees Nepali citizens a freedom to acquire, possess, own, sell and otherwise dispose of the property. *Id* Art 15 stated; "No one will be deprived of property save by authority of law." *cf* 1990 NEP. CONST. (1990) which is as follows.

"Article 17. *Right to Property:* (1) All citizens shall, subject to the existing laws, have the right to acquire, own, sell and otherwise dispose of, property.

(2) The State shall not, except in the public interest, requisition, acquire, or create encumbrance on, the property of any person.

(3) The basis of compensation and procedure for giving compensation for any property requisitioned, acquired or encumbered by the state in the public interest, shall be as prescribed by law.

105. For detail ed discussion on this *see supra* ch 2.2.2.2
106. The Court, in this case, seems to have been guided by two factors; (a) the use of term "freedom" in Art 12(2); and (b) the feeling that freedom under Art 12(2)(e) is not an independent provision. A close look of the Part III of the present Constitution will enable one to infer that the Constitution uses "right" in a generic sense to include freedoms, liberties, immunities etc. For a detail ed discussion on this *see supra* Ch 2.2
107. JEREMY BENTHAM, BENTHAM'S THEORY OF LEGISLATION (Bombay, N.M. Tripathy) (arguing that actual possession is a title to property which precedes all others and may hold place for them.)
108. NSAC, NEPAL HUMAN DEVELOPMENT REPORT ii (Kathmandu, Nepal South Asia Centre 1998)
109. Sita Bista Chhetri v HMG/Ministry of Home Affair, NKP 1994 (2051) p. 852
110. *Id.* at 859
111. For detail ed discussion on the constitutional premise see *supra* ch 2.5.3
112. NEP. CONST. Art 17
113. For a detail ed discussion *see supra* ch 2.5.2
114. Netraraj Upadhyaya v HMG/Dept. of Industry, NKP 1968(2025) p. 308
115. LAA, 1961 S 3(b). Under this state is empowered to acquire land for companies "if it was to be utilised for the construction of dwellings for staff, labour or for any other amenities for any other work benefiting general public".
116. *Id.*
117. However in this case the court did not further zero down and say that first the acquisition should be for a construction and secondly the thing so constructed should be for the benefit of general public.
118. Netraraj Upadhyaya v HMG/Dept. Of Industry, NKP 1968(2025) p.308
119. Under LAA, the government was empowered to acquire land for company, "if it was to be utilised for the construction of dwellings for staff, labour or for any other amenities for any other work benefiting general public. *See id* S 3(b).
120. Netraraj Upadhyaya v HMG/Dept. Of Industry, NKP 1968(2025) p. 308, 316-17

121. The State did away with the effect of the ruling in Netraraj Upadhyaya v HMG/Dept. of Industry, NKP [1968(2025) 308] by deleting the provision which required of a written undertaking by the institution requesting acquisition of land. *See* the LAA 1977, S 4(1)(a) and 4(2)(b). However, the 1977 Act provided that except for research or experiment purpose, no land shall be acquired for farming. *See id* S 4(3)

122. Sumitra Devi Marwadi v HMG/Ministry of Industry and Commerce (writ no 742 of the year 1973(2030)—unpublished judgment dated Aug 26,1975(2032/5/10 BS) in the file of the Supreme Court archives).

123. LAA 1961 required the corporation to sign a deed stating under what conditions the public is entitled to use the facility from the proposed construction. *See Id* S.7 (3)(d). It further provided that the bond signed would be published in Nepal Gazette and the conditions laid down therein would hold as good as law, *Id* S.7(4)

124. Sumitra Devi v HMG/Ministry of Industry and Commerce (writ no 742 of the year 1973(2030)

125. *Cf* LAA, 1894 (India) S. 3(f)(v)

126. Ram Kishore Prasad v HMG/Ministry of Food and Agriculture [Writ no 1177 of the yr. 1971(2028) judgment dated July 26,1971 (2028/3/10/4) holding resettlement of flood victim was a public purpose]; Sita Bista Chhetri v HMG/Ministry of Home Affairs NKP 1994(2051) p. 852 (holding resettlement of the victims of land slump was a public purpose).

127. Netraraj Upadhyaya v HMG/Dept of Industry, NKP 1968 (2025) p 368; Ram Kishore Prasad Singh v HMG/Ministry of Food and Agriculture [Writ no 1177 of the yr. 1971(2028) judgment dated July 26,1971 (2028/3/10/4); Krishna Bahadur Gurung v HMG/ Cabinet Secretariat NEP 1995(2052) p. 227

128. Krishna Bahadur Gurung v HMG/Cabinet Secretariat, NKP 1995(2052) p. 227 The case involved acquisition for the Police Training Centre. The claim of the petitioner was that the compensation was fixed arbitrarily.

129. *Id.* at 237

130. *Id.*

131. LAA 1977, S.14

132. So far at least two ministries, the Ministry of Water Resources and the Ministry of Transport, have issued Guidelines for to be applicable for the Arun III Hydro-power Project, and the Multi

Model Transport and Transit Facilitation Project respectively. *See* Land Acquisition Guidelines, 2045 (Jan 5, 1989)(henceforth Guidelines) issued by the Ministry of Transport and the guideline with the same title issued by the Ministry of Water Resources in 1992—a copy verbatim of the former. As the Arun III project was shelved in 1995 and the Multi-model Project ended with land purchase, these project specific Guidelines have not been applied in any projects so far in Nepal.

133. Guidelines, S 3(c)

134. The Guidelines define PAF as "a family who is adversely affected by the project, including those whose assets although not compulsorily acquired for the Project, are nevertheless damaged by the construction activities thereunder," *see* S 2(h). Similarly Guidelines define SPAF as "a project affected family (I) whose main source of income is derived from or dependent upon a land holding (whether agricultural land or house plot or business) which is under their direct cultivation or management either as owner, tenant, or physical possession; or (ii) whose main residence, place of business or main source of income earning activity is a house/house plot either as owner, tenant or physical possessor, and who as a consequence of the acquisition for, or damage by, the project of such land holding, house or house plot is either: (a) left with holdings of such land, house plot or house which are not adequate to ensure them that after a reasonable transition period they will at least regain the standard of living enjoyed prior to the implementation of the project.", *Id.* S 2(I).

135. This has been reflected in the definition of the PAFs and the SPAFs, and also in the guiding principles stipulated for the Acquisition Resettlement Committee (henceforth ARC). For instance, the Project Manager while conducting the survey, census and valuation of assets is required to assess the standard of living of the population to be affected, identify the population by their main and secondary avocation which could be utilised in the preparation of the compensation statement. *See Id.* S. 3(a)

136. *Id.* S. 3(b)

137. *Id.* S. 5(b)(d)

138. *Id.* Ss. 3(a), 4(d), 5(a). The Acquisition and Rehabilitation Committee (ARC) is mainly an official body consisting of the Chief District Officer, the Land Revenue Officer, Representative of the District Development Committee, the Land Reform Officer of the district, the Project Manager and such other person(s) as appointed by the government.

139. It requires the project manager to commence execution of compensation package. Once the project manager prepares the statement of compensation on the basis of the survey, census, assessment of the standard of living, loss of the source of income etc, it has to be sent for the approval of the ARC. After the compensation statement is approved by the ARC the Project Manager informs the PAFs and SPAFs about the package and gives them a period of 30 days to react. The compensation statement includes all the components of compensation and rehabilitation measures to be provided with the amounts and timing of delivery *See id*

140. The Guidelines S. 4(b)

141. The Guidelines S. 4(c)

142. With regard to the substitute asset the SPAF is given a choice either identify a substitute asset, negotiate its price on the basis of the market price within a ceiling price or accept the substitute asset offered by the government. If the SPAF opts for the first option, then he needs to identify the land within 30 days, and negotiate the price either by himself or with the assistance of the Project Manager. Once the price is negotiated and agreement is reached on the purchase price, the same is paid by the government directly to the owner of the asset. If, however the SPAF goes for the second option and accepts the substitute asset to be offered by the government, the government needs to ensure that such property is of equal productive potential and in near vicinity. However, if the SPAF and PAF do not accept any of the options offered by the Project Manager, the latter need not wait any longer. He can deposit the compensation amount in the escrow account (suspense account) in the name of the SPAF and PAF and go ahead with the construction work.

The Guidelines also allow the ARC to acquire land and other assets through direct negotiation with the PAFs, if it is deemed appropriate in their best interest. Similarly it can also enter into negotiation to obtain land on behalf of the SPAFs, if necessary. *See Id.* S. 4 (c)(e) and S. 6

143. LAA 19777 S. 16(1)

144. *Id* S. 13, Guidelines. S. 5(a).

145. Guidelines S. 4(d)

146. Ananda M. Bhattarai, Participatory Forest Management in the Mountain (1997) (LLM dissertation submitted to NLSIU, Bangalore India (quoting J. Bandyopadhyay).

4

THE PROJECT AFFECTED PERSONS UNDER INTERNATIONAL LAW AND THE INSTITUTIONAL POLICY REGIME

4.1 Introduction

In the previous two chapters an attempt was made to present an overview of the domestic legal regime where mismatch between the constitutional promise and the law and practice was highlighted. In this chapter a brief account of those aspects of international law having a bearing on the issues relating to PAPs will be presented. While doing so, provisions of international treaties, covenants and declarations as well as current efforts in evolving norms on the subject of the project induced displacement and rehabilitation will also be analysed.

As a matter of fact, international law and the domestic law are no more considered as two parallel lines never mixing or intersecting each other. The interaction between these two laws in recent times has been very much enriching for both the regimes. Countries traditionally following the dualist views are also slowly gravitating towards monism and thereby making direct application and employment of the international law in the settlement of disputes in domestic courts possible. While this is so in case of the municipal law, international law, especially the treaty law, has also been benefited from several principles developed in the former.[1] Besides direct application, international law impacts the domestic law in a number of other ways as well. It sets standard for action, imposes obligations on the state and other entities, and provides guidelines for domestic legislation. It also serves some educative purpose by sensitizing people on various aspects of their rights, entitlements and goods. The purpose here is to discuss those aspects of international law, which help to further the interest of the PAPs and draw inferences for evolving norms and standards for action. The exercise will begin with a correct understanding of the constitutional position of Nepal via-a-vis international law. To what extent the principles of international law as laid down in the covenants, treaties, and declarations etc can be employed in the settlement of disputes by the courts of Nepal will be the main focus here. This will be followed by a discussion on the rights of the PAPs under international human rights law. The international policy on human rights and the subsequent conventions, declarations have not only elevated the status of individuals from an 'object' to 'subject' of international law, they have also at the same time made human being the central subject of the development discourse.[2] The effort here will be to highlight those aspects of rights, which can be effectively used to protect the rights and interest of the PAPs, either through adjudication or legislation. Besides, the purpose here is also to see in what way and to what extent the PAPs can take recourse to the institutional structure devised in the International Bills on Human Rights. This will be followed by a discussion on the rights of the PAPs under international environmental law. Here again the purpose is to bring forth those rights and highlight the emerging trends, which have a bearing on the rights and interests of the PAPs. This will be further followed by a discussion on the ILO norms and standards for the protection of the indigenous and tribal interests. After this the policies of the international financial institutions like the World Bank and OECD, Asian Development Bank etc., will be examined. Finally, an effort will be made to draw refrains from the international law, which could be used for drawing a suitable legal regime for the protection of PAPs in Nepal.

4.2 The Complementarity of the Domestic and International Legal Regimes

The treaty making power of the State is considered to be a sovereign power and is generally exercised by the executive organ of the state. But this, as a matter of principle, cannot be exercised contrary to the provision of domestic law.[3] Nor by such exercise of power can the state adversely affect rights and interests of a person under municipal law. Within the constitutional limits of the state, such an exercise of power is possible only through legislative authorization.[4] However, if the state becomes a party to international convention, it cannot abdicate its responsibility of fulfilling its obligations solemnly affirmed in the international arena by putting forward an excuse that the fulfilment of such obligation is impeded by a provision in the domestic law.[5] This is because in the international arena the activities of the state are adjudged by reference to the principles of international law and not by its domestic laws. Every State, in the international arena, is required to carry out its obligations arising from treaties and other sources of international law in good faith. But the same cannot be true in the domestic plane unless the Constitution of the state makes provisions to that effect. Generally, the state is under a moral duty to enact laws in conformity with the commitment it has made to the international community, but the failure to fulfil such a duty does not automatically make domestic law invalid unless some provision of the domestic law provides for the same.[6] So long as the Constitution of a state keeps a wall of separation between the international and municipal law, the former cannot make an intrusion into the domain of the latter. Therefore, the correct approach to understand the relation between the two laws in the context of domestic law would be to look at the role that the domestic law offers to the international law.

The Constitution of Nepal declares itself as the fundamental law of the land.[7] It is the source of all legal norms existing in the country. Any law, inconsistent with the Constitution either by reason of imposing unreasonable restriction on the fundamental rights or on any other grounds, cannot stand as law.[8]

The treaty making power, which by its very nature is a sovereign power of the state, also emanates from the Constitution. In Nepal, this power is exercised jointly by the executive and the legislative organs of the state, though the Constitution is not very explicit on the point.[9] Going by the scheme of the Constitution, while the power of negotiating and signing of treaties lies with the executive,[10] the power of ratification or accession or approval of the treaty and agreement is vested in Parliament.[11] Generally, Parliament can enact law and lay down procedures for ratification of a treaty or agreement but on certain subjects the Constitution lays down conditions that need to be included in the law to be enacted by Parliament.[12] The ratification, accession, acceptance or approval completes the process of formalization of the treaty. Only after that, rights and duties and obligations to the people emanating therefrom follow. The Constitution clearly provides that unless a treaty or agreement is ratified, acceded to, accepted or approved, it shall not be binding on the government or the Kingdom as against its own subjects.[13] It is here that one needs to read the Constitution between the lines.

The Constitution nowhere mentions that after the process of ratification is over such treaties will form part of domestic law and shall be binding between the state and the people and can be enforced through the courts.[14] Unless the Constitution expressly mentions so, it will be quite implausible to hold that provision of the treaties impose obligations on the court to interpret them as though they were a part of the domestic law. However, in the Nepali context the problem does not end here. We need to have a look at section 9(1) of the Nepal Treaty Act 1990. It reads:

> If any provision of the treaty of which His Majesty's Government or the Kingdom of Nepal is a party, after such treaty is ratified, acceded, accepted or approved, is inconsistent with any law in force, such law to the extent of such inconsistency, shall be void and the provision of the treaty shall come into force as law of Nepal.

A cursory reading of this provision gives an impression that the legal system of Nepal follows the principle of monism and not dualism. The cardinal feature of the monist system is the supremacy of international law. In countries following monism, supremacy to international law is accorded by the Constitution itself. For instance, the US Constitution provides; "... all treaties made, or which shall be made under the authority of the US, shall be the *supreme law of the land*. And the *judges in every state shall be bound thereby*, anything in the Constitution or law of any state to the contrary notwithstanding."[15]

The two expressions viz., "supreme law of the land" and "judges ... shall be bound thereby" used in the US Constitution enumerated above are important for our purpose. It should be noted that a treaty could have an overriding effect over federal or state laws only if it is "made under the authority of the US [Constitution]."Only such a treaty binds the judges even if anything contrary is written in any Constitution or law of the state.

In countries following monist system also, Parliament retains the power to repeal or overrule or modify the treaty by subsequent legislation.[16] Similarly, where an Act of

Parliament already exists, a self-executing treaty can supersede such law, but if a treaty requires a domestic legislation, such a treaty *ip so facto* cannot be executed.[17]

Conversely in countries following dualism, the Constitution or an Act of Parliament is the supreme law. A treaty concluded and ratified by the executive does not automatically become part of the domestic law until an incorporating legislation is made by the Legislature.[18]

Courts are not bound to refer to international law in the settlement of disputes. International law is outside the purview of the domestic courts. The position is well expounded by Judicial Committee of the Privy Council in one of the influential labour Convention cases[19] where it was observed:

> Within the British Empire, there is a well established rule that the making of a treaty is an executive act, while the performance of its obligations, if any, entail alteration of the existing domestic law, requires legislative action ... If the national executive, the government of the day, decides to incur the obligations of a treaty which involve alteration of law they have to run the risk of obtaining the assent of Parliament to the necessary statue or statutes.[20]

The point that can be inferred from the elucidation of the Privy Council is that so long as the treaty does not entail any alteration of the domestic law, there is no problem in the execution of a treaty; such a treaty can be enforced by executive action.[21] It is only when an alteration in the law is required to execute a treaty obligation, an Act of Parliament should be in place.

In states following dualism also a practice exists where the court of law invokes international law if: (a) the contracting parties in a domestic contract have chosen to incorporate the provision of the treaty,[22] or (b) the domestic law, expressly or by necessary implication, requires the reference to international law.[23] Besides this, international treaty law may also be invoked to resolve the ambiguity of an incorporating statute even when the statute contains no direct reference to the provision of an international treaty.[24]

The relationship between the domestic law and the customary international law, as compared to the treaty law, in the dualist countries is considered to be a rather controversial one. Initially the English courts also followed the Blackstonian dictum and considered customary international law as part of common law[25] but a change in this position was witnessed in 1876 when Cockburn CJ. in *R v Keyn*[26] observed that the English tribunals are not authorised to apply international law without an Act of Parliament. Lush J. took the same view when he held that international law cannot enlarge the area of our municipal law, nor would treaties with all the nations of the world have that effect. That can only be done by an Act of Parliament. [27] However, the widely accepted view with regard to the customary international law is that so long as there exists a statute, a precedent or a rule of common law to the contrary, English courts are not at liberty to follow international law. But where the law is silent or where the law has not been settled, i.e. where there are no precedents, courts will, if they can, apply the rules of international Law.[28]

Of late, courts in countries following the principle of dualism have taken a rather flexible approach towards international law while interpreting cases in domestic jurisdictions. As put by Chief Justice Anand of the Supreme Court of India; "It is often considered within the proper nature of the judicial process and well established judicial function to have regard to international obligations which a country undertakes—whether or not they have been incorporated into domestic law—for the purpose of removing ambiguity or uncertainty from national constitutions, legislation or common law."[29] This by and large is the position in India than in other countries particularly in the second half of this century. A perusal of Indian case laws will enable one to cull out the trends in capsular form broadly as follows:

- Where national law is clear on the point, it has to be followed irrespective of the fact that such a provision contradicts with international law; [30]
- Where the domestic law is ambiguous or possible of two contradictory constructions, the interpretation which brings the statute in harmony with international law or treaty obligations, should be preferred;[31]
- Where the domestic law is silent on the point, resort to norms of international law can be had if it does not result in any inconsistency; [32]
- Where Provisions of treaty law which elucidate and go to effectuate the fundamental rights guaranteed by the Constitution, they can be relied upon by courts as facets of fundamental rights and hence enforceable as such;[33]
- Where a law to the contrary has been already laid down in several cases providing compensation to the victims of state atrocities, notwithstanding a reservation with regard to the payment of compensation while signing the Covenant, international law can be invoked;[34]
- Where rules of international law do not conflict with an Act of Parliament, to that extent, they are considered to be a part of national law and incorporated in the national law;[35]
- Where any international Convention not inconsistent with the fundamental rights but rather is in harmony with its spirit and may promote the

> object of constitutional guarantee by enlarging the meaning and content, the same can be relied upon.[36]

Besides the above, Indian courts have referred to various principles of international soft laws as well as treaty laws for making a case for evolving environmental doctrines, or issuing guidelines in the domestic legal regimes[37] a detailed discussion of which is perhaps beyond the scope of the present study. Suffice here to say that the principles culled out above, in spite of their inherent discrepancies and inconsistencies, are indicative of a new trend. The trend is geared towards increasing use of international law and norms for several purposes, like giving vigour to domestic law in the protection of rights, or enunciating new principles like the principles of public trust,[38] or precautionary principles or the principle of sustainable development[39] for curbing the unaccountable power of the state and other entities.

Against the back drop illustrated above especially in view of the evolving trends in countries traditionally following dualism, it is submitted that growing reference to international law has become the rule of the day even in these countries. It has no doubt influenced the interpretation of municipal law. But it would, however, not be legally correct to state that the wall of separation between domestic and international law has become redundant.

While examining the Nepali position, the most important thing that needs to be kept in mind is the structure of the Constitution itself. The Constitution of Nepal no where declares the supremacy of international law.[40] Historically also the constitutional system contained more characteristics of dualism than monism. The commitments made by Nepal to the international community were executed through domestic legislation wherever it was felt to be necessary.[41] Never ever in the courts of Nepal international law was recognised as a source of municipal law in connection to any acts of commission or omission by the state. But now, as the power of ratification of the treaty rests with Parliament,[42] and the Judiciary is also empowered to deliver justice in accordance with "the recognised principles of justice,"[43] there exists a great likelihood of the incorporation of international law and norms in the settlement of disputes in the domestic legal regime. This is more so in view of the provision of Nepal Treaty Act, which provides primacy to the treaty law over domestic law.[44]

In spite of its incongruence, so long as this provision is not declared *ultra vires*, there is a likelihood of international law overriding the domestic law.

4.3 Right of the PAPs under the International Human Rights Law

The development of the human rights law[45] is the most outstanding achievement of the international community in the last fifty years. Before the Second World War, no body would think that an access would be provided to the individual as 'subject' to the domain of law of the nations.[46] The Charter of the UN for the first time declared that the UN bodies constituted under the Charter are results of an agreement between the people of the world. And then it continued to declare that nation-states would work to provide human rights to every individual.[47] Thus theoretically, individuals became subjects of international law than remaining mere objects. Thanks to the development in human rights law, now the presence of individuals as subjects in international law is not only entrenched, to dispute them as subjects of international law will be considered a controversial statement-legally as well as morally.

Human rights law, thus, seems to have buried the traditional and doctrinaire dichotomy between the municipal law and international law in relation to individuals.[48] Invocation of the norms of international human rights law has been one of the noticeable features of the judicial process in the domestic legal regimes.[49] The principle that domestic law should be interpreted in conformity with the international human rights norms has been entrenched in both domestic and international law. In Nepal, the possibility of direct reference to the international human rights laws is even more because of the two distinctly important legal developments which have occurred in this country. First, is the provision of the Nepal Treaty Act, which has given overriding effect to international law over domestic law in case of conflict. This has offered avenues to individuals to invoke international human right instruments in domestic courts against authorities for obtaining remedies against the violation of human rights.[50] Secondly, as Nepal is a party to the Optional Protocol,[51] in addition to the domestic remedy, an access is now open to individuals to make written communications to the Human Rights Committee for redressal of the violation of human rights.[52]

One fundamental difference between the human rights laws and other international laws is that the former are the claim of individual against his/her own society and the state while it is not necessarily so in case of the latter.[53] The obligations that human right law imposes on the state are nothing but to respect the inherent human dignity of its own people—citizens or aliens who live within its jurisdiction. The purpose of human rights law is to remove the deficiency of the domestic law and improve economic, social and political conditions in which everyone can enjoy freedom of speech and belief, and freedom from fear and want.[54] This is attempted not only by recognizing rights but also by creating conditions under which realization of civil and political as well as economic, social cultural and developmental rights becomes possible.[55]

Right from the establishment of the United Nation, the promotion of social progress and better standards of life in larger freedom, and employment of international machinery for the promotion of the economic and social advancement of all people became one of the founding objectives of the international community.[56] This process was further concretised with the adoption of the Universal Declaration on Human Rights 1948 (henceforth UDHR) as a guide for the protection of not only civil and political rights but also economic, social and cultural rights. The two human rights Covenants viz., the International Covenant on Civil and Political Rights 1966 (henceforth ICCPR) and the International Covenant on Economic Social and Cultural Rights 1966 (henceforth ICESCR) recognised the rights of all the people to freely pursue their economic social and cultural development,[57] and also declared the indivisibility of civil and political rights as well economic social and cultural rights.[58]

The very notion of inalienability and indivisibility of all human rights in the first place rejects the notion of trade off between the rights and the social economic goods. Secondly, the concept of interdependency and inalienability of all human rights also made the prioritization of one right over another irrelevant.[59] The concept of indivisibility of the right also offered a space for autonomy in the exercise of economic, social, cultural and other rights in the same footing as it does to political rights. It means to say that normally, people are entitled to the enjoyment of their rights without the intervention of the state. The state should be obliged to respect the necessary freedoms and resource base of the people which is necessary for their livelihood so that they are able to take care of their own needs.[60] However, the responsibility of the state does not end here. It is also required to facilitate the enjoyment of these rights by introducing institutional and legislative changes wherever necessary.[61] To elucidate this point further, a few rights, for example, the right to life, liberty, equality, property, subsistence, adequate standard of living the security of tenure freedom of movement etc. can be taken.[62] The state is required to create conditions in which the enjoyment of these rights become possible.[63] No doubt, this demands a multi-pronged strategy on the part of the state including affirmative actions. For instance, where the right to a resource use by the community is being threatened, either due to the deficiency in the legal system of state or due to other direct or indirect interventions like the construction of projects. The state is not only required to refrain from threatening the use but is also required to respect such rights by removing the deficiency existing in its legal system and insulate individuals against such threats. The imposition of such a duty on the state is obvious because the state is "in no case empowered to deprive people of their means of subsistence"[64] recognised by the ICESCR almost in absolute terms, though this right still remains to be sufficiently highlighted. The state obligation at another level may call for a more assertive role in order to curb the chances of more powerful economic interests taking inequitable benefits by depriving the resource users of their means of subsistence. Similarly, the improvement of the productivity of the resources, and distribution mechanisms may also surface as state responsibility still at another level.[65]

With regard to the affirmative action of the state in the context of prescriptions of the ICESCR, it is sometimes argued that the duty of the state for the realization of the rights is subject to the available resources.[66] But it is difficult to accept this view because, the language employed in Art 2 creates an obligation to an increased level of commitment on the part of the state. The state cannot simply neglect its duty to respect these rights by giving priority to other areas.[67] Secondly, the state can not waver from its duty of protecting human rights where its activities directly or indirectly result in discrimination between persons, *inter alia,* on the ground of social origin, birth or other status, for such action would be considered as infraction of the state obligation.[68]

International human rights law has established norms and principles touching virtually all facets of life. This is reflected in the consistent reaffirmation of the international community of the indivisibility and interdependence of all human rights, whether civil and political or economic, social and cultural or developmental. Such interdependence becomes more evident especially while examining the violation of not just one right but a broad range of human rights. One comes across such violation of a broad range of rights in the practice of project induced displacement—the eviction of individuals, families, and communities from their homes, land and neighbourhood, against their will by acts directly attributable to the state.

There is a tendency to view the project induced displacement not as an issue of human rights but rather as a simple side effect of development. But this would be a faulty approach. The removal of people from their homes or lands without payment of, or with inadequate payment of, compensation or inadequate resettlement are fit cases to be dealt with under the international human right law. What essentially makes such cases fit cases for intervention under the human rights law is the amount of coercion and the involvement of the state in eviction.

In spite of the convergence of project induced displacement with other forms of displacements caused by factors like the racist policies, war, or ethnic cleansing etc., the international community has been reluctant as of now to extend any substantial support to project induced displacees. Despite the violation of a broad range of human rights like the right to life, housing, security of person, family, tenure, privacy, education etc displacement of people in the name of development is still considered as a subject to be dealt with under the domestic jurisdiction of the state. It is only recently that the issue has become a subject of discussion at human rights forums at the international level. A brief look at these developments, therefore, will be useful for our purpose.

In the recent human rights literature one generally finds the use of two terms viz., "forced eviction" and "displacement" to include displacements caused by a multitude of factors attributable to state action or inaction. In the parlance of the Committee on Economic Social and Cultural Rights (henceforth the Committee), "forced eviction" is the "permanent or temporary removal *against the will* of individuals, families, and/or communities from homes and/or land which they occupy *without the provision of access to appropriate forms of legal or other protections.*"[69]

Despite offering a very broad definition to "forced eviction" the Committee, however, does not term forced eviction illegal in all circumstances. It acknowledges the legality of evictions carried out by the state or its agencies in accordance with law and in conformity with the provisions of the international human rights Covenants.[70] But the general approach of the Committee is that "instances of forced eviction are *prima facie* incompatible with the requirements of [ICESCR] and can only be justified in the most exceptional circumstances and in accordance with the relevant principles."[71]

The use of expression "exceptional circumstances" here indicates that such circumstances should be narrowly interpreted. To further buttress the same approach the Committee in General Comment No 7 stressed that "in cases where eviction is considered justified, it should be carried out *in strict compliance* with relevant provisions of international human rights law and in accordance with general principles of *reasonableness and proportionality.*"[72]

The international human right law creates obligations requiring states to take legislative and other measures to ensure that the beneficiaries of such rights are protected from violations as well as ensure that effective remedies are guaranteed in case the rights are infringed. Where evictions are permissible in "exceptional circumstances" as indicated in the General Comment No 4, it is the view of the Committee that relevant legislation must specify in detail the precise circumstance in which such eviction would be permissible. Such a law not only requires to be in consonance with the principles of human rights, but also needs to be reasonable and weigh the "proportionality" of cost and benefits including the human and environmental cost. According to the Committee, this is mainly so because under Art 4 of the ICESCR any provision imposing limitation on the exercise and enjoyment of human right is permissible only to the extent that such limitations may be compatible with the nature of rights, and are imposed solely for the purpose of promoting the general welfare in a democratic society.

The international human rights law is yet to explicitly recognise the individual's right not to be arbitrarily displaced[73] but there are several provisions in existing Covenants and Declarations, which in effect endorse this right. For instance, the right to housing has been recognised and protected under international human right law.[74] The Committee is of the view that as Art 17(1) of the ICCPR complements the provision of the ICESCR, the provision, *inter alia*, recognises the right to be protected against "arbitrary or unlawful interference" with ones home—a right unqualified by considerations relating to the availability of resources.[75] The Committee emphasises that the state itself must refrain from resorting to forced eviction and also should ensure that the law is enforced against its agents or third parties carrying out forced eviction.[76]

Similarly, another right affected by forced eviction is the security of tenure. The Committee stressed the need to recognize the security of tenure irrespective of the type of tenure and accord legal protection against forced eviction, harassment or other threats. Furthermore, it called on the State parties to take immediate measures aimed at conferring legal security of tenure upon those persons of households currently lacking such protection in genuine consultation with the affected persons or groups.[77]

The Committee acknowledges the interrelation and interdependence of all human rights like the right to life, right to family life, right to security of person, tenure, right to peaceful enjoyment of one's possessions, right to education etc. In view of the fact that forced eviction affects these rights in different degree, the Committee also implicitly recognises the right not to be arbitrarily displaced. It maintains that forced eviction frequently violates other rights as well[78] Therefore, it emphasises that eviction should not result in rendering individuals homeless or vulnerable to violation of other human rights[79]

The main focus of the Committee seems to be to avoid and minimise eviction. It requires states to look for " all feasible alternatives in consultation with affected persons prior to carrying out any evictions." Where evictions are carried out it emphasises legal remedies or procedures to those affected by the eviction order.[80]

The principle of strict compliance of the international human rights law and the principles of reasonableness and proportionality emphasised by the Committee can be realised only when eviction is controlled by a meticulous observance of procedures and abidance to the due process of law. The Committee felt the need for broad procedural safeguards in order to protect the right against arbitrary eviction. These include:

- an opportunity for genuine consultation with those affected;
- adequate and reasonable notice for all affected persons prior to the scheduled date of eviction;

- information on the proposed evictions where applicable, on the alternative purpose for which the land or housing is to be used, to be made available in reasonable time to all those affected;
- especially where groups of people are involved government officials or their representatives to be present during eviction;
- all persons carrying out evictions to be properly identified;
- evictions not to take place particularly in bad weather or at night unless the affected person consent otherwise;
- provision of legal remedies; and
- provision, where possible, of legal aid to persons who are in need of it to seek redress from the courts.

In the event of eviction the displaced and other affected persons are entitled to restitution of their original position. It is here that one can recall the resolution of the Commission on Human Rights. The Commission stated; "all governments [should] provide immediate restitution, compensation and/or appropriate and sufficient alternative accommodation or land, consistent with their wishes and needs, to persons and communities that have been forcibly evicted, following mutually satisfactory negotiations with the affected persons or groups" [81]

While the above mentioned general comments and resolutions require compliance by the state and other agencies, the Committee seems to be aware that it is not only the government but also international financial institutions which have played a controversial role in promoting the practice of forced eviction. It, therefore, requested these agencies to scrupulously avoid involvement in projects which involve large eviction or displacement of persons, without the provision of appropriate protection.[82] It further stressed that efforts required to be made at every step that human rights are observed at each phase of development project.[83]

Thus the General Comments of the Committee as well as the resolution of the Commission on Human Rights certainly testify to the concern of the international human rights institutions on the issue of forced eviction. They cover almost all the areas of concern. They feel the need to recognise the right not to be arbitrarily displaced and call on the states to look for less displacing alternatives. Where eviction is inevitable, they lay down the procedures to be followed. They also require the state and other agencies to restitute the evicted persons through appropriate means of redress. More importantly, they emphasise that the law permitting eviction needs to conform to the principles of international human rights law and also needs to be reasonable. True, the comments and resolution have only persuasive value, nevertheless they are so strongly embedded with reason that it will be difficult for any state to neglect or by pass them on the ground of legality. The fact that the Committee has called on states to furnish information relating to eviction also makes it difficult for them to opt for non-compliance.[84]

Apart from the General Comments of the Committee on ESCR and the Commission on Human Rights another noteworthy development of recent origin on the issue of project induced displacement are the UN Guiding Principles on Internal Displacement (henceforth Guiding Principles).[85]

The most significant aspect of the Guiding Principles for our discussion is the inclusion of the project-induced displacees within its framework. The Guiding Principles identify the rights of the internally displaced people and guarantee them the right against forced displacement, and provide assistance during the displacement as well as during settlement.[86] According to the definition offered by the Guiding Principles:

> Internally displaced persons are persons or groups of persons who have been forced or *obliged to* flee or to *leave* their homes or places of habitual residence, *in particular* as a result of or in order to avoid the effects of armed conflict, situations of generalised violence, *violation of human rights* or natural or human made disasters, and who have not crossed on internationally recognised state border.[87]

This definition is comprehensive enough to cover any action of the State resulting in the forced eviction. Further, the use of the qualifier "in particular"in the definition makes clear that the internal displacement is not limited to causes mentioned in the definition alone. Upon a close reading of the definition one gets an impression that the idea of the framers is to keep the definition flexible so that it can be expanded to cover any unforeseen eventuality in future.[88]

Besides the definition, the Guiding Principles have attempted to establish an explicit right against arbitrary displacement. They guarantee every human being a right to be protected against being arbitrarily displaced from his/her home or place of habitual residence.[89] The Guiding Principles also lay down grounds which may amount to arbitrary displacement. In cases of large-scale development projects the right against displacement is recognised if the projects "are not justified by compelling and overriding public interest".[90]

The Guiding Principles cast a duty on the concerned authorities to explore all feasible alternatives before taking any decision on the project in order to avoid displacement altogether. They further provide that where no alternative exists, it is mandatory for the authorities to undertake all measures to minimise displacement and its adverse effects.[91] Special obligation is imposed on the state to protect against the displacement of indigenous peoples, minorities, peasants, pastoralists, and other groups having a special dependence and attachment to their land.[92]

Where the project has to be taken up for "compelling and overriding public interest," the government is required to take "specific decision" in this regard[93] and respect the right of the prospective displacees by taking adequate measures. These measures include the supply of "full information on the reasons and procedures for their displacement and, where applicable, on compensation and relocation."[94] While the Guiding Principles require the authorities to seek the informed consent of those to be displaced,[95] they at the same time recognise the right of the displaced persons to the planning and management of their relocation,[96] and also to "an effective remedy including the review of such decisions by appropriate judicial authorities.[97]

During displacement the Guiding Principles recognise the rights of the displaced persons to several rights guaranteed by the human right instruments. They include the right to dignity and physical, mental and moral integrity, non discrimination, security of persons, freedom of movement and choice of residence, respect of family life, adequate standard of living etc.[98] The Principles also cast a duty on the authorities to undertake affirmative actions to protect the women, the children, the elders, the disabled etc. during displacement.[99] They also guarantee the displaced persons same rights and freedoms under international and domestic law as any other persons in their country.[100]

The Guiding Principles cast a primary duty and responsibility on the national authorities for providing humanitarian assistance to the displaced persons. They also recognise the right of international humanitarian organizations and other appropriate actors to offer service in support of the displaced persons.[101] Similarly, the national authorities are also required to grant and facilitate international humanitarian organizations and other actors a rapid and unimpeded access to displaced persons.

Although the Guiding Principles are not binding instruments, they have immense practical value. They provide yardsticks for the state party to act upon and also form basis for international human right and humanitarian organization to monitor the treatment meted out to displaced persons. They may strengthen the advocacy work of NGOs and other human right organizations on behalf of displaced persons and can also be of use to governments in drafting laws to protect displaced persons. The importance of the Guiding Principles also lies in their potentiality to provide practical guidance and act as an instrument for public policy education and raising of consciousness.[102] At the moment, the Guiding Principles can be taken as authoritative statement of the Human Right Commission on the displaced persons. Over time they might contribute to the creation of a moral and political climate in which these principles might attain the force of customary international law.[103]

4.4 The Rights of the Project Affected Persons Under International Environmental Law

The correct understanding of the right of the project affected persons under the international environmental law would require one to understand the right in the general setting of the discourse. Taken from that point of view, the most noteworthy development in the domestic legal regime witnessed in the last two decades or so in South Asia is the expansive interpretation of rights. The right to a healthy or ecologically balanced pollution free environment is one of such right. This right has been entrenched as a fundamental right in several countries of South Asia mostly through judicial enunciation.[104] However, the development should be seen in the light of general environmental awareness created at international level especially after the 1972 United Nation

Conference on Human Environment, popularly known as the Stockholm Conference. Now at the national level, the awareness has given birth to constitutional and legal prescriptions world over.[105]

Despite being recognised as a right at several domestic jurisdictions, at the international level, the right to a healthy environment as a substantive right is yet to be entrenched in the international treaty law. A noble effort towards this was made at Stockholm. The Stockholm Declaration provided; "Man has the fundamental right to freedom, equality and adequate conditions of life, in an environment of a quality that permits a life of dignity and well being".[106]

However, the initial emphasis on the human right perspective to environment subsequently waned.[107] At the Rio Conference the State Parties refrained from making similar pronouncements despite according the human person the central place in the environmental discourse. The human person was entitled a healthy life not "in an environment of a quality" but "in harmony with nature."[108]

The Rio Declaration's failure to give a similar emphasis on human right to environment is indicative of the continuing debate on the correctness as well as usefulness of the right perspective to environmental problems that the world is facing today.[109] However, it would be a mistake to say that the jurisprudential debate has discouraged the recognition of environment as a right. A healthy environment has been recognised as a right in some form or the other in several international and regional Conventions and Protocols.[110] This apart, the central role accorded to the human being in the Rio Declaration is a testimony to the recognition of the intrinsic relation that the human being has with the environment. Though short of recognizing environment as a right, the Declaration contains several provisions which accord implicit recognition to several procedural rights. But before dwelling on this aspect it is worthwhile to examine the linkage between the international environmental and human right laws which is considered to be one of the cardinal features of environmental law in recent times.

The international environmental law establishes linkage with the international human right law through an overarching concept called "sustainable development". The concept is by and large based on the report of the Brundtland Commission. The Brundtland Report defined sustainable development as "development that meets the needs of the present without compromising the ability of future generations to meet their own needs."[111]

One of the core components of this concept is inter-generational equity- a concept which links the past generation in terms of right and the future generation in terms of obligations.[112] The idea springs from the realization that if the human race is to continue perpetually it should not cause irreversible damage to the resource base which may affect the ability of future generations to meet their own needs. The conservation of the natural eco-system, which the inter-generational equity demands, in the first place, requires conservation of the natural and cultural resource base and its diversity in such a way that it does not impose undue restrictions on the options available to future generations. Secondly, it refers to the maintenance of the quality of the planet so that it passes on to the future generation in no worse condition than it was received. Finally, it also refers to the maintenance of equitable access of each generation. This means that each generation should provide its members with equitable rights to access to the legacy of past generations and should conserve this access for future generations.[113]

In the context of the right and obligations of the project

affected persons, though all the three aspects of inter-generational equity are equally important, the main focus would fall on the third aspect, i.e., equity of access to resources. Generally speaking, the equity of access to natural resources in the context of the displacement means that where the members of the community are already enjoying the resource, they should not be denied of such enjoyment unless it causes undue deprivation of others. Secondly, it refers to the right of the person to demand the access to natural resources or the benefits that result from its sustainable use, and exercise of a right to protest against all measures which result in denial of the access to resources, where alternative resources are not availed.[114]

The concept of inter-generational equity in its embryonic form was first stipulated in Principle 2 and 3 of the Stockholm Declaration[115] after which it almost became a routine to incorporate this principle in environmental conventions, agreements or declarations.[116] The Rio Declaration, in most specific terms, linked development with inter-generational equity and declared environmental protection an integral part of sustainable development.[117]

Though the idea of sustainable development appears to be a simple concept, there are substantial controversies with regard to its translation into practice and development of standards and indices to access the achievement. Nevertheless, the Rio documents lay down certain processes, which enable one to examine the concept from the perspective of rights. It provides:

> Environmental issues are best handled with the *participation of all concerned citizens* at relevant levels. At the national level, individual shall have *access to information concerning environment* that is held by public authorities, including information on hazardous materials and activities in their communities, and the

> opportunity to *participate in decision making process*. States shall facilitate and encourage public awareness and participation by making information widely available. Effective access to judicial, administrative proceedings, including redress and remedy shall be provided.[118]

The provision stated above does not use the language of right as one would desire, however, it certainly casts a number of duties on the state with regard to environmental protection. One such duty is the dissemination of information concerning environment. In fact, access to information is a pre-requisite for a meaningful participation in the identification or selection of the project, or in carrying out environmental impact studies. This has been made a mandatory process to be followed before undertaking any project that is likely to cause significant adverse effect on the environment or bio diversity.[119] Another component of the participatory right emphasised above is the access to administrative and judicial remedy. The Declaration casts a duty on the state to provide access to such remedy including the redressal of disputes.

It should be noted that the Rio Declaration is not the only document attempting to lay down participatory rights. A resonance of Principle 10 can be found in the Convention on Biological Diversity[120] and several other regional conventions.[121]

The bridging of human rights and environment has been a matter of growing concern. Such attempts have been made at different fora. One such attempt of recent origin is the Ksenteni Report and the Draft Principles on Human Rights and Environment (henceforth Draft Principles).[122] The Draft Principles have formulated a host of procedural and substantive rights. A few of them are:

- the right to information concerning environment;[123]
- the right to receive and disseminate ideas and information;[124]

- the right to participation in planning and decision making process, including prior environmental impact assessment;[125]
- the right to freedom of association for the purpose of protecting the environment or the right of persons affected by environmental harm;[126] and
- the right to effective remedies and redress for environmental harm in administrative or judicial process.[127]

The Ksenteni Report and the Draft Principles do not limit themselves to declaring procedural rights only. In line with the Stockholm Declaration, the Draft Principles recognise people's right to a secure, healthy and ecologically sound environment-an environment which is adequate to meet equitably the needs of present generations without impairing the rights of the future generations to equitably meet their needs.[128] Besides this, they also recognize a few substantive rights, like the right to equality and non-discrimination, the right to freedom from environmental degradation, the right to preservation of soil, air, water, flora fauna etc. The right to health, free from environmental harm, the right to safe and healthy food and water, right to adequate housing, land tenure, and living conditions in a secure, healthy and ecologically sound environment are also guaranteed in the Draft Principles.[129]

In the context of project induced displacement the most important contribution of the Draft Principles is the recognition of the right of the people not to be evicted from their homes and lands. The rights enumerated in the Draft Principles include:

- right not to be evicted from their homes or land for the purpose of or as a consequence of decisions or actions affecting the environment except in emergencies or due to a *compelling purpose* benefiting *society as a whole and not attainable by other means;*[130]

- right to participate effectively in decisions and to negotiate concerning their eviction, and in case of eviction, the right to timely and adequate restitution, compensation and/or appropriate and sufficient accommodation or land; [131]
- right to timely assistance in the event of natural or technological or other humanly caused catastrophies;[132]
- right to benefit from the conservation and sustainable use of resources;[133] and
- right to preservation of the unique heritage sites.[134]

The Draft Principles also recognise rights of indigenous people to control their land, territories and natural resources and to maintain their traditional ways of life. The rights include the right to security in the enjoyment of their means of subsistence. It also recognises the right of indigenous people to protection against any action or course of conduct that may result in destruction or degradation of their territories.[135]

It is true that the Draft Principles proposed in the Ksenteni Report do not recognise the right against eviction as an absolute right, nevertheless, by providing a very narrow opening for lawful displacement,[136] they accord much force to the right not to be arbitrarily displaced. It may take some time for the principles laid down in the Report to transform into principles of international law, but looking at the dexterity and reason with which the right to environment and rights to development are integrated in the Draft Principles, there is reason to surmise that they have the potentiality of influencing the development of similar norms in the domestic legal regime.

4.5 The ILO Regime and the Project Affected Persons

Parallel with the legal and other developments under the

umbrella of the United Nations and its various agencies, the exercise undertaken at the International Labour Organization (ILO), has also been enriching for protecting the rights and interests of the labour, indigenous and tribal population.[137] One such exercise undertaken by ILO related to Indigenous and Tribal population.[138] This Convention (Popularly known as ILO Convention No 107) made an attempt to protect the indigenous, tribal and semi-tribal populations and facilitate their progressive integration into the national mainstream.[139] However, the assimilative approach, which the Convention adopted, was criticized in the subsequent years.[140] Therefore, keeping in mind the criticism an attempt was made in 1989 to foresake the assimilationist orientation of the Convention no 107 by adopting a new Convention (popularly known as the ILO Convention 169) in 1989.[141] The ILO Convention No 169 basically adopts a multi-pronged strategy with respect to indigenous and tribal people. It includes:

- protection of their self identity as an indigenous or tribal group as a fundamental criterion and respect for their integrity, recognition and safeguarding of their identity, institutions, culture, environment, language, religion, laws, values, custom etc;[142]
- enabling them to enjoy on an equal footing the human rights and fundamental freedoms and other socio-economic good enjoyed by the members of the mainstream society by assisting them to eliminate the socio- economic gaps between them;[143] and
- consultation and consent and participation, development of their own institutions, recognition of their right to decide their own priorities for the process of development.[144]

With regard to protection of land belonging to indigenous

community, the Convention casts on the government a duty to respect the relationship of these people with lands and territories (which they occupy or use, individually or collectively) and also the total environment of the area. It also requires the states to recognize the rights of ownership and possession of land which indigenous and tribal people traditionally occupy or have access to their subsistence and traditional activities.[145]

Where such rights are likely to be affected due to exploration or exploitation of such resources, the state is required to consult these people, wherever possible encourage their participation in sharing the benefit from such activities, and pay fair compensation for any damage caused by such activities.[146]

Where indigenous and tribal people are required to be removed from their lands, the Convention No 169 makes it a mandatory requirement that such people should be relocated with free informed consent. In such cases land based relocation is the rule under the Convention and cash compensation an exception. In case any person belonging to an indigenous or tribal group is paid compensation in cash or kind, he can be so compensated only under appropriate guarantee. The Convention also provides that the tribals are provided in all possible cases with lands equal in quality and legal status at least to that of the land previously occupied by them, which is suitable to provide for their present needs and future development. The convention also requires that the persons, thus relocated, get fully compensated for any loss or injury.[147]

Apart from the above, the ILO Convention No.169 touches upon several other issues. Responsibilities are assigned to the government in relation to the recruitment and employment,[148] vocational training, handicrafts and rural industries,[149] social security and health,[150] education and means of communication[151] and contact and communication across borders.[152] All of these can be taken as additional responsibilities to the minimum that the state is required to follow in relation to the protection of land rights of the indigenous and tribal people. The importance of ILO Convention No 169 lies in the fact that it recognises the right to livelihood of indigenous people, and where relocation is permissible (and inevitable) requires the state to ensure that resettlers are as well off after resettlement as before.[153]

The responsibility for implementing the Convention has been assigned to the government.[154] However, in the event of failure of the government to discharge its responsibility neither any recourse has been provided to indigenous and tribal people nor any international sanction is possible to be wedged against the state.

In the context of displacement every section of the population, irrespective of its ethnic origin, is a deserving candidate for such protection. Therefore, ethnicity as the only criteria for extending protection, which the Convention adopts, may not be of comprehensive canvas as one would desire. Where poverty and deprivation on account of being rooted in one particular locale spreads to each and everyone, the distinction of population in terms of ethnicity may also look spurious. There is no doubt that everyone directly dependent on natural resources for subsistence requires support and protection. All the same it is also true that the most affected groups are indigenous and tribal people. The ILO Convention No 169 in fact opens up the possibility of extension of similar protection to other deserving groups. Therefore, the contribution of the Convention in setting up of parameters for relocation, protection of identity and basic human rights is appreciable. The Convention, in spite of Nepal not acceding to it as of now, provides strength to the contention that state authorities should obtain informed consent of the DPs, involve them in planning and execution of rehabilitation and compensate them in such a way that an equally respectable and dignified life is possible.

4.6 The Institutional Policy Perspective and the Project Affected Persons

The rethinking on the issue of displacement dawned at the international level especially among the international financial institutions around the late seventies and early eighties. The resettlement programme of the World Bank and other financial institutions are the products of this new thinking.[155] While the Operational Directive issued by the World Bank in 1980 was refined and improved upon in the subsequent years finally culminating in the issue of a new Directive on Involuntary Displacement and Resettlement in 1990.[156] A similar Directive was issued by the Bank the following year for Indigenous and Tribal Peoples.[157] Refinement, improvement of Operational Directives is a regular feature of Banks initiatives.[158] The initiative taken by the Bank had two direct impacts. On the one hand, other Banks and donor agencies replicated the initiative, and on the other, the Directives implicitly encouraged similar policy formulations and legislative efforts in several countries. Now, almost in similar format, Directives are issued by the Organization of the Economic Cooperation and Development (henceforth OECD)[159] and a few other Banks like the Inter American Bank and the Asian Development Bank, in line with the guidelines issued by the World Bank. Besides, the Operational Directives the World Bank has developed the in-house mechanism for project preparation, appraisal, supervision and for correcting the non-compliance with the policies through an Inspection Panel. A quick perusal of these mechanisms will be worthwhile here.

4.6.1 The Operational Directives

The two main Operational Directives directly relevant to the issue of project induced displacement are the OD 4.30

and OD4.20.[160] But, there are a number of other policy formulations of the Bank, which have a bearing on the issue of displacement and rehabilitation.[161] Taken together, these guidelines set out considerations, yardsticks and procedures that the borrowing state need to follow. Besides, they also form a framework for action while undertaking the project appraisal, review and supervision by the Bank staff as well as provide guidelines for investigation by the Inspection Panel. The basic elements of the Bank's resettlement policy are:

- Involuntary displacement should be avoided, or minimised whenever feasible, exploring all alternative project designs, because of the disruptive and impoverishing effect.[162]
- Where displacement is unavoidable, the objective of the bank policy should be to insure that the population displaced from the project receives benefits from it.[163]
- Displaced persons should be given opportunities to share benefits and improve their earning capacity and production levels or at least to restore them.[164]
- Resettlement operations should be carried out in a participatory manner.[165]
- Social and economic integration of the resettlers with the host community should be the goal of resettlement.[166]
- The PAPs should be provided with land, housing, and infrastructures. Legal and customary rights should be taken into view while paying compensation.[167] Preference should be given to land-based resettlement strategies for people dislocated from agricultural settings.[168]
- Moving people in groups can cushion disruptions. Minimizing the distance between departure and relocation sites can facilitate the resettlers' adaptation to the new natural and socio-cultural

environments. The trade offs between distance and economic opportunities must be balanced carefully.[169]

- Resettlers' and hosts' participation in planning resettlement should be promoted. The existing social and cultural institutions of resettlers and their hosts should be relied upon in conducting the transfer and reestablishment process.[170]
- Indigenous people, ethnic minorities, pastoralists, and other groups that may have informal customary rights to the land or other resources taken for the project, must be provided with adequate land, infrastructure, and other compensation.[171]
- Resettlers should be integrated socially and economically into host communities so that adverse impacts on host communities are minimised.[172]
- The environment impact study of the relocation site and the mitigation plan should be a mandatory requirement of the resettlement package.[173]

Generally, the involuntary resettlement component is considered as an integral part of the main project component.[174] The purpose of integrating involuntary resettlement in the main project is to avoid the laxity on the part of the officials in relation to resettlement, and to execute the component as a development programme, and thereby provide the resettlers an opportunity to reap benefits from the project.[175] However, depending on the country specific situations and the size of the main project, the Directive allows the design of an involuntary resettlement project as a stand-alone project. Whether in the form of an integrated project or a stand alone one, the main emphasis of the Directives is to draw a detailed resettlement time table, budget and ensure institutional readiness to execute the project in a most possible short duration.

Another characteristic feature of the Directives pointed out above is the object of restoration of the earning capacity of the affected people to what they were before the move. The major obstacle to this goal is faulty compensation package.[176] The Directives require the planners to take into account all the sources of income in the base line survey before designing the compensation package. The broad indicators determined for the baseline survey largely conform to the objectives of restoration of the earning capacity, and minimization of the effect of socio-cultural destabilization, and execution of the resettlement programme in a participatory manner.

As to the package, the emphasis of the Directives, especially in case of agrarian, rural, tribal and other indigenous families is on the land-based resettlement. Where land based resettlement package is adopted the Directives require the project authorities to ensure the equal productive capacity of the land and establishment of the other infrastructural facility.[177]

The movement of resettlers in group as part of the existing community is one major consideration of the Directives as such a move would enable the resettlers to keep their social, cultural and religious fabric intact. Secondly, it would provide more security to them in the new environs. Similarly, the relation between the host and the resettling community is one very vexing problem in the resettlement. Generally the attitude of the host community remains hostile to the resettlers. It is more so where the hosts are not the beneficiary of the project and where the social, religious and cultural differences are stark. The solution indicated by the Directive is multi fold. First, it attempts to forge the participation of the host community along with the resettlers in the planning and implementation of the package. Secondly, through a timely environment impact assessment of the relocation site and by undertaking appropriate measures, it attempts to mitigate the adverse impact. And finally, it includes affected hosts also as the beneficiary of the project and endeavors to restore their earning capacity along with the resettlers.

One major component of the Directive relates to the legal framework. The Directives call for a proper understanding of the existing legal and institutional framework. The Directives require the planners to understand the nature of the legal framework including:[178]

- the scope of the power of eminent domain, the nature of compensation associated with it both in terms of its valuation, methodology and timing of payment;
- the legal and administrative procedures applicable, including the appeal process and the normal time frame for such procedures;
- land titling and restoration procedures ;and
- laws and regulations relating to the agencies responsible for implementing resettlement and those related to land compensation, consolidation, land use, environment, water use and social welfare.

An understanding of the existing legal framework is required for several other purposes as well. For instance, one needs to study the legal provisions relating to transfer of title, the registration fee involved in it, and various resource uses like the common property resources, the occupation and use of undocumented land etc. To take a concrete example, the existing legal system of Nepal and India do not recognise the interest of stakeholders on CPR. Nor do the existing Land Acquisitions Acts recognise the right of the occupants, encroachers etc to claim compensation. Village artisans, forest dwellers etc are never considered as persons having a claim on compensation in the event of eviction. Thus, it is difficult to comprehend how, in the absence of the legal system endorsing major considerations of the Operational Directives and streamlined accordingly, mere payment of special attention to the legal arrangements concerning land title, site, occupation etc or publication of legal provisions among affected population,[179] would help the planners to achieve their objectives.

4.6.2 *Project Preparation, Appraisal, Supervision and Evaluation*

The project preparation, appraisal, supervision and evaluation is another mechanism devised by the World Bank to ensure the compliance to its Directives of the Bank and thereby, reducing the involvement of the Bank in environmentally unsound projects or projects entailing heavy human cost. By evolving an in-house mechanism, the Bank in every stage of the project right from its inception to the post scheme evaluation, tries to strengthen the positive out put and reduce the negative effects of the project.

The process of project preparation begins with the preparation of the initial executive project summary by the Task Manager (henceforth TM). [180] Where there is a possibility of involuntary resettlement, the TM is required to briefly summarize the magnitude, strategy and timing of the resettlement and carry out other necessary works.[181] Similarly, where the project affects indigenous people, the TM should ascertain the relevant government policies, laws and plans for indigenous people and should signal the indigenous issues and the overall project strategy in the IEPS.[182]

Once the TM, in concurrence with the Regional Environmental Division (henceforth RED), determines the nature of the project and the type of the EA to be carried out by the borrower the same is generally mentioned in the terms of reference (henceforth TOR) The project which involve involuntary displacement fall under category A requiring EA.[183] In such type of projects the TM is required to inform the borrower Bank's policy on resettlement, and wherever possible, ensure that resettlement is avoided or minimised and where occurs ensure that the laws concerning displaced people provide compensation sufficient to replace all lost assets and that displaced people are assisted to improve or at least restore their living standard.[184]

One of the objectives of the EA in projects entailing displacement is to maintain transparency. The borrower while conducting the EA is required to keep the work transparent.[185] This provides an opportunity to the prospective displacees and other affected groups to familiarize themselves with the project. The EA report prepared by the borrower forms a part of the overall feasibility study.[186] In projects which involve a resettlement component, the feasibility of the resettlement must be established, a strategy for resettlement should be agreed upon, and the resettlement plan and budget estimate should be prepared. The Bank Directives clearly maintain that the full costs of resettlement should be identified and included in the total cost of the main investment project.[187]

Once the borrower submits the EA, the Feasibility Report and other necessary documents to the Bank, the process of assessment begins [188] following which the Appraisal Mission conducts the field visit. During this, the Mission reviews both the substantive and procedural elements of the EA with the borrower. It also resolves any issue that comes up, assess the adequacy of the institutions responsible for environmental management in the light of the EA's findings, and ensures that the mitigation plan is adequately budgeted and determines if the EA's recommendations are properly addressed in the project design and economic analysis.[189] Similar conditions for appraisal are set where the projects are likely to affect indigenous people.[190]

Following the Appraisal Mission's field visit the RED issues formal environmental clearance. The Regional Vice President then authorises negotiation for loan sanction.[191]

The supervision and review of the project financed by the Bank is a feature of the in-house monitoring by the Bank. The supervision of the project is based on the EA recommendations. Compliance with the environmental commitments, the status of mitigatory measures, and the findings of monitoring programmes are parts of borrowers reporting requirements and project supervision.[192] It is mandatory for the Bank to supervise resettlement component throughout the implementation. The Directives warn that laxity in supervision jeopardizes the success of the resettlement. It requires that the review and supervision should be planned from the outset.[193] The Directives also require post-project evaluation.[194]

The yardsticks developed by the bank for the environmental assessment, involuntary resettlement, protection of indigenous peoples, cultural and natural heritage and the detail procedures underlined therein for project preparation, appraisal, supervision review and ex-post evaluation are very useful. If properly followed these yardsticks have the potentiality of preventing blunders being committed against humans and the environment in the name of development. To what extent these directives are followed is a different question altogether.

4.6.3 The Inspection Panel

The Inspection Panel created by the World Bank is another very important institutional effort to evaluate the extent of pursuance of the policies and procedures by the bank itself.[195]. The Panel also provides a forum for people affected by the Bank funded projects to raise their concerns about the breach of the policies and procedures laid down by the Bank where they have either been rejected or not heard by the implementing agencies, host government or the Bank staff.

The framework for the Panel's action is contained in the various operational directives.[196] The Resolution[197] and the

Operation Procedures[198] of the Inspection Panel provide the different ways for bringing forward claims alleging the violation of the Bank policy which are as follows:[199]

- Two or more people living in a country or an area of a Bank-financed project and directly affected by the violations of Bank policies can allege that they have been or could be harmed by those violations.
- A local representative such as a NGO, producing authorization can represent the affected people.
- In exceptional circumstances where local representation is not available[200] a non-local representative with proper authorization with the approval of the Board can present such representation.[201]

Besides, the Executive Director, in special cases of serious alleged violations of such policies and procedures may ask the Panel for an investigation. Similarly, the Executive Directors, acting as a Board, may at any time instruct the Panel to conduct an investigation.

In order to meet the Panel's eligibility criteria the claimants, apart from alleging that they have been harmed or is likely to be harmed by the violation of the bank policies, should state that they have attempted to raise their concerns with the Bank Management and are not satisfied with the response. Such claims should be lodged with the Panel when the project is under consideration or has been approved by the bank, and the loan has not yet been substantially disbursed. However the Panel is specifically prohibited from hearing claims about:[202]

- actions which are the responsibility of the government or the implementing agency and which do not involve any commission or omission on the part of the Bank;

- claims by potential or actual suppliers of products or services relating to procurement;
- requests filed after the closing date of the loan financing the project or after the loan financing the project has been 95% disbursed;
- claims into matters that have already come before the Panel if no evidence of changed circumstances has been presented; and
- claims involving projects financed by the IFC or the MIGA.

Once the claims meet the eligibility requirements enumerated above, the Panel registers the claim in its registry following which it sends a copy of the claim to the Bank's President who represents the Bank for response. The Management gets twenty-one days to respond to the claim. After the response of the Management is filed with the Panel, the Panel is required to make a preliminary assessment of the request within 21 to 40 business days by evaluating the claim and management's response. In the evaluation process the Panel is entitled to review Bank files, interview Bank staff, and visit the project area if required.[203]

After the preliminary assessment is over the Panel recommends to the Board of Executive Directors whether or not the claim should be investigated. However, after this stage the Panel requires the approval of the Board of Executive Directors if it intends to proceed further.[204]

If the Directors approve an investigation, the Chairperson of the Panel designates one or more Panel members to conduct the investigation and prepare a report on the findings. Unless the Board restricts the Panel's term of reference,[205] the Panel exercises full access to Bank staff and Bank files in conducting its investigation, as well as site visits and meeting with the claimants, members of civil society and other affected people by the project. However, prior to the site visit by the Panel, the permission of the country where the project is located is required.[206]

After the investigation is complete, the Panel submits its report to the Executive Directors and the President. The Management is also to required to submit its recommendation by way of response to the findings made by the Panel within six weeks. Based on these two reports the Executive Directors decide the future course of action in response to the claim.[207]

The recommendatory power apart, the Panel does not hold any powers with regard to investigation. Every major step of the Panel is required to have the approval of the Board of Executive Directors of the Bank. Besides, the condition that the request should be filed before the closing date of the financing or disbursement of the loan also prevents the Inspection Panel from checking the post disbursement deviance.[208] Nevertheless, the Panel processes over the years have proved to be fairly effective in curbing default of the whole bunch of the Banks policy guidelines.[209] In several cases the deviation or derailment of the Bank policy have been corrected by the Management or the borrowing country by reforming policies and redesigning Action Plans as an alternative to an investigation. Neither the Bank nor the borrowing country has so far claimed that it need not follow the Bank Directives. The provision permitting the anonymity of the claimants, the possibility of the cause being represented by the NGO, and the scope for field visits by the Panel generally produces positive results. However, looking at the overall controlling power of the Board, and the power of the borrowing country to resist field investigation, the Panel does not appear to be too independent as it is proclaimed to be.[210]

4.7 Refrains of International Law on the Protection of the Rights of Projected Affected Persons in the Domestic Legal Regime

As discussed earlier, the relevance of international law in the context of displacement is two fold. First is the possibility of invoking the provisions of international treaty law and other recognised principles of justice in the domestic courts. The legal system of Nepal has now opened up this avenue. Secondly, with Nepal's accession to the Optional Protocol, she has opened up one more avenue for individuals to make communication to the Human Rights Committee against the violation of human rights by the State. Perhaps these two are the most visible notes that one needs to keep in mind. But as pointed out at the beginning of this chapter, an understanding of the rights of the project affected people under international law serves several other purposes as well. The reference to international law can be made, for instance, for drawing out standards and creating norms for domestic legislation. International legal norms would also influence the overall decision making process in the domestic legal and policy regimes. For instance, the concepts for development propagated by the UN Declaration on Right to Development and the concepts for sustainable development propagated by the international environmental law are likely to be taken as very important considerations in the domestic legal and policy regime. As principles of human rights are interspersed in both concepts, development cannot be reasonably advanced as a justification for the violation of human rights nor possible violation of human rights for non-development. It is here that the reiteration of the statement in the Vienna Declaration on Programme of Action becomes pertinent. It said; "while development facilitates the enjoyment of human rights, the lack of development may not be invoked to justify the abridgement of internationally recognised human rights."[211] The preeminence of international law can be assessed from the fact that no country ever maintains that she need not keep in mind the international norms while taking policy decisions.

The most enduring contribution of international law on the question of displacement that is emerging is the recognition of "a right not to be displaced."[212] Even though domestic courts in some countries of South Asia have given expansive interpretation of the right to life to include right to shelter[213] the recognition of a right not to be evicted from the shelter is still not recognised as a concomitant of the right to shelter or life. It is in this context that the recognition of the "right not to be arbitrarily displaced," which is being recognised in the burgeoning human rights literature assumes importance.

Apart from the substantive "right not to be displaced," a host of other substantive and procedural rights, like the right to information about the project as well as its environmental impact, the right to participate in the decision making process, and the right to be benefitted from the project including the right to compensation and restitution, the right to effective remedy through administrative and judicial process are some other important rights applicable in the context of displacement.

Primarily, the obligation to respect the rights of the displacees, mitigation of their hardships, restoration of their income lies with the concerned state. It is perhaps for this reason that the people displaced by development project have not received any international assistance. The UN Guiding Principles on Internally Displaced People now recognise the power of international humanitarian organizations and other actors to offer services in support of the displaced persons. National authorities are now required to grant access to such international organs and actors in extending assistance to the displaced persons.

Besides the general protection offered to the displaced persons international legal regime requires the states to undertake special protective measures for the protection of women, children, tribals and other indigenous people. If any project is likely to displace indigenous and tribal people the authorities are required to take informed consent of these people, involve them in the planning of the resettlement programme, as a necessary precondition.

Another significant development is the mendatory requirement for EIA in project involving displacement. EIA is required to be carried out through a participatory process. This has partially been incorporated in national legal regimes but still much needs to be done in this area, for which international norms may come into use.

At the national level, especially in the third world, the policy makers have a tendency to neglect human rights and environmental considerations so long as adherence to such norms is not mandatory. Now, as these norms to a great extent are incorporated in the Guidelines of the funding agencies like the World Bank, OECD etc. adherence to such norms at domestic level has also become a policy imperative. The access provided by the World Bank Guidelines to individuals for pointing out the infraction of the Guidelines, the possibility of investigation by the Inspection Panel and consequential reprimand have created a better environment for compliance of the Guidelines. Further the emphasis of the World Bank on the development of appropriate legislative norms at the domestic level has a likelihood of providing positive results, though as of now the adoption of ad-hoc policies rather than universal norms is the practice. In conclusion it is submitted that the authorities in Nepal (as well as other domestic regimes for that matter) may not find the adherence or compliance to international law very appealing, but adherence to it is less likely to be an option than a duty in the coming days.

REFERENCES

1. One such principle developed in the Trail Smelter case that no state has the right to use or permit the use of territory in such a manner as to cause injury in or to the territory of another or the properties or persons therein, when the case is of serious consequences and the injury is established by clear and convincing evidence. The principle was endorsed in the UN Declaration on Human Environment UN Doc. A/CONF. 48/14(1972) reprinted in 11 ILM 1416(1972) Principles 21, 22. *See* Trail Smelter Arbitration 35 AJIL 716 (1941). *See also* GURDIP SINGH, ENVIRONMENTAL LAW 231-234 (New Delhi, Lawman, 1995). The ICJ some times refers to and applies municipal law as it did in the Barcelona Traction, Light and Power Co II phase judgement, ICJ Reports 1970 at 3, 37-38 (applying the veil principle in the interest of shareholders). *See* P. C. RAO, INDIAN CONSTITUTION AND THE INTERNATIONAL LAW 51-52 (Delhi, Taxman, 1993) Similarly precautionary principle which originated in Germany in now a recogised principle both in the international and domestic law. *See* Michael Anderson, *Overview* in HUMAN RIGHTS APPROACHES TO ENVIRONMENTAL PROTECTION (Alan Byole and Michael Anderson eds.)(Oxford, Clarendon Press, 1996). *See also* NARAYAN BELBASE, THE IMPLEMENTATION OF INTERNATIONAL ENVIRONMENTAL LAW IN NEPAL 9-11(Kathmandu, IUCN, 1997).
2. The UN Declaration on Right to Development, 1986, U.N.G.A.Res. 41/128, 4 December 1986.
3. It is said that the executive authority of the State cannot acquire new rights against citizens by making treaties with foreign powers. *See* Maganbhai Patel v Union of India, AIR 1969SC 783,792 (per Hydayatullah CJ).
4. P.C RAO, *supra* note 1, at 12-13.
5. *See* The Vienna Convention on Law of the Treaties, 1969, reprinted in 8 ILM 679 (1969), Art 27 (providing that "a party may not invoke the provisions of its internal law as justification for its failure to perform a treaty.")
6. *See* P.C. RAO, *supra* note 1, at 18-19.
7. NEP.CONST. Art 1.
8. *Id.* Art 88(1).
9. Some Constitutions contain very clear provisions regarding

this. For e.g. the FRENCH CONST. States "The President of the Republic shall negotiate and ratify treaty"(Art.52).

10. NEP.CONST. Art 35.
11. *Id.* Art 126;The treaty making power of the executive, however, is not absolute. The Constitution imposes restriction on the treaty making power in matters detrimental to the territorial integrity of the Kingdom of Nepal. *Id.* Art 126 (4).
12. *Id.* Art 126(2) provides: "[In case of the following subjects] the laws to be made pursuant to clause (1) shall, *inter alia,* require that the ratification of, accession to, acceptance of or approval of treaties or agreements be done by a majority of two-thirds of the members present at a joint sitting of both Houses of Parliament:-
    (a) peace and friendship;
    (b) defence and strategic alliance;
    (c) boundaries of the Kingdom of Nepal; and
    (d) natural resources, and the distribution of their uses."
13. *Id.* Art 126(3) provides; "After the commencement of this constitution, unless a treaty or agreement is ratified, acceded or approved in accordance with this Article, it shall not be binding on His Majesty's Government."
14. Monist Constitutions contain such provisions, *See e.g.* the Constitutions of US CONST. Art 6(2); ITALY CONST. Art 10; GERMAN CONST. Art 25; FRENCH CONST. Art 52-55.
15. US. CONST. Art 6 (2). Not only the treaty law, in case of customary international law also, the US practice is guided by the Blackstonian doctrine which considers international law as part of the common law. *See* P.C. RAO, *supra* note 1, at 52-53.
16. It is now a settled rule in the US that the Congress can by law overrule a treaty stipulation, where there exists a strong reason for such congressional action. *See id.* at 54.
17. *Id.*
18. *Id.* at 55.
19. Attorney General of Canada v Attorney General of Ontario 1937 PC 326.
20. *Id.* at 347.
21. *See* P.C. RAO, *supra* note 1, at 62 (quoting Francis Vallant 1966).
22. Philipson v Imperial Airways Ltd (1939) AC 332.
23. *See* P.C. RAO, *supra* 1, at 58 (citing Zoerhsch v Waldock (1964)1 WLR 675).

24. Salomon v Commission of Customs and Excise(1967)2 QB 144; Post Office v Estuary Radio Ltd. (1968)2 QB 740

25. In Buvot v Barbuit [(2737) Cas. T. Talbot.281]Lord Talbot in this case reiterated Blackstone and held that "the law of the nation is here adopted in its full extent by the common law, and is held to be a part of the law of the land". Similar stand was taken in Triquit v Bath [(1764) 4 Burr. 1478, 1479] and Heathfield v Chilton [(1787) 4 Burr.2016. *See also* P. C. RAO, *supra* note 1, at 62-63.

26. (1876) 2 Ex.D. 63 cited in *id. at 62-63.*

27. *Id.*

28. IVOR JENNINGS, THE LAW AND THE CONSTITUTION 173 (5TH ed. Kents, ELBS/Holder & Stoeghton, 1979).

29. A.S. Anand, inaugural address on *The Domestic Application of International Human Rights Norms,* Bangalore, Dec.27,1998 at 4.

30. Jolly George Varghese v Bank of Cochin AIR 1980 SC 470.

31. A.D. M. Jabalpur v Shivakant Shukla (1976) 2 SCC 521, 542 (per Khanna J); Tractoroexport, Moscow v M/sTarapore & Co. (1969) 3 SCC 562,571; Similar positions are taken by courts of other common wealth countries as well; *see* A.S. Anand *supra* note 28 (citing Minister of Immigration and Electric Affairs v Toeh 69 AUST.LR630(1995); Quin v Ryan (1965) Irish Report 70; Byane v Ireland (1972) Irish Report 241; Simpson v Attorney General(1994) New Zealand Reports 667).

32. Visakha v State of Rajasthan JT 1997(7)SC 384;AIR 1997 SC 3011, 3014.

33. People's Union for Civil Liberties v Union of India, JT 1997(2)SC 311.

34. Nilabati Behra v State of Orissa (1993) 2 SCC 746; AIR 1993 SC 2366.

35. Gramophone Company of India v Birendra Bahadur Pandey, AIR 1984 SC 667, 671; (1984)2SCC 534; *See also* Michael Anderson, *International Environmental Law in Indian Couris,*7 RECIEL 25 (1996).

36. Visakha v State of Rajasthan AIR 1997SC 3011.

37. *See* Rural Litigation Entitlement Kendra v State of UP, AIR 1985SC539; AIR 1985SC 652 (referring to 1972 Stockholm Declaration and African Charter on Humans and People's Rights in order to make out a case for the right to live in a healthy environment with minimal disturbance to ecological balance); *see also* Vellore Citizens Forum v Union of India AIR 1996 SC

2715, (1996)5SCC 647(holding that the precautionary principle and the polluter pays principle are part of the concept of sustainable development); S. Jagannath v Union of India (1997)2 SCC 87.

38. Kamalnath v Union of India (1997)1 SCC 388.

39. Vellore Citizens Forum v Union of India AIR 1996 SC 2715, (1996)5SCC 647.

40. *See e.g.* the earlier Constitutions of Nepal, THE NEPAL GOVERNMENT ACT, 1948, THE INTERIM CONSTITUTION, 1951, THE CONSTITUTION OF THE KINGDOM OF NEPAL, 1959, THE CONSTITUTION OF NEPAL 1962, declared such supremacy.

41. *See e.g.* The Extradition Act 1988, The Breton Woods Act 1961, The Plant Protection Act 1977, The Right of the Child Act 1992, the Nepal Treaty Act 1990 are some of the Acts in point.

42. NEP. CONST. Art.126.

43. NEP. CONST. Art 84 provides; "Powers relating to justice in the Kingdom of Nepal shall be exercised by Courts and other judicial institutions in according to the provisions of this Constitution, the laws and the recognised principles of justice."

44. Nepal Treaty Act,1990, S. 9.

45. By the expression "human rights laws" the researcher proposes to include both the hard and soft laws as well as other practices which could possibly form the part of customary international law.

46. In 1922 Oppenheim wrote; "Law of Nation is a law between States only and exclusively. States only and exclusively are subject of law of Nation". *See* the relevant excerpt in LOUIS B. SOHN & THOMAS BURGENTHAL, INTERNATIONAL PROTECTION OF HUMAN RIGHTS, 1 (New York, The Bobbs-Merril Co Inc.,1973) The views of Oppenheim were considered valid till the World War Second. However, a change occurred in this line of thinking even among the jurists taking traditional view with regard to the subject of international law. Lauterpacht, while revising Oppenheim in 1955 wrote; " ... Individuals are the *ultimate* objects of international law ... Law of Nations is *primarily* a law between States, States are to that extent, the only subject of the Law of Nation ... Individuals are not *normally* subject of international law", *see id.* at 5-6 (italics supplied).

47. *See* UN CHARTER, Preamble (stating "we the peoples of the United Nations ... have resolved to combine our efforts to accomplish these aims.") *See also* Art 1(3)(setting promotion

and encouraging the respect for human rights and for fundamental freedoms as one objective); Art 55 (providing that the UN shall promote universal respect and assurance of human rights and fundamental freedoms for all without distinction as to race, sex, language or religion); Art 56 (providing for joint and separate action for the achievement of the purposes set forth in Art 55); Art 76 (providing for respect for human rights and fundamental freedoms as one objective of trusteeship system).

48. *See* LOUIS HENKIN, *Introduction* in THE INTERNATIONAL BILL OF RIGHTS, 6 (Louis Henkin ed New York, Columbia Univ. Press, 1981); *See also* Imre Szabo, *Historical Foundations of Human Rights and Subsequent Development* in 1 INTERNATIONAL DIMENSIONS OF HUMAN RIGHTS 35 (Paris, UNESCO, 1982).

49. Domestic courts in India have quite often referred to the international human rights law in interpreting the rights guaranteed by the domestic laws and in developing guidelines for immediate implementation in the absence of appropriate laws. Similar developments are occurring in other countries as well. *See e.g.* Peoples' Union for Civil Liberties v Union of India (1997)1 SCC 301; Samatha v State of AP (1997)6SCC 47; Life Insurance Corporation of India v Consumer Education and Research Centre(1995)5SCC 482 Visakha v State of Rajasthan AIR 1997 SC 3011 (developing guidelines for immediate action till the Parliament enacted the law).

50. Nepal Treaty Act 1990, S. 9.

51. Nepal acceded to the International Covenant on Civil and Political Rights, the International Covenant on Economic, Social and Cultural Rights (henceforth ICCPR and ICESCR respectively) and the Optional Protocol to the International Covenant on the Civil and Political Rights (henceforth referred to as the Optional Protocol I) on 14th May, 1991. This year she has also acceded to the optional protect on Right of the Child. For the Human Rights Instruments either ratified or acceded by Nepal. *See* Annexure 3.

52. The Human Right Committee constituted under Art 28 of the ICCPR can now receive written communications from individuals after the exhaustion of domestic remedy. *See* Optional Protocol I G.A. Res. 2200 A (XXI), 21st Session. 16 Dec. 1966, Supp. No 16 at U.N. Doc A 6316, Art 1, 2.

53. MYERS S. MCDOUGAL ET AL, HUMAN RIGHTS AND THE WORLD PUBLIC ORDER 64 (New Haven, Yale Univ. Press, 1980).

54. *See* the Universal Declaration on Human Rights, G.A. Res. 217

(III), U.N. GAOR 3rd session,10 December 1948, at U.N. Doc A 810 (1948), Preamble.

55. *Id.* Art 28.
56. UN CHARTER, Preamble; Art 55, 56.
57. ICCPR, G.A. Res.2200A, U.N. GAOR, 21st Session,16 December 1966, Supp No 16 at 53 U.N. Doc A 6316 Art 1(1); ICESCR, G.A. Res. 2200A 21st Session, 16 December 1966, Supp. No 16 at 49 ,U.N. Doc. A 6316.
58. *Id.*, Preamble.
59. John O'Manique, *Human Rights and Development*, 14 HUMAN RIGHT QUARTERLY 78-197 (1992).
60. Asbjorn Eide, *The Human Rights Movement and the Transformation of the International Order*, ALTERNATIVES 367, 373 (1986).
61. *Id.*
62. *See* UDHR, *supra* note 54, Art 3, Art 17, 22, 25; ICESCR ,*supra* note 57, Art 2(2), 9, 11(1); ICCPR, *supra* note 57, Art 2, 6, 26. According to Art 4 of the ICCPR Art 6,7,16,18, are non-derogable even in emergency. *See also* Maria, Stavropoulau, *The Right not to Be Displaced*, 9 AMERICAN UNIVERSITY JOURNAL OF INTERNATIONAL LAW & POLICY 689,737-739 (1998) (arguing that freedom of movement which includes right to remain, or right to stay or even the right to return is inherently breached when displacement occurs, because the displaced are restricted invariably in their movement. This right is subject to restriction only for national security, public order, public health or morals or rights and freedoms of others and consistent with right recognised in the Covenant) *See also* ICCPR, *supra* note 57, Art 12(3).
63. *See* ICCPR & IESCR, *supra* note 57, Preamble.
64. *See* IESCR, *supra* note 57 Art. 1(2); *see also* Asbjorn Eide, *Economic, Social and cultural Rights as Human Rights*, in ECONOMIC SOCIAL AND CULTURAL RIGHTS: A TEXT BOOKS 37 (Asbjorn Eide et al eds, Dordrch,Martin Nijhoff, 1995).
65. ICESCR, *supra* note 57, Art 11(2) ; *see also* Asbjorn Eide *id.* at 37-38.
66. ICESCR, *supra* note 57, Art 2(1).
67. David Trubek, *Economic Social and Cultural Rights in the Third World: Human Rights, Law and Human Needs Programmes* in HUMAN RIGHTS IN INTERNATIONAL LAW AND POLICY ISSUES, 214, 215 (Theodor Meron ed.) (Oxford, Clarendon Press, 1983).

68. ICESCR, *supra* note 57, Art 2(2).

69. *See* Committee on Economic Social and Cultural Rights, General Comment No 7 (para.4), U.N.Doc.E/C.12/1997/4(1997)(italics supplied) (henceforth General Comment No 7).

70. *Id.*

71. *See* Committee on Economic Social and Cultural Rights, General Comment No 4 U.N. Doc. E/C 1992/23 annex III, (henceforth General Comment No 4).

72. *See* General Comment 7,*supra* note 69, (para 15); *see also* the Human Right Committee General Comment No 16 U.N. Doc. HRI/GEN/i/Rev.1 (29 July 1994), (in relation to Art 17 of ICCPR, states that interference with a person's home can only take place "in cases envisaged by the law." The [Human Right] Committee further observed that the law "should be in accordance with the provisions, aims and objectives of the Covenant, and should be in any event reasonable in the particular circumstance". The Committee also indicated that "relevant legislation must specify in details the precise circumstances in which such interference may be permitted."

73. However, the burgeoning literature on the subject is moving towards recognizing this right.

74. ICESCR, *supra* note 57, Art 11; ICCPR, *supra* note 57, Art 17.

75. *Id.* Some have even argued that "home" constitutes not only a means of "shelter", but also a means of placing a person in a social and physical space, and of circumscribing a person's private life and social interaction see Maria Stavropoulin, *supra* note 62, at 717.

76. General Comment No 7, *supra* note 69, (para 9). For similar principles in the domestic legal regime, *see* PUDR v Union of India AIR 1982SC 1473,1490 (holding that state is under an obligation to ensure the enjoyment of fundamental rights).

77. *See* General Comment No 4, *supra* note 71 Annex III. This issue was discussed by the Human Rights Committee in 1991 while offering general comments on right to housing. *See also* UN Doc HRI/GEN/i/Rev.1 (29 July, 1994).

78. General Comment No 7, *supra* note 69, para 5.

79. *Id.* para 17.

80. *Id.* para 14. The Committee also recalled Art 2(3) of ICCPR, which requires the State Parties to ensure an "effective remedy" for persons, whose rights have been violated.

81. UN Commission on Human Right Resolution 1993/77 para 4 (March 10, 1993).

82. Committee on Economic Social and Cultural Rights, General Comment No 2 (1990) para 11, UN Doc. E/C 1992/23 Annex III.
83. Reemphasized in General Comment No 7, *supra* note 69, (para 18).
84. Committee has requested the States to furnish information relating to (a) the number of persons evicted within the last five years and the number of persons currently lacking legal protection against arbitrary eviction or any other kind of eviction; (b) legislation concerning the right of tenants to security of tenure, to protection from eviction, and (c) legislation prohibiting any form of eviction. *See* General Comment No7, *supra* note 69, (para.20).
85. *See* UN Doc. E/CN 4/1998/53 Add. 2, February 11, 1998. These Principles entitled "Guiding Principles on Internal Displacement" were prepared by Mr. Francis M. Deng, representative of the UN Secretary General on Internally Displaced Person and presented to the Commission at its 54th session in 1998. (henceforth Guiding Principles).
86. Scope and Purpose.
87. *Id.*, Principle 1(2)(italics supplied).
88. Roberta Cohen, *Recent Trends in Protection and Assistance for Internally Displaced People* in INTERNALLY DISPLACED PEOPLE 4 (Janie Hampton ed.) London, Earthscan,1998).
89. Guiding Principles, *supra* note 85, Principle 6(1).
90. *Id.* Principle 6(2)(c).
91. *Id.* Principle 7(1).
92. *Id.* Principle 9.
93. *Id.* Principle 7(3)(a).
94. *Id.* Principle 7(3)(b).
95. *Id.* Principle 7(3)(c).
96. *Id.* Principle 7(3)(d).
97. *Id.* Principle 7(3)(f).
98. *Id.* Principles 1, 4, 11, 12, 17, 18.
99. *Id.* Principles 4(2) and 19(2).
100. *Id.* Principle 1(1).
101. *Id.* Principle 25.
102. Report of Mr Francis Deng, E/CN 4/1998/53, *supra* note 85.
103. Roberta Cohen, *supra* note 88, at 1.

104. *See e.g* Surya P. Sharma Dhungel v Godavari Marbles NKP Golden Jubilee Issue 1995(2052) 169 (Nepal); Mohiddin Farooque v Bangladesh 48DLR 1996 (Bangladesh); Subash Kumar v State of Bihar AIR 1991SC 420(India); Shehla Zia v WAPDA, PLD 1994 SC 693(Pakistan).*See also* Martin Lau, *Islam and Judicial Activism: Public Interest Litigation and Environmental Protection in Islamic Republic of Pakistan* in HUMAN RIGHT APPROACHES TO ENVIRONMENT, *supra* note 1, at 285-301; Michael Anderson, *Individual Right to Environmental Protection in India, id.* at 199-220.

105. As of now more that 60 constitutions of the world contain some sort of provision relating to environmental protection. *See* James Cameron and Ruth Mackenzie, *Access to Environmental Justice and Procedural Rights in International Institutions, id.* at 13.

106. 1972 Declaration of the UN Conference on Human Environment, U.N. Doc. A/CONF. 48/ 14(1972), 11 ILLM 1416(1972), Principle 1 (henceforth Stockholm Declaration).

107. The World Commission on Environment and Development (WCED), for instance, recognised the right to environment but not in as forceful terms as the Stockholm Declaration. In the Proposed Legal Principles it stated; "All human beings have the fundamental right to an environment adequate for their health and well being.", Principle 1, WECD, OUR COMMON FUTURE 248 (Annex 1), (Delhi, Oxford University Press, 1987).

108. UN Declaration on Environment and Development, U.N. Doc. A/CONF. 15/25 Vol.1 (1992), reprinted in 31 ILM 876(1992), Principle 1.

109. The basic objection to adopting a right perspective is its anthropocentric orientation whereas, according to critics, environment possesses intrinsic values by itself. Beside this, the necessity of preventive and precautionary measures for environmental protection, the indeterminancy in fixing standard, determining the holders of right and duties are arguably the obstacles in recognizing environment as a right. *See generally*, J.M. Merrills, *Environmental Protection and Human Rights: Conceptual Aspects*, in *supra* note 1, at 25-42; Alan Byole, *The Role of International Human Rights Law in the Protection of Environment, id.* at 43-65.

110. *See e.g* the African Charter on Human and Peoples' Right, June 27, 1981 Art 24; OAU Doc.CAB/LEG/67/3 rev.5, reprinted in 21 ILM 58 (1982); the Additional Protocol to American Convention in the Area Social and Cultural Rights, OAS Treaty Series No.69 (1988) Nov.17, 1988, Art 11 (assessed on Oct 25,1999);

The Convention on the Right of the Child, 1989 U.N.GA Doc A/RES/44/25 (12,Dec.1989), Art 24 (in a limited form); The Convention Concerning the Protection of Indigenous and Other Tribal Populations (ILO Convention No 169 reprinted in 28 ILM 1382(1989)) (in an indirect form).

111. OUR COMMON FUTURE, *supra* note 107, at 42.The report further states;" Sustainable development is not a fixed state of harmony, but rather a process of change in which the exploitation of resources, the direction of investments, the orientation of technological development and institutional change are made consistent with future as well present needs." *Id.* at 9. And further states; "The concept of sustainable development does not imply absolute limits but limitations imposed by the present state of technology and social organization on environmental resources and by the ability of the biosphere to absorb the effects of human activities...meeting essential needs requires not only a new ear of economic growth for nations in which the majority are poor, but an assurance that those poor get their fair share of resources required to sustain that growth,"*id.* at 8.

112. Edith Brown Weiss, *Our Rights and Obligations to Future Generations*, 84 AJIL 198 (1990) where she writes; "The purpose of human society must be to realise and protect the welfare and well being of every generation. This requires the sustaining of the life support system of the planet, the ecological process and the environmental conditions necessary for a healthy and decent environment", *id.* at 199.

113. Weiss calls these three as conservation of option, conservation of quality and conservation of access respectively, *id.* at 202.

114. The resonance to this logic may be found in the concept of intra-generational equity which Weiss advocates, *See id.* at 202; *See also* Luthar Gundling, *Our Responsibility to Future Generation*, *id.* at 211.

115. Stockholm Declaration, *supra* note 106, Principle 2 provided; "The natural resources of the earth including the air, water, land, flora and fauna ... must be safeguarded for the benefit of the present and future generations through careful planning or management as appropriate." Similarly, Principle 3 provided; "The capacity of earth to produce vital renewable resources must be maintained and wherever practicable restored or improved"

116. *See e.g.*, the Convention on the Protection and use of Trans-boundary Water Course and International Lakes, reprinted in 31 ILM 1312(1992) Art 2; The UN Framework Convention on

Climate Change, U.N. Doc. A/AC. 237/18, reprinted in 31 ILM 849(1992) Art 3; the North American Agreement on Environment and Cooperation, reprinted in 32ILM 1482(1993), Preamble and Art.1; the Convention for the Protection of the Marine Environment of the North East Atlantic, reprinted in 32 ILM 1969(1993) Preamble and Art 2; The UN Convention on Biological Diversity, reprinted in 31ILM 818(1992) Preamble and Art 10; Agreement Governing the Activities of States on the Moon and Other Celestial Bodies, reprinted in 18 ILM 1434 (1979) Art 4.

117. UN Declaration on Environment and Development U.N. Doc. A/CONF. 15/25 Vol I (1992) 14 June 1992, reprinted in 31 ILM 876(1992) Principle 1,3 and 4, (henceforth Rio Declaration).

118. *Id.* Principle 10 (italics supplied).

119. The UN Convention on Biological Diversity, reprinted in 31ILM 818(1992), Art.17.

120. *Id.* Art 14.

121. For instance, the EC Convention on Environmental Impact Assessment 1991 reprinted in 30 ILM 802(1991) Art 2(6) and 3(8); Council of Europe Convention on Damage Resulting from Activities Dangerous to Environment 1993, reprinted in 32 ILM 1228 (1993) Art 14, 15 and 16; EC Convention on Access to Information Public Participation in Decision-Making and Access to Justice in Environmental Matters reprinted in 38 ILM 517 (1999), Preamble, Art 3(g) (recognizing right of the public to "access to information, possibility to participation decision-making and have access to justice in environmental matters without discrimination as to citizenship, nationality, or domicile"; *see also id* Art 6, 7, 8 (participation in decision making, planning etc); 9(access to Justice). In addition to the above certain themes of the Stockholm and Rio Declarations for instance, liability and, compensation for victims of pollution and other environmental damages and prescriptions for EIA studies before undertaking any project activities that are likely to have adverse environmental effects also need to be recalled here. Similarly, the protection of the interests of indigenous people and other communities, provisions relating to environmental migration and displacement also carry the same theme. It provides that demographic concerns, including concerns for environmental migrants and displaced people should be in the programmes for sustainable development. *See* Stockholm Declaration, *supra* note 106, Principle 13,14; Rio Declaration, *supra* note 117, Principle 13, 20.

122. UN Commission on Human Rights, Sub Commission on

Prevention on Discrimination and Protection of Minorities, Final Report of the Special Rapporteur on Human Rights and Environment (popularly known as Ksenteni Report) UN Doc. E/CN 4/sub.2/1994/5 (6 July 1994).

123. Draft Declaration of Principles on Human Rights and the Environment, http://www.tufts.edu/departments/fletcher/multi/www/1991-decl.html accessed on Dec 14, 1999, Principle 15.
124. *Id.* Principle16.
125. *Id.* Principle 18.
126. *Id.* Principle 19.
127. *Id.* Principle 20.
128. *Id.* Principle 4.
129. *Id.* Principles 5 to 10.
130. *Id.* Principle 11(a)(italics supplied).
31. *Id.* Principle 11(b).
132. *Id.* Principle 12.
133. *Id.* Principle 13.
134. *Id.*
135. *Id.* Principle 14.
136. Namely, emergencies, and/or compelling purpose benefiting society as a whole and not attainable by other means.
137. The Convention Concerning the Protection of Indigenous and Other Tribal Populations 1989, reprinted in 28 ILM 1382 (1989) (henceforth ILO Convention No169) does not offer any formal definition of the indigenous and tribal population. However, the Convention applies to those people in independent countries who are regarded as indigenous on account of their decent from the populations which inhabited the country or a geographical region to which the country belongs, at the time of conquest or colonization or the establishment of present state boundaries and who, irrespective of their legal status retain some or all of their social, economic, cultural and political institutions, *id.* Art 1(b). Tribal people are the people whose social, cultural and economic conditions distinguish them from other sections of the national community and whose status is regulated wholly or partially by their own customs and traditions or by special laws or regulations, *Id.* Art 1(a).
138. Convention Concerning the Protection and Integration of Indigenous and Other Tribal and Semi Tribal Populations in

Independent Countries, 1957, 328 UNTS 247, (henceforth ILO Convention No 107).

139. The Convention developed standards for their protection by recognizing their land rights and limiting the scope of state intervention. It also provided that tribals can be removed from their habitual territories only for (a) national security, (b) national economic development and (c) the health of the tribal population. The Convention also laid down that the displaced tribals shall be provided with lands of quality at least equal to that of the lands previously occupied by them suitable to provide for their present needs and future developments. It also cast duties on the governments to develop systematic and coordinated action, which would ultimately encourage the Tribal and Indigenous people to gravitate towards the mainstream culture. *See Id.* Art 3,11,12,13.

140. *See* Convention No 169 Background, in http://www.ilolex.ch1567/script-s/convde.pl?=(169)queryo=169 accessed on June 17,1999.

141. The new Convention also tried to keep abreast the development that had occurred over time in the situation of indigenous and tribal people. The Convention specifically took note of the inability of the indigenous and tribal people to enjoy their rights. The erosion of the laws, values, customs of these people was also kept in mind while revising the Convention no 107 in 1989. So far only 10 countries have ratified this Convention. Nepal has not acceded to the Convention. As per Art 38(2) ratification by two countries is sufficient to bring the convention into force.

142. *See* Convention No 169, Preamble, Art 1,2,4, 5,8, 9, 10.

143. *Id.* Preamble, Art 2.2(C) , Art 3.

144. *Id.* Art 6 and 7.

145. *Id.* Art 13 and 14.

146. *Id.* Art 15; The land relation is dealt in Chapter II (Art 13-19)

147. *Id.* Art 16.

148. *Id.* Art 20.

149. *Id.* Art 21-23.

150. *Id.* Art 24,25.

151 *Id.* Art 26-31.

152. *Id.* Art 32.

153. The message of the ILO Convention is resonated in a number of

subsequent literature. *See e.g.* the World Bank OD 4.20. *See also* the Vienna Declaration and Programme of Action, U.N. Doc. A/CONF 157/23, 12 July 1993, Art 20, (recognizing the inherent dignity and unique contribution of indigenous people to the development and plurality of society and strongly reaffirming the commitment of the international community to their economic, social and cultural well-being and their enjoyment of the fruits of sustainable development, and also calling to ensure the full and free participation of indigenous people in all aspects of society, in particular in matters which concern them). *See also* Agenda, 21 A/CONF 15/26 Vol 1, 14 June 1992, Ch 26.

154. *See* the Convention No 169, *supra* note 137, Art 33.

155. *See* Michael Cernea, *Public Policy Responses to Development Induced Population Displacement*, 31(24) EPW, 1515, 1519 (1996)(arguing that the World Bank by formulating the operational guidelines (a) rejected the argument that impoverishing DPs was unavoidable, (b) predicted policies on the argument that operational strategies could produce broader outcomes, and (c) imposed responsibility on borrowers to carry out resettlement programmes).

156. OMS 2.33 issued by the Bank in 1980 were refined and improved in 1986 and 1988 and finally a new Operational Directive, OD 4.30 was issued in 1990, *see* OD 4.30, Involuntary Displacement and OD.4.20, Indigenous People in http://www.worldbank.org/inv.res.htm accessed on Sept. 2,1999.

157. The Operational Directive, OD 4.20. Though the OD 4.20 does not define the indigenous people it sets out the following criteria for determining the identity of these people. These are: (a) a close attachment to ancestral territories and to the natural resources in these areas; (b) self identification and identification by others as member of a distinct cultural group; (c) an indigenous language often different from the national language; (d) presence of customary social and political institutions; and (e) primarily subsistence oriented production.

158. The Bank at the moment is in the process of refining and improving OD 4.30. The Draft OD. 4.12 which is in circulation is not a revision of the current Bank policy but conversion into new format. It intends to expand the coverage of OD to both physical economic displacement resulting from the taking of land and other assets or from the restriction of access to legally designated parks and protected area. The policy does not however cover indirect social or economic impacts, or situational where is resettlement is voluntary. The language of the Draft has been

changed to suit broad spectrum of project and harmonizing policy with Bank's new lending instruments handling of projects involving Parks and affected areas.

159. The World Bank, at the request of the OECD provided support in preparing resettlement Guidelines, congruent with the Bank Guidelines in 1991.WB, RESETTLEMENT AND DEVELOPMENT: THE BANKWIDE REVIEW OF PROJECTS INVOLVING RESETTLEMENT, 9 (Washington DC.,1996). *See* OECD Guideline Doc.OECD/GD(91) 201 (1991) reproduced in REHABILITATION POLICY AND LAW IN INDIA; (Walter Fernandes and Vijay Paranjpye eds.)(Delhi: Indian Social Institute, 1997).

160. OD 4.30 is in the process of refinement and improvement. *See* draft 4.12 Involuntary Resettlement, circulated by the Bank in CODE on Nov 21, 1997 (CODE 97-74) For highlight of the same *see* OED, RECENT EXPERIENCE WITH INVOLUNTARY RESETTLEMENT, (Washington DC, The World Bank, 1998) (henceforth OED 1998).

161. *See e.g.*, OD 4.01 Environmental Assessment including annexure (Oct 1991); OD 4.00 Annex B Environmental Policy for Dams and Reservoir Projects (Apr.1989); OP 4.04, Directives on Natural Habitat (Sept. 1995); OP 4.04, Economic Evaluation of Investment Operations (Sept.1994); OD 13.05, Project Supervision (March 1989); OP 11.03, Management of Cultural Property in Bank Financed Project (Sept 1986); BP 1755, Inspection Panel (Feb.1997).

162. OD 4.30 para 3(a); *see also* the OECD Guidelines for Aid Agencies on Involuntary Displacement and Resettlement in Development Projects para 5 and 6 (a)(b) (henceforth OECD).

163. *Id.* para 3(b) provides; "All involuntary resettlement should be conceived and executed as development programmes, with resettlers provided sufficient investment resources and opportunities to share in project benefits." *See also id.* para 6; OECD. para 2,4,6.

164. *Id.* para 3(b) provides; "Displaced persons should be (i) compensated for their losses at full replacement cost prior to the actual move;(ii) assisted with the move and supported during the transition period in the resettlement site; and (iii) assisted in their efforts to improve their former living standards, income earning capacity and production levels, or at least to restore them. Particular attention should be paid to the needs of the poorest groups to be resettled." *See also* OECD para 6(b).

165. *Id.* para 3(c) provides; "Community participation in planning and implementing resettlement should be encouraged.

Appropriate patterns of social organization should be established, and existing social and cultural institutions of resettlers and their hosts should be supported and used to the greatest extent possible." *See also* OECD para 6(c)(d).

166. *Id.* para 3(d) provides; "Resettlers should be integrated socially and economically into host communities so that adverse impact on host community are minimised. The best way of achieving this integration is for resettlement to be planned in areas benefiting from the project and through consultation with the future hosts."

167. *Id.* para 3(e) provides; "Land housing, infrastructure and other compensation should be provided to the adversely affected population, indigenous groups, ethnic minorities, and pastoralists who may have usufruct or customary rights to the land or other resources taken for the project. The absence of legal title to land by such group should not be a bar to compensation." *See also id* para 17.

168. *Id.* para 4.

169. *Id* para 7 provides; "Most displaced people prefer to move as part of a pre-existing community, neighbourhood, or kinship group. The acceptability of a resettlement plan can be increased and the disruption caused by resettlement can be cushioned by moving people in groups, reducing dispersion, sustaining existing patterns of social organization, and retaining access to cultural property (temples, pilgrimage centers, etc.), if necessary relocation of the property. *See also* OECD para 6(c).

170. *Id.* para 8 provides; "the involvement of involuntary resetlers and hosts in planning prior to the move is critical ... to obtain cooperation, participation and feedback, affected hosts and resettlers need to be systematically informed and consulted during preparation of the resettlement plan about their options and rights. They should also be able to choose from a number of acceptable resettlement alternatives." *Id.* para 9 provides; "The plan should address and mitigate resettlement's impact on host populations. Host communities and local governments should be informed and consulted." *See also id.* Para 19.

171. *Id.* para 16 maintains; "Vulnerable groups a particular risk are indigenous people, landless and semilandless households headed by females who, though displaced, may not be protected through national land compensation legislation. The resettlement plan must include land allocation or culturally acceptable alternative income-earning strategies to protect the livelihood of these people. *See also id.* 3(e); OECD para 6(e); OD 4.20 para 8 (providing

that the policy of the Bank is that the strategy for addressing the issues pertaining to indigenous peoples must be based on informed participation of the indigenous people themselves).

172. *Id.* para 3(d). It further provides; "The best way of achieving this integration is for resettlement to be planned in areas benefiting from the project through consultation with the future host.."

173. *Id.* para 20.

174. *Id.* para 1(providing that planning and financing resettlement components for free-standing projects are an integral part preparation for projects that cause involuntary displacement).*See also id.* para 6.

175. *Id.* para 3(b).

176. The Directives require that the base line survey should contain (a) magnitude of displacement, (b) information on full resource base of the affected person including income derived from informal sector and non farm activities and from common property, (c) the extent to which the groups will experience total or partial loss of asset, (d) public infrastructure and social services that will affected, (e) formal and informal institutions (such as community organizations, ritual groups etc) that can assist with designing and implementing the resettlement programme, and (f) attitude on resettlement options. *Id.* para 11.

177. *Id* para 13 (provides; "for land based resettlement, the new site's productive potential and locational advantage should be at least to those of the lost land ... for rural resettlers irrigation, land reclamation, tree crop development intensification of production, and other innovations often can provide adequate production potential on land limited amounts of land to resettle agriculturalists, even in countries with high population densities."

178. *Id.* Para 11.

179. It is required by *id.* Para 14.

180. OD 4.01 Annex D. para 1 where he is required to indicate (a) the key environmental issues, (b) the project category and the type of environmental work needed, and (c) a preliminary environmental assessment schedule.

181. OD 4.30 para 28 provides; "The possibility of involuntary resettlement should be determined as early as possible and described in all project documents. The TM should (a) briefly summasize in the Initial Executive Project Summary (henceforth IEPS) the magnitude, strategy and timing of the resettlement (b) inform borrowers of the Bank's resettlement policy, (c)

review past experience with similar operations, (d) invite agencies responsible for resettlement to discuss their policies, plans and institutional, consultative and legal arrangement, and (e) where appropriate, ensure that the technical assistance is provided early to borrowers. Such assistance should include the use of project preparation facility (PPF) resources for planning resettlement and building institutional capacity."

182. OD 4.20 para 16 provides; "During project identification, the borrower should be informed of the Bank's policy for indigenous people. The approximate number of potentially affected people and their location be determined and shown on maps of the project area. The legal status of any affected group should also be discussed. The TMs should ascertain the relevant government agencies, and their policies, procedures, programmes and plans for indigenous peoples affected by the proposed project. TMs should also initiate anthropological studies necessary to identify local needs and preferences. TMs, in consultation with the REDs, should signal indigenous peoples issues and the overall project strategy in the IEPS.

183. The classification of each proposed project depends on the type of location, sensitivity and scale, and nature and impact of its potential effect. Projects that are likely to have significant sensitive, irreversible and diverse adverse impact are categorised as type A project requiring EA. Similarly, projects that may have less significant adverse environmental impact are categorised as B type requiring only Environmental Report (ER). Projects unlikely to have adverse environmental impact for instance education, family planning, institutional or human resource development projects are categorised as type C. These project do not require EA. *See* OD 4.01 Annex E.

184. OD 4.30 para 24.

185. OD 4.01 para 21 The borrower is required to inform the affected groups and members of civil society (with relevant information) about the project by providing a summary of the project describing its objectives, potential adverse impact prior to consultation. Similarly, after the EA report is prepared the borrower is required to provide to the affected group a summary of the conclusions in a plain and simple language.

186. OD 4.01 Annex disabilities para 1-7.

187. OD 4.30 para 29. It also maintains that the cost of resettlement should be treated as a charge against the economic benefits of the investment project that causes relocation.

188. OD 4.30 para 27. Here the TM with the advice of the RED

assesses the EA taking into account the TOR agreed upon. The TM also ascertains the nature of consultation undertaken by the borrower with affected groups and NGOs. Similar assessment of EA is also conducted by the RED. In projects which involve major resettlement, the Regional Vice President of the Bank should be informed and his guidance sought where necessary. Similarly, the Legal Department (henceforth LEG) and the resettlement specialists in Sector Policy and Research (henceforth PRS) are also required to be consulted or included as necessary in peer reviews on involuntary resettlement issues throughout the project cycle.

189. OD 4.01 Annex disabilities para 8; A time bound resettlement plan is also a condition of appraisal for project involving resettlement. The Mission is required to ascertain: (a) the extent of the involuntary resettlement and human hardship and whether the borrower can manage the process, (b) the adequacy of the resettlement plan including the time table and budget for resettlement and compensation; (c) soundness of the economic and financial analysis; (d) the availability and adequacy of sites, funding for all resettlement activities; (e) the feasibility of implementation arrangements; (f) the extent of involvement of beneficiaries. *See also* OD 4.30 para 30.

190. OD 4.20 para 18.

191. OD 4.01 Annex disabilities para 9-12. While sanctioning the loan the Bank may also outline measures critical for sound project implementation in the project conditionality. In projects having resettlement components, the Directives require that the Bank and the borrowers agree on the resettlement and such agreement be reflected in the legal documents. *See also* OD 4.30 para 30.

192. OD 4.01 Annex, disabilities, para 13.

193. OD 4.30 para 31; OD 4.20 para 19.

194. OD 4.01 Annex disabilities para; OD 4.30 para 32 During this (a) environmental impacts, (b) effectiveness of the mitigation measures (c) institutional development and training (b) resettlement and its impact and standard of living of the resettlers and the host population is evaluated.

195. IBRD Res. 93-10/IDA 93-06.Resolution establishing the Inspection Panel. The Panel came into force in 1994.The Panel is composed of three members nominated by the President of the Bank and approved by the Board of Executive Directors. Though the Panel is financed by the Bank, attempts have been made to keep the Panel independent by imposing certain disqualification to

the members. For instance, any Panel member should not have worked for the Bank at least two years prior to the serving on the panel, nor can they work with the Bank after expiry of their terms. The power of the Inspection Panel extends to the lending made by IBRD and IDA. Recently IFC also accepted Bank's draft 4.12 with minor modification to apply to its private sector operations. *See* Draft IFC Environmental and Social Policies and Procedures, Part II Corrigendum (IFC/ R 97-208/1) Nov. 26, 1997 cited in OED 1998 *supra* note 159. The Inspection Panel for its origin owes to the international campaign against the Sardar Sarovar Dam Project on the Narmada river in India in which the Bank for the first time, appointed an independent Commission to review the Bank's role in the project. The two member Commission popularly known as the Morse Commission scathingly indicted the Bank for its failure to enforce its policies and for tolerating Government of India's failure to mitigate social and environmental impacts. This and a few other factors like the pressure from NGOs, donor countries and the Bank's own realization about the adoption of a "culture of approval" rather than the implementation of the policies and procedures were responsible for the Bank to create the Panel. *See* DANA CLARK AND MICHAEL HSU, A CITIZEN'S GUIDE TO THE WORLD BANK INSPECTION PANEL 3 (Washington, Centre for International Environmental Law, 1997).

196. *See supra* note 161.
197. IBRD Res, *supra* note 195.
198. Inspection Panel Operating Procedures adopted by the Panel on Aug 19, 1994.reproduced in DANA CLARK & MICHAEL HSU, *supra* note 195.
199. IBRD Res., *Supra* note 195, Clause 12.
200. Which presumably could include countries where local NGOs are not allowed to operate or where there is a risk of retaliation.
201. In all these three instances the actual claimants can request anonymity while making the claim.
202. *Id.* clause 14.
203. DANA CLARK & MICHAEL HSU, *supra* note 195, at 11.
204. By a very recent resolution adopted by the Board it is now clarified that if the Panel recommends, the Board is required to authorise investigation without making a judgment on the merits of the claimant's request and without discussion. *See* Conclusion of the Board's Second Review of the Inspection Panel April 20, 1999, http:/www.worldbank.org/html/inc-panel/hrm accessed on July 10, 1999.

205. As was done in the NTPC Power Generation Project at Singrauli in India and Yacyreta Hydro Project in Argentina/Paraguay *see* DANA CLARK & MICHAEL HSU, *supra* note 195, at 11.

206. *Id.*

207. *Id.* Copies of the recommendations of the Panel and the Management as well the decision of the Executive Directors is provided to the claimants within three days of the Board's consideration of the Panel's report.

208. A similar problem exists with the implementation of OD 4.30. There is no provision to check such deviation in the Directives. Further, the post resettlement evaluation aspect of the OD is also utterly weak.

209. *See supra* note 161. *See also* IBRD Res No 93-10/IDA 93-06 (Resolution Establishing the Inspection Panel, Sept 1993); Operating Procedures as adopted by the Panel on August 19,1994); BP 17.55 (Inspection Panel, Feb 1997); BP17.55 Annex B (Review of the Resolution Establishing the Inspection Panel: Clarification of Certain Aspects of the Resolution-Feb 1997). In a very short period, the Panel has recommended for detailed investigation in a number of projects funded by the Bank.209 *See* DANA CLARK AND MICHAEL HSU *supra* note 195 at 11.

210. Though an attempt has been made to increase the independence of the Panel staff from the Bank by laying down condition that the Panel members cannot have worked for the Bank for at least two years prior to serving on the Panel. They also cannot work again for the Bank after serving on the Panel. *See* DANA CLARK AND MICHAEL HSU *supra* note 195 at 3.

211. Vienna Declaration and Programme of Action 1993(Adopted by the UN World conference on Human Rights on 25 June 1993), Principle 10.

212. *See* Draft Principles on Environment and Development 1994, supra note 123, Principle 11(a); UN Guiding Principles on Internally Displaced Persons, 1998 supra note 85, Principle 6 (1).

213. Chemile Sing v State of UP (1996) 2 SCC 549; New Riveria Housing Society v Special Land Acquisition Officer (1996) 1 SCC 731; UP Avas Evam Vikash Nigam v Friends Coop Housing Society Ltd 1995 Supp(3)SCC 456; State of Karnataka v Narusimhamurthy (1995) 5 SCC 524; P.G. Gupta v State of Gujarat 1995 Supp (2) SCaC 182.

5

ACQUISITION OF PROPERTY, RESETTLEMENT AND REHABILITATION OF PROJECT AFFECTED PERSONS: SOME CROSS-CULTURAL EXPERIENCES

5.1 Introduction

Project induced displacement is not a problem of one country or region. It is an experience common to all humanity. But, despite the magnitude of the problems involved, and the research findings on the adverse effects of displacement, precious little has been done in terms of correct understanding of the problem, formulating proper policies and laws and seriously implementing them. In most of the countries a remnant of law exists to deal with land acquisition, but extension of the same law or formulation of another set of law to address the problem of resettlement and resettlement is a rare sight. Resettlement and rehabilitation operations in most of the countries are carried out apparently in a policy and legal vacuum. Project specific ad-hoc policies are brought out in some countries as fire fighting measures to deal with the opposition to displacement. Of late, however, a shift in this scenario is slowly emerging. A few countries in Asia, Africa and South America are moving towards developing uniform norms on resettlement and rehabilitation.[1]

True, a law or a policy alone cannot be a handy tool in finding the solution to the problem of project-induced displacement, resettlement and rehabilitation. There is no guarantee that a good law always produces desired results. The interplay of other variables like the political will, institutional capacity and preparedness, timely and suitable allocation of budget, technical know-how are also equally important. Besides, support of people to government decision to launch a project is also seminal in bringing about desired results. Nevertheless, an appropriate law is the first right step for and all other things to follow. When a legal framework is developed and major contours for action fixed, it becomes difficult for any one to deviate later and blur the contour. It is for this reason an attempt has been made in this chapter to trace out the legal and policy regimes on acquisition of property, resettlement and rehabilitation. The exercise will begin with a discussion on the land acquisition laws in South Asia.[2] This is followed by brief discussion of the resettlement policies of a few Asian countries like India, China, and Bangladesh. The objective in presenting cross-cultural experience here is to highlight policies and laws. The discussion on implementation, wherever done, is only of peripheral concern. The purpose of comparative studies however is not mere description but also the assessment of the relative merits of the rules, which may provide insights for the development of norms to address the problem under study.

5.2 Acquisition of Property and the Normative Framework in South Asia

The existence of a pro-state and pro-industry law is the general feature of the normative framework on the acquisition in south Asia. Owing to the British legacy, three countries of the region, viz., India, Bangladesh and Pakistan operate under the Land Acquisition Act of 1894. Some minor modifications have been made here and there after 1947 in respective countries, but by and large the old structure of the law still remains intact. Though Nepal was never a part of the British India, the law on acquisition has remained heavily influenced by the law of its southern neighbuour. The Sri Lankan law on acquisition shows some substantial difference from its Indian counterpart, but it is also not free from the inherent shortcomings that the laws on acquisition of other countries in South Asia contain. Both Maldives and Bhutan do not have a separate law on acquisition but contain some provisions, which can be of interest to other countries at least on some points. As almost all the countries are at the same stage of development and face similar constraints and challenges against human and environmental destruction, a quick look on the existing legal framework of these countries may provide us some clue to address the problems and evolve a comprehensive law on the subject. It is from this point of view that a brief account of the legislative framework on land acquisition is presented in this section.

5.2.1 *India, Bangladesh and Pakistan*

As stated earlier, the Land Acquisition Law of 1894 enacted by the British still remains the governing law in all the three countries. A comparative study of the Acts of the three countries shows that the Indian law has witnessed more legislative amendments than its counterparts, but by and large the structure still remains intact. Therefore, while presenting salient features of the laws, it is submitted that unless mentioned otherwise, the description represents a commonality and not the differences.

Under the LA laws, the state is empowered to acquire any quantum of land for public purpose[3] and for companies.[4] The law does not require the government to inform public in detail about the project by supplying information like the nature of the project, its usefulness to public, whether other alternatives were searched or not and the result of such search if any, steps taken or intended to be taken to minimize hardship, nature and type of compensation etc.

The Act comes into operation after publication of the notification under S. 4(1) of the Act after which the preliminary investigation begins.[5] Any person interested may lodge objection to the acquisition of his/her land or any land in the locality to the collector within 30 days.[6] After the preliminary investigation is over, if the government is satisfied that the land is required for public purpose or for a company a declaration to that effect is made by the government and is published in the official gazette.[7]

After the publication of the second notification, the next step is the determination of compensation.[8] The persons eligible to make complaints are 'persons interested'[9] who may claim compensation on account of acquisition of land. The law does not envisage determination of compensation by an independent body, nor does it envisage the participation of PAPs in the determination of compensation. The collector conducts inquiry about the claims and objections and pronounces his award.[10] If the person interested in land does not accept the award, and by written submission requests, the matter needs to be referred to the court. The Collector while doing so is needed to submit his side of the story. [11]

The reference to the court does not, however, open the matter fully. The scope of inquiry is restricted to a consideration of the interest of the persons affected by the decision to acquire.[12] In no case the compensation awarded by the court should be lesser than the amount awarded by the collector.[13]

One interesting part of the award of the court is that, if the court on such reference, awards any amount of compensation in excess of the amount determined by the Collector, such awards benefit all other persons whose land is being taken by the same notification[14] irrespective of the fact that they had not complained against the award of the collector. The law requires the Collector to re-determine the amount of compensation on the basis of the court's ruling.[15]

In normal circumstances the occupation of land is possible after the award by the Collector is made. The payment of compensation prior to occupation is not mandatory.[16]

Under the law, monetary compensation is the norm. Land in lieu of monetary compensation is left to the discretion of the authorities.[17] The law lays down certain yardsticks for the determination of compensation of which the market value is the one. As the cut off date for determining the market value of the land is the date of the first notification under S 4(1) of the Act, this value turns out to be a historic value. There are other yardsticks also that the Collector should keep in mind while determining compensation,[18] but taken together, these yardsticks do not recognize replacement value as criterion for compensation. The payment of replacement value is beyond the consideration of law.

In India and also in Bangladesh and Pakistan, acquisition of land for companies is possible either for the erection of dwelling houses, or amenities for the companies or for any construction work, which is likely to prove useful to the public.[19] Where acquisition for the company is sought, the company is required to execute an agreement with the government laying down the conditions for acquisitions and for the use by the public. Such agreement is published in the gazette and forms the part of the law.[20]

The general shortcoming of the laws on acquisition in India Bangladesh and Pakistan has mainly arisen due to the lack of understanding of the emerging social realities. Whereas the availability of land due to the growth in the population has shrunk; the states instead of adopting cautious approach to 'public purpose' have expanded the scope of acquisition of land.

The near non-existence of the judicial review of the stated purpose,[21] non inclusion of several interests in land, for instance, the loss of the common property resources, loss of environment, health etc. in the assessment of compensation, exclusion of agricultural laborers, unrecorded tenants, village artisans, pastoralists, forest dwellers and tribals are some of the major problems of the Act. The law is also criticized for adopting irrelevant and faulty considerations in the determination of compensation, over reliance on documentary evidence rather than the factual occupation or use etc. non-linkage of displacement with resettlement and rehabilitation etc.[22]

5.2.2 Sri Lanka

The Sri Lankan Law on land acquisition[23] is slightly different than the Indian, Bangladeshi and the Pakistani law, though it also contains similar inadequacies and shortcomings. The most interesting feature of the Sri Lankan law is its procedure relating to the hearing of objections and its concern about informing the parties at every major step.

Under the Sri Lankan law, the process of acquisition commences with the publication of notification under the instruction of the concerned Minister.[24] Once the Minister decides to acquire the land, it is deemed to be for public purpose.[25] After the Minister takes a positive decision, he makes a written declaration to this effect and such a declaration is published in the gazette.[26]

Once the notification is published, the acquiring officer makes the call for the claims for compensation and related rights on the land or the servitude to be acquired by the government and the hearing on such claims begins.[27] The beauty of the Sri Lankan law is that even those people who fail to present their claims with regard to the right, title or interest over the land within the stipulated time may do so any time before the conclusion of the inquiry. The acquiring officer is also required to entertain oral claims as well and make a record of the same.[28]

Once the inquiry is over, the acquiring officer either makes a decision on every claim made by any person to any right, title or interest or refers the dispute to Primary Court/ District Court. Where he himself makes a decision, the aggrieved party can request him to refer the matter to the court.[29] After the decision of the acquiring officer or the Court[30] becomes final, the acquiring officer proceeds to make the final award. This helps the acquiring officer to avoid repetitive exercise in the determination of compensation. The award, *inter alia,* fixes the compensation that the expropriated owner is entitled to receive.[31] The basis of compensation so determined is the market value of the land. The market value is explained as the amount which a willing seller is expected to realise if sells by in the open market as a separate entity on the date of publication of the third notice in the gazette.[32] Other considerations are similar to India.[33] Like the other Act of the subcontinent, the Sri Lankan Act also does not include various other factors, as for instance, the loss of the common property resources, loss of earning from land, loss of environment etc in the assessment of compensation.

If the person having interest in land does not accept the award pronounced by the Acquisition Officer, he can appeal to the Board of Review.[34] The Board of Review is a 16 member permanent body.[35] The Board while hearing the appeal against the award exercises the power of the District Court. The Sri Lankan Act also makes provision of appeal against the decision of the Board of Review to the Court of Appeal on the point of law.[36] On the whole, the Sri Lankan law, except on the question of providing recourse to the affected persons at various stages, is as regressive as the laws of the other countries of the continent on the subject.[37]

5.2.3 *Maldives*

The Constitution of Maldives is the only Constitution in South Asia, which explicitly guarantees the right to a "just compensation" in the event of acquisition of property by the state in the interest of general public.[38] When, in the interest of the state or the citizens, any property, including land homestead etc is to be acquired authorization of the Ministry of Justice or the High Court of Maldives is required.

The Maldivian law differs from other laws in the sense that the whole proceeding is conducted on the authorization of the Ministry of Justice or the High court of Maldives. Once the authorization is given a committee for valuing the land to be acquired is set up. The committee values the land justifiably and submits the report for the approval of the Ministry or the Court. Another noteworthy feature of the Maldivian law is the mandatory requirement of the payment of compensation before taking the land in possession.[39] However, the mandatory provision is often bypassed in case of *wakf* property by transferring the property in other islands. Once it is done the property becomes the property of the government for use of which no compensation needs to be paid to anyone.[40]

5.2.4 *Bhutan*

As stated earlier, the Himalayan Kingdom of Bhutan does not have a separate law for acquisition and resettlement[41] . Still the land code of Bhutan contains some provisions, which may be indicative of the legal regime of Bhutan on acquisition and resettlement. A good provision of law worth mentioning in this context relates to the landless people in Bhutan. The law casts a duty on the government to provide land to landless citizens free of costs.[42] Similarly, it provides that if the government takes away the registered and cultivated land of the citizen, it is required to pay compensation by taking into consideration the class and type of land. In addition to this, the government is also required to provide a fallow land to the person whose land is thus taken away. However, such person will not have a right to choose the land and if he declines to take the land given by the government he forfeits the right to claim alternative land in addition to compensation.[43]

5.3 The Resettlement and Rehabilitation: The Asian Experience

The continent of Asia is not only the largest in terms of size and population it is also a place where a strong wind of displacement and involuntary migration blows.[44] The magnitude of displacement in Asia is still high.[45] At present, three of the four largest displacing countries of the world, China, India and Indonesia fall in Asia[46] In the recent review of the World Bank, Asia presents both the best and the worst case scenario. The grass root movement against displacement is also high in some of the countries of this region. In a few instances, this has even compelled the governments to shelve controversial projects.[47] Whereas the implementation of resettlement and rehabilitation operation in countries like China and Thailand is much appreciated, the performance of countries like India and Indonesia is rated to be poor.[48] A few countries like China, Bangladesh, India and Laos[49] have developed resettlement laws or/and policies or are in the process of developing them. Besides, countries like India and Thailand have developed some sectoral policies as well.[50] It is in this context that an attempt has been made here to cull out the salient features of the policies developed in these countries.

5.3.1 India

As mentioned earlier, India is considered as one of those countries which has a very high incidence of project induced displacement.[51] The pace with which industrialization, infrastructure development and urbanization are taking pace in India during the last ten years or so, a rapid surge in the numbers is imminent.[52]

Now, whereas the figure of displacement in India is high, the number of people resettled is very low. Even the government estimate does not go beyond 25 per cent. [53] This means that a great majority have been left to fend for themselves. [54] Studies have shown that many of the DPs have become prey to multiple displacements.[55]

Despite the high incidence of displacement due to gigantic projects in the post independence era, for a long time the issue of displacement was considered as a byproduct of development and was tackled within the framework of the *Land Acquisition Act 1894*. The restoration of the livelihood of the displaced population was beyond the scope of this Act.

5.3.1.1 The Narmada Water Dispute Tribunal Award

Nearly after 30 years of India's independence, for the first time, the inadequacy of the *Land Acquisition Act* was at least implicitly acknowledged in the form of Narmada Water Dispute Tribunal Award in 1979.[56] By virtue of the award, for the first time the people to be dispossessed by the Sardar Sarovar Project (henceforth SSP) were entitled to benefit what amounted, as was declared, to an opportunity for economic and social progress through the package of resettlement.[57] The award provided not only monetary compensation for property lost, but also indemnification through rehabilitation grants and grants in aid. It required the states to establish civic amenities in new or existing villages where the PAPs were to be resettled. The award required the states to allot house plot apart, agricultural land of equal size for every displaced families losing more than 25 per cent of its holdings, subject to land ceiling laws with minimum of two hectares.[58] It required the preparation of a comprehensive Master Plan for resettlement. The Tribunal in no uncertain terms made the resettlement and rehabilitation of oustees a necessary precondition for submergence of the areas inhabited by them.[59]

The directives of the NWDT are of immense significance. These were stipulated even before the much applauded World Bank guidelines were formulated[60] The importance of the award lies in its response to the inadequacy that existed in the prevailing system of displacement. Viewed from this perspective, the award appears to endorse the overarching principle, later evolved by the World Bank, that the economic status of the PAPs should be restored at least to the pre-move level.[61] Over and above, the very idea of setting up of resettlement and rehabilitation as a precondition for displacement indicates the strong resolve of the Tribunal not to make it an issue to be forgotten later in the actual implementation of the project.

While discussing about the award of the NWDT award, attention is often drawn to the shortcomings of the award.[62] True, there were some inherent defects in the award. But it also needs to be remembered that any court or tribunal delivers its ruling or award on the basis of information submitted to it. When the Tribunal was seized of the dispute, many issues that were raised later were not studied at all. Given the overall orientation of the Tribunal on the issue of resettlement and rehabilitation, there is reason to believe that many shortcomings would probably have been corrected had it been supplied with sufficient information, projections of needs or action plan.[63]

Some inherent defects notwithstanding, the award of the NWDT is remarkable in several respects. For instance, the award in the first place, is a product of continuous search for an equitable distribution of burden and benefits. Second, the guiding principles carved out by the Tribunal are not mere hypothetical contemplation, but are possibly the reflection of India's bitter experience with displacement and resettlement during the fifties and sixties, which by that time had already come to public knowledge. The Tribunal was probably concerned about the possibility of the replication of the same phenomena. And finally, the message handed down by the NWDT is clear at least to the extent that if development projects were not to be carried out at the expense of vulnerable section then rehabilitatory measures setting out bottom lines for actions were a must.

5.3.1.2 Post NWDT Scenario: The Emergence of State Laws

Subsequent to the pronouncement of the NWDT award, a stage was set in for further concretization of the norms on resettlement and rehabilitation. But, the progress was not very commendable in this regard for several years during the 1980s. On the contrary, what is witnessed is that despite the directives of the Tribunal all the three states involved themselves in exploring escape routes.[64] However, bowing to public pressure and also to the goading by the world Bank all the three states brought out policies and action plans on the SSP in the latter half of the 1980s and early 1990s.[65]

Besides state policies on SSP, another interesting development of the 1980s is enactment of laws on resettlement and rehabilitation by the three States—Maharastra, Madya Pradesh and Karnataka.[66] These Acts tried to cater to the interest of the PAPs by expanding the scope of the Act beyond the owner or tenant or the easement holder of property. [67] Resettlement planning [68] option for resettlement,[69] development of basic amenities,[70] emphasis on resettlement in the benefited zone,[71] are other features of these Acts.

On a cursory look, one will find that the three state Acts of India on resettlement falter on several fronts. Most glaring shortcoming is that except in case of the Maharastra Act the other two Acts do not contain provisions for automatic application.[72] Similarly, none of these Acts requires updating of the land record. The Acts are silent on the market survey of the land to be acquired or availed for resettlement. The assessment of the livelihood, occupation, and source of income, skills and job opportunities in the original and resettlement sites, the resource base of area, inventory of heritage sites and other infrastructure, the environmental impact study of the original and resettlement sites, which are integral part of a detailed planning of the main project and resettlement package, however, do not find a mention anywhere in the Act. The facilities assured for resettlers by these Acts are minimum of grant or grant in aid (which do not exceed thousand rupees), a house plot and agriculture land. The minimum guarantee of land made by the Act also falls quite below the minimum agricultural land suggested by the NWDT award.[73] Besides, none of the Acts requires studying of productivity of the land to be given. Similarly, transitional help for construction of house, food supply, seed, measures to protect the health, provisions for education, welfare measures for women, children, the aged and physically or mentally handicapped are kept outside the scope of these Acts. Similarly no attention has been given to training and employment, skill development etc. These Acts are silent on the involvement of the DPS/PAPs at any level of project inception or planning and implementation of RR. The grievance redressal mechanism is also weak. There is no scope for the involvement of civil society or local self-government in the planning and implementation of the resettlement and rehabilitation package. The Acts apparently endorse the idea of stand-alone projects. But where the issue of resettlement and rehabilitation is so much neglected integration of the RR component with the main project, internalization of the cost of RR and other social and environmental cost would perhaps infuse more accountability among the planners and policy makers.

5.3.1.3 The Resettlement and Rehabilitation Policies

While the 1980s in India witnessed a growing unrest against the dominant approach to development.[74] The state on its part is also seen adopting some fire fighting measures in the form of project specific policies and state laws, the present decade has witnessed a slight change in the perception of the government on the issue of project induced displacement. This has resulted in formulation of a few sectoral and state policies as well as draft national policies on resettlement and rehabilitation (henceforth RR) of the project affected people.[75] Most of the drafts have convergence at several fronts.[76] Therefore, here a quick visit of the latest Draft on Resettlement Policy of the Ministry of Rural Development is made. The recent draft of the Ministry of Rural Development addresses most of the criticisms made of the earlier drafts.[77] The Draft National Policy enunciates the following principles.

- Displacement should be minimised. So people displacing projects should be the last option after studying non-displacing and least displacing alternatives.[78]
- Displacement results in "state- induced impoverishment"[79] and that "no developmental project can be justified if a section of society is pauperised by it."[80]
- Informed consent of those to be affected by it should be mandatory. The project needs to be explained to them.[81] They may question every aspect including its public purpose and environmental impact.[82]
- The definition of the DPs/PAPs goes beyond the landowners to include those who depend for sustenance on land owned by other or on the common property resources (CPR) and also persons whose economy is dependent on the community and the people who face dislocation. Similarly, every adult member, his/her spouse, along with unmarried minor children below 18 is considered as separate family unit. The policy prescribes for

payment of compensation for the loss of CPR and the loss of livelihood.[83]

- The welfare of DPs/PAPs is a pre-condition of the project. Rehabilitation is mandatory and should go on side by side with the project and should be prior to dislocation. The DPs should be resettled in communities. And should have a better life after displacement than before it because they pay the price of development. They should be the first beneficiaries of jobs and other project benefits.[84]
- Land for land is recommended as compensation to all the DPS/PAPs and is mandatory for tribals.

On the one hand, the policy gives a very wide definition of the PAPs not to exclude anyone who is residing in the project site,[85] it on the other, limits the range and extent of the policy by excluding certain cross-section of the people, for instance income tax payees, absentee landlords, persons/families getting compensation above certain amount,[86] persons/families who even after acquisition of land would be having an income three times more the property of people falling below the poverty line.[87]

Another aspect of the policy, which merits a mention here, is its gender consciousness and its proper understanding of the vulnerability of the tribals and other disadvantaged sections. In the case of women, the policy attempts to give them a proper representation in the planning and implementation RR[88] and in getting of benefits. It treats them in equal footing with men in recognizing their status as an individual and as a member of family. It recommends the accrual of benefits in the form of homestead, grant etc to them jointly and separately. For instance, the policy prescribes for allotting agricultural land in the joint name of husband and wife. In case where agricultural land or a job could not be given, grant assistance goes in the joint name of husband and wife. The policy also stresses on designing of programmes education, health, family welfare and employment opportunities for women as an integral part of the RR plan.[89]

In case of tribals apart from mandatory requirement of agricultural land, other interests, like the use of CPR and forest resources, protection of their language, culture and rituals are also taken into consideration in the policy.[90] Similarly, the interests of other disadvantaged sections irrespective of the legality of their occupation is taken care of. They are provided with minimum benefits in the form of a homestead, grants, training and employment so that a life above the poverty line becomes possible.[91]

There are several other attractive provisions in the policy. For instance, the policy discourages multiple displacement. It provides that in case of second displacement occurring within a period of 20 years, such families will be entitled for double benefits prescribed under each of the items of RR package.[92] Similarly, by assuring the land to be allotted to the PAPs to be free from all encumbrances, the policy attempts to give a whiff of relief to the PAPs.[93] There are provisions for civic amenities,[94] and also for the improvement of the quality of land, for agricultural inputs and implements.[95] Another major improvement in the present draft over previous drafts is the institutional arrangement.[96] It also imposes obligation on persons manning such institutions for speedy execution of the RR plan.

In a comparative sense, the latest Draft National Policy brought out by the Ministry of Rural Development appears to be progressive than the earlier drafts. It has incorporated most of the suggestions made in the alternative draft prepared by the Indian NGOs. Still the Draft National Policy is not free from weaknesses. For instance, the Policy does not define "public purpose." It also does not give adequate importance to the cultural aspects. It also does not contain any provision on post resettlement support and subsequent evaluation of the restoration of the livelihood of PAPs. Similarly despite its concern for the DPS/PAPS it does not recognise the "right not to be displaced" as a right.[97] Over and above the draft contains several provisions which cannot be implemented without a suitable law in place.[98] Therefore, the latest draft also gives rise to doubts about it being internalised in the actual implementation of the RR operations.

5.3.1.4 The Draft Land Acquisition Bill 1998

In India, when questions relating to the protection of rights of the displaced and other affected people are raised the civil society and other enlightened sections prefer the intervention of the central government. The preference for a central policy and law to address the issue of displacement is a testimony to this.[99] It is perhaps for this reason that the Draft Bill introduced in the Parliament in 1998 to amend the Land Acquisition Act has been received both with interest and criticism. [100] The Bill, for the first time, attempts to link land acquisition with resettlement and rehabilitation. The Bill also tries to introduce transparency and accountability by requiring the Collector to conduct a public hearing on the suitability of the proposed site for acquisition and other objections.[101] He is even empowered to recommend the government against acquisition, keeping in mind the public disagreement.[102] There are quite a few other attractive provisions in the draft. For instance, for the first time the procedure for the determination of market value is laid down.[103] While computing compensation the draft also takes into consideration the loss of livelihood, profession or business.[104] Another noteworthy feature of the draft is the incorporation of principle of constructive or regulatory taking.[105]

Despite some good efforts, the proposed draft amendment appears to be inadequate as the Land Acquisition Act still contains major shortcomings. For instance, the problem created by the inclusive definition of' public purpose' has not been sorted out.[106] Moreover the provision, which empowers the government to acquire land for companies, has been left untouched. The draft also does not embrace the policies underlined in the Draft National Policy on Resettlement. Therefore, it is submitted that whatever has appeared in the form of the Draft Bill, it is still short of the expectation of the critiques of the Act.[107]

5.3.1.5 The Judicial Response to Resettlement and Rehabilitation

As far as mega projects are concerned, the role of the Indian courts so far has not been very encouraging. Many a time serious questions as to the environmental and social impacts of mega projects have been brought to several courts in India, but very little seems to have been done by the judiciary to provide justice to the PAPs or address environmental issues.[108] Apparently, the reason for such reluctance on the part of the judiciary to seize upon the matter seems to be the linking of the project with national development. Often the judicial reasons is also weighed in favour of continuance of the project on the ground of investments already made on them. It is very rarely that the courts intervene on such matters. One such rare instance comes from the Karnataka High Court where the court stayed a project, which purported to acquire 700 ha of lush green forest in Karnataka and asked the government to reconsider the matter and take a *de novo* decision.[109] Barring this and a few other cases like the *Banwasi Sewa Ashram*[110] or the *Gramin Seva Samstha,*[111] *Karjan Jalasay*[112] case, the mass violation of the basic human rights of the displaced persons have remained unattended.

Thus, the brief account of the policy and legal regime of India on displacement, resettlement and rehabilitation of the project affected persons indicates that the issue of project induced displacement in India still remains a neglected subject.

Despite a heavy emphasis on gigantic schemes right from the 1950s for almost three decades after independence, India relied on an archaic law of Victorian vintage under which monetary compensation was the norm.

Despite realising the inadequacy of the Land Acquisition Act in the form of Narmada award in 1979, even earlier than it was felt anywhere else, India could not benefit much from it. Instead of further concretizing and building up on the award subsequent years saw states exploring escape routes[113]

Except some project specific policies where foreign finance was expected or availed of and the three non-functioning state laws, the decade of 1980s was wasted in debate and deliberation. After a strong indictment by the World Bank and consequential backing out in 1992 for India's failure to abide by the NWDT award and the conditions laid down by the loan and credit agreements, the present decade saw some sectoral, state and central policies either under the pressure of the funding agencies or as responses to the opposition by the NGOs and other affected people. Yet the policies are still to be officially adopted and announced in India. In a few sporadic decisions the Supreme Court has also tried to issue guidelines though it is yet to cast aside the old cloak of non-intervention.

In a nutshell, a detailed paper work is being done in India on the issue of resettlement and rehabilitation, but very less of it has been brought into practice. India still presents a not so good scenario on RR. The total absence of resettlement plans even after the completion of major civil works,[114] preparation of ad-hoc plans *pari pasu* with construction work,[115] non-allocation of sufficient budget[116] and on the top of it lack of political will and institutional capacity and preparedness can be attributed as salient features of the Indian scenario on RR.[117]

5.3.2 *China*

China is not only the most populous country in the world but also the one causing high displacement.[118] China ranks first in one recently conducted study of the World Bank having the highest figure of displacement in bank assisted projects.[119] Most of the displacement in China occurs due to dam projects, which she has taken with much fervour.[120] But despite high incidence of displacement, China is generally taken a country having good implementation of involuntary resettlement and rehabilitation package, though the history of its good performance is not very old.

China was involved in the development of massive infrastructure projects from 1950s itself. But the question of involuntary displacement was not seriously taken in China until a series of laws and regulations were adopted and refined in steady succession from 1978 to 1992, for several sectors like water, hydropower, transport, industry and urban development. Some regulations were issued in 1952. These regulations prescribed for minimization of project related resettlement, payment of adequate compensation to both resettled population and host communities and the integration of resettlers in their new communities. The regulations also called for the protection of living standard of both hosts and restttlers. However, the law remained neglected during Cultural Revolution and the great leap forward.[121] People displaced from development projects were simply pushed into surrounding communes with little compensation for lost asset.[122] In several instances, displacees were transported to the less populated western interiors or the border areas of the northeast. The tragic results of mass impoverishment that occurred in the first two decades were realised by Chinese authorities in the 1970s after which corrective measures were undertaken by formulating a policy and legal framework.[123] Going by the review reports of the World Bank, China now appears to be one of the very few countries that have introduced the concept of "productive resettlement" or "resettlement with development" and trying to earnestly implement it. The initial policy guidelines of China were independent of the World Bank, but since mid 1980s China had several rounds of policy dialogues with the Bank especially in the reservoir sector.[124] The major highlight of China's resettlement and rehabilitation policy is as follows.[125]

- The population subject to resettlement should not only maintain its current standard of living but should also *directly share in project benefits*
- The resettlement transition period should be minimised and adequate support of both social and economic nature provided during the transition period.
- Resettlement should achieve *complete social and economic re-establishment* of those dislocated, on a *viable productive basis*, through the creation of project funded new industries, service sector and agricultural employment and activities.
- Insofar as changes in occupation are necessary, occupational replacement opportunities should properly recognise the social, communal, cultural, educational and vocational profile of those affected and any such changes in economic activity should be introduced on a voluntary basis.
- Resettlement of agricultural population should be land based wherever possible.
- Land sharing with host villages should be based on the *principle of mutual acceptance* and should be planned so as to provide higher incomes (from all sources) for relocatees and hosts.
- Resettlement plan should have broad-based popular acceptance, and the affected population should be consulted.

- Relocation distances should be minimal, and opportunities for resettling people in-groups and communities should be provided.
- House plot and dwelling size allocation at new town and village sites should ensure improved standards and conditions.
- Resettlement plans for towns, villages and enterprises should minimise *the loss of existing agricultural lands.*
- Resettlement plans should have adequate institutional arrangements to ensure effective and timely implementation, and adequate monitoring and evaluation arrangements.
- Financial resources to carry out the relocation and resettlement development proposals should be available when and where required. Development plans should be prepared in concert with relocation plans.
- The impact of resettlement on the natural and socio-economic host environment should be mitigated and offset.
- Only those enterprises that will be economically viable should be considered for relocation, and the compensation for the assets of non-viable enterprises should be used to create new employment opportunities.
- Inundated items of infrastructure such as roads, bridges etc should be replaced so that the previous level of service is maintained or improved.
- If sharing farmland doesn't result in achieving target incomes, some of the labour force may be offered non-agricultural employment opportunities.
- Family members of farm workers may be transferred to non-farm status if they so desire, and then be

employed by the units for which the workers are working or by the local govt.

The operationalization of the policy prescriptions in China is done right from the planning and design phase to implementation and post implementation support programme. At the planning phase, planners are required to look for less displacing alternatives.[126] The baseline survey of the socio-economic, infrastructural and other assets of the people living in areas to be inundated is carried out with the help of local leadership at the village, township (*Xiang*), and county level.[127]

Subsequent to the baseline survey the resettlement plan is prepared keeping in mind the basic tenet of the Chinese resettlement policy. Efforts are made to ensure for resettlers and host community a standard of living at least equal to their pre-project conditions and enable them to share in overall project benefits. The preparation of resettlement sites with adequate infrastructure, detailed scheduling of relocation and synchronization with the construction activity and inclusion of the relocation and rehabilitation costs in the detail estimate of the project costs are some of the features of the current Chinese practice. The resettlement package is also kept flexible so as to allow the authorities to exploit emerging benefits in favour of resettlers.[128]

As elsewhere, the most complicated part of the resettlement programme is the determination of compensation. In China, attempts have been made to resolve this by identifying the opportunities for land based employment and then broadening the search for other sectors.[129] In conformity with the World Bank norms, replacement costs of the lost assets and incomes have been made the guiding principle for determining compensation.[130] As no private holing on agricultural land exists in China the compensation for the loss of land is paid to the commune which agrees to resettle the project affected families at mutual consent. An agreement is signed between the Resettlement Office and the concerned commune before relocating the PAFs.[131] In order to ensure that resettlement ensures improvement of livelihood for both resettlers and hosts, before entering into agreement with the host commune several factors like the total area of farm land available, the productivity, the availability of undeveloped sub-sectoral niche, carrying capacity, environmental impacts are required to be studied thoroughly. For the improvement of livelihood, intensive farming, income through horticulture, livestock, forestry, aqua farming in the reservoir (if it is a dam) and other agro- based enterprises are required to be launched.[132] If because of some unforeseen circumstances, the productive capacity of the resettlers is not restored, the resettlers and the hosts get support from the county revenue, and if required, some of the labour force is diverted to the non-agricultural occupation as a measure to obviate the implementation failure.[133]

Though land based resettlement for agricultural population is a policy prescription, wherever possible, the land based resettlement is guided by socio-economic, educational, health and other profiles of the resettlers along with their choice and readiness to learn new skills. As part of the resettlement strategy, families are encouraged for non-agricultural occupation as well.

The involvement of local leadership in several aspects of resettlements is a unique practice in China.[134] Local leaders at village, township, county and provincial level work in tandem with the resettlement officers in their respective areas.[135] They also find solution to grievances that the resettlers or the host make. They are also held accountable if the resettlement package fails to bring about the desired results. In fact, by routing resettlement through local government in China, a possibility is created to draw diverse technical skills and development opportunities in the whole exercise.[136]

Another equally important aspect of China's resettlement programme is the post resettlement support. Unlike in other countries, the support does not end with the completion of the project.[137] The creation of Reservoir Area Support Fund and allocation of 0.01per cent of the revenue from power generation to be used for resettlement support is one good example of post resettlement support in China. This Fund in fact works as a safety net. If the resettlers or hosts are unsuccessful in achieving satisfactory income levels, they will have recourse to the Fund which guarantees minimum income should farm or non-farm livelihood fail to meet their minimum needs. Applications to the Fund by PAFs are referred through their village leaders to the County Resettlement Officer. This Fund remains in place until the Ministry of Water Resources deems that the relocatees and affected hosts are no longer at risk. This Fund also supports the entire village should that be necessary[138]

Given the magnitude of displacement caused by big projects, especially the reservoir projects, it would be illogical to claim that China presents a best case scenario in the resettlement and rehabilitation of project induced displacees. China herself is very conscious not to feel complacent by the positive review of the financing agencies or its own researchers.[139] The resettlement experience of the most controversial Three Gorge Project currently under construction in China, which is much criticised for its deficient execution of the RR package resulting in serious violation of human right, also indicates that everything is not so good as is often stated.[140] The most frontal attack on Chinese resettlement and rehabilitation policy comes on the non availability of appeal mechanism and the absence of independent monitoring and involvement of the state in silencing dissent.[141] Nevertheless the Chinese experience, for a few explicitly visible reasons like the emphasis on distributive justice and equitable benefit sharing, rejection of the policy of development of some areas at the cost of others and the introduction of the concept of "resettlement with development" makes a clear departure from the officially adopted policy of several other countries. If the successive reviews of the World Bank are any indication, China not only ranks first as the largest displacing country but also holds a very appreciable record on resettlement and rehabilitation.[142] The bank has cited several Chinese projects where the review team has found income restoration and improvement happening. For instance, in 1993 citing the execution of resettlement package in Shukoi project, which was then under construction, the Bank Review Team wrote; "it demonstrates that involuntary resettlement can be done well, relocated people can share in project benefits, and can improve their livelihood."[143] When the project was completed the bank again reviewed the Shukoi and one more project in 1998. The Bank Review Team wrote; "the two projects in China show how resettlement can work when executing agencies are prepared to use any tools and take whatever opportunities are available."[144] In yet another place the Bank wrote, " borrowers exceed bank standards and are actually leading and teaching the Bank."[145] In China there are also evidences of uniform application of resettlement policy in projects not financed by the World Bank as well.[146] As the resettlement policy is uniformly applied in all provinces it is believed that it is also used in other types of projects besides hydropower projects. The setting up of a network of resettlement offices at the county and province level in China,[147] her effort to develop research capacity on resettlement[148] indicate her seriousness towards policy promises on project induced displacement, resettlement and rehabilitation.

5.3.3 Bangladesh

Though Bangladesh does not have a recent experience on heavy displacement due to high dam,[149] the trauma caused by partition, yearly floods and other nature and human induced displacement are certainly not uncommon in Bangladesh. As till recently Bangladesh did not have a resettlement policy, the problem of land acquisition, displacement and resettlement was dealt within the framework of the Land Acquisition Act 1894. But a few years back Bangladesh framed Draft National Policy on resettlement and rehabilitation in the context of the Jamuna Multipurpose Bridge project (henceforth JMBP).[150] The policy was operationalised in the form of resettlement action plan for the JBMP which was again revised at the insistence of financing agencies and the Revised Resettlement Action Plan (henceforth RRAP) was endorsed by the government in October 1993.[151] The RRAP, which is modelled after the World Bank Directives, is tailored to suit the need of Bangladesh. The RRAP calls for avoidance or/and minimization of the incidence of displacement. Where displacement occurs it states that emphasis should be given on the restoration of the income and livelihood of the affected persons at least to the pre move level. In other words, it emphasizes on rehabilitation rather than relocation or resettlement. Emphasis is also given on the dissemination of information, baseline survey and consultation of the PAPs with regard to the choice on relocation. The planning and implementation of R & R as a development project is the major thrust. Replacement cost is the basis of determination of compensation and absence of legal title is no bar for claiming compensation. Support to PAPs in the transition period provision for training, and post training credit support service and post resettlement support, development of adequate infrastructures in the relocation site, institutional support for resettlement—provision for monitoring and supervision, participation of the PAPs and NGOs in the execution of the rehabilitation are other features of the RRAP.[152]

5.4 Refrains of the Cross-Cultural Experience

The brief account of LAA of South Asian Countries demonstrates the existence of an archaic legal regime incapable of handling the issue of displacement holistically. The laws of India, Pakistan and Bangladesh for the reason of having common ancestry are also similar in their deficiency. These laws come into operation only after the project decisions are taken, and therefore virtually offer no opportunity for questioning the usefulness of the project for the public.

Though the Land Acquisition Act of Nepal 1977 is modelled after the Indian Act of the same nomenclature, it seems to be still more deficient. For instance, the law of Nepal offers wider avenues to institutions to take the intervention of the state. It also does not require the publication of any of the notices in the newspaper. It also does not set a complete time frame for completion of acquisition proceedings. It is not even specific about the market value in determination of compensation. Similarly, in the event of unsatisfactory decision by the acquiring authorities, either with regard to the exclusion or inclusion of land measurement or valuation of compensation, or the distribution of the same, the Act does not provide the interested person recourse to the court.[153]

The law of Sri Lanka seems to be little influenced by Indian law but its framework does not seem to be significantly different from its Indian counterpart except on the question of hearing. The Constitution of Maldives leaves an encouraging note with regard to compensation, but in the absence of an independent judiciary to review executive action, how will the right to property be effectively protected is difficult to say. Still the laws of South Asian countries contain some scattered provisions, which can be picked up while improving the normative framework on displacement, resettlement and rehabilitation. For instance, the publicity aspect of the Indian and Sri Lankan law, the concept of just compensation and authorization by the court enshrined in the Maldivian law, the land plus compensation concept of Bhutanese law provide some insights for the development of a legal framework.

As it is clear from the brief account of the cross cultural experience on resettlement and rehabilitation that most of the countries handle the issue of project induced displacement and resettlement either in a policy vacuum or through some ad hoc project specific policies. The development of general norm is rare, and rarer still is its honest implementation.[154] Even in countries where neat paper works have been done, the same seems to have been hardly actuated in implementation.[155] Of late, countries are gradually moving towards formulating policies, and in a few instances implementing them though the pace is slow and tardy.

Secondly, while in countries like China and India, resettlement guidelines were developed even before the formulation of the much acclaimed World Bank guidelines, there was a serious lapse when it came to implementation. The 1952 law of China was completely forgotten during the period of Cultural Revolution and the Great Leap Forward. Similarly, the policy formulations brought out in the form of Narmada Water Dispute Tribunal award, instead of being further concretised and developed, were not honestly implemented even in the projects in the Narmada basin. Most of them remain unimplemented even today.

In a wide spectrum of cases, the policies of countries not only postdate the World Bank guidelines but also are heavily influenced by them.[156] In the Bank financed project, the view that the bank should, instead of emphasizing on project specific policy, focus on the development of general norm, is gaining currency.[157] It is also being suggested that bank should expertise and even provide resources to countries for developing laws and policies on resettlement. Given that most of the Regional Banks and funding agencies like OECD, NORAD etc. have now either endorsed the World Bank Policies or have formulated their own policies on resettlement and rehabilitation, it has become difficult for any country to approach these banks and funding agencies without a policy on resettlement and rehabilitation or at least a plan on paper to address the issue. This is another factor which compelled a few states to develop law and policy on RR.

Apparently reflection on the World Bank guidelines in framing policies by countries owes much to the non-existence of an alternative model.[158] In fact there is no harm to resonate to time tested principles developed elsewhere provided such importation conforms to the constitutional framework and respects the basic and inalienable rights of the people and suits the socio-economic reality of that particular country.

The resettlement policies and laws of various countries discussed here clearly recognize that displacement and resettlement are interrelated issues. The policies also endorse the overarching principle that, wherever possible, displacement should be avoided or minimized. The participation of PAPs and hosts in the planning and implementation of resettlement, integration of RR in the project design, sufficient allocation of budget, development of infrastructures, transitional support and the like are common features of resettlement policies. But as to the measures to be taken where displacement is unavoidable, while China seems to be more forthright in endorsing the policy of productive resettlement, other countries still cling to the policy of restoration of asset and earning capacity of the people to be affected by the project as a bottom line for action.[159] On the question of post resettlement support also one witnesses a variation in policies. This is a neglected issue in the World Bank Guidelines[160] and except in China post resettlement support is not much emphasized in other policies.[161] Similarly, while the draft Indian policy makes land based resettlement mandatory only in case of tribals, in China land based resettlement is prescribed for all rural community and the World Bank guidelines recommend land-based resettlement for all agricultural families. However, the

Chinese policy is also not free from defects. As stated earlier, the absence of independent monitoring and evaluation and absence of judicial recourse are the weakest part of Chinese resettlement. Another notable feature of the policies is that while the policies contain convergence in several areas they are at the same time tailored to the country specific requirements and suitability.[162] Tailoring policy to country or region or project specific requirements is an ongoing process. In what way and to what extent can the cross-cultural experience be resonated in formulating norms for RR in Nepal is reserved for chapter VII.

REFERENCES

1. They include China, India, Bangladesh, Laos, and Turkey in Asia, Central African Republic, Uganda and Cote De Ivor in Africa, Brazil, Columbia and Costarica in South America. *See* Roli Astha, *Involuntary Resettlement: Survey of International Experience,* 31(24) EPW 1468(1996); *see also* MICHAEL CERNEA; AFRICAN INVOLUNTARY POPULATION RESETTLEMENT IN GLOBAL EONTEXT (Washington DC, World Bank 1997); NTFC, NAM THEUN 2 HYDROELECTRIC PROJECT RESETTLEMENT ACTION PLAN (Ventine, 1998).
2. As almost all the countries in the world have some remnant of laws on acquisition, for geographical and cultural proximity, legal similarity and the similarity of problems that the South Asian countries face in relation to development the study is limited to South Asia. Of course, space and time are other considerations to leave out other countries.
3. An inclusive definition of public purpose given in the Act is being expanded time and again. Where as the Pakistani and Bangladeshi law includes provision for village sites as public purpose, the Indian Act adds to the list entries like, the provision of land for town and rural planning, for planned development of cities, for a corporation owned and controlled by the state, for residential purposes to the poor landless or person affected by the reasons of the implementation of the scheme, for carrying out any educational, housing, health slum clearance etc for government sponsored or approved schemes etc. *See* the Land Acquisition Act 1894, S 2 f(f).

4. *See* the Land Acquisition Act 1894, preamble and S.4 (1) of the Act. In India the expression "or for the company" is added by the 1984 amendment.
5. This includes the survey to ascertain the suitability of the land, setting out of boundaries etc. *See* S. 5 of the Act. In India, after the 1984 amendment publication of the notification in the newspaper is mandatory, as it added " and in two daily newspaper circulating in that locality of which at least one shall be in the regional language"
6. *Id* S5A (1)&(2). A person is defined to be " interested" if he is entitled to claim an interest in compensation if the land were acquired.
7. The declaration, apart from being published in the gazette should also be published in two daily newspapers circulating in the locality, in which land is situated, of which at least one should be in the regional language. Though the reviewability of the declared purpose by the court is not ruled out, but the law shows a kind of bias against such measures by maintaining that the publication of the declaration shall be of conclusive evidence that the land is needed for public purpose or for a company; *see Id* S 6 *Id* S(2) Under the Indian law by virtue of the 1967 amendment, several declarations in respect of different parcels can be made.
8. For this the Collector issues a public notice and informs the persons interested in land to make their claims to compensation, their objections to measurements, or value of the land. *See Id* S.9
9. Persons interested include all persons claiming an interest in compensation and person having easement rights. *See id* S 3(b)
10. *Id* Ss 10,11. The collector issues a public notice and informs the persons interested in land to make their claims to compensation, their objections to measurements, or value of the land; *Id S. 9* The Act by requiring the Collector to take the approval of the government before the pronouncement of the award, leaves very little space for the sue of his discretion.
11. He needs to give detailed statement about the situation and the extent of land to be acquired, names of interested person, amount awarded for damages and paid, and compensation, the ground of determination of compensation etc. But, instead of requesting for reference if the person interested in land accepts the award the matter ends there and the award given by the Collector is final; *See id* Ss 18 & 19.

12. *Id* S 21
13. *See* 31 AIR MANUAL 5D 922 (1989) [citing (1912) 1 Ind Cas. 270,273 (DB) (Mad)].
14. That is the S 4(1) notification.
15. *Id* S 28 A
16. In case of urgency taking possession of land is possible even before the announcement of award. *See id* S 17
17. *Id* S 31(3)
18. Other considerations are the damage sustained by persons (a) by reason of taking of standing crops and trees, (b) by reason of severing of land, (c) by reason of the acquisition or injuriously effecting his other property, d) diminution of profit of the land between the second notification and possession. Where the person is compelled to change his residence or place of business reasonable expenses incidental to such changes is also taken into consideration. An amount to the tune of 12 per cent of the market value is awarded as interest to setoff the loss caused due to the time lag between the S 4(1) notification and the actual possession. *See id* S 23(2). Whereas the Indian law prescribes for 30 per cent on the market value as solatium, under the Bangladeshi and Pakistani Law it is 15 per cent. However, under these laws where the purpose of acquisition is the establishment of industry by a person other than the government, the solatium is 25 per cent of the market value.
19. Indian Law has made a little departure on this. For instance, under s 40(1)(aa) and 41(4A) of the Indian Land Acquisition Act, acquisition is possible for the construction of some building or work for a company which is engaged or is taking steps for engaging itself in any industry or work which is for a public purpose. But this scope is not available for private companies. *See* S 44 B of the Act.
20. *Id* Ss39,41,42
21. This has been discussed in *supra* Ch 2.5
22. *See generally* Vasudha Dhagambar, *The Land Acquisition Act: High Time for Changes* in REHABILITATION POLICY AND LAW IN INDIA: A RIGHT TO LIVELIHOOD 111-117 (Walter Fernandes and Vijay Paranjpye eds. Pune/Delhi, Econet/ Indian Social Institute 1997)
23. The Land Acquisition Act 1950 (Sri Lanka)
24. If, after the preliminary investigation, it is found that the land is suitable for a public purpose, the Minister directs the acquiring

officer to issue a notice to the concerned owner giving him an opportunity to file objections, if he has any on such decision to the appropriate Secretary.After an opportunity of hearing is given, the appropriate Secretary makes his recommendation to the appropriate Minister who in turn makes reference to the Minister who is the final authority to decide whether a particular land or a servitude should be acquired or not. *See id* S 2(1) *See also* S 4(1), 4(3)(c), 4(4)(5).

25. On the face of it the power of acquisition of land seems to be limited only for "public purpose" but public corporations wholly or partly owned by the government as well as other authorities, persons or bodies (by the reason of being allowed to acquire land by any other law of the land) are also allowed to approach the Minister and take his intervention for acquisition *See Id* S 49, 49 A.
26. *Id* S 5(1) the declaration is published in Tamil, Sinhala, and English languages.
27. *Id* S 7(1)
28. *Id* S 16
29. *Id* S 10. If the claim to compensation is less than Rs 1500 it is referred to the Primary Court, otherwise to the District Court.
30. *Id* Ss11-16. The court includes the Court of Appeals as well.
31. *Id* S 17
32. The other considerations for the assessment of compensation are damage sustained by person by reason of the severance of the land from his other land, (up to 20 per cent of the market value of the land) other injuries caused to other property, loss of earnings from any business carried on the land to be acquired (up to 3 times the annual net profits from the business), other reasonable costs. *See Id* S 45(1). This section refers to the notice under section 7, which is the third notification. Before this, the notice for preliminary investigation u/s 2 and notice u/s 4 giving opportunity *id* S 46(4) are required to be published.
33. For instance, major considerations for compensation etc.
34. *Id* S 22.
35. The Board of review consists of eight lawyers and the remaining either members having adequate knowledge of the valuation of land appointed by the President on the advice of the Judicial Service Commission *see Id* S 19.
36. *Id* S 28.
37. Despite these elaborate provisions on the appeal at various

stages of hearings, the Sri Lankan law is weak on the question of compensation. While the Act does not make it mandatory to pay full compensation before taking possession of the land, it also keeps silence on the question of resettlement. Landless labourers, village artisans, forest dwellers and other occupants of land are kept outside the purview of the law.

38. MALD. CONST. Art 23(2). Besides, Art 18 also guarantees the inviolability of homes save according to the procedure laid down by the law.

39. S.7 of the General Laws (statute no 4J/68-11/11/1968)

40. *See* the Law Relating the Transfer of *Wakf* Property in Male to Other Islands and Abolition of *Wakf* Property in Male (statute not 2J/70 - 12/4/1970). Under this provision the government transferred a vast area of *Wakf* property of Male—the capital city—to other less important islands and took over the property.

41. As besides the already operational Chukha Hydropower project, Bhutan has embarked upon the construction of three other projects viz., Kurichu Hydropower in Mongar, Basochu hydropower in Qangduephodrang and Talas hydropower in Chukha, the displacement due to hydropower projects is likely to surge in the coming days in Bhutan. Information based on telephonic conversation with Mr Choining Dorji, Legal Officer at the Public Service Commission, Thimphu, Oct 21, 1999.

42. LAND CODE, Bhutan Ch 6 "Definition of Government and its Distribution" S 9.

43. *Id* S 8 & 9.

44. Where as in a span of 40 years between 1950 and 1990 China displaced some 10.2 million people by the construction of dams alone, India displaced 21 millions during the same period. Major dams like the Mahabali Dam in Sri Lanka, Tarbela and Mangla Dam in Pakistan, Kaptai (Karnafuli) in Bangladesh, Sanmensia, Danjiangkou, Sianjiang dams in China, Hirkud, Ukai, Pong, Bhakra Srisailam etc in India are considered to be major causes of displacement. *See* PATRICK McCULLEY, SILENCED RIVERS 1-7 (London, zed Books).

45. One world bank studies shows 67 per cent of displacement over the world occurs in Asia. *See* OED, RECENT EXPERIENCE IN INVOLUNTARY RESETTLEMENT 32 (Report no 17538 Washington DC: Operation and Evaluation Department/ World Bank, June 2, 1998) (henceforth OED 1998).

46. These countries rank first, second and fourth respectively leaving Brazil the third slot. *See id.*

47. The shelving of Silent Velley Project in India in 1970s and the recent shelving of Kalbagh dam downstream of the Tarbela Dam on the Indus river in Pakistan can be taken as examples of this; *see* ARMIN ROSENCRANTZ ET AL, ENVIRONMENTAL LAW AND POLICY IN INDIA 278-87(Bombay: NM Mani Tripathy, 1991); *see also* Kalpana Sharma, *Dams Projects Must Take into Consideration Social Factors* THE HINDU Dec 12, 1998 at 14 and http://www.bangladesh.web.com/news/dec/19/Zu3n/o/.htm accessed on 6th Aug, 1999

48. *See generally* OED 1998 *supra* note 45

49. Laos first developed a Resettlement policy for its 681MW(and US $ 1.5 billion) Nam Theun 2 project in 1996. This was later expanded and converted into the Draft National Policy on Resettlement. *See* NTFC *supra* note 1.

50. *See for e.g.* National Thermal Power Corporation Ltd. (India) Rehabilitation and Resettlement Policy; the Resettlement and Rehabilitation of Coal India Ltd. reproduced in REHABILITATION POLICY AND LAW, *supra* note 22 at 314-344. Similarly the Electricity Generating Authority of Thailand (EGAT) is known to be one of the government undertaking having resettlement policy. EGAT formulated resettlement policy in 1970s and got the reputation for resettlement performance. Its resettlement policy on Pak Mun dam project is much appreciated by the World Bank. *See* OED 1998 *supra* note 45 at 37-38, 47-48, 52-53, 56

51. ARMIN ROSENCRANTZ, ET AL, *supra* note 47 at 276. The recent World Bank study conforms this see OED 1998 *supra* note 45. Though there exists no official account, one estimate shows the number of people displaced by major projects like dams, mines, industries, wildlife projects in between 1950-1990 to be 21,300,000 people. If all types of projects are included the number stands some where around 35 million during the same period Walter Fernandes 1994, reproduced in REHABILITATION POLICY AND LAW IN INDIA; *See supra* note 22 at 17

52. Now number of displacees is put some where around 50 million. *See* Arundhaty Roy *The Greater Common Good,* FRONTLINE July 14, 1999 at 5 (quoting N.C. Saxena, Secretary to the Planning Commission).

53. Draft National Policy of the Ministry of Rural Development (para 1.9, reproduced in *supra* note 22 at 62

54. Recent studies in India have demonstrated that around 50 per cent of the displacees are tribals whereas their total strength in

the country is merely 7.8 per cent. Similarly Dalits constitute another 20 per cent of such displaces. *See* Walter Fernandes and Vijay Parenjpye, *Introduction* in *supra* note22 at 18.

55. There are several instances of multiple displacement in India. For instance, some people displaced by Rihand dam in 1964 were later displaced by Singrauli Project and then by mines, railways, urban development etc; *See* Smitu Kothari, *Whose Nation, The Displaced ad Victim* 31(24) EPW 1478 (1996). Similarly the displacees of Tehri Dam were displaced again by the Rajaji National Park. *See* MRIDULA SINGH, DISPLACEMENT BY SARDAR SAROVAR AND TEHRI 137 (Delhi: Multiple Action Research Group 1992); Similarly the Displacees of Mangalore Port in 1960s were displaced again by the Konkan Railways and Tribal displacees of Kabini and Tharak Dam in Karnataka were displaced again by Nagarhole (Rajiv Gandhi) National Park. *See* M.K. Ramesh and Francis Guntipally, *A Critique of the Karnataka Resettlement of the Project Displaced Persons Act 1989*, in *supra* note 22 at 205.

56. The Tribunal was constituted in 1969 on the complaint of Gujarat government over the water sharing arrangement of Narmada under the Interstate Water Dispute Act, 1956.

57. The award required the Gujarat government to establish rehabilitation villages in Gujurat in the irrigation command area of the SSP for the rehabilitation of the families should they elect to settle in Gujarat. *See* clause XI Sub-clause IV(1) of the Award, reproduced in MRIDULA SINGH *supra* note 55 at 151

58. *See* in *id* clause XI sub clause IV(2); IV(3);IV(4); IV(7).

59. It stated; "In no event shall any areas in MP and Masharastra be submerged under the Sardar Sarovar unless all payment of compensation, expenses, and costs as aforesaid is made for acquisition of land and properties and arrangements are made for the rehabilitation of the oustees therefrom in accordance with these directions and intimated to the oustees." *Id* clause XI sub clause IV(6)(II)

60. The World Bank began evolving guidelines only 1980 onwards.

61. This is visible from the approach that the Tribunal took on several issues. The recognition of adult sons as a separate family entitled for equal benefit, directives for creating resettlement villages with a modicum of infrastructure and civic amenities are all indicative of the orientation of the Tribunal for rehabilitation. Though there was a dispute on whether adult sons as a separate family were eligible for house plot and

other benefits or they were also entitled for a minimum of 2 ha of land as stipulated by the Tribunal, the govt. of Gujarat which was assigned with a major responsibility of resettling people finally agreed to provide them every benefit as a separate family. *See* MRIDULA SINGH *supra* note 55 at15-16; *see also* BRAFORD MORSE & THOMAS BERGER, SARDAR SARJOVAR: REPORT OF THE INDEPENDENT REVIEW 138-139(Ottawa, Resource Future inc. 1992)(henceforth MORSE COMMISSION REPORT)

62. For instance, it is often argued that the award was not sufficiently wide in its definition of "oustees" or that the award relied on the Land Acquisition Act 1894 in granting a minimum of two hectares of land and thereby ignored encroachers, tribals, or that it did not take into account the tenurial practice and reliance of people on natural resource base around their habitation, or that it talked only about the submergence area and thereby neglected the displacees of the dams, dykes, infrastructure colony, canal, the catchment area treatment, compensatory forestry or that it did not utter a word about the displacees of Gujarat etc. Sometimes, the award is also criticized for its lack of appreciation of the environmental aspect or future expansion of the resettlement sites also.

63. MORSE COMMISSION REPORT *supra* note 61 at 62.

64. Whereas Gujarat wasted a long time by not coming promptly to undertake responsibilities as desired by the award, the other two states perhaps thought it wise not to create an environment where by the oustees, instead of opting Gujarat, would elect to stay back in their respective states. For detail discussion, *see* MORSE COMMISSION REPORT *supra* note 61 at 84-89, 138-144, 154-180.Another reason for the search of escape routes (rather than the compliance) by formulating of progressive policies and implementation of the same was the general fear of a spill over effect. *See id* at 79-80 (on the stand of MP) and at 142 (on the stand of Maharastra). Though Gujarat brought out a fairly comprehensive policy in 1988 it has also maintained that the policy applies only the SSP.

65. *Id*

66. *See* the Maharastra Project Affected People Rehabilitation Act 1989 (henceforth Mah Act); Madya Pradesh Pariyojana ki Karan Visthapit Vyakti Punarsthapan Adhiniyam 1985 (The MP Project Displaced People Resettlement Act, henceforth MP Act); The Karnataka Resettlement of Project Displaced Persons Act 1987 (henceforth Kar Act). Though the present Mah Act came into

being in 1989 its history goes back to 1976 when the Act was first enacted. *See* R.V. Bhuskute, *The Maharastra Rehabilitation Act 1989* in *supra* note 54 at 169-191

67. For instance, the Mah. Act gives a very wide definition of "Project Affected Person" to include occupants, tenants, agricultural labourer, labourers, members of Hindu joint family having a share on the joint property, persons having land in Gaothan which is acquired irrespective of the size persons whose holding has been reduced to less than one ha or has been rendered fragmented or uncultivable. The MP and Kar. Acts use the term "Displaced Person" to mean any tenure holder, tenant, government lessee, owner of the property. Agriculture labourer residing in affected area for one year immediately before the declaration of affected zone is also included in the displaced person. However, none of these Acts include encroachers, village artisans, pastoralists, tribals in DPs/PAPs. See S 2. of Mah Act, MP Act and Kat Act.

68. *See* Mah Act Ss 11, 12, and 13; the MP Act Ss 10 & 11, 12, 14; the Kar Act Ss 9 & 10 11,13

69. The MP Act S18; the Mah Act S 15; the Kar Act S 18

70. Only Mah Act is explicit on this. The amenities include the dugwell or borewell or piped water supply, school with play ground, Chavadi or Samaj Mandir, internal and approach roads, electric supply, cremation or burial ground, open built up gutters, public latrines, land for cattle stand, land for pick up shed for MSRTC bus service, land for thrashing ground floor, pasture land for market and future expansion of Gaothan, The Act further provides that the expenditure on all such amenities shall be part of the cost of project. *See* The Mah Act S 10.

71. The Mah Act S 10; the MP Act s 18; the Kar Act S 10.

72. For instance, the Mah Act is automatically applicable to certain types of projects like irrigation projects where affected zone exceeds 50 ha, or the area of benefited zone exceeds 200 ha or a Gaothan is affected. In other types of projects it becomes applicable only if the government so notifies. *See also* Mah Act S 1(4); MP Act S 10, Kar Act S 9.

73. Whereas the NWDT required the states to provide a minimum 2 ha of land the minimum land prescribed by all the state Acts is quite less than that. For instance the minimum agricultural land guaranteed is 40 ares (2 acre ?) in Maharastra 40.47 ares in MP and almost the same in Karnataka . *See* schedules of the respective State Acts.

74. For instance the famous Narmada Bachao Andolan (NBA), the Tehri movement, the movement against the Keol Karo projects to name a few, can be taken as notable movement against dams. *See generally* Satyajit Singh, *Introduction* DAMS AND THE NATION: DISPLACEMENT AND RESETTLEMENT IN NARMADA VALLEY 1-23 (Jean Dreze et al eds. Delhi, Oxford Univ. Press 1997); S. Parasuraman, *The Anti-Dam Movement and Rehabilitation Policy* in *id* at 26-65; *See also* MRIDULA SINGH *supra* note 55 at 5-7

75. So far two public sector undertakings the Coal India limited (in 1994) and the National Thermal Power Corporation (in 1993) and two states Rajasthan and Orissa have brought out policies on resettlement and rehabilitation. At the Central level the Ministry of Water Resource and the Ministry of Rural Development have formulated draft policies on the issue. *See* the documents in appendix in *supra* note 22

76. For detail discussion on these policies, *see generally* Walter Fernandes, *The Draft National Policy for Rehabilitation of the Displaced Persons: Is Displacement Inevitable*? In *supra* note 22 at 35-54; Nikhil Verma, *A Critique of the Draft Rehabilitation Policy of the Ministry of Water Resource Development*, *id* at 118-130; Vijay Paranjpye and Lolita Sewarstamani, *Swamped by NTPC Fly Ash: A Review of the Rehabilitation Policy*, *id* at 131-148; Arvind Anjumand Manthan, *A Reviw of the Policy of Coal India*, *id* at 149-168; Aniniddha Dey , *A Critique of the Orissa Rehabilitation Policy*, *id* at 215-230

77. For instance, it acknowledges that displacement pauperises the people, degenerates and compels them to lead a life of destitution with traumatic psychological experiences, that cash compensation alone does not enable them to acquire new means of livelihood on their own, and that it hits the people falling on the lower socio-economic bracket very badly. It also acknowledges that unsatisfactory arrangement for rehabilitation and resettlement creates opposition to acquisition of land. Most importantly the policy feels the necessity to bring into existence operation of an uniform policy, packages and guidelines to provide minimum basic resettlement and rehabilitation benefits to such vulnerable group of citizens/families *See* MRD/ GOI, the National Policy, Package and Guidelines for Resettlement and Rehabilitation-1998, the preamble (hereinafter referred to as National Policy 1998)

78. *Id* para 2.1a and 3.1.3

79. *Id* para 2.1a

80. *Id* para 3.1.2(further stating that the welfare and envelopment of PAPs is a precondition, an inseparable part of the project itself and not merely an unwanted appendage to be executed unwillingly).
81. *Id* 2.1d
82. *Id* 3.1.3 and 3.1.25
83. *Id* para 3.1.5
84. *Id* para 2.4(c) (stresses that DPs and other PAPs have a standard of living superior to the one before their displacement and in any case, have an income above that prescribed as the poverty line) 3.1.2, 3.1.4 (calling for synchronizing resettlement with implementation of the project); 3.1.9 (stresses that no dislocation without prior implementation of resettlement);3.1.10 (stresses for advance planning) 3.1.12 (stresses for life above poverty line); 3.1.13 (providing CPR for Trebles), *See also* 3.1.14, 3.1.18-23.
85. *Id* Para 3 of the Policy. The policy includes only those who were residents of the area three years prior to the notification under 4(1) of the Land Acquisition Act, 1894.
86. For instance persons/families/displaced from urban areas and awarded Rs 5 lakh as compensation or persons/families/ displaced from rural areas and awarded a compensation of Rs 3 lakh or more are excluded form taking other benefit expect the homestead on full payment of cost See para 4.1 and 4.2 of the Policy.
87. *Id* One may have reservations about the inclusion or exclusion of people but by and large this is one criteria of maintaining the balance between the capacity of the government to deal with the situation and the demands of justice and equity.
88. *See id* Para 3.1.24, 11 and 15
89. *Id* para 3.2.24 and 5.2.1
90. *Id* para 3.2.2; 5.2.2; 7 and 9
91. Like, occupants of land without legal status, the cultivators of river bed lands, fisher folks, cattle rearers, occupants of forest, revenue, community or command lands, sanctuaries, farmers and fisher folk down stream of major reservoirs, agricultural labourers, petty traders, ST/SC etc. *See Id* para 2.1(c); 3.1.12; 3.2.1; 3.2.5; 3.2.5; 3.26; 3.1.15
92. *Id* para 3.29
93. *Id* para 5.2.8

94. *Id* para 10
95. *Id* para 5.2.3; 5.24; 5.2.5; 5.2.10
96. Apart from the R & R cell, also requires for the establishment of Implementing and Monitoring Authorities at the District level, the State level and at the National level with comprehensive representation of the PAPs including the ST/Sc, women. *See Id* para 14 and 15
97. *See generally*, Walter Fernandes, *Land Acquisition (Amenement) Bill, 1998: Rights of the Project Affected People Ignored* 33(42&43) EPW 2703-2706(1999)
98. *See for e.g.* 3.1.17 (on debt recovery) 3.1.11 (on emergency acquisition)
99. In several instances such interventions through legal and policy measures have also proved to be effective. The enactment of the Forest Conservation Act 1980 is one of such example.
100. *See generally*, Walter Fernandes, *supra* note 97 2703-2706
101. Ss 2, 5, 20(3) of the Draft Land Acquisition (Amendment) Bill, 1998
102. The Collector is also required to prepare and display a summary of the acquisition, resettlement and rehabilitation proceedings and publish the same in official gazette, in addition to making it available, in a booklet form free of cost to all person interested.*See id* S 16(2)
103. *Id* S 1
104. *Id* S 11(5)
105. *Id* S 6(4)
106. *Id* S 3(3)
107. *See for e.g.* Vasudha Dhagambar *supra* note 22 Walter Fernandes *supra* note 97 *See also* Usha Ramanathan, *Displacement and the Law* 31(24) EPW 1486-1491 (1996)
108. *See* For instance in Dahanu Taluka case where the petitioners raised a very strong case of violation of the recommendations of the Environment Assessment Committee appointed by the government itself. They also contended that the respondent company had violated conditions and guidance laid down for setting up a Thermal Power Plants. Instead of probing deep into the matter, the Supreme Court turned a blind eye and just asked the government to investigate the matter to put petitioners' apprehensions at rest. Almost a similar approach was taken by High Courts in several other cases. Dahanu Taluka

Environment Protection Group v Bombay Suburban Electricity Supply Co AIR 1991 SC 910; *See also* Goa Foundation v Konkan Railway AIR 1992 Bombay 471.

109. Hannovara Taluka Parisara v State of Karnataka dated 2/11/1990 (writ no 8170 of 1988 Karnataka HC) cited in the ENVIRONMENTAL ACTIVIST HANDBOOK (Gayatri Singh et al eds. Bombay , 1992(?), p. 463

110. Banwasi Seva Ashram v State of UP AIR 1992 SC 920. In this case the SC turned a letter into a PIL and gave detailed instructions for the resettlement of the evictees of the Rihad Super Thermal Power Project of the National Thermal Power Corporation.

111. Gramin Seva Samstha v State of MP 1986 (supp) SCC 578. In this case the court directed the M.P. Government to consider the application of MP Project Displaced Person Settlement Act 1985 to the Hasdeo Bango Dam. It also gave direction to the State government for making provisions for resettlements of Tribals as per various guidelines including World Bank Guidelines.

112. Karjan Jalasay Yojana Assargasth Sahkar Ane Sangarsh Samiti v State of Gujarat AIR 1987SC 352. In this case the Supreme Court issued detailed guidelines for resettlement of the evictees of the Karjan Dem Project.

113. The state policies of all the three riparian states of Narmada viz., Gujarat, Maharastra and Madya Pradesh clearly testify this. See the discussion on these policies in MORSE COMMISSION REPORT in *supra* note 61 at 84-89, 138-144, 154-180.

114. For instance in Krishna Irrigation Project in Karnataka the resettlement plan was not prepared even after completion of the first project. *See* OED,1998 *supra* note 45 at 39

115. For instance Tehri Project *see* MRIDULA SINGH *supra* note 55 at 93-106

116. For instance in the Maharastra Irrigation Project III out of the four components of R&R, viz., civic amenities, house improvement grants, income generation grants and irrigation for those settled in the command area , except for civic amenities no budget was allocated in other three components; *see* OED 1998, *supra* note 45 at 40

117. *See Id* at 57. It states that Indian projects have failed in terms of planning, budget allocation, institutional preparedness, involvement of PAPs in resettlement, execution of resettlement and post resettlement support. About the two cases the WB studied it wrote, " The two project [viz Upper Krishna Project

and the Maharastra Canal Irrigation Project III] in India are even more troubling in terms of borrower performance and are treated here as a special case of failure " *see id* at 57.

118. Around 10.2 million people are reported to have been displaced by the construction of dams alone in China during the last 40 years or so including those displaced by the giant projects of 1960s and 1970s like the Sanmenxia dam, Danjiangkou, Xinanjiang projects which displaced 410,000 , 380,000 and 280,000 people respectively. *See* Wu Ming, *Resettlement Problems of the Three Goreges Dam: A Field Study Report* [International River Network, Berkeley 1998], http://www.hrichina.org/reports/3gorges.html accessed on 23.12.1998. Another study shows the displacement of 30 million people due to major capital investment programme. *See* John Bizer and Tod Ragsdale, *The Development of Resettlement Policy in China: Two Case Studies in Sichuan and Hebei Provinces*, http://www.his.com/~mesas/chinapol.htm accessed on 22.12.1998

119. India, Brazil and Indonesia rank second third and fourth respectively see OED 1998 *supra* note 45 at 32.

120. The country had only eight large dams at the time of its revolution in 1949.;40 years later had around 19, 000. *See* PATRICK McCULLEY *supra* note 44 at 2-4

121. John Bizer and Tod Ragsdale, *supra* note 118.

122. MICHAEL M CERNEA, HYDROPOWER DAMS AND SOCIAL IMPACTS: A SOCIOLOGICAL PERSPECTIVE 13 (Social Assessment Series (44 Washington DC: World Bank 1997)

123. China has been frank enough to acknowledge that roughly 70 per cent of its early reservoir relocatees were living in extreme poverty. In eighties the government launched measures to rehabilitate them. For instance in 1986 the Ministry of Water Resources earmarked 1.9 billion yuan rehabilitation programme at 46 sites of completed water projects where 5 million people had been resettled. However, despite this hundred of thousands of resettlers were still struggling for survival. In 1994 the World Bank cited Chinese government saying that 46 per cent of Chins's resettlers were yet to be properly resettled. *See* Wu Ming *supra* note 118

124. WB, RESETTLEMENT AND DEVELOPMENT 99 (Bank wide review of projects involving Involuntary Resettlement 1986-1993, Washington DC: World Bank 1996) (henceforth REVIEW)

125. The policy stipulations are broadly based on Reservoir Resettlement Law and Regulation 1981, Regulation on the

Acquisition of Land for State Construction Projects 1982, Land Administration Law 1986 (amendment 1988), The Reservoir Resettlement Design Requirement 1985(Issued by the Ministry of Water Resources), The Law of Land Management 1987,' The Regulation for Land Requisition, Compensation and Resettlement Provision for Large and Medium sized Water Conservancy and Hydro power Projects issued by the State Council Degree no 74 PRC May 1991.The major policy high lights are produced in EIA/1997 Update for XIAOLANGDI MULTIPURPOSE DAM PROJECT STAGE II 4.40 (Prepared by Yellow River Reconnaissance, Planning Design Institute(RPPI) for Resettlement Office(RO) of Yellow River Water and Hydropower Development Corporation, Feb. 1997)(the project is considered as one of the mega project over Yellow river currently under construction in China generating 1800 MW of power and displacing 181,000 people).

126. There are several examples to testify this. For instance in Shanghai. Sewerage Project, planners were required to re-site the and use tunnel to save more than 4000 people from resettlement. Other examples of such types are the Beiliugang Thermal Project, Zouxian Thermal Project, Taihu Basin Projects. *See* REVIEW *supra* note 124 at 106.

127. Dissemination of information about the project through public lectures, consultation with local residents, distribution of questionnaire, and direct interview of the villagers are important features of the EIA and resettlement requirement at the planning phase. More particularly the resettlement team is required to give attention to the opinions/ wishes of the affected resettlers families and the affected host communities. It is also required to launch a door to door campaign for soliciting the opinion of each and every resettler family on resettlement destination and resettlement programme. For instance, in Xiaolangdi Project, beside door to door visit by the Resettlement Team, the authorities consulted 173 village committees, 30 *Xiangs* in the flooded counties including 152 public lecture , 500 interviews with villagers and 50,000 questionnaires (with 80 per cent return rate); *See* EIA/1997 Update for XIOLANGDI MULTIPURPOSE DAM PROJECT STATE II *supra* note 125 at 4.30 and 4.31.

128. The experience in the recently completed Shuikou project in China testifies this. Here the implementing authorities were quick to exploit the economic boom in China's eastern coast. *See* OED 1998 *supra* note 45 at 48.

129. *Id supra* note 45 at 7.

130. This in operational terms means several things. For instance, for a rural family, depending on the choice, a house and with a yard more spacious than the family was previously holding. Similarly, urban resettlers receive houses with two to three times their current living space. As people in rural area live in congested house or cave, providing more housing space is the official polity executed in several projects. *See* REVIEW *supra* note 125 at 80.

131. In fact the compensation payment provides a strong incentive to host communes as this offers them an opportunity to the surplus land in exchange for compensation. In some cases communes even bid to receive resettlers. This generates funds for the commune to improve their land or to invest in other enterprises. This should not, however mean that it is a free for all bid. *Id* at 122 (Quoting China Country Department).

132. OED 1998 *supra* note 45 at 50.

133. REVIEW *supra* note 125 at 122.

134. *Id.*

135. *Id* at 80.

136. *Id* at 122.

137. Constant supervision, review enables the authorities to make corrections if something goes wrong during the execution, provisions are also made to support the resettlers and hosts for a considerable period of time until the income or productivity is restored and improved. Such support not only insulates them against sudden break down of the family, but also enables many to use it as an opportunity launch new enterprises that they previously would not be in a position to afford, *see id.*

138. EIA/1997 UPDATE FOR XIAOLANGDI MULTIPURPOSE DAM PROJECT STAGE II *supra* note 125 at 4.11.

139. For instance, in 1998 Chinese authorities asked the Review Team of the World Bank to cite Shuikoi Project only as exceptional and not to imply that such high standard prevails throughout the country. *See* OED 1998 *supra note* 124 at 58.

140. According to the official record the 3200 MW Three Gorges Project over Yangtze river in China displaces 1.2 million people. However, international NGOs estimate that the actual number will be in between 1.6 to 1.9 million people . *See* Wu Ming *supra* note 118. Wu Ming criticises the resettlement programme for a wide spread mismanagement, discrimination, official corruption, inadequate compensation, routine falsification of figures of resettlement, suppression of media and other opposition through

the use of state machinery etc. See also Martin Stein, *The Three Gorges: The Unexamined Tales of Development Induced Displacement*, http://www.nrc.no/global_idp_survey/FMR/1998-1/stein.htm accessed on Aug 6, 1999 Further, Chinese leaders are now realizing the unrealistic claims about the project and the difficulty of resettling peoples, writes New York Times, *see* hp://www.irn.org/programs/threeg/991018 artb.html accessed on Nov.18,1999. In December 1998 Primer Zhou Rongi toured the Three Gorge for project and sacked more than 100 officials stealing huge amount of money, *See* Jasper Berker, *Dam Cadres Steal $ 217 Million,* South China Morning Post Feb.14, 1999 p. 1, in http://www.irn.org/programs/threeg/coverage 99018.html accessed on Nov.18, 1999.

141. Martin Stein *id.*
142. For instance, the 1994 update of the Environment Department (Now Social Department) of the World Bank evaluated as many as 27 projects in China as having one rating on resettlement. *See* ENV, REGIONAL REMEDIAL ACTION PLANNING FOR INVOLUNTARY RESETTLEMENT IN WORLD BANK SUPPORTED PROJECTS: A REPORT ON ONE YEAR FOLLOW UP TO RESETTLEMENT AND DEVELOPMENT 6 (Washington DC: World Bank 1994)
143. REVIEW *supra* note 124 at 80.
144. The second project was Yantan Hyrdopower Project.
145. Here the reference was made to China and Thailand (after the review of Pakmun project) *see* OED 1998 *supra* note 45 at 65.
146. For instance the policy has been uniformly implemented in dam projects in Hongjaidu Project in Guizhou Province, Defeng Hydro Project and projects in Sichuan or Hubei Provinces, *see* John Bizer and Tod Rasgdale *supra* note 118.
147. *Id.*
148. In Early 1990 China set up a National Research Center on Resettlement at Hohai University (Nanking). Since then important advances have been made in the Centre in the research methodology of investigating resettlement. MICHAEL CERNEA, HYDROPOWER DAMS AND SOCIAL IMPACTS A SOCIOLOGICAL PERSPECTIVE 14(Washington DC: World Bank 1997) citing several Chinese research reports.
149. Bangladesh, the then East Pakistan had constructed Kaptai (Karnafulli) Dam in 1960s with installed capacity of 1400MW which submerged 65,600 ha of land and displaced 100,000 people id Appendix 1.

150. Jamuna Multipurpose Bridge Project is a US $ 900 million project linking two north-western districts of Tangail and Sirjgong districts with the eastern part of Bangladesh. An area of 5800 acre of land was acquired for the project which affected 16,341 households (i.e. about 100,000 people and required the relocation of a quite a number of community and educational institutions. See Tasheem Siddiqui, *Jumuna Bridge Project Policies and issues in Resettlement of the Displaced*, DAILY STAR 1(147) Jan 8, 1998, http://www.banglanet.html, accessed on Dec 23, 1998 , *see also* MD. Shahid Alam, *A Short Paper on the Resettlement Operations of the Jamuna Multipurpose Bridge Project, Bangladesh*, paper presented at the workshop on the Development Induced Displacement and Impoverishment, Jan. 3-7, 1995 Wadham College Oxford.)

151. *See* Tasheem Siddiqui *id.*

152. *See id; See* also Shahid Alam *supra* note149.

153. A detail discussion on all these aspects of Nepali Law is made in Ch. 3.2

154. The predominant pattern of policy stipulations is the formulation of project specific policies. *See e.g.* the Land Acquisition Guidelines of Nepal. A discussion on this is made in *supra* Ch 3.5

155. *See* OED 1998 *supra* note 45 at 65 (lessons and recommendation where it after reviewing 8 project is stated; "planning received disproportionate attention in comparison with results...While in other parts of the portfolio, better planning usually translates into better implementation, this assumption has not held up for involuntary resettlement ...resettlement continues to receive inadequate attention during implementation from the executing agency and from Bank supervision." *See also* MICHAEL CERNEA *supra* note 1 at 31 (highlighting implementation in Africa).

156. For instance the resettlement policies of Laos(draft), Uganda, Cote De Ivore and the resettlement laws of central African Republic are modelled after the World Bank Guidelines. *See supra* note 1.

157. *See* Michael Cernea, *Public Policy Responses to Development Induced Population Displacement* EPW 31(24)(1996) 1515, 1519 (arguing that Bank's effort to promote an improved policy for resettlement for borrowing countries will be more consequential than assistance provided to individual resettlement operations)

158. Though the Chinese Policy seems to be still one step ahead to the World Bank guidelines, however whether similar policies will suit other countries or now is also a point to be considered.

159. *See* OED 1998 *supra* note 45 at 16.

160. Except requiring the borrowing country to submit post resettlement evaluation report Bank does not undertake any responsibility after the disbursement of the loan or credit amount. *See for e.g.* OD 4.30 para 22, 32 reproduced in *supra* note 22 Annex.

161. For e.g. The Draft RR policy of India is silent on this issue.

162. For e.g. the Draft National Policy of India excludes certain section of PAPs from the benefit of RR. *See* the Policy at para 3. It also emphasizes on giving additional benefit to the victim of multiple displacement. *See id* at para 3.29. The RRAP of Bangladesh applied in JBMP is unique in its compensation package. It provides compensation to those who lose land due to bank erosion both on upstream and downstream of the river. *See* Tasheem Siddique *supra* note 149, *see also* Shahid Aslam *id.*

6

PROJECT INDUCED DISPLACEMENT AND REHABILITATION IN NEPAL: REPORT OF THE TWO PROJECTS OF FAR WESTERN AND WESTERN NEPAL

6.1 Introduction

A brief overview of the project induced displacement scenario in Nepal presented in the first chapter indicated the absence of the uniform policy and legal regimes. The main focus of inquiry in this chapter is to examine how the issue of displacement is addressed in the absence of a uniform policy and law and how the resettlement operations are carried out in the real field situations. For this purpose, two projects, namely, the Royal Suklaphanta Wildlife Reserve (henceforth RSWR) Project in the far western Nepal and the Pokhara Airport Project in western Nepal are selected for study. In the two projects, different strategies are adopted for the removal of persons from project areas. Whereas in the RSWR project a land for land policy was adopted, in the airport project the government limited itself to the distribution of cash compensation. Secondly, while in the airport project the distribution of compensation was by and large completed by late 1980s, the displacement and resettlement operation in the RSWR project is yet to be completed. The main purpose of study in the RSWR project is to examine compelling reasons, objective stipulations for initiating the extension programme and strategies adopted for execution of the project. The problems encountered in the execution and the intervening forces which led to the present situation are also studied here. What policy imperatives can one draw both for the short-term solution of the resettlement and extension programme as well as long term handling of similar programmes is also the focus of study in the RSWR.

In the Pokhara Airport Project, the inquiry relates to both the process of implementation and the impact on the PAPs. For this, an attempt has been made to inquire about the compelling reasons for undertaking the project, to examine the extent of displacement, the efficacy, adequacy or inadequacy of law to address the issue of displacement and the impact of displacement on the project affected persons. After presenting the detail of the empirical study of the two projects, a comparative analysis in the light of research questions formulated in the first chapter will be presented.

6.2 The Royal Suklaphanta Wildlife Reserve Project

The RSWR is one of the seven wildlife reserves that have been opened up in Nepal. The reserve is situated in Kanchanpur—a Terai district of Far Western Nepal. The district geographically falls in the tropical region between 28°32' to 29°8' north latitude and 80°3' to 80°33' east longitude. The area comprises flat and gently rolling hills with an elevation ranging from 176m to 1528m from the sea level. The northern part of the district comprises the southern watershed of the Churia range and the Bhavar, a zone of hill wash. India borders this district in the west and south and Kailali district in the east and Dadeldhura district in the north.

Till recently Kanchanpur was called as Naya Muluk implying, thereby, the land regained from the British as a gift for the service rendered by Nepalese forces to quell the 1857 Indian mutiny. But due to a large spatial distance from the hill centers and the capital Kathmandu, and also because of the malarial scare, Naya Muluk virtually remained a forest district till 1950s—with very sparse and scattered settlements of indigenous Tharu communities and a few zamindari holdings of hill feudals cultivated by Tharus. The area around Bellauri—the district head quarter till 1964—was known by a nickname of "Death Valley." Any posting of government officials to this district used to be considered as a punishment posting. But by late fifties things began to change. The Government initiated the malaria eradication programme in Nepal. Along with this, the government also launched the resettlement programme in the frontier districts of southern Nepal for the people for instance, the landless, the victims of natural calamities, the Burmese expatriates, the ex-service men etc. This brought in a totally different demographic scenario in the region.[3] The district of Kanchanpur, which had a population of only 17,000 in 1961—the lowest of any Terai districts—became a major destination of the hill migrants. This resulted in a rapid population growth. So much so that by 1991 the population of the district reached 257,906.[4]

The dramatic change in the demographic characteristics of the district is partly due to the official resettlement programme, but largely due to illegal occupation of the forestland. Since early sixties the district of Kanchanpur began to be infested with massive forest encroachment which is yet to get subsided. Today, out of the 88,200 ha of officially declared forest area of the district around 10,000 ha is encroached upon and cultivated.[5] Though the programme of settling landless in the Terai was officially discarded in 1989, the government, however, does not appear to be firm on this issue.[6]

The latest land use scenario of Kanchanpur is presented in Table 6.1.

TABLE 6.1

Kanchanpur District: Major Land Use Pattern

Land Use	*Area in Hectare*	*Percentage*
Forest	**88,200**	**53.9**
The Royal Suklaphanta Reserve	30,500	34.58
Area allotted for Resettlement of the oustees of the Reserve	2000	2.26
Area under encroachment	10,000	11.33
Agricultural land	**62,500**	**38.18**
Other land	**12,978**	**7.92**
Total area	**163,678**	**100**

Source: LRMP 1986, DFO Office, Kanchanpur, March 1999

6.2.1 The Establishment of the Reserve

The shrinkage of forest, the loss of habitat of the fauna and preservation of the biodiversity are the stated reasons for the establishment of the RSWR.[7] Originally, the Reserve was a sanctuary, but by an official notification it was declared a Royal Sikar Reserve, and was closed for shooting for the public in 1964 (2021 B.S.). The RSWR was officially declared as a Reserve by the Gazette notification in 20th July 1976. (i.e. Shrawan 4, 2033 B.S.)[8]. A few settlements which fell within the boundary of the Reserve (i.e. the original 155 sq. km) were evicted and resettled around Mahendra Nagar—the district head quarter.[9]

The RSWR was considered a good habitat for unique fauna species[10] amphibians[11] and birds.[12] A total of 268 species of birds have been recorded in the Reserve.[13] Large grass lands like the Suklaphanta, and Jhilmila swamps like the

Ranital and Solgaudi Tal (i.e. lake) along with the tropical and subtropical forests of the reserve were supposed to provide adequate habitat to animals, birds and amphibians. However, surreptitious cutting of trees and grazing of domestic animals inside the reserve hindered conservation efforts at the RSWR. The determination of the boundary of the reserve also took a long time.[14]

6.2.2 Extension of the Reserve

One may look at the extension programme of the RSWR as a response to the overall deterioration of the environment of Kanchanpur as well as an effort of the authorities to boost up the conservation of the Reserve. It was felt that both the resettlement policy of the government and the illegal poaching of flora and fauna in the forest of Kanchanpur had a massive adverse effect on the local environment. The habitat loss had limited the movement of wild animals in the district. The development of settlements in the southern part of the district around Beldandi and Sripur had posed a stress on the environment of the Reserve. In 1980 it was revealed to the disquiet of the government that except in the Churia region in the north of the district, there was not any large stretch of forest in the district, which did not have illegal settlements inside it. As such, the encroachment of forest was a problem in almost all the Terai districts, but it was severer in the Far Western Terai region.

It was under these circumstances that the extension programme for the reserve by another 155 sq km was launched in 1981. The extension programme had the following main objectives:

- Extension of the reserve to strengthen the conservation of the flora and fauna of the area.
- Establishment of a corridor which could link the reserve to the Churia forest, and via this to the Royal Bardia National Park

With a view to addressing the problem of deforestation in the district of Kanchanpur as well as to initiating programme of implementation of the extension of the RSWR the government constituted a committee named "The Forest Sector Strengthening High Powered Committee"(henceforth the Committee) under the chairmanship of Justice Sarbagya Raj Pandit.[15] The Committee was high powered in terms of responsibilities power as well as the profile of its members.[16] It was vested with wide ranging legal and administrative powers and responsibilities. The major responsibilities given to the Committee, inter alia, were:

- the removal of encroachment to forest;
- the prevention of further encroachment;
- drawing of the internal demarcation for the settlements which had grown inside forest areas;
- resettlement of those occupants who had squatted inside or near the forest areas; and
- settlement of all the claims of occupation, encroachment and title in and around forest areas and to resettle or pay compensation to all those bonafide titleholders or occupants, in the course of strengthening the forest areas .

As such the strengthening of the forest area and the extension the RSWR was a very onerous task that the Committee was supposed to shoulder. By the nature of the job the Committee required not only administrative but also quasi-judicial and judicial power as well. Therefore, the government constituted a Special Court under the chairmanship of the person heading the Committee, and vested with the following powers:[17]

- power to put any person under preventive detention in case of breach of public law and order under the Public Security Act, 1961;

- power assigned to the concerned Officer to demarcate and determine the boundary of the forest under the Forest Act 1961, and punish the offender in case of violation of the Forest Protection(Special Provisions) Act, 1967;
- power to survey and measure the area of any land, determine the area, provide the ownership title to the concerned person under the Land (Measurement) Act, 1962;
- power to regularize the unregistered or fallow land in the name of squatters under the Revenue Act, 1977 where such a need arises;
- powers vested to the Chief District Officers under the Local Administration Act, 1971 and the Some Pubic (Offences and Punishment) Act, 1970; and
- powers to be exercised by the Departmental Head to conduct departmental inquiry in the case of breach of duty by any officials under the Civil Service Rules, 1964.

6.2.3 The Settlements in the Proposed Extension Area

A large section of the proposed area of the reserve consisted jungle, but a sizable area of it also had human settlements scattered in 17 blocks of five VDCs. The name of the villages and Settlements is presented in Table 6.2.

Almost all the settlements mentioned in Table 6.2 do not have a very long history. In most of the cases, the land record in the District Revenue Office does not go prior to 1950s when the first land survey was conducted. Only a few blocks like Bhatpuri, Andaiya, Pataiya etc had zamindari holdings. Whatever be the history of holdings almost all the blocks had registered (Numbari), unregistered (i.e. *ailani*) holdings,[19] as well as large parcels of lands with illegal occupations. Except Padao, all other blocks have inhabitants of mixed ethnic origin though the dominant groups in these blocks are that of the hill migrants from the far western region.[19] Padao is a block inhabited by two sub-sects of Tharus, namely Dagoras and Ranas—the original inhabitants of the Terai. In other blocks like Pipladi and Jhalari they are mingled with other hill migrant groups.

TABLE 6.2

Settlements in the Proposed Extension Area of the RSWR

Name of the villages	*Name of the Blocks*	*Remarks*
Rauteli Bichuwa (From ward no 1 to 6 in full and 7 and 8 in part)	Badani Kheda, Andaiya, Pateiya, Darak, Lalpani, Tikasuwa, Bhursa, Radhapur	
Pipladi (Ward no 1 and 2)	Tarapur, Bhatpuri, Padao, and Khajuwa	
Jhalari (Ward no 1 and 8)	Hirapur , Arjuni	
Dekhatbhuli (Ward no 1 and 5)	Dhakka , Hatiya	
Daiji	Chataiya	

Source: RSWR, March 1999

6.2.4 The Royal Directives and its Implementation

Under the constitutional set up of the pre -1990 era, the Palace was the real centre of power, though the day to day administration of the county used to be carried out by the cabinet. Every major decision either used to be taken by the King or used to have his approval. It is a common knowledge that the Palace had taken special interest in the establishment of National Parks and other protected areas in Nepal, which was true with the RSWR as well. Several visits of the King to the RSWR demonstrate his keen interest in the establishment, management and extension of the Reserve. The Royal directives issued by the King on 16th Jan 1982, in connection with the extension of the RSWR, with regard to the resettlement of the people of the proposed extension site contained the following:[20]

- That the displacees be given land for land which they would loose as a result of the extension of the Reserve;
- That the land to be given to the displacees should be cultivable; and
- That the social and cultural composition of the displacees should not be disturbed while resettling them.

6.2.5 The Strategy for Implementation

It seems that, despite the King's directives, the government did not have a clear vision as to the implementation of the extension programme, nor did it have the detailed work plan prepared beforehand. It was found from the government records that for almost a period of eight years, the government tried to implement the extension programme through the Committees / Commissions constituted for strengthening the forest sector of the district.[21]

However, despite a heavy logistic support and sweeping administrative and judicial powers, the implementation programme could not really take pace for a long time. Instead, it was found that due to slow pace, several unanticipated problems cropped up in the course. To cope with the situation, the government, therefore, created a separate Extension Office headed by Mr. Damodar Parajuli to implement the extension of RSWR and issued a gazette notification to this effect. As the Committee, which was already functioning for the same purpose was not relieved of its responsibility, Mr. Parajuli was required to work under the supervision of the said Committee.[23] The Gazette notification required the Extension Office, inter alia, to allot land to the evictees, to provide financial support to transport belongings to the new place, to get the forest clear felled through the Timber Corporation.[24] However, before Mr. Parajuli could complete the

TABLE 6.3

Committees / Commissions Constituted for the Settlement Of the Problem of Extension of the RSWR

S.N	*From*	*To*	*Committee/Commissions headed by*	*Members*	*Remarks*
1	Jan 3,1982	Jan 6,1988	1 high Powered Commission and 3 Committees/Commissions, headed by Sarbagya Raj Pandit, Yuganath Sharma, Sudarshan Bahadur Singh, Omkar Prasad Gauchan and Ghanashyam Giri(except Mr. Pandit all others were politicians)	14 Max	
2.	Jan 8, 1988	July 18, 1990	Damodar Parajuli (Bureaucrat)		Ext. Off
3.	July 19, 1990	July 20, 1992	No work done		
4.	Jul 21, 1992	July 14, 1995	Lalit Bahadur Thapa, Subarna Lal Shrestha, Hiramani Bhandari, Ramaadev Joshi (all CDOs in official capacity)	5	
5.	Jul 15, 1995	Nov 1, 1995	Badri Prasad Khatiwada (politician)	4	

contd....

6.	May 17, 1996	Jan 16, 1996	Dr Devi Prasad Ojha (retired CDO)	8
7.	Jun 13, 1997	Dec., 1997	———— Mukarji Giri (politician)	11
8.	Apr. 29,1998	June, 1998	Devi Prasad Bhattarai (CDO in official capacity)	7
9.	Sept. 29, 98	Feb. 29, 1999	Puskar Raj Ojha (Politician)	13
10.	Marh 1, 1999	To date	Sthaneswar Prasad Devkota (CDO in official capacity)	7

Source: Nepal Gazette; RSWR March 1999; DNPW, Apr 1999

implementation work, Nepal was engulfed in a political movement for the restoration of democracy. This abruptly brought the implementation programme to a halt.[25] After the restoration of democracy in 1990, a totally different scenario emerged. Almost with a parallel speed ran the political unrest and the encroachment of the land in Terai. As the interim government that came into the place of the old Panchayati government was busy in the drafting of the Constitution, and conducting the general election in the Kingdom, it could not look into other problems. Therefore, during this phase of transition, nothing could happen with regard to the extension of the RSWR. The extension programme of the RSWR could not resume for another two years.

In July 21, 1992 the government constituted a five member Committee under the chairmanship of the Chief District Officer to settle the issue of extension and resettlement in RSWR. Though the Committee worked for almost two years the records do not show any thing substantial being done by the Committee. As a result, the problem relating to the extension of the RSWR not only remained unresolved but also got further complicated due to some intervening forces.

It appears that the frequent change of the political leadership badly affected the extension programme. The political masters began to be guided by some extraneous and irrelevant considerations rather than finding a solution to the problem. The appointment of people with political background to Committees testifies to this.[26] The list of the Committees/ Commissions constituted so far for the settlement of the issue of extension is presented in table 6.3.

As one can see from Table 6.3, there were intermittent time gaps in the constitution of the Committees during the first phase i.e. between 1982 and 1990 and also after 1990. For almost two years in between July 1990 and July 1992 there was no office to carry out the execution of the project work.

And between July 1992 and July 1995 phase when the RSWR Extension Problem Settlement Committee was constituted under the ex-officio chairmanship of the Chief District Officers (CDO). The frequent transfer of CDOs seems to have affected the project work.[27] In the post 1995 phase, the political instability that the country faced due to frequent change of government also got reflected in the frequent dissolution and constitution of Committees.[28]

As one can also see from Table 6.3, there were intermittent time gaps in constituting new committees continued subsequently as well. This had several implications. For instance, as none of the Committees were permanent Offices, the support staff it employed used to be either temporary or in deputation. Therefore, with every new constitution or the dissolution, the movement of staff would generally follow. This would affect the record keeping system. Secondly, once a new Committee was constituted the first thing that it was required to do was to apprize itself of the activities of its predecessor(s) and take stock of the prevailing situation. This is essentially a time taxing job. But over and above, such time gap had the chances of providing a breathing space to those who were against the extension program or were looking for an opportunity to take undue advantage of the situation either by giving false statement or producing fake records. Apart from these inherent strategic defects there were several other reasons which had a bearing on the perpetuation or aggravation of the problem. But before we move to that, it would be worthwhile to have a brief look at performance aspect of the project.

6.2.6 *The Extension and Resettlement Programme: A Performance Audit*

The performance audit of the resettlement and extension programme of the RSWR can be summed up in a few words by stating that, despite efforts of almost two decades, the project is still incomplete and seems to be in a total mess. What has been done in both extension and resettlement aspects of the project is highly unsatisfactory and ad hoc. Therefore, instead of presenting an anecdotal detail of the activities of each committee, it is therefore, more worthwhile to present a summary of the activities that have been carried out so far.

6.2.6.1 *Identification of Evacuation and Resettlement Sites*

After confusion of several years, the boundary of the Reserve is now determined conclusively[29] (See Map no 2). With the determination of the boundary of the Reserve, the villages and blocks that require to be relocated are also determined. The name of such villages and blocks is presented in Table 6.2 above.

But with regard to the total number of the households and the number of people to be relocated and resettled, it has remained the most complex and vexing problem at hand for several reasons. First, the household survey was not conducted in time. When it was finally conducted in 1987 by Mr. Parajuli, the total number of families requiring resettlement was recorded as 1518 of which only 463 households were *numbariwalas* and the remaining1055 were recorded as encroachers.[30] However, this census was relied on only during his tenure, as there existed no law, which would provide legal sanctity to the household survey. Nor was there any procedure laid down prescribing guidelines for conducting of the survey, hearing of the complaints arising in the course and finalize of the same once for all. Since there was no bar for the subsequent Committees to conduct resurvey and prepare list of people requiring resettlement afresh, they seem to have chosen to follow the more convenient recourse to preparation of a new list. Therefore, in spite of the fact that some of the DPs were resettled in different blocks, the number of DPs kept on increasing in the subsequent years.[31]

The staggeringly slow pace of execution of the project fostered encroachment as well. The serious infiltration of encroachers in all the five blocks allotted for resettlement occurred between 1990 and 1992, during which there was no office to carry out the project activities. This appeared to be breathing period for the encroachers to take every benefit of the government inaction. There was a feeling that the post 1990 political scenario had also emboldened the encroachers. The decision of the Committees constituted after 1995 to resettle all the encroachers by preparing a fresh list seems to have been influenced by this emergent reality.

The heavy increase in the number of people requiring resettlement was a result of this decision. So much so that by 1997 the number of families requiring resettlement was reported to be 3000 households.[32] This number further increased in the ensuing years. The latest figure of families requiring resettlement is shown as 4319.[33] Among these the number of encroachers in the resettlement blocks is reported to be 1018 families.[34] The details of families requiring resettlement as reported by the Pushkarnath Committee is presented in Table 6.4.

TABLE 6.4

Households Requiring Resettlement as per the Pushkar Nath Committee

S.N.	*Village*	*Types of holdings*	*Number of households*
1	2	3	4
1	Rauteli Bichawa -1	Aileniwalas	173
		Those having names in the field books (Field bookwalas in short)	17
		Those who have got a land certificate from the Regional Housing Office (certificatewalas in short)	10

cont....

1	2	3	4
2	Rauteli Bichawa -2	Aileni wala	132
		Land less agri. Labourers	27
		Certificatewalas	5
		Field bookwalas	8
3	Rauteli Bichawa -3	Aileniwals	511
4	Rauteli Bichawa-4	Aileniwals	302
4	Rauteli Bichawa-5	Aileniwala	9
6	Rauteli Bichawa-6	Aileniwala	75
7	Krishnapur VDC	Encroachers (in Bani)	29
8	Hirapur	Field bookwalas	4
		Landless agri. Labourers	4
9	Bandarpur	Encroachers	468
10	Pipladi -1	Ailaniwalas	1144
11	Pipladi - 2	Ailaniwalas	466
12	Dekhatbhuli-1	Ailaniwalas	110
13	Dekhatbhuli-5 (Hathia)	Ailaniwalas	304
14	Buttabari	Encroachers	441
15	Dhakka	Encroachers	80

Source: RSWR Office, 1999

6.2.6.2 The Resettlement Criteria and Resettlement

On this score after a confusion of eight long years Mr. Parajuli could develop clear criteria for resettlement.[35] One major consideration in determining the size of the plot in the resettlement site was the type of holding that the DP has in his original site. Besides this, other factors like the proximity of the site to the highway or the district head quarter, availability of irrigation, the type and fertility of the soil etc were also

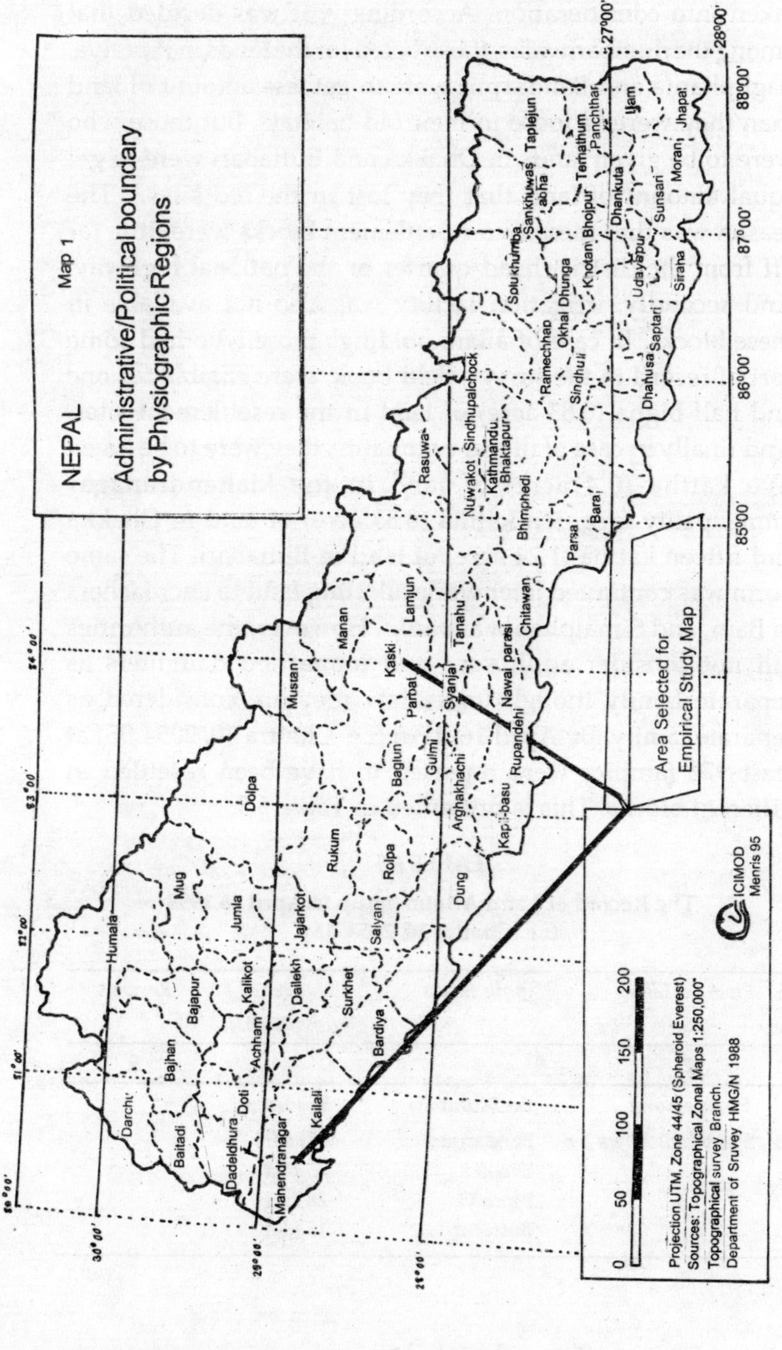
NEPAL
Administrative/Political boundary
by Physiographic Regions
Map 1
Area Selected for
Empirical Study Map
Projection UTM, Zone 44/45 (Spheroid Everest)
Sources: Topographical Zonal Maps 1:250,000'
Topographical survey Branch.
Department of Sruvey HMG/N 1988
0 50 100 150 200
ICIMOD
Menris 95
Darchula
Baitadi
Dadeldhura
Bajhan
Doti
Achham
Kailali
Mahendranagar
Bajapur
Humala
Kalikot
Mug
Jumla
Dailekh
Jajarkot
Surkhet
Bardiya
Salyan
Rukum
Rolpa
Dolpa
Dung
Arghakhachi
Kapilbasu
Gulmi
Baglun
Rupandehi
Syanja
Parbat
Mustan
Kaski
Nawal parasi
Tanahu
Manan
Lamjun
Chitawan
Bhimphedi
Parsa
Bara
Nuwakot
Rasuwa
Kathmandu
Bhaktapur
Sindhupalchock
Ramechhap
Sindhuli
Dhanusa
Okhal Dhunga
Saptari
Solukhumba
Khotam
Udayapur
Sirana
Sankhuwas
abha
Bhojpur
Dhankuta
Sunsari
Taplejun
Terhathum
Panchthar
Moran
Ilam
Jhapa
30°00'
29°00'
28°00'
27°00'
28°00'
84°00'
85°00'
86°00'
87°00'
88°00'

taken into consideration. Accordingly, it was decided that among the numbariwalas, those opted for the lands in Pipraiya, Baghphanta and Bandarpur were to get less amount of land than they were to loose in their old habitats. But those who were to be given lands in Dhakka and Buttabari were to get equal amount of land that they lost in the old sites.[36] The reason was that these two resettlement blocks were little far off from the district head quarter or the national highway. And secondly, irrigation facility was also not available in these blocks. In case of ailani holdings those who had some sort of record in the survey field book, were eligible for one and half bigha (0.83 acre) of land in the resettlement sites. And finally in case of illegal occupants, they were to be given five kattha (0.41acre) of land in the Mahendranagar municipality area, ten kattha (0.83 acre) of land in Dhakka and fifteen kattha (1.24 acre) of land in Buttabari. The same norm was continued later while allotting land to encroachers in Bani, and Simalphanta as well.[37] However, the authorities did not consider adult sons and unmarried daughters as separate family though under law they are considered as separate family. By April 16, 1998 (i.e. Chaitra 30, 2054 BS) at least 972 families were reported to have been resettled in different blocks. This is presented in Table 6.5.

TABLE 6.5

The Record of Land Allotment up to April 16,1998 (i.e. Chaitra 30, 2054 BS)

S. No.	*From the Blocks*	*in the Blocks*	*Number of. Households (HH)*	*Remarks*
1	2	3	4	5
	From among	**the Numbari**	**holdings**	
1	Rauteli Bichawa 1-8	Bandarpur	171 HH	
		Dhakka	73 HH	
		Pipraiya	28 HH	
		Buttabari	15 HH	

cont....

1	2	3	4	5
2	Jhalari VDC			
	Hirapur	Baghphanta	51HH	
		Pipraiya	1 HH	
	Arjuni	Baghphanta	16 HH	
		Pipraiya	11 HH	
3	Pipladi VDC-1	Dhakka	53 HH	
		Baghphanta	31 HH	
		Pipraiya	4 HH	
4	Daiji VDC Chaitaiya	Baghphanta	20 HH	
5	Dekhatbhuli	Buttabari Baghphanta	27 HH	
	From among	**the Aileni Holdings**		
6	Rauteli Bichawa	Dhakka	158 HH	
7	Jhalari VDC			
	Hirapur	Buttabari	134 HH	
		Baghphanta	1 HH	
	Arjuni	Baghphanta	5 HH	
		Dhakka	2 HH	
		Buttabari	19 HH	
8	Pipladi VDC-9	Dhakka	21 HH	
		Baghphanta	3 HH	
		Buttabari	1 HH	
9	Dekhatbhuli VDC	Baghphanta	2 HH	
		Dhakka	2 HH	
10	Mahendranagar 1,15,18	Buttabari	3 HH	
11	Baghphanta	Baghphanta	20 HH	
	From those	**Having names in the**	**Field**	**Books**
12	Rauteli Bichawa	Baghphanta	28 HH	
		Pipraiya	2 HH	
13	Pipladi -9	Pipraiya	13 HH	
		Dhakka	33 HH	
		Baghphanta	24 HH	

Source: RSWR Office March 1999

Besides, the Pushkarnath Committee also decided to allot land to different categories of people from the extension sites

MAP 2

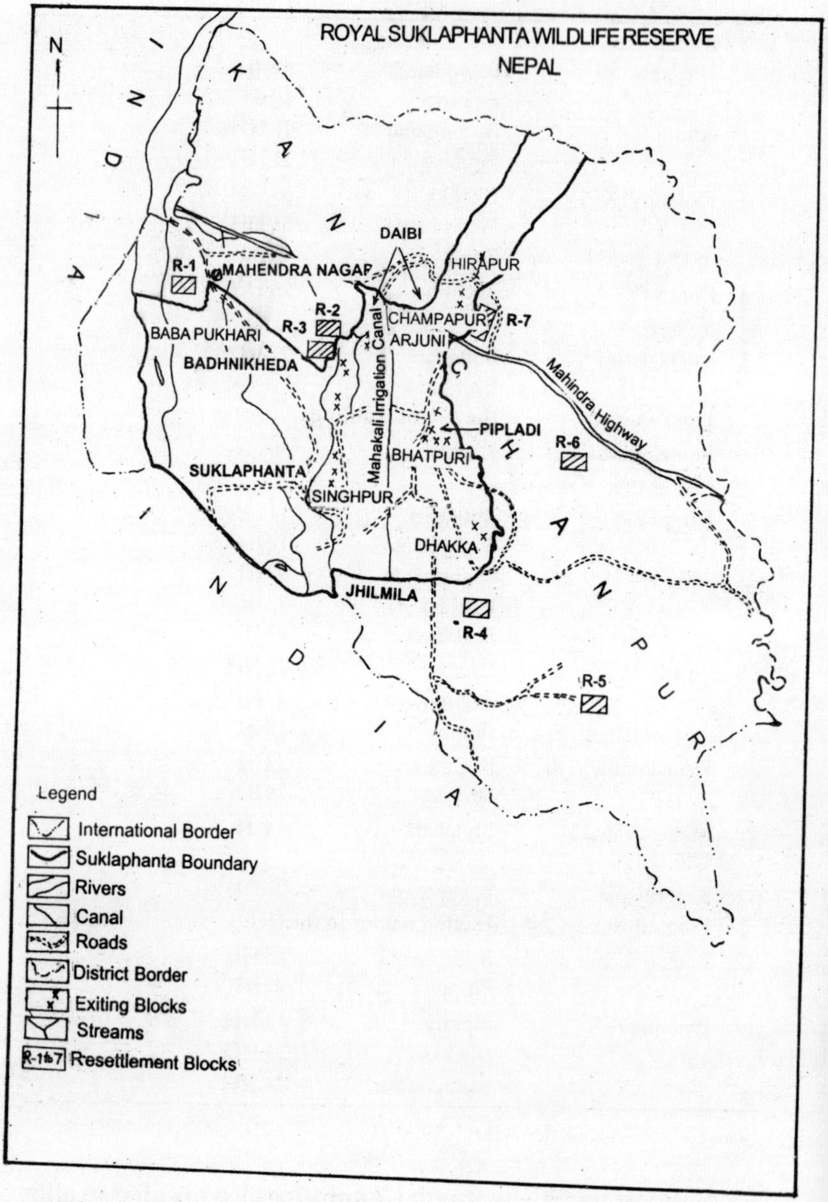
ROYAL SUKLAPHANTA WILDLIFE RESERVE
NEPAL
N
KANCHANPUR
DAIBI
HIRAPUR
R-1
MAHENDRA NAGAR
R-2
R-3
CHAMPAPUR
R-7
ARJUNI
BABA PUKHARI
BADHNIKHEDA
Mahakali Irrigation Canal
Mahindra Highway
PIPLADI
BHATPURI
R-6
SUKLAPHANTA
SINGHPUR
DHAKKA
JHILMILA
R-4
R-5
INDIA
Legend
International Border
Suklaphanta Boundary
Rivers
Canal
Roads
District Border
Exiting Blocks
Streams
R-1 to 7 Resettlement Blocks

in different blocks. But before the Committee could complete the resettlement and evacuation proceedings it got dissolved. However, as the site for resettlement was already allotted by the Ministry of Forest, people began to occupy the land without waiting for the official order. The details of the land allotment for resettlement by the Pushkarnath Committee is presented in Table 6.6.

TABLE 6.6

Land Allotted by Pushkarnath Committee

S.N.	*Allottees of the Village*	*Name of the Resettlement block*	*Number of households*
1	Rauteli Bichawa-1	Bani	121
		Simalphanta	93
2	Rauteli Bichawa-2	Simalphanta	120
3	Jhalari VDC- 1	Bani	11
4	Suda VDC-5	Simalphanta	27
5	Krishnapur VDC-2	Bani	29
		Total	**401**

Source: RSWR March, 1999

6.2.6.3 Infrastructure and Support

So far at least seven blocks have been identified for resettlement purpose. These blocks vary in a number of respects like their size, proximity to the district head quarter and the national highway, availability of irrigation facility and fertility of soil etc.[38] The name and size of these blocks is presented in Table 6.7.

With regard to development of infrastructure, some effort was made in the initial phase to provide irrigation and agriculture support service to the resettlers, but it was not consistently followed throughout.[39] The official record depicted no facilities for schools, health post, community development,

TABLE 6.7

Resettlement Sites and Size for the Displacees of the Royal Suklaphanta Wildlife Reserve

S.N.	*Name of the Blocks*	*VDC/Municipality*	*Size in Bighas*	*In Ha*	*year of Creation*
1	Pipraiya	Mahendranagar	170	118.01	1981
2	Baghphanta	Do	832	554.69	1981
3	Bandarpur	Suda VDC	320	213.34	1981
3	Buttabari	Kalika VDC	418	278.68	1987
5	Ratanpur Dhakka	Beldandi VDC	1000	666.7	1987
6	Banijhala	Dekhatbhuli VDC	200	133.34	1997
7	Simalphanta	Jhalari VDC	160	106.67	1997

Source: Field study 1999

Note: One bigha is equivalent to 0.5218 ha

and recreation site. Some sites like Pipraiya, Baghphanta, and Bandarpur, by virtue of being closer to the district headquarter, were not so much deprived of these facilities, but the absence of such provision in sites like Buttabari, Dhakka and Bani seems to have badly affected the resettlers. There was no school in Buttabari, while in Bani the resettlers had established a thatched school by raising money in a vacant plot. There were no blackboards, no furniture, and no rooms and not even provision for drinking water. When the author visited the place there was a person involved in teaching. Upon inquiry it was found that he was not a teacher but, as the lone teacher had gone to the city, he was doing his duty only as a helper. In Dhakka the condition of the school was not enviably better. Some classes were still conducted in a thatched shade though the school had now obtained formal recognition and was getting some financial support.

Except in Pipraiya, which fell inside the Mahendranagar Municipality, there was no provision for water supply in other blocks. The supply of electricity in resettlement sites was limited to blocks like Prpraiya, Bandarpur, and Baghphanta. Provision for link and feeder road was made only in the plotting of lands. Though all the resettlement plots were formerly the forestland which had been clear felled for resettlement, no support was extended for the families to remove tree stumps and make the land suitable for cultivation. In Bani and Simalphanta, while allotting the land for resettlement of the DPs no instructions were issued for removing the timber and other forest produces. It was witnessed during the study that the resettlers were clear felling the trees and clearing the land for cultivation causing serious misuse and abuse of the forest resources.[40]

So far as the support to the displacees is concerned, except for Rs 2000 for shifting belongings, provision for timber for construction of dwelling at a concessional rate and Rs 5000.00 for uprooting the deep bore wells (if the displacees had any in the extension sites), virtually no support was extended to the resettlers.[41] Even the claim for the compensation for the loss of fodder was rejected.[42] There was no support for transition period. However, the displacees were allowed to cultivate the land until the crop in the new settlement became ready. The absence of support put the displacees under much stress. Many of them had to sell a portion of their land or take loans to shift and settle in the new place.[43]

In spite of the third directive of the King, which called for non-disturbance of the social and cultural composition, very little seems to have been done to keep the social fabric and cohesion intact. The concept of group settlement seems to be foreign to the authorities. One does not find any conscious attempt being made to protect the interests of the threatened community. Even where the whole block (such as Padao) is inhabited by indigenous Tharus, one does not find, from the deliberation of the authorities or from official record, any attempt to resettle such community in-group.[44]

6.2.6.4 The Present Situation

When the author reached Kanchanpur for his fieldwork in the first week of March 1999, the Puskarnath Ojha Committee had just been dissolved and a new Committee, under the chairmanship of the CDO was constituted.[45]

The Ojha Committee had functioned for around six months during which it had prepared a list of families requiring resettlement by dispatching teams to all the extension sites and resettlement blocks.[46] The Committee had also decided to allot land for resettlement of 401 families in Simalphanta and Banijhala. (for details see table 6.6), but before the Committee could complete its work, snap poll was announced in Nepal and the Committee was dissolved. Though, the subsequent Committee constituted under the chairmanship of CDO had all the powers that the Ojha Committee exercised excepting the power to allot land, it showed no sign of executing the works commenced by the its predecessor.[47] The direct impact of this official lethargy was the encroachment of land in the newly allotted blocks like Banijhala and Simalphanta. The process of occupation of land by clear felling the trees and raising huts had started before the plots were cleared of timber and other forest produces and the allottees were helped to identify their plots.[48]

During the field study it was found that there was no official presence to monitor the activity. Nobody knew among the occupants how many were real resettlers and how many of them were encroachers. In Banijhala some people had even begun encroaching forestland and the forest officials were trying to prevent this. It appeared that the whole exercise was nothing but the repetition of the same old story of encroachment and mismanagement.

During the study it was also found that almost all the resettlement blocks, except Pipraiya, were infested with the problem of encroachment. Even in Pipraiya, no one could say for sure how many of the resettlers had really vacated their old sites and were not involved in double cultivation.[49] Double cultivation was a normal phenomenon. In many resettlement sites and also in the original settlements quite a few people openly admitted that they were involved in double cultivation.

In the official records old blocks like Arjuni, Khujua and Hirapur are shown to be completely vacated, but when the author visited these sites in second week of March 1999, the scene was found to be little different. Among the three blocks stated above only Khajua was totally vacated. But in Arjuni there were still four thatched houses existing. Similarly, in Hirapur the author found at least 25 houses.

Apart from the above mentioned settlements all other settlements of the extension areas like Rauteli Bichawa, Pipladi, from where hundreds of families have already been resettled showed no sign of evacuation. Neither the Officials of the Reserve, nor the Army had taken charge of the vacated lands though officially all the area falls under the Reserve.[50] Thus, in a nutshell, the present situation with regard to displacement and resettlement operation in the RSWR project has been found to be chaotic. In what follows, a brief discussion on the causes and intervening forces that seem to be responsible for the present state of affairs will be made.

6.2.7 Causes Responsible for the Present State of Affairs

The extension and resettlement programme of the RSWR is one of the most chronic problems relating to the management of protected area in Nepal. A programme that was considered noble in its objective over the years transformed to be a chronic problem mainly due to the gaps in policy formulation and other strategic blunders. A discussion on this aspect is necessary not only to find out solution to the instant problem but also to take inference for future policy formulations and legal reforms. By and large the problems relating to the extension and resettlement of the RSWR seem to be as follows.

6.2.7.1 The Absence of Clear Vision

One thing very visible in the resettlement and extension of the RSWR is the absence of a detail plan of action. No study on socio- economic, environmental aspects of the project was carried out, nor was a detailed work schedule prepared prior to the launching of the project. Even after the issuance of King's directives the executing authorities spent a lot of time deliberating on whether a particular area should be included in the Reserve or not.[51] The controversy about the boundary of the Reserve remained unresolved till 1994.[52]

The resettlement part of the project was beset with several problems. First, the government did not have any information about the population, the number of households, their size and the occupation of the DPs, the area under cultivation, the productivity and similar other social, economic and cultural statistics. No census of the proposed extension site was conducted before the programme was announced. Even after that, it took eight long years for the authorities to conduct a household survey. Until then the implementing authorities had with them only sketchy records of the people and their property. It is found that even the household survey conducted by Mr. Parajuli, had serious flaws. For instance, he recorded the size of the family but did not record the name of all the members nor did he record their sex and age, or their family history. Therefore, down the line, this survey record could not be used to ascertain whether the person claiming land in the resettlement area constituted a separate family or the part of the old family. Secondly, as no record of ailani land or lands under illegal cultivation was available with the government, the authorities could not use the household survey record to solve complications and decide who was the original inhabitant and who had crept into the area after the announcement for the extension of the Reserve. With the time gap in the execution of the project, authorities had to bear the burden of allotting land to several joint families that broke up in due course. This apart, the infiltration of encroachers put further stress on the implementing authorities. In the absence of an appropriate record and a concrete policy as to the cut off date the authorities could not rely on anything for denying the claims of displacees or encroachers.

One of the directives of HM the King was to provide land for land under the resettlement programme. But despite this a broad approach to resettle the ailani holders and illegal occupants of lands together with the holders of registered land (i.e. the Numberiwalas) was not adopted. The authorities first decided to resettle the numbariwalas. The Numbariwalas were initially given lands in Bandarpur, Baghphanta, and Pipraiya.[53] As all the blocks had ailani holdings as well as illegal occupants, so long as these holders were allowed to occupy the land, the resettlement of the numbariwalas alone would not solve the problem. It seems that the authorities failed to understand this reality, and instead of finding an overall solution, they stuck to the piece meal approach which led to further complications in the form of further encroachment of the vacated land, continuation of cultivation etc.[54]

A connected problem with respect to the implementation of the extension and resettlement programme is the lack of logistic support. Though the security of the original area of the RSWR is entrusted to the army, it had not been moved into the extension area, which were vacated by the displacees. Upon inquiry it was found that the army was reluctant to take charge of the area until budget was allotted to it for infrastructure development for the increased strength.[55]

Another problem related to this was the absence of land survey before the initiation of the resettlement process. The land survey of the evacuation site has not so far been done. In the absence of this, the total area under cultivation in various forms either as registered, or ailani or as illegal cultivation is not known till date. It has also affected the extension and the resettlement as confusion always existed about the actual amount of land required. This has led to ever increasing demand for land for resettlement[56] which has not ended even today.[57]

6.2.7.2 The Problem of Encroachment

Of late the encroachment in any vacant plot or forestland in Terai has surfaced as a national problem. But in RSWR this appeared in an aggravated form. By and large the encroachment in the RSWR extension programme has surfaced in the following forms:

- encroachment in the resettlement sites,
- encroachment through transaction in legal holdings,
- encroachment in *ailani* holdings, and
- encroachment through illegal occupation in resettlement sites and vacated blocks.

(a) Encroachment in the Resettlement Sites

As mentioned earlier problem of encroachment in the resettlement site surfaced right in 1981. When the Sarbagya Raj Committee began distributing land in Bandarpur and Baghphanta encroachers began flocking around the resettlement sites.[58] Later the same syndrome got repeated in other blocks as well. The latest record, which shows the number of encroachers in different resettlement blocks, is presented in Table 6.8.[59]

TABLE 6.8

Distribution of Encroachers in Different Resettlement Blocks

S.N.	*Name of the Block*	*Number of Encroachers*
1	Bandarpur	468 households
2	Banijhala	29 households
3	Buttabari	441 households
4	Dhakka	80 households

Source: Field Study, March 1999

(b) Encroachment through Transaction in Legal Holdings (Numbari lands)

One finds two types of encroachments in legal holdings. The first is a direct encroachment of government land by virtue of a legal holding in a particular parcel of land. In such type of cases families occupy more land than they are legally entitled to.[60] The second is an indirect form of encroachment. In this case, families either go for partition or indulge in other forms of divisions or transactions with a view to get more benefits from the resettling authorities. For instance, when a plan was made to take care of the interests of small farmers of Rauteli Bichawa and offer them a sizable amount of land required for cultivation in Bandarpur and other places, a spur of land transactions occurred in numbari holdings. By the time authorities finally banned such activities much damage was already caused.[61]

(c) Encroachment in Ailani Holdings

An *ailani* holding is a cultivation of which no formal record exists in the official ledgers. The *ailani* holdings were common in all the blocks delineated for extension. This apart, in the proposed extension site, there were holdings which had some sort of mention in the survey field books but the occupants did not have a proper title document which is called the Land Ownership Registration Certificate. For resettlement purposes, these people were also treated like those pure *ailaniwalas*.[62] The absence of record creates a number of problems with regard to the size of the holding, its ownership or interest, the quality of land etc. As the King's directive was to give land for land which the displacees were to lose, the *ailani* holders resorted to practices like grabbing more land, creation of more families by dividing land with an intention to obtain more land in the resettlement sites. The rate of encroachment in this type of holding was higher than in others.[63]

(d) Encroachment in the Resettlement Site and Vacated Blocks.

The encroachment in the resettlement sites occurred because of a host of factors like delay and intermittent discontinuity in action, lack of coordination among various organs of the governments, and lack of administrative and logistic support.

As it was witnessed, all the resettlement sites were forest areas clear felled for the purpose. The responsibility of clearing these areas was given to the Timber Corporation of Nepal (TCN). The TCN did not begin the exercise in tandem with the implementing authorities, and cleared blocks long before the authorities were ready for evacuating the displacees. As the hunger for land in the district was high people began to settle down in these resettlement sites once they saw the land lying vacant for a considerable length of time. However, instead of first dealing with these encroachers and removing them from sites and then allotting the same to the displacees, land allotment and removal of the encroachers were attempted simultaneously. It was found that resettlers occupied the allotted land in the resettlement site wherever it remained vacant, but in case of those resettlers whose land was already occupied by others stayed back in the original sites. This gave rise to two kinds of interconnected problems. First, when the resettled families found that some families were staying back, they also could not resist the temptation of continuing cultivation in the old sites. Secondly, when the resettled families found that no stringent action was being taken against encroachers they also began to occupy any vacant land that was available in the adjoining plot or in any other place in the same block.[64] Where direct occupation was not possible the resettlers themselves invited their kith and kin to occupy land.[65] As no amendment was made in the strategy to address the emergent situation and the authorities just went ahead allotting the land the same syndrome got repeated everywhere with new allotment.

As for almost two years between 1990 and 1992 there was no official presence at the site, things went beyond control and the situation further worsened. The encroachers got tremendously emboldened to occupy land.

Later when the officials tried to remove them from the land allotted to the DPs, serious resistance was experienced.[66] So much so that once they found that a certain patch of land was being sanctioned for the resettlement of the displacees of the Reserve, they would flock around and start occupying that land. This happened in Bani block and is happening in Simalphanta this year.[67]

6.2.7.3 Absence of Monitoring and Evaluation

The author found no record of systematic monitoring and evaluation of the implementation of the project, nor was there any monitoring or evaluation cell constituted at the central level. For almost eight long years the government relied on the High Powered Committees for the implementation of the project. No reflection of the emergent reality was found in the orders issued to these Committees. With the constitution of a separate Extension Office in 1987 it appeared for some time that the government was taking the problem seriously. But the evaluation of the achievements and the shortcomings of activities of the Extension Office was not done while constituting Committees in the ensuing years. No record of deliberation exists either at the central or field office even on the appropriateness of the idea of allotting land to the encroacher of the resettlement sites nor does there exist any record of public discussion or deliberation on the issue.

The vertical communication between the Center and the field officeals seemed to be poor. For example, the request of the sanction of new lands for resettling the DPs and encroachers, which was demanded by various Committees, remained unheard for a long time. Similarly, when instructions from the centre were sought with regard to the forest produces of Banijhala and Simalphanta, there was no response from the government at all.[68]

6.2.7.4 Lack of Appropriate Legal Regime

The lack of an appropriate legal regime with regard to the displacement and resettlement made several actions of the executing authorities legally questionable. For instance, the Land Acquisition Act, 1977 was never invoked for the acquisition of the land, nor was the procedures laid down therein ever followed.[69] There exists no legal basis for the allotment of less land in the resettlement blocks than the land PAPs lost in the original place. This apart, there were other types of problems as well. For instance, no space was provided for complaint against the arbitrary decisions of the authorities. As no law existed to give finality to actions and check the repetition, the same problem had to be looked into again and again. The survey of the households for resettlement is one example to illustrate the point. There was no law to reject the claim of the encroachers for settlement or resettlement. It was felt during the study that running of the resettlement programme in a legal and policy vacuum was responsible for several problems. Further, no international standards seem to have been followed in the displacement and resettlement programme.

6.2.8 Policy and Legal Imperatives for the Solution of the Problem

As examined earlier, the extension and resettlement programme of the RSWR today stands in a precarious state. In the past 18 years not even a thought seems to have been given to the fulfilment or non-fulfilment of the King's directive. It is found that whatever good effort was made in the latter half of 1980s also could not be concretised and seriously followed. As there exists no programme for transitional or post resettlement support, the primary consideration of the government seems to be the removal of the people from the extension area. While this is true in case of DPs and PAPs in the post 1990 scenario, legitimization of encroachment and pursual to some fire fighting measures seems to be the primary concern. Keeping in mind the several variables, that have surfaced identification of the real DPs and other PAPs, linking of the resettlement with poverty alleviation measures, stringent action against the encroachers and other pseudo DPs and PAPs seem to be desirable steps. Besides, sufficient budget allocation, creation of permanent office to handle the issue, horizontal communication and coordination among various departments of the government are other considerations desirable for the solution of the extension and resettlement programme of the RSWR.

6.3 The Pokhara Airport Project

Pokhara is a valley, little smaller than Kathmandu, along the middle and high mountains in western Nepal. It is 200 km west of Kathmandu and is linked both by all weather road and air. Geographically Kaski district, of which Pokhara is the centre, falls between 28° 6' to 28° 38" north longitude and 83° 46' to 84° 12' east latitude. The district is basically a mountain district with an area of 2017sq km. The total population of the district is 292,945.[70] In total there are two municipalities and 57 villages in the district. The density of population is 145.2 per square kilometer.[71]

The Pokhara valley is oval in shape with an east west axis. According the census of 1991 the city had a population of some 95000. With an annual population growth rate of 2.01 per cent the population by now is believed to have crossed one lakh. Pokhara is also the headquarter of Zonal and Regional Offices.

Climatologically the valley lies in the subtropical region of Nepal at an elevation of 384 m from the sea level-100m lower than Kathmandu. Therefore, comparatively it is little warmer as well. Pokhara extends to the crest of famous Annapurna Range with peaks ranging from 7219 m to 8091 m. One can have a majestic view of Mt. Dhaulagiri (8167 m) Lamjung Himal (6983 m) and a host of other peaks like Mt Machhapuchhre (Fish Tail Peak), Himalchuli, Varahashikhar, Gangapurna etc at a horizontal range of 25 miles. The lush green forests of the surrounding hills, the old and unspoiled countryside, and many sprawling lakes have added to its beauty.[72] Pokhara is known by a few sobriquets such as " the city of seven lakes" "the Cherapunji of Nepal" etc.[73]

The physiography of Pokhara is very strange. It has rugged terrain with subterranean streams, caves, sinkholes etc. Except in places where traditional or modern canal systems have given a coating of fine alluvial soil, a boulder mixed rock even at the depth of one meter is a normal sight. In the plains of Pokhara no trace of old primeval forest is found though one may see some patches of recent afforestation.[74] Geologists have indicated that the plains of Pokhara had once been washed away and badly affected by the glacial lake burst in the Himalaya.[75] The infertile condition of soil and the lack of forest corroborate this.[76]

Pokhara has been traditionally an inter-pot of trading junction for east-west as well north-south trade.[77] In spite of this, human settlements in the plains of Pokhara do not have a very long history. The barrenness of the land, the malarial scare due to the presence of a number of lakes and swamps, acted as inhibiting factors for early settlements. Some agricultural parcels of Kundahar, Khudi, Sishuwa, Arghaun, Baidam, either did not have settlements or had very sparse and scattered ones.[78] Because of its trading importance a small bazar along the north south route was set up in 18th century and Newar community (which is a trading community from Bhaktapur) was invited for settlement.[79] However, till

1950, the town remained a dwelling of a few thousand people only.[80]

Once Nepal opened up to the external world in 1950, an airport was constructed in Pokhara, which linked it up with Kathmandu. By 1969, a north south highway linking the valley with India was constructed with the cooperation of India. And in 1970a another highway was constructed which linked Pokhara with Kathmandu.

As Pokhara is a place of exceptional beauty, it has grown over time as a major tourist destination as well as an entry point for mountain trekking in the western Nepal. The growth of commercial, educational and tourism opportunities in the city have attracted both well to do and business oriented people. Now, Pokhara is the second largest city in the hill regions of Nepal and also the largest in the western region. It is also one of the fastest growing city in the country.[81]

6.3.1 Settlements and Life Pattern

The largest settlement in the valley is concentrated within the limit of the Pokhara Municipality. The peripheral area of the municipality consists of Chauthe, Majeri Patan, Daduwa Kharka, Chhinidanda, and Dhungasahgu in the east, Batule Chaur in the northwest. On the eastern limit of the city lies a huge flat agricultural land now irrigated by the Seti Canal and a seasonal spring source called Kahun Khola. The Seti Canal also irrigates other areas of the valley. Though the trading community is growing in the valley, still the predominance is of farming households mainly concentrated in the suburb.

6.3.2 The Proposed Pokhara Airport Project.

The proposal for the construction of another airport began more than three decades back.[82] The reasons advanced for such an airport seem to be (a) construction of an alternative international airport sufficient for the operation of big planes, and (b) opening up Pokhara as a major tourist destination to the outside world through air linkage.[83] The new airport was planned to have a runway of 5,700 ft to be extended to 10,000 ft. in future.[84] For this purpose the government decided to acquire a vast tract of agriculture land having settlements, almost 4 km east of the existing airport along the Prithwi Highway. (See Map No 3)

Most of the land in the proposed airport site was owned by inhabitants of settlements like Majeri-Patan, Chhinedanda, upper and the lower Daduwa Kharka and Dhungasaghun. These were peripheral settlements of Pokhara and were inhabited by people of mixed origin, though Chhetriyas and Brahmin (in one block) were the predominant castes. Other occupational castes like Kami, Damai, Sharki, and Gurung and Magars comprised the minority. Originally these five blocks were spread in three wards of Chinnedanda Panchayat. Later they were merged with the Pokhara Municipality forming three wards. The total population of these areas today is around five thousands.

The major occupation of the people in these settlements was agriculture. As a canal from Kahun Khola irrigated the land it was used for growing double crops. Given the proximity to the core of the city this part of Pokhara was also famous for cash crops. For many families cash crop was a major source of earning. But for the rest, the land was used for producing staple crops like paddy, wheat, cereals etc.

6.3.3 The Land Acquisition

Though the preliminary investigation for the project began in 1967, except for cessation of land transfer and land survey, nothing happened for almost a decade. And finally, acquisition of land for the airport project began in 1978. The Ministry of Works and Transport published a notification to this effect in

MAP 3

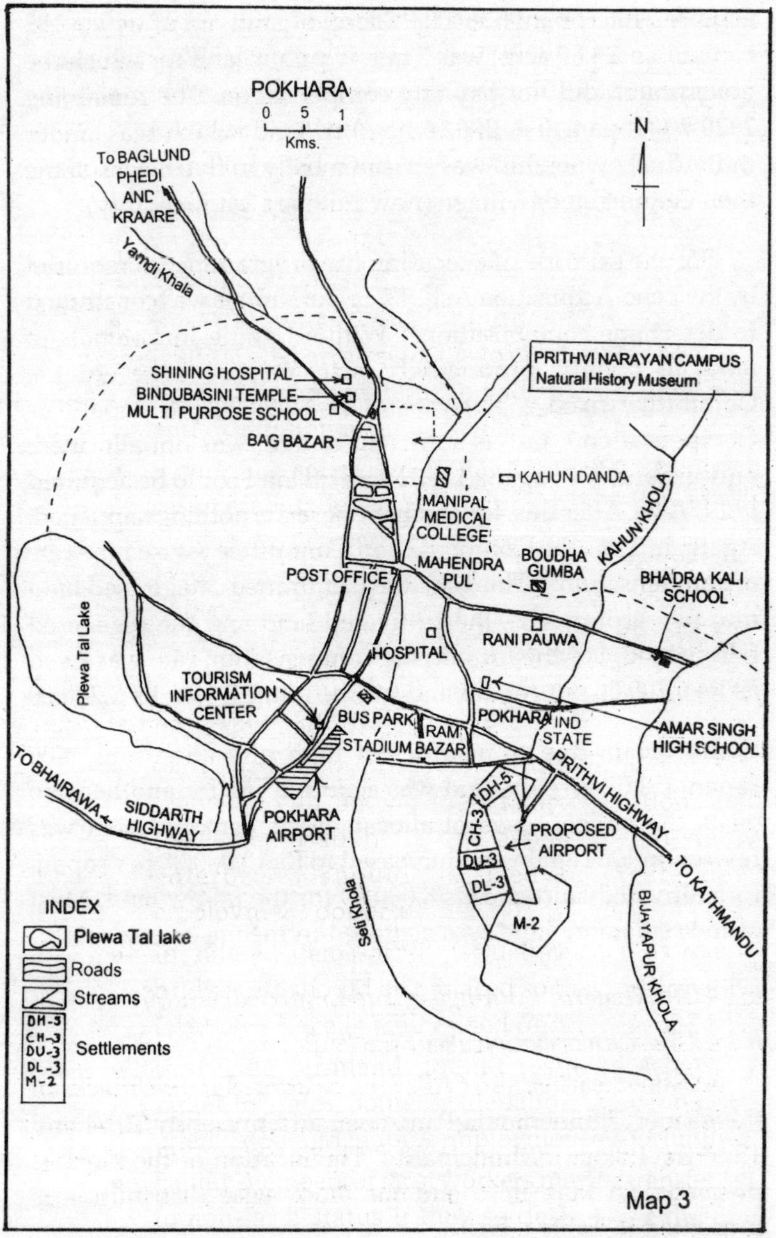
POKHARA
0 5 1
Kms.
N
To BAGLUND PHEDI AND KRAARE
Yamdi Khala
PRITHVI NARAYAN CAMPUS
Natural History Museum
SHINING HOSPITAL
BINDUBASINI TEMPLE
MULTI PURPOSE SCHOOL
BAG BAZAR
KAHUN DANDA
MANIPAL MEDICAL COLLEGE
KAHUN KHOLA
MAHENDRA PUL
BOUDHA GUMBA
POST OFFICE
BHADRA KALI SCHOOL
Plewa Tal Lake
HOSPITAL
RANI PAUWA
TOURISM INFORMATION CENTER
BUS PARK
RAM BAZAR
POKHARA IND STATE
AMAR SINGH HIGH SCHOOL
STADIUM
TO BHAIRAWA
SIDDARTH HIGHWAY
POKHARA AIRPORT
PRITHVI HIGHWAY
DH-5
CH-3
PROPOSED AIRPORT
DU-3
DL-3
M-2
TO KATHMANDU
Seti Khola
BIJAYAPUR KHOLA
INDEX
Plewa Tal lake
Roads
Streams
DH-3
CH-3
DU-3
DL-3
M-2
Settlements
Map 3

Nepal Gazette in 1976.[85] In total the government intended to acquire 3106 ropani (i.e.400.04 acre) of land out of which 185 ropani (i.e. 23.80 acre) was a fallow public land for which the government did not pay any compensation. The remaining 2920-7-0 ropani (i.e. 376.16 acre) of land which was under individual ownership was spread mostly in five blocks of the then Chinnedanda village (now Pokhara Municipality).

For the purpose of executing the programme, as required by the Land Acquisition Act 1977, a Committee was constituted to determine compensation.[86] Without going into details of land, its quality, productivity, size, market value etc. the Committee fixed a flat rate of Rs 4000.00 per ropani as Compensation.[87] But as sufficient budget was not allocated, only around 250 ropani (i.e. 32 acre) of land could be acquired in 1977/78. After this, for another two years nothing happened. Again, in 1980, the Compensation Committee revised the rate of compensation.[88] This time the Committee categorised land into two groups viz., the cultivated land and the registered fallow land. For the former, the compensation rate was fixed as Rs 6,700.00 per ropani and for the latter it was Rs 5,200.00

But again due to insufficient fund allocation, only 400 ropani (51.52 acre) of land was acquired. As for another two years the budget was not allocated, the compensation was revised in 1982 again and increased to Rs 10,000.00 per ropani for cultivated land and Rs 8,000.00 for the fallow land. Most of the remaining land was acquired in the ensuing years.[89]

6.3.4 The General Findings of the Empirical Study

6.3.4.1 Basic information about the PAPs

As stated earlier, the PAPs were scattered in five blocks of the former Chhinedanda Panchayat and presently 10,14 and 15 of the Pokhara Municipality. The location of the block is presented in Map no 3 and the block wise distribution is presented in Table 6.9.

TABLE 6.9

Distribution of Project Affected Families in the Pokhara Airport Project

S.N.	*Blocks*	*Ward No*	*Description of PAPs losing*			
			Houses, cattle shed other structures and land	*Cattle shed, Other Structures and land*	*Land Only*	*Total*
1.	Chhinedanda	5	27	12	21	60
2.	Daduwakharka U	3	30	12	24	66
3.	Daduwakharka L	3	13	6	20	39
4.	Dhunagsagu	5	17	8	23	48
5.	Majari Patan	2	61	26	48	135
	Total	18	148	64	126	348

Source: Field Study Feb. 1999

The ethnic composition of the PAPs resonates to the ethnic composition of the entire blocks. This is presented in Table 6.10

TABLE 6.10

Ethnic Composition of The Project Affected Families

S.N.	*Blocks*	*Ward*	*Ethnic Composition in percentage*				
			Number of HHs	*Brahmin*	*Chhetris*	*Other Castes*	*Remarks*
1	Chhinedanda	5	60	70.3	22.22	7.4	
2	Dhungasagun	5	48	5.2	89.0	5.8	
3.	DaduwakharkaU	3	66	6.6	83.3	10.0	
4.	Daduwakharka L	3	39	4.5	79.9	15.3	
4.	Majeri Patan	4	135	3.2	93.6	3.2	
	Total		348				

Source: Field Study, Feb. 1999

For the purpose of the study a sample of 20 per cent of the total PAPs from each of the blocks was selected through a systematic random sampling. The block wise distribution of respondents is presented in Table 6.11

TABLE 6.11

Block-wise Distribution of Respondents[90]

S.N.	*Blocks*	*Frequency*	*Per cent*	*Valid Per cent*	*Cum. Per cent*
1.	Chhinedanda 5	12	17,9	17.9	17.9
2.	Dhungasagun 5	8*	11.9	11.9	29.9
3.	Daduwakharka L-3	7*	10.4	10.4	40.3
4.	Daduwakharka U-3	14	20.9	20.9	61.2
5.	Majari Patan 2	26*	38.8	38.8	100.00

Valid cases: 67 Missing cases 0

Source: Field Study Feb. 1999

Among the respondents 28.4 per cent are females and 71.6 per cent are males. There is the predominance of family heads among the respondents. The age wise distribution of the respondents is presented in Table 6.12.

TABLE 6.12

The Age-wise Distribution of the Respondents

S.N	*Value Label*	*Frequency*	*Per cent*	*Cum. Per cent*
1.	Up to 25years	2	3.0	3.0
2.	26 to 30 years	4	6.0	9.0
3.	31 to 40 years	10	15.0	23.9
4.	41 to 50 years	10	15.0	38.8
5.	51 to 60 years	22	32.8	71.6
6.	More than 60 years	19	28.4	100.0
	Total	67	100.0	100.0

Source: Field Study Feb. 1999

A majority of respondents are found to be literate (79.1 per cent). This, in general parlance, means that the stated per cent of the respondents can read and write the vernacular language. When it came to gainful education (i.e. SLC and above) the percentage was only 22.4 per cent. Similarly the percentage of graduates (i.e. B.A and above) was only 4.5 per cent. The percentage of literacy among female respondents was quite lower than the male folk.

6.3.4.2 The Process and Procedure of Acquisition

As prescribed by the Land Acquisition Act, 1977 the preliminary work for the acquisition begins with a notification declaring the intention of the government to acquire land.[91.] Such notification needs to be fixed in the concerned VDC Office, public place around the land to be acquired, and most importantly on the house, or compound wall where such house or compound wall is to be acquired. But the survey sample showed that in none of the cases the procedure was followed. None of the respondents stated that such a notification was fixed at his/her house/shed or compound wall, or a personal notice was served to him/her. Most of the respondents came to know about the acquisition when the land survey was conducted, due to rumor that spread in the village. In 19.4 per cent of cases the informal source of information was the family head. Only in 7.5 per cent of cases the respondents said that they came to know about the project from the village leaders. In 71.6 per cent of the cases there was no particular source but the rumor in the village.

The respondents were neither informed nor explained about the need for such an acquisition, nor any publicity was made about the need of the airport at Pokhara. The respondents do not remember any official meetings to have taken place to inform and explain about the project. Similarly neither the family survey nor the survey of household income was conducted by the project authorities.

The government surveyors conducted the survey of the land to be acquired. Though nearly 93 per cent of the respondents or their family members were present during the land survey, and nearly 96 per cent of them were present when the measurement of the house or cattle shed or other structures was taken, none of them were explained about the measurement or the result. All they were asked to do was to sign a paper that the surveyors had brought with them. No receipt or acknowledgement was given to them.

When the survey results were published, in 9 per cent of the cases it was shown more and in 22.4 per cent it was shown less. That way, in 31.4 per cent (19cases) of the cases the survey varied with the previous record of the government.

But no system existed for automatic updating of the record where excess land was shown and no mechanism for explanation or correction where it was shown to be less. In all the cases the respondents could register the excess land shown by the survey only after complaint. But where the land was shown to be less only 40 per cent (6 cases) of the respondents could complain and get the measurement of land corrected, but 60 per cent (8 cases) of them could not do so. As no mechanism existed for recheck or correction of the measurement of the house and other structure, whatever grievance that the respondents had remained unheard.

6.3.4.3 Land Distribution and Acquisition

The project area is a flat land within the Pokhara valley having the potentiality of irrigation subject to the availability of water. Partly due to this and also by virtue of being relatively old settlements, the illegal occupation was almost nil. Whatever village commons was left after some of it was used for the government owned Sheep Farm, the villagers had jealously guarded it against encroachment. The author found no case of illegal occupation in the project area where the land was taken without paying compensation. Only one respondent said that after displacement he now holds a small patch of land under occupation. The distribution of land before acquisition shows the predominance of small farming households. Whereas 98.5 per cent of the respondents had less than 20 ropani (i.e.,2.56 acre) of Bari land [92] 56.59 per cent had less than 20 ropani (i.e.,2.56 acre) of irrigated land and another 31.3 per cent had irrigated land between 20 to 30 ropani (i.e., 2.56 to 3.86 acre). There existed no land under tenancy.[93] The distribution of land ownership is presented in Table 6.13

TABLE 6.13
Distribution of Land Ownership before Acquisition

Amount of Land	*Bari Land*	*Irrigated d land*	*Land under Tenancy*	*Land under Occupation*
No land	—	2 (2.9)	65 (97.1)	—
Up to 10 Ropani	46 (68.65)	8 (11.9)	2 (2.9)	—
10.1 to 20 Ropani	20 (29.8)	28 (41.79)	—	—
20.1 to 30 Ropani	—	21 (31.3)	—	—
30.1 to 40 Ropani	1 (1.4)	4 (5.9)	—	—
40.1 to 50 Ropani	—	3 (4.4)	—	—
More than 50 ropani	—	1 (1.4)	—	—
Total Number of Respondents	67	67	67	67
Average land holding	8.72	20.21	0.22	0.00

Note: (a) one ropani = 0.1288 acre or 0.05218 ha
(b) Figures in the parenthesis indicate per cent to the total.
Source; Field Study Feb 1999.

The above table shows that the respondent held more irrigated land than Bari land. The mean land holding among the respondents before acquisition comes out as 29.15 ropani (i.e. 3.46 acre).

The acquisition of land began in 1978/79. Around 14.9 per cent of the respondents began to get compensation that year whereas 31.3 per cent began to get it in 1980/81 and 52.2 per cent in 1982/83.The author found that at least two people in the project area are yet to get compensation. The distribution of people losing land is presented in Table 6.14.

TABLE 6.14

Percentage of Respondents Losing Land Due to Acquisition

S.N.	*Value Label*	*Frequency*	*Per cent*	*Cum. Per cent*
1.	Up to 25% acquired	13	19.4	19.4
2.	25.1 per cent to 50% acquired	17	25.4	44.8
3.	50.1 per cent to 75% acquired	22	32.8	77.7
4.	More than 75% acquired	15	22.4	100.0
	Total	67	100.0	100.0

Valid cases: 67 Missing Cases 0
Source: Field Study Feb. 1999

In terms of area of land lost due to acquisition the respondents in an average lost 4.13 ropani of Bari land and 10.79 ropani of irrigated land and thereby, making the total land lost as 14.93 ropani (i.e.,1.92 acre) per family. No land under tenancy or occupation was acquired for the project. Whereas all the respondents had Bari land before acquisition, the percentage of people without any Bari land increased to 26.86 after acquisition. Similarly, whereas the percentage of people not having irrigated land was 2.9 before acquisition it shot up to 23.88 per cent after acquisition. In an average also, whereas the total holding per family was 29.15 ropani before acquisition, it came down to 14.22 ropani per family after acquisition. This shows a clear decline in the land holding size after the acquisition among respondents. The distribution of land after the acquisition is presented in Table 6.15.

6.3.4.4 Payment of Compensation

Though the Act gives discretion to the state to devise and offer land package to the PAPs,[94] none of the respondents said that they were given such an offer. The official memo shows no record of determination of the compensation on the

TABLE 6.15

Distribution of Land After Acquisition Among the Respondents

Land Holding Group	*Bari Land*	*Irrigated land*	*Tenancy land*	*Occupied land*
No land	18 (26.86)	16 (23.88)	65 (97.1)	67
Up to 10 Ropani	41 (61.19)	27 (40.2)	2(2.9)	—
From 10.1 to 20 Ropani	8 (11.94)	17(25.3)	—	—
From 20.1 to 30 Ropani	—	3(4.4)	—	—
From 30.1 to 40 Ropani	—	2 (2.9)	—	—
From 40.1 to 50 Ropani	—	2 (2.9)	—	—
Above 50 Ropani	—	—	—	—
Total	67	67	67	67
Average Holding Size	4.58	9.41	0.22	0.00

Note: (a) figures in parenthesis indicate percentage to the total
(b) One Ropani = 0.1288 acre or 0.05218 ha

Source: Field Study Feb. 1999

basis of productivity, land use or its indispensability for the farming household. It also does not show any evidence of land market survey around the project area before fixing compensation. The official memos state no reason for the determination of compensation or its subsequent revision.[95] Whereas the first Committee fixed a flat rate for all type of lands, a distinction between fallow land and cultivated land was made in the subsequent revision.[96] Though under the land tenure system of Nepal, depending on the productivity, both unirrigated up land and irrigated lands are classified into four categories, this was not followed as yardstick by the Committee constituted for the payment of compensation.[97]

As the government could not pay in a single instalment, the compensation for the land to be acquired was revised at least three times. But no revision was made to the compensation determined on a lump sum basis for the house, cattle shed and other structures. The flat amount fixed in 1978/79 was continued throughout.[98] Besides, none of the respondents were paid for the loss of trees or fodder. Similarly, though the Land Acquisition Act 1977 empowers the state to devise special assistance schemes for those who are to be physically displaced,[99] no such assistance in the form of house grant, grant in aid, solatium, grant to demolish the house, cattle shed, transport of belongings was extended to the DPs. None of the DPs were given any transitional support either in the form of food subsidies, or support for the loss of income. Even for the loss of public infrastructures like school[100] and *Panchayat Ghar*, compensation was paid only for the removal of buildings but not for the loss of land.[101] There was a strong feeling about the compensation among respondents. Their main complaint was that the compensation was determined without consulting them. There was a feeling that the amount paid to them was quite below the price of the land in the surroundings. They also felt that the slow and tardy pace of payment of compensation adversely affected them.

6.3.4.5 Impact of Acquisition and the Present Situation

The impact of acquisition among the respondents was visible in varied forms. One of such impacts is the loss of agriculture land. In an average of loss of total land per family was 14.93 ropani (i.e. 1.92 acre) the average purchase of land per family from compensation amount remained only 4.69 ropani (i.e. 0.60 acre). This is very significant especially in view of the agriculture being the main occupation and the primary source of income for the family. The study showed only a slight change in the second important source of income for the family. For instance, whereas 83.6 per cent of the respondents stated self employment and daily wages as second important source of income before acquisition, it came down to 65.7 per cent around the time of interview. Similarly, a slight increase in the employment in the government sector from 7.5 per cent to 10.4 per cent, a moderate increase in employment was seen in other organised sectors from 1.5 per cent to 13.4 per cent and a nominal increase in foreign employment from 1.5 per cent to 3 per cent during the same interval. The earnings from these sectors have only supplemented the earning from agriculture sector.

TABLE 6.16

Change in Primary and Supplementary Occupation

S.N	*Item*	*Per cent Then*	*Per cent Now*
	Primary Occupation		
1.	Agriculture	100	100
	Supplementary Occupation		
2.	Government service	7.5	10.4
3.	Employment in other sectors	1.5	13.4
4.	Self Employment	83.6	65.7
5.	Foreign Employment	1.5	3.0
6.	Business	1.5	4.5
7.	Industry	0	0

Source: Field Study Feb. 1999

The importance of agriculture is also seen from another set of data. Whereas the present average holding excluding land under tillage and occupation remains 14.22 ropani, on account of tillage and occupation and the purchase the net holding has increased by another 3.61 per cent to make it 17.83 ropani per family.[102] The land holding pattern among respondents before and after acquisition, and the present situation is graphically presented in Figure 6.1

The average loss of 14.93 ropani per family due to acquisition is a real slump in the land holding pattern among respondents. The increase in tillage (i.e. 2.87 ropani) should also be seen against the popular practice among farmers that they hardly cultivate the land of other persons so long as their own land meets the food requirement of the family. The present distribution of land holding is presented in Table 6.17

FIGURE 6.1

The Change in Land Holding Pattern Before Acquisition, After Acquisition and Now

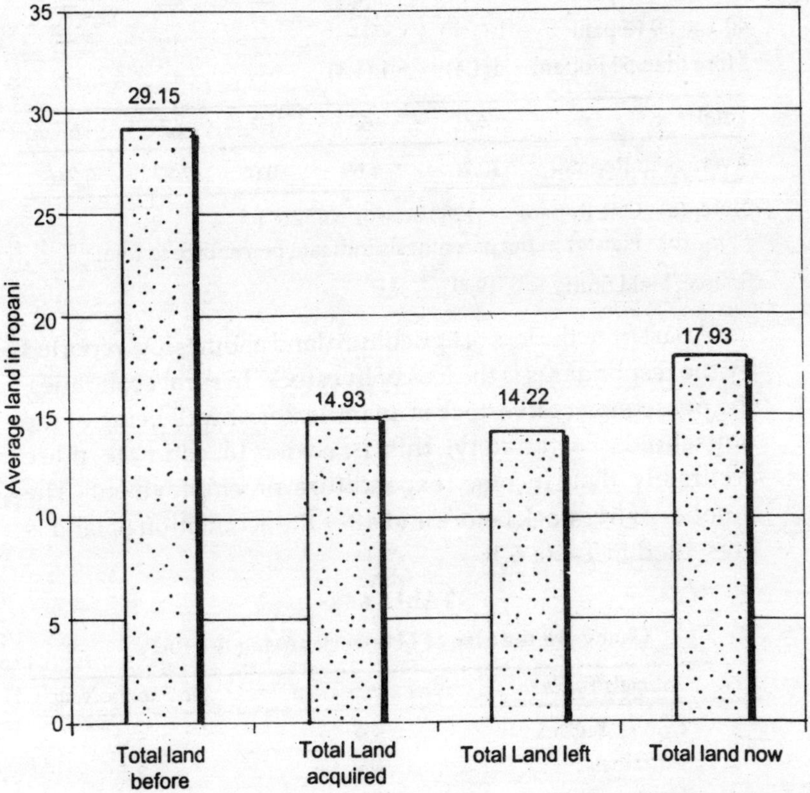

TABLE 6.17

The Present Land holding Pattern Among Respondents

Groups	*Land Left Purchased Area Under Compensation*	*Land*	*Purchased from Other Tillage*	*Area Under*	*Area Under Occupation*
No land	12 (17.9)	26 (38.8)	—	46 (66.6)	66 (98.5)
Up to 10 Ropani	29 (43.2)	35 (52.2)	—	13 (19.4)	1 (1.4)
10.1 to 20 Ropani	16 (23.8)	3 (4.4)	—	8 (11.93)	—
20.1 to 30 Ropani	8 (11.94)	—	—	—	—
30.1 to 40 Ropani	—	3 (4.4)	—	—	—
40.1 to 50 Ropani	1 (1.4)	—	—	—	—
More than 50 Ropani	1(1.4)	1 (1.4)	—	—	—
Total	67	67	67	67	67
Average in Ropani	10.20	4.69	0.0	2.87	0.746

Note: (a) One Ropani = 0.1288 acre or o.05218 ha

(b) Figures in the parenthesis indicate percentage to total.

Source: Field Study Feb. 1999

Apart from the loss of agriculture land another loss reported by the respondents is the loss of livestock. In rural economies, the possession of livestock is an indicator of well being of the household. Fortunately, this is easier to estimate more accurately than income, expenditure or employment. The number of livestock before and after the acquisition of land is presented in Table 6.18.

TABLE 6.18

Change in the Size of Livestock among the PAPs

S.N.	*Animals/Fowls*	*No/Family-Then*	*No/Family-Now*
1.	Cows/ Bullocks	8.9	5.0
2.	Buffaloes	4.5	2.5
3.	Goats/ Sheep	11.9	7.9
4.	Fowls	8.5	8.7
5.	Pigs	0.2	0.2

Source: Field Study Feb.1999

TABLE 6.19

Investment of Compensation in Sectors in Order of Priority

Agriculture			*House site*			*Construction of House*			*Business*			*Transport*			*Family Expense*		
P	F	%	P	F	%	P	F	%	P	F	%	P	F	%	P	F	%
1	22	32.8	1	2	3.0	1	29	43.3	-	-	-	1	4	6.0	1	9	13.4
2	13	19.4	2	2	3.0	2	15	22.4	2	2	3.0	2	2	3.0	2	24	35.8
3	7	10.4		-	-	3	4	6.0	-	-	-			1.5	3	24	35.8
4	2	3.0		-	-	-	-	-	-	-	-				4	4	6.0
X	23	34.3	X	63	94.0	X	19	28.4	X	65	97	X	60	89.6	X	6	9.0
	67	100.0		67	100		67	100		67	100		67	100		67	100

Note: a) P= Priority, F= Frequency, % = Percentage, X= No response

While before acquisition respondents on an average held 8.9 cows and bullocks the number.declined to 5.0 around the time of study. Similar change also occurred in rearing of buffaloes and goats/sheep as well. Whereas on average respondents owned 4.5 buffaloes before land acquisition, the number slumped to 2.5 at present. Similarly, whereas the respondents on an average owned 11.0 sheep/goats before land acquisition the number got reduced to 7.5. There is not significant change in the number of fowls and pigs. When asked about the cause of such decline 41.8 per cent reported loss of pasture and space as the cause for decline while 49.3 per cent of the respondents felt that it was due to shortage of manpower.

In spite of agriculture remaining the main occupation and the first source of income, it is found that not much money was invested in purchasing agriculture land. It was found that only 32.83 per cent (22 cases) of the respondent said that purchase of agriculture land was their first priority. Conversely 34.3 per cent (i.e. 23 cases) of the respondents did not spend any amount in agriculture. Similarly the construction of house for family got precedence over the purchase of agricultural land among 43.28 per cent (i.e. 29 cases) of the respondents. These respondents on an average purchased only 2.27 ropani (0.29 acre) of agriculture land. The investment of compensation amount in preferential order is presented in Table 6.19.

The above given table however does not show the distribution of money among co-parceners. In a few cases the compensation money has been distributed among the co-parceners as well. For the non- investment of money in agriculture family expenditure appears to be the major reason. The Table 6.19 also shows that a whopping 91 per cent of the respondents used certain fraction of compensation money in family expenses. Similarly, at least 72.6 per cent of the respondents used some amount of money in construction of house. As the project area falls in the suburb of Pokhara municipality the proclivity to spend more money on house construction is understandable. Besides, demolition of old house or the need of a new house where the family breakup had occurred was also important causes responsible for high investment in the construction of dwellings. The first priority sector of expenditure is graphically presented in Figure 6.2.

FIGURE 6.2

Investment of Money in the First Priority Sector

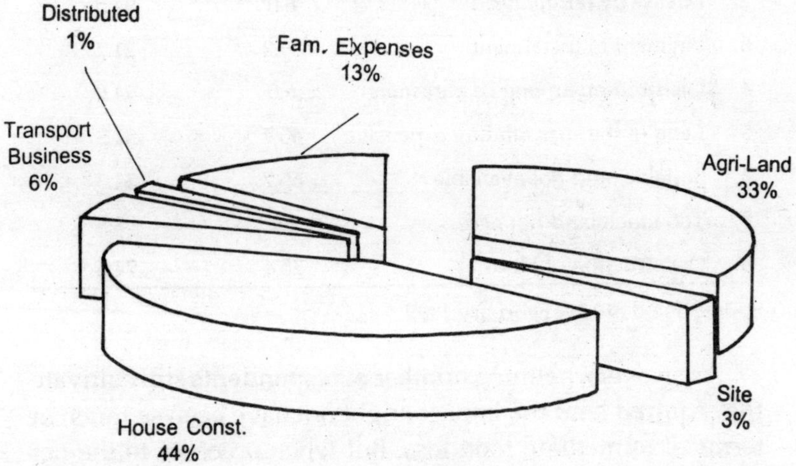

Where the respondents indicated that they could not spend much of the compensation money on agriculture land they were asked about the reason for the same. The answer is given as below in Table 6.20.

The table shows family expenses, payment of compensation in instalment, the non-availability of suitable land in the surrounding and the shooting up of prices of the land as four dominant causes responsible for non-investment in agriculture land. Despite general perception in the project area, very few respondents indicated the misuse by family head or "Karta" to be a major cause. This is partly because a majority of the respondents were family head themselves. After all confession is a very painful thing.

TABLE 6.20

The Reasons for Non-Investment in the Purchase of Agriculture land

SN.	*Reasons for non Investment*	*Response*	*Non Response*
1.	Family expenses	78.6	22.4
2.	Misuse by family head	6.0	94.0
3.	Payment in Instalment	79.3	21.7
4.	Distribution among co parceners	6.0	94.0
5.	Land in the surrounding expensive	65.7	34.3
6.	Suitable land not available	65.7	34.3
7.	Too much land not necessary	1.5	98.5
8.	Construction of House	25.4	74.6

Source: Field Study, February 1999

As an overwhelming number of respondents still cultivate the acquired land the impact might not have been so much in terms of immediate food loss. But when it comes to the net loss in agriculture land it is clear and stark. Such a loss obviously contains multiple ramifications economic and otherwise. Though in terms of availability of basic amenities like electricity, water supply, irrigation facility (due to the construction of a canal) roads, and schools visible changes have occurred, it is mainly due to the locational advantage of the area. These have not enabled the PAPs to reap substantial benefits in terms of earning or employment. During the survey the 64.2 per cent of the respondents reported that they feel that they are worse off now than before acquisition. Only 3 per cent felt that the land acquisition helped them to improve their economic status.

6.4 Comparative Analysis of the Empirical Study

In spite of the difference in the objectives and strategies adopted types of projects, a lot of commonalties emerge from the study. Here both commonalties and differences will be highlighted. While doing so an attempt will also be made to find answer to some of the questions raised in Chapter 1.

(i) The most prominent commonality in both the projects relates to the primary objective. In both the projects the primary motive seems to be the removal of people from the project site. In the Pokhara Airport Project, monetary compensation was thought to be a sufficient consolation to the economic, social and psychological loss that the PAPs would incur. Therefore, no effort was made to design a resettlement plan and execute it in this project. In case of the RSWR, though a land for land policy was followed, still the primary consideration seems to be the removal of the DPs and other PAPs and not the restoration of their earning capacity or mitigation of the economic, social or psychological. The study presents several examples to illustrate this. For instance, criteria developed for allotting land contained serious flaws. There exists neither the upper ceiling in allotting land to the numbariwalas nor is there any lower limit fixed. Though at one stage in earlier phase, an attempt was made to allot sizable plots to small holders, who were basically, numbariwalss, in Bandarpur, this policy was discarded later. Under the present policy plots of five katthas (i.e 0.41 acre) ten katthas (i.e. 0.83 acre) and fifteen katthas (1.24 acre) are allotted to the DPs and other PAPs. Given the very small size of the plots, viable cultivation does not seem to be possible. Further, there exists no system of transitional support, infrastructure development, health care plan etc.

In both the projects adult members of the family especially sons, brothers, unmarried daughters were not considered as separate family. As a result, they got no support for resettlement or any sort of compensation. While a land survey was carried out in Pokhara Airport Project, no survey to ascertain the actual occupation of land was carried out in the RSWR project. The absence of family or land survey before launching the evacuation and resettlement package created a lot of complications at a later stage in RSWR.

While in the Pokhara Project no grant, or solatium was provided, in the RSWR project a provision for the grant of Rs 2000.00 per family was made for shifting the belongings, and a grant of Rs 5000.00 for uprooting and shifting the borewell was made (if the DPs had any). In a nutshell, while resettlement was out of the purview in the Pokhara project, rehabilitation was out of consideration in the RSWR.

(ii) In both the projects the PAPs were neither informed nor consulted about the project before a decision to launch the project was made. Subsequent to the project decision also there exists no record of consultation of PAPs in any of the activities like fixing of compensation, measurement of dwelling and other structures or in the resettlement planning.

(iii) In the RSWR project, the Land Acquisition Act 1977 was not applied nor was the procedure laid down therein followed for the acquisition of property.[103] This posed a serious question about the legality of the whole exercise though nobody has so far challenged the project decision to requiring the person to vacate the land.

(iv) Invasion to the right to information was very much visible in both the projects. Information regarding the project was not disseminated. At no stage, the PAPs were explained about the necessity or the purpose of the project, its benefits to the community, or the possible adverse environmental and social impacts. No EIA study was conducted in both the projects. So much so that even after the Environment Protection Act, 1998 coming into force, and despite the request of the District Forest Officer, no EIA study was carried out before the government issued its consent for clear felling a natural forest at Simalphata and Banijhala in the RSWR project.

(v) Though the RSWR project is yet to be completed, looking at the criteria adopted for allotting land it seems to be unlikely that the PAPs will be rescued from the poverty trap. The threat of impoverishment looms large among the PAPs. The absence of transitional support, grants, aids food and seed supply, employment or income generation scheme is likely to have serious implications as there exists no plan to involve them in benefit sharing from the conservation exercise. No attempts have so far been made to include the PAPs in the sharing of benefit under the Buffer Zone Regulation, 1996.[104]

In case of Pokhara Project, though most of the families are still cultivating the acquired land, the adverse impact is felt in terms of net asset loss. In an average per family loss of agriculture land is estimated to be 14.22 ropani (1.89 acres) Already 26.86 per cent and 23.88 per cent of the respondents do not possess any bari or irrigated land respectively.[105] It is likely to have serious economic implications among most of the PAPs who are already marginalised lots.

(vi) Another adverse impact is felt in terms of scattering of communities. Though it is not seriously felt in the Pokhara project, as there the DPs have shifted in the remaining parts of the existing blocks, which have fallen outside the project, its effect seems to be serious among the DPs of the RSWR. Except Baghphanta and Bandarpur, all other resettlement sites are quite apart from each other. Two of them, Dhakka and Buttabari fall on the southern side of the RSWR at a distance of 25 to 35 KM from the district head quarter and the national High Way where as the original blocks were at a

TABLE 6.21

Comparative Analysis of the Research Findings

S.N	*Querries*	*RSWR Project*	*Pokhara Airport Project*
1.	Inception of the project	1982	1964
2.	Primary Motive	Removal of DPs	Removal of DP
3.	Strategy adopted	Land for land	Cash compensation
4.	Objective of the project	Extension of the Reserve	Constr. of alternate airport
5.	Basis of compensation	Land holding	Land holding (reg.only)
6.	Adult Sons/Daughters considered as separate family	No	No
7.	Any support provided	Rs 2000.00 for transporting belonging and Rs 5000.00 for removing bore well	No
8.	Infrastructure Development	No	No
9.	Information sharing/ consultation/participation	No	No

10.	Was LAA applied for the acquisition of land	No	Yes
11.	Legal basis of resettlement	Executive decision	No resettlement component
12.	Whether EIA study conducted	No	No
13.	Present status	Incomplete, people still occupying proposed extension sites	Land acquisition by and large complete, but except the construction of access road, garage and office, no construction work has begun.
14.	Impact	Not studied	Net loss of agricultural land and livestock found.
15.	Scattering of community	Seems to be the natural consequence of resettlement	Not significant

Source: Field Study, 1999.

distance of 3-5 km from the highway and almost the same distance from the district head quarter. As the authorities have no plans to resettle the DPS in-groups scattering of the family seems to be the natural consequence of resettlement. This has a likelihood of seriously affecting the indigenous Tharu community who live in a closely knit surrounding.[106] But despite the King's directives there exists no plan to resettle these the Tharu communities in a group. The researcher found Tharu houses scattered in Dhakka, Bani and Buttabari. There exists no plan to resettle the Tharus of Padao in on resettlement site.

(vii) As the resettlement operation is launched in a policy and legal vacuum there exists no uniformity in approach and consistency in action. The absence of permanent institution to handle the issue of displacement and resettlement in both the projects is felt. The ad hoc approach adopted in the extension and resettlement programme of the RSWR is likely to have very wide adverse effect on the PAPs and on the environment.

The comparative analysis of the research findings of the RSWR project and the Pokhara Airport Project is presented in capsular form in Table 6.21.

In a nutshell, the findings and the comparative analysis show that the approach of the Nepali government on the issue of displacement is traditional. In both the projects, primary concern of the implementing authorities seems to be the removal of people from the project site. The restoration of earning capacity, alleviation of poverty etc seems to be beyond the scope of the projects. While on the one hand the deficiency of the Land Acquisition Act affected the displacement of people in the Pokhara Airport project, the absence of an appropriate law and policy affected the resettlement operation in the RSWR. Though there seems to be little scope for questioning the benefit of the conservation likely to accrue to the public in the RSWR project, whether an alternative airport in a small valley of a mountainous region will serve long term benefits of the local people is open to debate. But leaving aside the question of long term benefits for a while, even when one looks at the rights and entitlement aspects, as analysed above, it becomes clear that the mismatch between the constitutional norms and the existing laws has been reflected in the practice of the government on the question of displacement and resettlement. The study also depicts an amount of obliviousness on the part of the government of Nepal to its international obligations with regard to the rights and entitlements of the displaced and other affected persons. What it implies in the broader context of project-induced displacement, resettlement and rehabilitation is the focus of inquiry in the next chapter.

REFERENCES

1. E.A. Smythies, a forest expert wrote in 1950s "although cultivation increased in recent years, the NAYA MULUK is essentially a forest district", *See* DIVYA D. BHATTA & T.K. SHRESTHA, THE ENVIRONMENT OF SUKLAPHANTA 11 (Kathmandu, Tribhuvan University, 1977) (quoting Smythies).
2. Tharus are a typical indigenous tribe inhabiting in the Nepalese Terai. In Kanchanpur district on finds two sub groups of Tharus-*Ranas* and *Dagauras*. Though their genealogy is not properly recorded they love to link themselves to the Rajputs of Indo-Gangetic plains who entered the Nepalese Terai owing to the threat of Mugals in India. Till 1970s Tharus were the most dominant community in the district, but the heavy influx of the hill population in the district in the last three decades reduced them to a minority. The 1991 census shows their population to be 59795 (i.e. 23.18 per cent). *See* CBSN, THE STATISTICAL YEAR BOOK OF NEPAL, (Kathmandu, The Central Bureau of Statistic, 1997).
3. Kanchanpur had one of the first five-resettlement projects launched by the Nepal Resettlement Company. The settlements like Tribhuvan Basti, Bhuvan basti, Kalike Basti, Buddha Basti in the southern part of the district, after the RSWR, have grown up as a result of this offical resettlement programme.
4. CBSN, *supra* note 2; *See also* DILLI RAM DAHAL, LAND AND

MIGRATION IN FAR WESTERN NEPAL 122, (Kathmandu, Tribhuvan University, 1977).

5. From the record of the District Forest Office obtained during the field study.
6. Even the post 1990 governments have constituted Sukumbasi Samasya Samadhan Aayog (The commission for the settlement of the problem of the landless) just to regularize illegally occupied land and offer title document to the encroachers and squatters. Such ad-hoc and often contradictory policies of the government have only emboldened the encroachers.
7. The official memo in the file of the Department of National Park and Wildlife, HMG dated March 15, 1970.
8. *Supra* note 1, at 3; *see also* E.W. BALSON, GENERAL REPORT ON THE ROYAL SUKLAPHANTA WILDLIFE RESERVE 2, (Kathmandu, NPWC Project/FAO/UN Sept., 1976).
9. The settlements which fell within the reserve were from Balma, Baskola and Kalikich area. *See id* at 13.
10. For instance, the Barasinga (Cervus duvauceli) the Chital (axis axis), the Blue Bull (Boselaphus tragocameles), the Barking Deer (Muutiacus muntjac), the Krishna Saar or the Black Buck (Antilope cervičapra), the tiger (Panthera tigris) the wild elephant (Elephas maximus) Ban Kukur (Canon alpinus) etc *See* E.W. BALSON *supra* note 8 at 1-7.
11. For instance, muggar, wolf snake, blind snake etc, *see id.*
12. For instance, the giant Tornbull (Buceros bicornis), King, Parakeets, Bank mynah, Black Partride etc, *see id.*
13. *See,* http://www.visitnepa.com, accessed on Apr. 15, 1999.
14. E.W. BALSON, *supra* note 8.
15. Similar Forest Sector Strenghtening (High Powered) Committes and Special Courts were initially constituted one each for Jhapa, Morang-Sunsari, Nawalparasi, Rupendehi-Kapilvastu, Banke-Bardiya, Kailali, Kanchanpur, and Makawanpur-Chitwan districts. These Committes were headed by retired judges of the Supreme Court or Regional Courts. *See* Nepal Gazette Jan 3, 1982 (vol 31 add.no 56, Paush 17,2038B.S.).
16. The members, among others, included the Zonal Commissioners, the Conservator of Forest, District Superintendent of Police, the Chief District Officer, the Revenue Officer, The Settlement Officer, The Director of the Department of Land Reform, the District Forest Officer, chief of the Resettlement Company, *see* Nepal Gazette Jan3, 1982 (vol 31 add no 56. Paush 17, 2038 B.S).

17. *See* Nepal Gazette, Jan 4 1982 (vol 31 add no 57 Paush 18,2038 BS) Apr. 21, 1982 (Vol 32 add.no 1, Baishak 5, 2039 B.S.); *id* Aug 1, 1983 (vol 33 add no 13.(e) Shrawan 15, 2040 B.S). However, none of the Gazette notifications make any mention of the land. *See also* Nepal Gazette, April 19, 1990 (vol 40 add. no 2 (A) Baisakh 3, 2047 BS).
18. *Ailani* holding is a holding which is not registered in the revenue records, but which is not prohibited land for cultivation.
19. The Far Western Region consists of Seti and Mahakali zones of Nepal.
20. From interview with Dr. Devi Prasad Ojha, the former Chairman of the RSWR Settlement of the Extension Problem at Mahendra Nagar on Mar 14, 1999.
21. Such commissions and committees were headed by People like Justice (retd) Sarbagya Raj Pandit, Mr. Sudarshan Bahadur Singh, Mr. Omkar Prasad Gauchan, Mr. Yuganath Sharma, and Mr. Ghanashyam Giri.
22. Nepal Gazette Jan 6, 1988 (Vol 37, no 37 Paus 20,2044 B.S.). The Extension Office functioned till June 18,1990.
23. According to Mr Parajuli, during his tenure as project chief, the Committees were headed by Mr. Omkar Prasad Gauchan and Mr. Ghanashyam Giri (Both Members of the then Rastriya Panchayat).
24. *Supra* note 22.
25. The people's movement of the restoration of democracy began in Nov. 1989 and culminated in a tripatriate agreement between the King and the Nepali Congress, and the United Left Front Apr 23, 1990.
26. The appointment of Badri Prasad Khatiwada, Dr. Devi Prasad Ojha, Mukarji Giri, and Pushkar Raj Ojha from July 1995 onwards clearly exemplify this.
27. In a span of three years four CDOs were transferred. *See* Table 6.3.
28. With the fall of the communist government headed by Mr. Man Mohan Adhikari in 1995, when the RSWR Extension Problem Settlement Committee headed by Mr. Badri Prasad Khatiwada got dissolved, it took five long months for the Sher Bahadur Deuba Government to constitute another Committee headed by Dr. Devi Prasad Ohja. And again as the Deuba government collapsed within a year the Ojha Committee could work only little more than seven months. As usual, the government the

next Committee headed by Mr. Mukurjee Giri got constituted only after a gap of six months. Table 6.3.

29. It is fixed in the east to Sihalinala right from the foot of Churia to near to Security Post at Dhakka down south. In the west it is fixed to border to Amakhiya nala till the nala reaches to Badanikheda of Rauteli Bichawa VDC. There the Reserve stretches further west to Chaudhar Nala for some time in Bandarpur and Baghphata (the two resettlement sites on the western bank of the Chaudar Nala). Though the course of these nalas keeps on changing still they, to a large extent, contribute to constrict the encroachment and movement of people and their domestic animals at least seasonally. *See* Nepal Gazettee, May 25, 1994 (Vol 43 no 5 Jestha 9 2951BS).
30. However, the term "encroachers" at this stage should be taken cautiously because except in Bandarpur till then there was not heavy encroachment in the extension sites. Those who were termed as "encroachers" by the authorities included both the *ailani* holders as well as the encroachers of forest land.
31. The number of families requiring resettlement was reported to be 1732 by 1992. *See* the Official Memo Department of National Park and Wildlife date Dec, 1997.
32. *Id.*
33. This figure was calculated from the minutes of the proceedings of the Puskarnath Ojha Committee kept in the custody of the RSWR Office by the author in March 1999.
34. *Id.*
35. *See* Nepal Gazette Jan 6, 1988 (vol. 37 No 37, Paus 20,2044 BS).
36. From personal interaction with Mr. Damodar Parajuli, the then head of the RSWR Extension Project and presently Joint Secretary in the Ministry of Forest and Soil Conservation at his office on March 29, 1999 and Mrs. Tara Bahadur Chand, Khadka Bahadur Bogati, and Ram Bilash Mahato, officials of the RSWR, March 18 at the RSWR Office, March 18,1999.
37. From interaction with the resettlers in these blocks March 1999.
38. While in Pipraiya, Baghphanta and Bandarpur, irrigation facility is available and soil condition is also reportedly good for cultivation, in Buttabari, Bani there is no irrigation facility. Dhakka has just begun to get irrigation facility but the soil condition was reported to be comparatively poor.
39. In Bandarpur Bagphanta and Pipraiya irrigation facility was provided and in Bandarpur, a pilot programme for agriculture development was launched in eighties.

40. The author personally witnessed this when he visited those sites on March 14, and 15, 1999. When inquiry was made with the DFO the author was told that the Simalphanta block alone had a timber worth of two crore rupees, but as the government did not send any instruction, he could not clear fell the site. Later when the same question was put to the CDO the same thing was repeated. It also came to the knowledge that due to government's negligence to the issue instruction heavy loss of timber occurred in 1998 in Bani block. Though to save their face the Mukurji Giri Committee had asked the resettlers to sign a bond to protect the trees which fell in their plots, it was hardly complied with.
41. The compensation for deep Tubewell was increased to Rs. 7,500.00, *see* the minute dated July 8, 1993 (i.e. Ashad 22, 2050 BS) in the file of RSWR Office.
42. The Hiramani Bhandari Committee rejected such a claim. *See* the minute dated Oct 9, 1994 (Ashwin 23, 2051 BS) in the file of RSWR Office.
43. From interview with Jayandra Bahadur Shah, Dhan Bahadur Thapa and Mandire Giri in Dhakka on March 17, 1999, with Jitandra Bishta Chairman, Pipladi VDC on March 18, 1999 and with Sarbe Nath, Janak Lawad Lalmani Bhatta resettlers of Buttarbari at Buttabari, March 19, 1999.
44. Though Mr. Parajuli, in his interview with the author, argued that people were given opportunity to choose their neighbour, this was not consciously followed throughout. As a result Tharus were interspersed and mixed with other hill migrants in Dhakka, Bani, Buttabari etc.
45. Other members of the Committee were Chief of the District Offices including the DFO, The warden of the RSWR. However, not even a single meeting of the Committee was held till the last week of March 1999 when the author visited the place.
46. It was in fact a follow up of the initiative taken by its predecessor.
47. It even did not monitor and control the indiscriminate felling of trees and land reclamation in Simalphanta which occurred immediately after the dissolution of the Puskarnat Ojha Committee.
48. When the author asked about the identity and whereabout of the people involved in clear felling, they told that they were from Rauteli Bichawa (i.e. one of the extension site), but to the surprise of the author it was revealed during conversation that even the people claiming to be hailing from the same village did not know each other.

49. This admission was made to the author by the people in Rauteli Bichawa when he visited the site on March 13, 1999.
50. Upon inquiry, it was found that both the Army and the Reserve had complains about the lack of physical strength for the protection. It was also revealed from the report of the Committees that for increasing the strength and establishing itself in the proposed area the Army had demanded a budget of five crore rupees and the Reserve office had requested for the increase of 30 game scouts. But the government met none of these demands.
51. For instance, the Sarbajya Raj Pandit Committee was for a long time bogged down to decide whether Jhilmila blcok falling under ward no 8 of Rauteli Bichawa, and settlements of Radhapur and Emilia should be included in the Reserve or not, finally these two blocks were included in the Reserve. *See* the decisions of the Committee dated June 20, 1982 (Ashad 4, 2039 BS) and Apr. 22,1984 (Baisakh 6,2041 BS) Similarly, Champapur block of Daiji VDC was finally excluded from the Reserve by the Yuganath Sharma Committee. *See* the decision taken by the Committee on May 22, 1986 (i.e. Jestha 2, 2043 BS) in the file of RSWR.
52. It was only in May 25, 1994 that a Gazette notification designating the boundary of the RSWR could be published. After this notification only the present area of the reserve i.e. 305 sq. km is considered as the area of the reserve in official documents, *see* Nepal Gazette, May 25, 1994 (Vol 43 No 5 Jestha 9, 2051).
53. These three blocks fall within the Mahendra Nagar Municipality, the site of the district headquarter. Later *numbariwalas* were given land in Dhakka and Buttarbari blocks.
54. When inquired about the reason for adopting such a view, Mr. Parajuli told the author that his mandate was limited to resettling only the *numbariwalas* and not encroachers. However, the gazette notification does not support his view. *See* Nepal Gazette, Jan 6, 1988 (Vol 37, No 37, Paush 20, 2044 BS).
55. Even today the Army, which has the strength of 205 personnel has not moved into the area designated by the extension notification of May 25, 1994.
56. Till 1987 the resettlement programme was limited to Bandarpur, Baghphanta and Pipraiya but later it was thought to be insufficient and resettlement sites created in Dhakka and Buttabari as well. Again after 1990 two more blocks were created in Bani and Simalphanta.
57. Both the Mukarji Giri Committee and the Pushkar Nath Ojha Committee had requested for additional land for resettlement.

The Giri Committee had demanded 1000 Bighas of land and The Ojha Committee repeated the same. The present chairman Mr. Devkota in his interview with the author went even further and said that if the problem has to be solved the government needs to allot another 2500 bighas of land.

58. *See* the decision of the Committee dated March 29, 1981 (Jestha 13,2038BS) and Aug 23,1983 (Bhadra 7,2040BS).
59. *See* The record prepared by the Puskar Raj Ojha Committee, in 1999, in the file of RSWR Office.
60. This kind of encroachment was there in RSWR right from the beginning. See Nepal Gazette, Jan 3, 1982 (Vol.31 No 56, Paush 17,2038 BS), para 13.
61. On Aug.20, 1981 the executing authorities sent a notice to the District Revenue Office tasking them not to register such land transactions, *see* the decision of the committee of the above date (i.e. Bhadra 4, 2038 BS.) in the file of RSWR Office.
62. S.5 of the Land Survey Act 1961 of Nepal contains provision for regularization of unrecorded cultivation on the basis of long term occupation. *See also* of the Land Revenue Act, 1977, S. 34 (providing for regularization of unrecorded cultivation).
63. From personal interaction with Khadka Bdr. Bogati, RSWR staff at Mahendra Nagar March 21, 1999.
64. From personal interaction with Jitendra Bistha, Chairman of Pipladi VDC and a member of the Pushkar Raj Ojha Committee march 10, 1999 at Mahendranagar.
65. From personal interaction with Mr. Baburam Yadav the then warden of RSWR and Member Secretary of the Mukarji Giri Committee at the Department of National Parks and Wildlife, Babarmahal, Kathmandu on Apr 4, 1999.
66. In one incident in Bandarpur a surveyor was attacked on June 25, 1993 and the theodolite was smashed when the authorities tried to make the 173 small farmers settle in the land allotted to them. From personal interaction with Officials of the RSWR Tara Bdr. Chand, Khadka Bahadur Bogati, Ram Bilash Mahato at the RSWR Office March 22, 1999.
67. The author witnessed it himself in Bani block and Simalphanta block during the field study in the second and third week of March, 1999.
68. From personal interaction with the DFO Mr. Man Bahadur Khadka at his Office at Mahendra Nagar on March 27, 1999.
69. *See* Nepal Gazette, Jan 3, 1982 (Vol 31 No 56, Paush 17, 2938 BS).

70. As per the 1991 census *See* CBSN, STATISTICAL YEAR BOOK OF NEPAL 1997 (Kathmandu, Central Bureau of Statistics).
71. *Id.*
72. http://www.al/pokkhara.htm, accessed on 14th Apr. 1999.
73. Out of the seven lakes a few lakes like the Phewa, the Begnas and Rupa worth the name but others like Khaste, Kadini, Maidi and Dipang are either swamp lands or small water bodies of the size of a big pond. Pokhara experiences an annual rainfall of 5000 ml, the highest in Nepal.
74. One of such forest is the Bairagiko ban on the ridge of Seti river, near the main bus stop at Pokhara.
75. Harka Gurung. Pokhara Valley, Nepal Himalays: A Field Study in Regional Geography (1965) (unpublished Ph.D thesis, Univ of Edinberg, (Edinberg). *See also* ICIMOD, *Occasional Paper No 1*, Kathmandu, International Centre for Integrated Mountain Development, 1985 at 1.
76. DOROTHY MIERO, THIRTY YEARS IN POKHARA 3 (Kathmandu, Ratna Books, 1998).
77. It is linked with Kathmandu in the east with other western hills on the one hand and Tibet and India in the north and south respectively, *see* http://www.windownep.com.pokhara.htm, accessed on Apr. 14th 1999.
78. The malarial scare was present till 1950s.
79. *Supra* note 76, at 5.
80. *Id.* at 19.
81. *Id.*
82. According to the displacees and other affected people of the airport area, the government froze the land transaction in the proposed area since 1967 (i.e. 2024 BS).
83. In the existing airport only small planes like Twin Otter, DC 10 etc can operate. The north south axis of the runway is supposed to have posed a problem for easy landing and take off. (From personal interaction with the Mr. K. Rayamajhi, the Chief of the Pokhara Airport) at his Office. The Fourth Development Plan Report sites the growth of economic activities in Pokhara as one reason for proposal, while the Fifth Plan mentions about developing an alternate airport. *See* NPC, THE FOURTH PLAN (1970-75) 155 and THE FIFTH PLAN (1976-1980) 331 (Kathmandu, National Planning Commission, 1976) (Nepali Text).

84. *See* THE FIFTH PLAN *Id.* at 331.
85. By this notification the government issued its final intention to acquire land for the purpose. *See* Nepal Gazette, March 18, 1976 (vol.25 no 48 Chaitra 2, 2032BS).
86. The Committee was headed by the then Zonal Commissioner, Ramchandra Bahadur Singh. Other members of the Committee were the Chief of District Revenue Office, The Engineer of the District Civil Construction Office and the Chief of Pokhara Airport. In spite of the legal requirement, the Committee did not have any member from the District Panchayat, *see also* the Land Acquisition Act, 1977 S. 13.
87. One Ropani is equivalent to 0.1288 acre.
88. *See* the decision of the Committee dated Apr. 151980 (2036/12/29 BS) in the file of the Pokhara Airport Office.
89. However, an area of 9.30 acre belonging to least two people, is yet to be acquired for the Project.
90. One respondent each from three blocks was not available for the interview, which is indicated by a symbol (*). Therefore, non response is only 4.3 per cent.
91. *See* the Land Acquisition Act, 1977 Ss 3, 4, 5, and 6.
92. Bari land is generally an unirrigated land.
93. Under the Land Act, 1964 a person who cultivates the land of other person for a year with his or his family's labour is eligible for acquiring tenancy right. *See* the Land Act 1964 Ss. 2, 25 and 34 (before the 1997 amendment).
94. Land Acquisiton Act, 1977, S. 14.
95. The official memo dated April 7, 1977 states, "for the land acquired vide Nepal Gazette vol.25 no 48 dated March 18, 1976 the compensation to be paid from allotted budget of Rs. 1,000,000.00 is determined by this Committee [CFC] to be Rs. 4000.00 per ropani." *See* the Memo in the file of Pokhara Airport Office.
96. While revising compensation also the committee gives no reason. *See* the decision of the CFC dated Apr 15, 1980 (Chaitra 29, 2036) in the file of Pokhara Airport Office.
97. *See generally* M.C. REGMI, LAND TENURE AND TAXATION IN NEPAL 53-71 (Kathmandu, Ratna Pustak Bhandar 1978).
98. *See* the memos dated April 7, 1977 and April 15, 1980 in the file of Pokhara Airport Office.
99. *Id* Ss 16(1)(b), S 29. h Laa 1977.

100. One secondary school, "Balabhadra Madhyamik Vidyalaya" existed in the project area.

101. Rs. 42,674/91 land Rs. 4,849/49 was paid respectively for the school and the Panchayat Ghar, *see* the official record in the files of Pokhara Airport Office.

102. Land under tillage here should be distinguished from the land under tenancy. Whereas a person cultivating land as a tenant under the Land Act 1964 used to acquire cultivating right, land under tillage here is a land under cultivation arisen out of informal agreement for crop sharing between the owner and the cultivator, with no legal protection of any sort to the latter.

103. *See* notifications in Nepal Gazette, Jan 2, 1982 (vol 31 add no 56, Paush 17, 2038BS); Jan 4, 1982 (vol 31 no 57, Paush 18, 2038 BS); April 19, 1990 (vol 40 add no 2(a) Baisakh 3, 2047 BS).

104. This Regulation provides for spending 30 per cent to 50 per cent of the revenue of the Park and Reserve in the Buffer Zone.

105. However, these are not mutually exclusive.

106. It is seen from the fact that in the whole block of Padao there hardly exists any house of family belonging. to non-Tharu community.

7

CRITICAL ESTIMATES AND SUGGESTIONS FOR REFORMS

7.1 Introduction and Critical Estimate

The main focus of the study on "Project Induced Displacement in Nepal" was to inquire into the nature and extent of protection available to the PAPs under the legal regime of Nepal and see how responsive the Nepalese state is on the issue. It was also to see how far the response of Nepal is in tune with the evolving international regime and the standards developed in some countries of Asia.

We began with a proposition that the Constitution of Nepal guarantees no fewer rights to the PAPs than it does to other citizens or persons.[1] But the foregone analysis of the Constitutional norms and other laws of Nepal revealed that there exists a striking mismatch between the two. Whereas the Constitution lays down a very bold framework of rights, the legal regime relating to the acquisition or requisition of property does not seem to portray same concern towards people and respect for the rights.

It was found that despite the recent initiatives in devolving powers on the institutions of Local Self Government, the introduction of environmental parameters, and a few judicial pronouncements have no doubt striven to change the traditional notion which used to take development as a privilege of the executive, the initiative is yet to be translated into practice. It was also found that the major problem of the Land Acquisition Act,1977 is its non-relevance to the present day situation and its parochial approach towards displacement and RR. A prior appraisal of the project with regard to its purpose, need and its impact on the population and environment are beyond the scope of the Act. It virtually imposes no restriction on the power of the state to acquire property. It does not even uniformly require the authorities to pay market value, let alone the replacement value, as compensation. The individuated notion of compensation does not take into consideration several sources of livelihood and pay for the deprivation of the same before displacing people. Resettlement is left to the executive mercy.[2]

It was also found that the legal regime and the practice of the government of Nepal is not responsive to the international norms nor is it informed of the norms developed to address similar issues in neighbouring and other countries of Asia.[3] This stands substantiated by the findings of the empirical study of the two projects viz., the Royal Suklaphanta Wildlife Project (RSWR) and the Pokhara Airport Project in the far-western and western regions of Nepal respectively.[4] It was found from the empirical study that the approach of the government of Nepal with regard to the project-induced displacement is traditional. The primary motive of the government in both the projects seemed to be the removal of people from the proposed project areas and not to restore their assets or earning capacity or to make them partners in or beneficiaries of development. Whilst the PAPs were adversely affected by a defective Land Acquisition Act, 1977, the approach of the government in the Pokhara Airport Project worsened their condition. The absence of an appropriate legal and policy regime was reflected at every stage of the displacement and resettlement operations in the RSWR project. It was also found that the whole operation in the RSWR was launched in a legal and policy vacuum. The non-abidance by the Kings directives or international standards, the adoption of an ad-hoc approach, absence of vision etc. posed serious adverse ramifications on the rights and entitlements of the PAPs. Whilst it was found that in the Pokhara project, the impoverishment of the PAPs in terms of net asset loss and the holding of livestock was striking, the resettlement operation of the RSWR was marred by lack of concern for alleviating the poverty of the PAPs, in spite of the fact that a majority of them belonged to the lower socio-economic bracket. The absence of plan, lack of transitional support, neglect in the development of infrastructures and basic amenities, absence of post resettlement support met with steep resistance on the part of the PAPs; the series of interruptions and other institutional weaknesses only further complicated the problem in RSWR. Therefore, in the light of the constitutional norms and international legal standards presented in earlier chapters and the findings of the empirical study, an attempt has been made here to address the following two questions which recur in the mind.

(a) What would be the correct approach to the question of displacement?; and

(b) If a project is permissible under the domestic and international norms what would be the correct approach with regard to the payment of compensation, resettlement and rehabilitation of the PAPs?

7.2 Approach to Displacement

As the issue of development and displacement are interlinked with each other, there is a need to look at them holistically.[5] It has been clarified earlier that displacement is not only a problem of development. It is more a human, social and human rights problem. Thus, guarantee of rights, the concern for social and economic justice, and the orientation of the Constitution to overall development, all taken together, fix benchmarks for evolving a set of yardsticks with regard to displacement. These have been discussed earlier in various places. We will cursorily touch upon them once again here.

7.2.1 Displacement in the Context of Rights

The rights which come to the fore in the context of displacement inter alia are rights to life, liberty, equality, freedom of movement, residence, right to information, right to privacy, right to culture, right to education, right to property etc.[6] The International Bills of human rights also seeks to guarantee similar rights.[7] The very purpose of incorporating these rights in the Constitution was to impose restrictions on the power of a transient majority. Once rights are guaranteed the government is not free to treat them as commodities of convenience.[8] To the extent rights are guaranteed they operate as a shield against certain types of governmental action regardless of the end that the government is professing to achieve as the framework of the Constitution is generally based on the primacy in individual rights and freedoms over social good. It is therefore said that rights create a space of autonomy.[9] So long as rights are exercised within permissible limits invasion to rights is proscribed. Modern constitutional jurisprudence goes beyond non-intervention and imposes a duty on the state to protect the rights against all possible threats as invasions are possible not only by the state but by other persons as well.[10] Facilitation of the enjoyment of rights by creating an appropriate environment, including legislative measures especially in the interest of weaker section, is another aspect of the state's duty.[11] Further, the guarantee of the rights and the imposition of limits on their derogation create a presumption in favour of the enjoyment of the rights. This essentially means that unless the proposed state action is permissible under the Constitution, the rights are considered inviolable.

In a democratic order the guarantee of rights besides

respecting individual freedoms and choices, also bears implications for the governance. Where the Constitution guarantees rights,[12] it would permit the scrutiny of state action[13] in the light of (a) its impact on the guaranteed rights, and (b) its conformity or non-conformity with the development objectives. The guarantee of constitutional remedy as a fundamental right, and the power vested in the Supreme Court to review any law or state action make the scrutiny a necessary and viable process under the Constitution of Nepal.

The legality of state action resulting in displacement is questioned mainly because of its discriminatory effect. The perceived discrimination in the context of displacement is two fold. On the one hand the exploitation and siphoning of resources deprives those directly dependent on it for their survival, on the other, the expropriation of property and means of livelihood without fully exonerating the affected person further generates and deepens inequitable living conditions. Any state action having discriminatory content or effect or, a state action, which is unfair, unjust or unreasonable or which invades other rights guaranteed by the Constitution goes against the letter and spirit of the equality clause.[14] Therefore, justness, fairness, and reasonableness of the policy decision are major considerations in the context of displacement which would all be judicially reviewable.

The legality of state actions leading to displacement also needs to be juxtaposed with the right to life. The emergence of the integrative approach to fundamental rights enables one to link various other rights, like the right to choose residence, right to trade, occupation, right to information etc. also as a corollary extensions of the right to life, though several of these rights are entrenched in separate provisions in the Constitution. The expansive connotation of right to life has added more petals into its foliage and thereby transcended its doctrinaire meaning. Now, right to life encompasses a right to life with human dignity and a few more attendant rights.[15] The Supreme Court of Nepal has already engrafted some of these rights, like the right to a healthy environment, right to culture and heritage as constitutive rights in the overarching sweep of right to life.[16] If the present trend is any indication, there is a likelihood of further expansion of right to life to include the right to subsistence conducive to a dignified life as forming a part of the right to life. The deprivation of life in the context of displacement would essentially mean that if the project in effect impoverishes the prospective oustees and other persons likely to be affected then it can be argued that it deprives them of their right to live with dignity and hence against the constitutional protection to the right to life.

State action affecting the right to life and personal liberty under a constitutional order is possible only when such action meets both substantive as well as procedural requirements.[17] This is also of immense significance in the context of displacement as most of the people to be adversely affected belong to the poor and the marginalised section. Life with human dignity would require the fulfillment of basic necessities like adequate nutrition, clothing shelter, educational facilities, means of expression etc. Logically where a person possesses some of these rights (for instance, shelter in this context) this would mean that he/she has a right not to be deprived of these rights. The declaration of these rights also means entitlement to these rights. In this sense the state is under a duty to fulfill these rights under Part IV of the Constitution. It is submitted that the possible impact of displacement on the right to life is one such substantive consideration that needs to be kept in mind while developing a correct approach on displacement. It is further submitted that the bottom line for any state action is that it should not result in deprivation of right to life.

Displacement also affects freedom of movement, residence, trade, occupation etc. Arguably, freedom of movement within its ambit also includes the freedom not to move. In case a person (in this context a citizen) is forcibly evicted, the freedom of movement probably includes a right to return to the original habitat. Like the freedom of movement, the right to freedom of residence also carries both positive and negative connotations.[18] The non-interference with residence and property is firmly entrenched in the Constitution of Nepal separately in addition to the freedom of movement and residence guaranteed under Art 12(2)(d). The interference with residence and property would be permissible only under conditions laid down by the law.[19] Where the state action results in interference to these rights it is also necessary to see that these restrictions are in consonance with the underlined principles recognizing these rights and are not confiscatory in nature even where interference with the right is permissible.[20] Therefore, in the context of the constitutional promise to ensure social and economic justice it seems very much plausible to argue that under the Constitution of Nepal a person(s) possesses "a right not to be arbitrarily displaced of his/her home or the place of habitual residence and environment under which he/she has been making living possible."

Besides, the Constitutional provisions, the International Bill of Human Rights guarantees a host of these rights.[21] These rights bear special meaning in the Nepalese context for several reasons. First, guarantee and respect for basic human rights is the promise of the Constitution of Nepal.[22] Secondly, the Nepalese legal system embraces possibility of application of international law in the domestic regime.[23] And, finally, as Nepal is a party to the Optional Protocol, access is now available to the people to make communication to the Human Right Committee for redressing violation of human rights.[24]

The issue of displacement is basically an issue of human rights. What essentially makes it an issue of human rights is (a) the adverse effect on a broad range of guaranteed rights and lack of protection to basic rights of PAPs, (b) the amount of arbitrariness involved in the decision making process, (c) the use of force, and (d) the involvement of the state in the operation.[25] Eviction of people without the provision of access to appropriate forms of legal and other substantial remedies are nothing but a violation on human rights.[26] In fact the international instruments of human rights carry the same tone and tenor and provide force to the rights entrenched in the Constitution. It is interesting to note that the constitutional recognition of "a right not to be arbitrarily displaced" is implicitly supported by international human rights law[27] and very explicitly supported by the emerging norms on human rights[28] and environment.[29] The possibility of international human rights instruments being interpreted as part of domestic law, further reinforces the right not to be arbitrarily displaced enshrined in the Constitution of Nepal.

Prima facie, invasion to rights without the authority of law is arbitrary. The "law" under which restriction on rights would be permissible should be a valid law and not a mere nomenclature. Secondly, it should be just, fair and reasonable and not confiscatory, fanciful, oppressive or discriminatory. This means to say that it should be fair, just and reasonable to the victims as well as the beneficiaries of development. Thirdly, it should not result in impairment of the guarantee of fundamental rights. Fourthly, it should also take into consideration the existing social practices rooted in the notion of survival. And finally, such law should contain a minimum moral content. But when one comes to the characteristics for a valid law in the particular context of displacement there are several areas where it becomes difficult to conclusively take a stand as to whether or not any intervention on rights is permissible or it would amount to arbitrariness. In what follows we will look into this issue.

7.2.2 *Displacement and Public Interest*

The Constitution provides an opening to the state to restrict some of the rights of the citizen in public interest. "Public interest" is a permitted ground to impose restriction on the freedom of residence, trade and occupation. The state is also empowered to acquire, requisition and create encumbrance in "public interest".[30]

The issue of "public interest" is a very thorny one in the context of displacement. The power of the state to acquire, requisition or encumber property is often linked with the power of eminent domain. The power of eminent domain is an attribute of sovereign power of the state arising out of public necessity. But it is not an absolute power. The very notion of a democratic order presupposes that the exercise of this power is to be limited by the constitutional confines. It was clarified that the concept of eminent domain is not a proprietary right of the state originating from the notion of the state as *parens patriae*. The constitutional requirement that the acquisition, requisition or creation of encumbrance on property is to be possible only by paying compensation rejects the notion of *parens patriae*.[31]

The concept of "public interest" is of course not a uni-dimensional concept. On what constitutes "a public interest" and what constitutes "a private interest" multitude of opinions and views may exist. The difference of opinion between economists and lawyers is also not less striking. Whereas any decision of the state, which results in general welfare of the community or a section thereof or any venture of the state resulting capital accumulation through revenue generating or export promoting schemes may be looked upon by economists as sufficiently serving "public interest," such a broad generalization may not be acceptable to lawmen. Though no fixed definition of "public interest" or other cognate expressions like "public purpose"[32] or "public use"[33] have been attempted by courts so far, certain yardsticks and assumptions have been developed in other countries to curb the abuse of power. Therefore, what needs to be reemphasized here is that the public nature of the project and the necessity of the state to involve in the project should be looked into while accepting the claim of "public interest". If the project is warranted by public necessity, does not deprive persons of their basic human rights, and the benefit to the community is direct and paramount and not merely incidental, then the project may be said to serve "public interest." On the contrary, if public benefits are merely incidental or if the private interest too clearly dominates, it is plausible to hold that such a project doesn't serve public interest as required by the Constitution.

The "Instruments of Instructions", as the Directive Principles are generally referred to, by laying down broad parameters for development, have, to some extent, made the job of both policy makers and judges easier in determining "public interest". However, as the Instrument of Instructions also contain some value premises requiring reconciliation,[34] they do not altogether eliminate the necessity for prioritizing existing value premises nor do they rule out the need to draw up new value premises for the greater good of the common.[35] Prioritization of value premises would provide better linkage to the concept of public interest and prevent the gratification of the naked preference of the stronger ones. This may sometimes appear to be disputable, but it is nevertheless desirable, when situation demands and the Constitution permits. The promise of "social, economic and political justice" and the "equitable distribution of economic gains," "promotion of human right," and a more categorical statement on the impermissible ends, for instance (a) concentration of available resources and means of the country in a limited section of the society or (b) economic exploitation of any class or individual, (c) damage to environment etc. would enable the policy makers and judges to review public preferences and interests that the proposed project is intended to serve. It is true that with the march of a nation on the path of development, the category of public values (interest) may expand or contract. Such expansion or contraction would not however change the permanent benchmarks pegged by the Constitution. In the context of displacement it is therefore submitted that any state action, which blatantly goes against the notion of economic and social justice enshrined in the Constitution, and more particularly a project which allows or facilitates the concentration of available resources and means of the country within a limited section of the society, or (b) directly or indirectly fosters economic and social inequalities, or (c) goes against equitable distribution of economic gains on the basis of social justice[36] will most unlikely to be in "public interest" and hence arbitrary.

The question as to who is to decide whether or not a project causing displacement serves "public interest" is an equally important one that needs to be looked into in the context of displacement. This question again takes us back to the issue of development, which is blended with a gloss of meanings and interpretations. Suffice here to say that the constitutional framework of Nepal proposes a right based concept of development. It sufficiently indicates that the objective of the development process envisioned in the Constitution is realization and enjoyment of rights even by persons at the lowest level of the socio-economic ladder. It rejects the traditional notion of development having over-reliance on the increment of national capital alone. Therefore, in the constitutional context, a suitable definition of development would be desirable. A more acceptable definition of development in the light of the constitutional premise of

Nepal appears to be the definition given by the UN Declaration on the Right to Development, which defines development as "a comprehensive, economic, social, cultural and political *process*". The aim of this process is the "constant improvement of the well-being of the *entire population and of all individuals* on the basis of *their active, free and meaningful participation* in the development and in the fair distribution of benefits resulting therefrom".[37]

A participatory process of development underlined in the UN Declaration on Right to Development brings the human person (both as individuals and collectivities) to the centre stage and makes them active participants and beneficiaries of development.[38] It also casts a duty on the state to formulate "appropriate development policies" through a participatory process.[39] The participation is required to be "active, free and meaningful." This is rather a pro-active form of participation and not a reactive one. The notion of appropriate development maintains a rational relation with participatory development. The dissemination of information, and creation of a dialogical space for stake-holders and civil society, which facilitates and fosters participation are prerequisites for active, free and meaningful participation. Any paternalistic development policy which takes the people as the object and not as subject of development stands delegitimised by the notion of appropriate development policy.[40]

The Constitution of Nepal, in tune with the emerging international norms ordains, a representative government and a participatory development process.[41] The guarantee of the freedom of opinion,[42] and the right to information,[43] calls for a transparent, people-centered, accountable and consultative process.[44] It should be noted that a citizen is empowered to seek information even from persons when the information sought relates to activities affecting other persons (i.e., an information of public importance). This has now been clearly recognised in the Constitution[45] as well as in the burgeoning norms on environment and human rights.[46] Now, with the incorporation of the right to information as a fundamental right, the Constitution has made open government a rule, and secrecy the exception. Where the exigencies require secrecy, the state can maintain it only by law and not by executive fiat. The implicit presumption on the matter is that the government documents are public unless a legal provision states otherwise. A right to access to such documents is proved when the person proves that the information sought is of public importance. Except this, the citizen seeking such information need not establish any *standi* for the same.[47]

Dissemination of information is a pre-condition for participation. A complete and thorough study of the project on the human, social, economic and environmental impact on present and future generation, a thorough debate on the public necessity, alternatives distribution of cost and benefits are basic considerations to be resolved through this process. A few case laws developed in Nepal lend support for and reinforce the right to information.[48] Therefore, it is submitted that in the context of displacement the PAPs collectively through their representatives are the persons to decide whether or not a project serves genuine public interest. Such a process, if established and institutionalised, will end the practice of putting project over people and the culture of benefiting a section of people at the livelihood cost of others.[49]

Secondly, when there arises a dispute as to whether or not a project serves "public interest," it has to be decided by the judiciary taking into view the possible human, social, economic and environmental considerations. The notion which offers more weights to executive wisdom over the rights of the affected persons would go against the constitutional promise of liberty, equality and justice, the notion of development discussed above and also the responsibility accorded to the judiciary as the custodian of the Constitution. Courts in other countries, more particularly in the US, have developed several yardsticks to determine a cognate expression "public use." A discussion on this has been made earlier while highlighting the US experience.[50] Some of the yardsticks developed there are also important for our purpose. Given the economic, and subsistence scenario in Nepal while determining whether or not a project serves "public interest", the judicial effort should be geared toward ensuring that in no case people's means of subsistence are snatched way. This is important because the state in no case is empowered to deprive people of their means of subsistence.[51] In the light of the constitutional responsibility it is submitted that the notion, which regards the executive as first judge or good judge or best judge, has ceased to have relevance in the Nepalese constitutional context, and therefore, need not be given any weight.

7.2.3 Displacement and Distributive Justice

In recent times, the question of distributive justice has assumed much importance in the context of project decisions and, more specifically, in projects involving heavy social and environmental costs.[52] Distributive justice in the form of social, economic and political justice is the signature tone of the Constitution of Nepal. It needs to be understood in the light of socio-economic reality of the country and not only in a doctrinaire sense.[53] Some factors, like heavy dependence of the people on agriculture, scarcity of land and low productivity of the available land, skewed distribution of land and income, concentration of social economic and political power in a handful of traditional elite[54] sufficiently indicate in whose favour should development plans be designed. The Constitution is not a colourless and neutral document or a dry and lifeless parchment. It is a document with a social purpose and an economic mission. It is an instrument heavily weighed in favour of the weaker section and promises to establish a new socio-economic order based on egalitarianism and social justice.[55] Therefore, it is submitted that any project which causes displacement should be "to the greatest benefit of the least advantaged"[56] of the PAPs so that they will be in a position to have a reach to other social economic goods, by exercising their other rights. Similarly, equitable distribution of the cost and benefit of the project also falls under the rubric of distributive justice. Linking of the displacement with poverty alleviation measures is one viable strategy ensuring distributive justice, which deserves attention in the context of displacement.

Another aspect of justice is the justice to resources. Distributive justice on the one hand demands equal access of the weakest section to the resources of the country; on the other, it also requires policy makers to look into the question of sustainable use of the resources in the interest of the present as well as future generation.[57]

A majority of the peoples in Nepal live in the mountain areas.[58] As most of these areas are food deficit,[59] people in these areas rely on narrow valleys, relatively flatter lands at lower elevation and river stripes for food supply. Besides, mountain areas are supported by the food production in Terai, which physically covers only 14.3 percent of the total territory. Therefore, any large project that comes up in the Terai land or the valleys and other low lying areas affects the life not only of those directly depending on the acquired land but also of all those in the far flung areas who depend on the food supply from the project areas. Therefore, in view of the need to ensure sustainable development and distributive justice one major consideration in the context of displacement would be the prioritization of preservation of the cultivated and culturable land, and also inclusion and evaluation of the social and environmental cost to be incurred by the project.

7.3 Approach to Compensation, Resettlement and Rehabilitation

The recognition of the "right not to be arbitrarily displaced," as argued earlier, does not rule out displacement altogether. It essentially requires the state to be more responsive and accountable, and attempts to usher a people centered development process by meeting certain substantive and procedural considerations. The very fact that rights are not guaranteed in absolute terms offers a space for maneuverability for the "greater good of the common". Though rights are claims on society, better protection of rights is possible only under an economically prosperous and vibrant society. Therefore, it is also necessary to have a correct approach to compensation, resettlement and rehabilitation with the presupposition that under the Constitution of Nepal avenues exist for the state to impose certain amount of restrictions on personal rights.

Displacement is not limited to the expropriation of property or removal of people and the payment of compensation. It involves larger issues and its effects are quite wide and deep. It uproots people from their homes, place of habitual residence, takes away employment and other sources of earning, fragments and destabilizes cultures etc. It is now felt that even with the best compensatory laws on expropriation of property, the risk of impoverishment would not be eliminated.[60] As the rights guaranteed by the Constitution or the international human rights instruments do not stop at the door of PAPs,[61] it is therefore necessary to take compensation, resettlement and rehabilitation as complementary and supplementary to each other and see that the rights of the PAPs are respected before displacement, during displacement and after resettlement as well.[62] There is no reason why PAPs should sacrifice their life for the benefit of others. So the overall objective of the integrated approach would have to be that the people affected by the project benefit from the project. Linking the project with poverty alleviation measure and restoration of assets and earning capacity of the PAPs to a higher level than pre-move level should be considered as bottom line for state action.

The governing law of Nepal on acquisition does not look at displacement, resettlement and rehabilitation in an integrative sense. Though attempts have been made to mitigate the rigor of the law through project specific guidelines, unless the question of legality of these Guidelines is solved and is given universal application, these Guidelines are unlikely to protect the interest of weaker sections.[63] The question of legal streamlining for the protection of PAPs has become paramount in the context of liberalization where more openings are created for private enterprises in areas traditionally assigned for the state like harnessing of water resource, mining etc.

There are various other considerations that need to be addressed to give effect to the integrative objective. These will be discussed while advancing suggestions for reforms.

7.4 Suggestions for Reforms

The suggestions for reforms are based on the discussion made in earlier chapters and the major findings of the empirical study. The mismatch between the constitutional and the international norms on the one hand and the existing legal and institutional arrangements on the other can be mitigated and harmonised through two process, viz., the judicial process and the legislative process. In some countries, the response to the issue of displacement, resettlement and rehabilitation in recent times is emerging in the form of either project specific or general RR policies or law.[64] Most of these policies are modeled after the Guidelines of the World Bank and other financial institutions and tailored to suit the domestic requirements. In fact, there is nothing wrong to find resonance of the policies developed elsewhere should that suit the local requirement. But any policy or law, which errs in favour of imitating than grasping local needs, retains less chances of success.

A connected question relating to reform is a choice between a policy and law on RR. There also exists a chance of adopting a mixed model of both law and policy, where the law would fix the basic parameters and the rest would be left to the realm of policy. But when there is a choice between a policy and a law the relative advantage or disadvantage of both needs to be examined.

A major advantage of a policy over a law is its flexibility and adaptability to the changing circumstance and time. But all the same, it contains some inherent weaknesses. First, when displacement is a legal consequence, an attempt to address RR through policy appears to be a lighter antidote. Secondly, fixing accountability on recalcitrant officials becomes difficult on the basis of a policy. Thirdly, as policies generally do not open up the jurisdiction of the court, redressing grievance through judicial institutions on the basis of a policy becomes unattainable. And, finally, a policy can any time be amended, withdrawn or even ignored. Thus, a law either enacted or judiciary made, appears to be more promising than a policy to be framed by the government. The law reduces the chances of dilution of commitment, once major contours are fixed, rights recognised and responsibilities assigned.

7.4.1 The Judicial Process

The Constitution of Nepal holds immense possibilities for judicial initiatives for protecting rights of the PAPs.[65] The notion of the system of justice envisioned by the Constitution is not only an "independent" but also a "competent" one.[66] The Supreme Court is the custodian of the Constitution.[67] The Constitution confers power on the courts and other judicial institutions to deliver justice "in accordance with the provisions of the Constitution, the laws and the recognised principles of justice."[68] Given the general premise of the Constitution, in the context of displacement it may be argued that the Constitution offers the possibility of judicial scrutiny of several issues including the "public interest" on a case to case basis.

Basing on a presumption in favour of rights one can contend that it would not be sufficient for the government to state that the project serves a "public interest" in vague terms, the burden would have to lie on the government to prove that the stated purpose genuinely serves public interest. The courts can examine whether or not there exists a sufficiently close connection between the stated purpose and the service the project offers or intends to offer. If the project fails to demonstrate sufficiently close connection then the averment on "public interest" would become suspect.

In the scrutiny of "public interest" by the court on a case by case basis, another issue that needs examination is the search for less displacing alternatives. Here courts can, by asking the government to furnish the report on the study on alternatives and by constituting its own team of experts, determine "public interest", should the exigency so require. In several instances courts have successfully brushed aside the skepticism that they lack the capacity to review government decisions which are based on economic or technical considerations. There is no reason, why the courts cannot adopt the same approach in reviwing the stated objective on a displacing project.

There are several other issues as for instance, issues relating to the environmental study, the adequacy or non-adequacy of compensation or congruence or non-congruence of the law, policy or practice on RR with the fundamental norms that generally come for redressal before the courts. In a liberal democratic order the role of the court in deciding both regulated and unregulated disputes need not have to be over-emphasised. Therefore, given the power, which the Supreme Court holds under the Constitution, and also the responsibility it is bestowed with to give effect to the human rights norms, it can very much look into both justiciability and of public purpose justifiability of the project, and issue guidelines to mitigate the hardships that the PAPs face.[69]

Despite such possibility, over-reliance on the settlement of every kind of dispute is, however, coupled with risks. There are some inherent weaknesses of the judicial process. In the first place, it judicialises the whole process. Secondly, owing to cost and time factors, the judiciary is beyond the reach of common masses. Finally, unless the courts issue uniform guidelines, judicial rulings are less likely to be uniformly abided. Therefore, social interest litigation may not always be a very viable option available to the PAPs.

7.4.2 The Legislative Process

Under this process either of the two options, viz., (a) the amendment and expansion of the existing law,[70] and (b) formulation of a totally new law by scrapping the deficient law, can be adopted. The important issues in either of the two relate to the basic objectives, major considerations, processes and procedures, institutional arrangement for implementation, grievance redressing system, horizontal and vertical coordination between the implementing agency and other organ provision for budget. Expanding the existing law or drafting a new law is therefore, only a matter of strategy. While a detailed law proposed on displacement, acquisition of property, payment of compensation, and resettlement and rehabilitation is appended as annexure, the basic framework of the law is outlined here.

7.4.2.1 Outline of the Proposed Policy and Law on Displacement, Resettlement and Rehabilitation

(a) Objective and Major Considerations

The main objective of the law should be to avoid and minimise displacement. And where displacement is unavoidable, the PAPs should benefit from the Project. The law should aim at restoring the asset and earning capacity to higher than the pre-move level, and in case of people falling below the internationally determined poverty line it should aim at restoring life above poverty line.

The law should recognise the rights of the prospective displacees and other persons (citizens and also non-citizens to the extent their rights are guaranteed by the existing law) likely to be affected from the project, not to be arbitrarily displaced. Where a project is permissible under the Constitution and the law, the law should recognise the right of the PAPs to be fully compensated, resettled and rehabilitated. Where the property acquired is not used for the stated purpose within a reasonable time, the law should reognise the right of the original holder to get back the property.

The prospective PAPs whose lives are likely to be profoundly affected by the project do possess a right to be informed and consulted before being displaced. A right to demand the supply of full information about the nature of the project, its size, its possible impact on human and environment (including a right to participate in the EIA studies), search for an alternative, and results of the search, strategies proposed to mitigate the hardship and mitigate adverse effects on environment, should be recognised. The right of PAPs to negotiate and actively participate in decisions concerning their displacement should be recognised. Where displacement occurs, the rights of the PAPs to timely and adequate restitution, compensation and resettlement should be recognised. Similarly, the right of the PAPs to preservation of the unique heritage and environment should be recognised.

It should be made mandatory for the state to bring out a clear statement of the project objective. It must provide a comprehensive listing of all options and comparative costing of all options for achieving the objectives. Similarly, the distribution of benefits among different sections of society and among different regions and in particular, the gender distribution of benefits must be revealed and clarified before the project gets sanctioned.[71] Further, the EIA study of both evacuation site and the resettlement site should be made a precondition for project initiatives. This will allow the person likely to be affected and the civil society to effectively question whether or not a project is in public interest.

Dissemination of information by radio, television and newspaper and a debate on appropriate representative fora (depending on the size effect of the project, House of Representative or other Institutions of Local Self-Government) should be made mandatory. Where the project is likely to affect socially and economically weaker sections their informed consent should be made mandatory

The protection and preservation of available cultivable land should be high priority in any development measure. The short term as well the long term impact on environment and the sustainability of resources at local regional and national level by projects should be included in major considerations in the planning process.

All those persons likely to be affected by the project, without discrimination of sex, age, race, caste or religion, marital status, holding, occupation, avocation or calling, who are residing in the area to be vacated at least three years before the decision to undertake a project should be eligible for claiming rights and benefiting from the project. Legality or illegality of holding or use of land or other resources should not be a ground for discriminatory treatment among PAPs. Those physically displaced as well as those economically displaced, including those who depend for sustenance on land owned by other or CPR or those whose life depends in some way on the economy of the area to be acquired should be considered as PAPs.

The cost of displacement and resettlement and rehabilitation including transitional support should form a part of the project cost. The loss of environment and other social cost should also be taken into view while determining the feasibility of the project.

A social and economic survey and population census should precede the determination of compensation. Updating of land records and survey of land should form a part of this process. Compensation should be based on the social, economic and family survey of the prospective PAPs. The loss of every source of income and subsistence for e.g., the loss of earning opportunity, loss of common property resource, culture heritage etc. should be accounted for while determining compensation. The basis of compensation should be the replacement cost. While determining the compensation not only the present value but also the future development possibility of the area to be condemned for the project should also be taken into view. In the case of PAPs falling below poverty line, restoration of life above poverty line should be the criteria for payment of compensation. The legality of holding should not be a basis for compensation. Where the resources are collectively managed for e.g. the community or religious forests, arrangements should be made in such a way that everyone gets his legitimate share of the compensation paid for.

Where the project is likely to adversely affect a person around the project whose land is not acquired but who is substantially adversely affected in terms of diminution of value of property, loss of productivity etc., such person should be eligible for claiming compensation and compensation should be paid or the same.

For determination of compensation, distribution of the same and other benefits, every member of the family irrespective of age and sex should be considered as a separate unit. In case of minor members their health, education and future dependence on parental property should be taken into view while fixing compensation. Local and customary rights of PAPs should also be taken into view while paying compensation.

Except in case of emergency there should be no displacement prior to the payment of compensation and arrangement for resettlement. Where natural calamities like sudden flood, change in the course of river, landslide or similar other situation require immediate eviction of people, a reasonable time for the transport of belonging, stored food and animals, and other movable property should be given. In such a situation, transitional requirements of the PAPs including shelter, food, and other minimum expenses for survival should be met by the authorities acquiring property and other resettlement and rehabilitation measures should be promptly followed.

The PAPs should be informed in advance about the amount and type of compensation that they are eligible to. Resettlement should be an integral part of the compensation package. In the case of families having agriculture as the main occupation, land-based resettlement should be mandatory.

The minimum amount of land to be provided should be determined by taking into account the availability of irrigation, productivity, price index of the region for settlement. The minimum land to be provided should enable the family to meet its yearly food requirement. Gender concerns should be kept in mind while transferring the land to the PAPs. The resettling authorities should ensure that no one is left homeless and without means of income after resettlement. Land to be given to the PAPs should be free from all encumbrances.

Option should be given to the PAPs either to accept or to decline the resettlement package devised by the authorities.

However, in case of tribals and other agro-based socially and economically weaker sections having no other viable means of income, the right to choose cash compensation in lieu of land should be supported by appropriate guarantee. The PAPs should be given at least one opportunity to review their decision either to accept or reject the land-based resettlement.

As far as possible, PAPs eligible for resettlement should be resettled in group. The distance between the original site and the resettlement site should be minimised. Group resettlement should be mandatory in case of agriculture based communities.

Acquisition of land by mutual agreement should not deprive the PAPs of the benefit of resettlement and rehabilitation.[72] However, the executing authorities may decline to avail land based resettlement to absentee owners and landlords, or PAPs who obtain compensation substantially higher (say 5 times) than the annual income of the person on the poverty line, or are left with land which is more in area than the land to be given to the PAPs in the resettlement site, or whose income from other sources is substantially higher (say at least five times more) than the income of the person from agriculture at the poverty line.

Multiple displacement should be avoided as far as possible. Where multiple displacement is unavoidable, the PAP should get at least double benefit that a PAP normally gets, if he/she is to be displaced or substantially affected within 20 years of the first displacement. The PAP should be eligible for similar benefits on every succeeding displacement.

The transitional support to the PAPs should accrue in the form of food support and subsidies, grant for house construction, land reclamation, fertilizer, seeds etc. In case of non-agricultural families provision for training, employment and other schemes of self employment and income generation should be made. Special attention should be given to the effect on health of women, children and elderly persons.

Resettlement should achieve complete social and economic re-establishment of those dislocated on a viable productive basis through intensive agricultural initiatives, establishment of industries, and development of service sector etc. Intensive farming, use of local niche etc can form the part of the strategy to raise income of PAPs.

The RR should to be to the mutual benefit of the host and the PAPs. Both PAPs and the host community should be involved in planning and execution of the RR package. Representation of women, and PAPs belonging to socially backward and economically weaker class should be ensured in the planning and execution of resettlement. Resettlement plan should be broad based and should have popular acceptance. The impact of resettlement on the natural and socio-economic environment should be mitigated and offset. Environmental impact assessment of the resettlement site through a participatory process should be made mandatory.

As far as possible, the PAPs should be resettled in the benefit zone of the project. Efforts should be made to improve housing condition, sanitation and general environment in the RR site. Care should be taken to meet the present and future need of the PAPs. Post resettlement support should be continued until PAPs do not re-establish in the new surroundings.

Project should contribute positively to the overall development of the surrounding community by catering the need of the community in education, health, sanitation, and by creating opportunity for income generation. Relocation of cultural and religious site should be mandatory.

(b) Process and Procedure

Displacement, resettlement and rehabilitation should be

based on a conscious and purposeful decision. PAPs should be given adequate and reasonable notice before the scheduled date of displacement. The eligibility for compensation, the method of valuation of compensation and procedure for addressing grievance on compensation should be adequately publicised. The compensation should be determined by a body having the representation of PAPs, and after giving a due hearing to claims of PAPs.

Identity of the executing authorities, their powers and function should be adequately publicised among the PAPs.

Authorities should ensure that except in case of emergency like sudden natural calamity and similar other grave situation no displacement occurs before compensation being paid or PAPs being resettled. Timely allocation of sufficient budget is important in successful execution of the resettlement package. The choice of the PAPs to opt for RR or cash should be recorded and sufficient time should be given to him to review his decision.

Development of infrastructure and basic amenities should be completed before resettling PAPs. The available facility in the resettlement site should be publicised well in advance so that the PAPs may make reasoned choice whether or not to take the RR package. Implementing authorities should be made accountable for failure to develop infrastructure after resettlement as a breach of contract. Resettlement should be completed at least before the land is condemned for the project. Rehabilitation process should synchronized with the main project component. Efforts should be made to minimise transition period. Time should be prescribed for displacement and the completion of RR package. PAPs should be given enough opportunity to plan their resettlement.

(c) Institutional Arrangement

Keeping in mind the magnitude, recurrence of displacement

and the type of RR plan, two types of institutional arrangements can be envisaged. Where RR operation is to be integrated with the main project component, the overall responsibility of executing the RR package should lie with the Planning, Implementation and Monitoring Committee (henceforth PIMC). Where RR is conceived as a stand-alone project the responsibility of executing it should lie with a permanent government or semi-government body with adequate representation of PAPs and non-governmental organizations in the planing and execution of the RR in coordination with the PIMC. The views of the PAPs should get priority about the kind of RR which would be suitable for them. Participation of PAPs through their representatives at every stage of RR should be made mandatory. Responsibilities should be assigned to a permanent government body to cause post rehabilitation evaluation. The state should encourage the involvement of civil society in tandem with PAPs in all possible spheres of activities right from the planning to the execution of the project, resettlement and rehabilitation operation, evaluation, monitoring, research and other activities.

(d) Grievance Redressing Mechanism

The right to remedy against possible human or environmental harm should be recognised. Similarly, the right of the PAPs to a hearing on the compensation and redressing of grievances relating to RR through appropriate fora including the court should be clarified in the law. The provision of punishment for failure to fulfil duty should be incorporated in the law.

(e) Coordination

It must be made a mandatory duty for every branch of the government to assist the authorities in planning and executing the project including the RR package. In case of any law and order problem arising due to encroachment by pseudo PAPs or any other eventualities, it should be a mandatory duty of the police and armed force located in the district to abide by the order of the Chief Executing Officer, and should be executed as the command of their own superior.

7.6 Concluding Remarks

The objective of presenting the outline of the comprehensive policy and law on displacement, resettlement and rehabilitation, as stressed earlier, is to remove the mismatch between the constitutional norm and the existing legal and institutional regime and to correct the inadequacy of the latter to protect the rights and interest of the PAPs. Though the outline of policy and legal reform will be handy for drawing both policy and legal regime on displacement, resettlement and rehabilitation, the objective in emphasis on framing a law, besides the reasons stated earlier, was also to make the state more responsive to its international obligations set out in international human rights and environmental law instruments.

The Constitution of Nepal envisages estabilishing a just system. It is a system of reason which is just even to those upon whose rights it intends to impose restrictions. And when one argues that under the constitutional framework PAPs do possess a right not to be arbitrarily displaced, it essentially means the law imposing restriction meets both procedural and substantive requirements as set by the Constitution.

It is no doubt that the formulation of a legal framework is only the first step. It is also true that a good law does not always ensure good result. The interplay of various factors like the institutional commitment, allocation of budget, evaluation monitoring and timely correction of mistakes and more importantly the support of the civil society and the PAPs is instrumental in turning impoverishment risks into an avenue of progress.

The proposed legal regime attempts to cover and correct all the adverse effects like landlessness, homelessness, joblessness, economic deprivation, and cultural scattering, etc. as illustrated in the First Chapter. For instance, the possibility of homelessness has been addressed by imposing the duty on the state to ensure that no one remains homeless because of displacement. The Draft Law (annexure 1) neatly draws a scheme aimed at addressing all the impoverishment risks. The proposed regime, however, leaves out several economic considerations and controversies related to resettlement and rehabilitation not because they are considered to be unimportant but because of the considered view that if human beings have a right to live with dignity the economic logic should follow the logic of rights. Therefore, it is submitted that if adopted and seriously implemented the proposed regime will herald a more people centered development process.

It is encouraging to note that in recent times quite a few countries have formulated law or policies on RR, but still one of the best kept secrets of resettlement is its implementation failure. The recent study conducted by the World Bank shows a rampant failure of RR operations in the Bank financed projects.[73] This is happening in many countries despite project specific or general policies being in place at the behest of the financing agencies.

It is now realised that a project with a good resettlement package will always have better chance of delivering more benefits than an ill designed project. Moreover, benefit sharing generates vested interest in the project and avoids adversarial relation and reduces resistance. It also establishes the moral base for the project as the benefits are not accrued to people at the expense of the PAPs. It is hoped that the draft law proposed here, if adopted into law and implemented honestly will solve most of these problems and end the pro-industry and pro-state bias of the existing law, help to evolve a balanced approach to development and make the state responsive to its constitutional and international obligations.

REFERENCES

1. For a detailed discussion on this, *see supra* ch 2.
2. This had been discussed in *supra* ch 3.
3. This has been highlighted in *supra* ch 4 and 5.
4. This has been highlighted in *supra* ch 6.
5. In the absence of a consensus on the concept of development, delimiting the ambit of displacement in the context of development is not an easy task. But is submitted that in view of the major contours being drawn in the form of constitutional prescriptions enshrined in Part III and Part IV of the Constitution of Nepal and the concept of development propagated in the UN Declaration on Right to Development, 1986, and the concept of sustainable development propagated by the UN Declaration on Human Environment 1972, and the UN Declaration on Environment and Development 1992, as discussed in previous chapters, drawing up of substantive and procedural yardsticks is now possible.
6. NEP CONST Art 11,12,16,17,22.
7. Displacement threatens a broad range of rights guaranteed various in Bills. *See e.g.*, life liberty and security of person, Universal Declaration on Human Rights [GS Res. 217 (III) A, U.N.GOAR 3rd Session, 10 December 1948 at 71 UN Doc. A 810 (1948) (henceforth UDHR)], Art 3; International Covenant on Civil and Political Rights, [G.A. Res 200A, U.N.GOAR 21st Session, 16 Dec. 1966, Supp. No 16 at 53 U.N. Doc A 6316 (henceforth ICCPR)] Art 6; right to freedom of movement and residence [UDHR 13 (1)] right against arbitrary interference with an individuals home and privacy (UDHR Art 12, ICCPR Art 17) right to property [UDHR Art 17 (2)], right to health [UDHR] Art 25(1), right to participate in the government (UDHR Art 21), right to social security (UDHR Art 22), right to health, family, housing (UDHR Art 25). Similarly a few rights are guaranteed in International Covenant on Economic Social and Cultural Rights [G.A. Res. 2200A U.N. GOAR 21st Session, 16 December 1966 Supp. No 16 at 49 U.N. Doc. A 6316]. *See e.g.*, right to pursue freely one's own economic, social and cultural development (Art 1), right to work (Art 6), right to family (Art 10), right to an adequate standard of living, shelter and food,

clothing, housing and continuous improvement of living conditions (Art 11), right to physical and mental health (Art 12), right to education (Art 13), right to participate in cultural life (Art 15). For detail discussion on the right of the PAPs under international human rights law, *see also supra* Ch 4.2.

8. SURYA DHUNGEL ET AL COMMENTARY ON THE NEPALESE CONSTITUTION 95 (Kathumandu, Delf, 1998) (quoting Ronald Dworkin).
9. *See* LOUS HENKIN, RIGHT OF MAN TODAY 2(London, Steven & Sons, 1978) arguing that rights are claims upon society, not against society as rights flourish only in a good society and further arguing that ideologically individual rights cannot be sacrificed even for the greater good of greater numbers, even for general good of all).
10. *See e.g.* PUDR v Union of India AIR 1982SC 1473,1490 (holding that the state is under an obligation to ensure the enjoyment of fundamental rights).
11. For a general discussion on the general premise of rights, *see supra* ch 2.2.
12. NEP. CONST. Art 23.
13. *Id.* Art 88.
14. *See* NEP. CONST. Art 11. This has now become possible because of the integrative principles evolved by the courts. *See also supra* ch 2.5.1.
15. The expansive interpretation of rights began with Maneka Gandhi v Union of India AIR 1978 SC 597. In Nepal the initiative is already set in with Leaders Inc. v Godavari Marble Industries 4S.Ct. Bulletin p. 1 Feb. 1997 (Magh 16-29, 2052); Yogi Naraharinath v Prime Minister 5 S.Ct Bulletin p.5,Aug.1998 (Bhadra 1-15, 2053).
16. *See* Leaders Inc. v Godavari Marble Industries 4S.Ct. Bulletin p1 Feb.1997 (Magh 16-29, 2052); Yogi Naraharinath v Prime Minister 5 S.Ct. Bulletin p.5, Aug. 1998 (Bhadra 1-15, 2053).
17. Yagyamurty Banjade v Bagmati Special Court NKP 1970 (2027 BS) p 5.
18. In India right to shelter has been interpreted as spring from right to residence under Art 19 and right to life under Art 21. *See* Chemile Singh v State of UP (1996) 2SCC 549; New Riveria Housing Society v Special Land Acquisition Officer (1996)1SCC 731; UP Avas Evam Vikash Nigam Friends Coop Housing Society 1995 supp (3) SCC 456; State of Karnataka v

Narasimhamurthy (1995)5SCC 524; P.G. Gupta v State of Gujarat 1995 supp(2) SCC 182.

19. This is in conformity with provision of the ICCR. *See supra* note 7 Art 17(1).
20. For instnace, while while restrictions can be imposed on the right to trade and occupation to protect public health or morality, to confer on the state the exclusive right to undertake specified industries, business or services, or to impose any condition or qualification for carrying on any industry, trade, profession or occupation, *see* NEP. CONST. Art 12(5); freedom of movement or residence can be restricted in the interest of general public or to restrict act jeopardizing harmonious relation among people [*Id* Art 12 (4)].
21. The UDHR, ICCPR, ICESCR are collectively called the International Bill of Human Rights. For the rights guaranteed under the Bill, *see supra* note 7.
22. *See* NEP. CONST, Preamble, Art 25(4).
23. *See* Nepal Treaty Act, 1990, S. 9.
24. This has been discussed in *supra* ch 4.3.
25. This has been discussed in *supra* ch 4.3.
26. *See* Committee on Economic Social and Cultural Rights. Gen. Comment No 7 (para 4) UN Doc E/C R 1997/4 (1997) *See also* http://www.umn.edu/humanrt/gencom/econ.html, accessed on July 10, 1999).
27. The International human rights law by guaranteeing the right to life liberty and security of person, [UDHP and ICCPR, *supra* note 7 Art 3]; a right against arbitrary interference with a persons home (except in cases envisaged by law, [ICCPR *Id* Art 17, right to property, UDHR *Id* Art 17 (2)] and categorical assurance that in no case a people be deprived of its means of subsistence, [ICCPR *Id* Art 1(2)] and a right to participate in the decision making process implicitly recognises a right not to be arbitrarily displaced. *See also supra* ch 4.2.
28. For instance, the Committee on Economic Social and Cultural Rights states "instances of forced eviction are prima facie incompatible with the requirements [of ICESCR] and can only be justified in most exceptional circumstances and in accordance with relevant principles. *See* General comment No 4 UN Doc. E/C 1992/23 III, http://www.umn.edu./humanrt/gencom/econ.htm accessed on July 10, 1999. The Committee further emphasises and ensure that the law is enforced against its

agents or third parties carrying out forced eviction. *See* General Comment no 7 (para 4) UN Doc E/C 12/ 1997/4. *See also* Draft UN Guiding Principles on Internal Displacement U.N. Doc. E/ CN 4/1998/53 Add. 2, 11 Feb. 1998, Principle 6(1) (guaranteeing every human being a right to be protected against being arbitrarily displaced from his/her home or place of habitual residence.

29. *See* the Draft principles on Human rights and Environment UN Doc. E/CN 4/sub.21994/5, 6 July 1994), Principles 11 (a) (guaranteeing right [of the PAPs] not to be evicted from their homes or land).
30. *ld.* Art 12(4) and Art 17(2)
31. *See supra* ch 2.4.2
32. IND.CONST. Art 31(2) (original Constitution)
33. US.CONST. amend V
34. For instance the concept of 'open society may be interpreted to go against imposing economic restraint in the name of ensuring social and economic justice. *See* NEP. CONST. Art 25(1)
35. Let it be contrasted with the much highlighted notion of greater good of the common.
36. NEP. CONST. Art 25.
37. *See* UN Declaration of the Right to Development, U.N. G.A. Res. 41/128, December 4,1986 (henceforth UNDRD), Preamble (italics supplied). It further provides: "The right to development is an inalienable human right by virtue of which every individual and all peoples are entitled to participate in, contribute to, and enjoy economic, social cultural and political development, in which all human rights and fundamental freedoms can be realised." *See id* Article 1(1)
38. *See* Upendra Baxi, *The Declaration of Right to Development* in HUMAN RIGHTS IN CHANGING WORLD 3 (E.S Venkatamaramiah ed.) (Delhi, International Law Association, India Branch, 1991). The new paradigm of development enunciated by the UN Declaration on Right to Development from other quarters as well. *See e.g.*, UNDP, HUMAN DEVELOPMENT REPORT 1(New York, Oxford University Press, 1991) (stating "men, women and children must be the centre of attention- with development woven around people, not people woven around them. Moreover, development must be participatory, and for this people must have opportunity to invest in the development of their capacity" at another place "the basic object of human development is to enlarge the range of peoples'choices to make development more democratic and

participatory." And further stating "the best way to achieve human development is to promote more equitable economic growth and more participatory development" *id* at 3. *See also* THE SOUTH COMMISSION, THE CHALLENGE TO THE SOUTH 10-13 (New Delhi, Oxford Univ. Press, 1990)(defining development as a process of self reliant growth achieved through participation of the people acting in their own interest as they see themselves and under their own control).

39. The UNDRD Art 2(3) provides; "States have the right and the duty to formulate appropriate national development policies that aim at the constant improvement of the well-being of the entire population and of all individuals, on the basis of their active, free and meaningful participation in development and in the fair distribution of the benefits resulting therefrom. *See also supra* note 38.

40. U. Baxi, *supra* note 38, at 4. The state is not only required to formulate appropriate development policies the Declaration summons the state to eliminate "obstacles to development" which mainly arise on account of the failure of the state to observe human rights and freedoms *See* UNDRD *supra* note 7, Art 6(3)

41. It attempts to promote conditions of welfare on the basis of the principles of an open society. *See* NEP. CONST. Art 25(1), to maintain conditions suitable to the enjoyment of the fruits of democracy through wider participation of the people in the governance of the country and by way of decentralization. *See Id.* Art 25 (4)

42. *Id.* Art 12 (1).

43. *Id.* Art 16.

44. The process has begun in Nepal in the form of strengthening the Local Self-government and formulation of some rules on EIA studies, but the planning process is still by and large top-down and paternalistic. *See also supra* ch3.1.1.

45. *See also supra* ch 2.6.3.

46. This has been discussed in *supra* ch 4.3 and 4.4.

47. DHUNGEL ET AL, *supra* note 8, at 166.

48. *See* Balakrishna Neupane v PM Girija Prasad Koirala 1(11) S.Ct Bulletin 1 1992 (2049); Gopal Sivakoti v Ministry of Finance NKP 1994 (2051) 0 256; Balakrishna Neupane v Ministry of Water Resource NKP 1007 (2053) P 210. For a detailed discussion, *see supra* ch 2.5.3.

49. *See* Niraja Gopal Jayal, *Displace Persons and Discourse of Rights* 33 (5) EPW PE 30-36 (1998).
50. *See also supra* ch 2.4.2.5.
51. *See* ICESCR, *supra* note 7, Art 2(1).
52. Social costs are defined as project costs that are left to accrue to the society outside the project, as opposed to the project's direct internal costs (labour, materials, equipment and so forth). But social costs are fully in that they would not accrue without the project. *See* Michael Cernea, *Why Economic Analysis is Essential to Resettlement* 34 (31) EPW 2149, 2954 (1999) The environmental costs refer to the loss caused to environment experienced by a wider community.
53. The dicta of distributive justice enumerated by John Rawls in the libertarians social order is encapsulated as follows:

    "First, each person is to have an equal right to the most extensive total system of equal basic liberties compatible with a similar system of liberty for all.

    Second, social and economic inequalities are to be arranged so that they are both:

    (i) to the greatest benefit of the least advantaged consistent with the just saving principle, and

    ii) attached to offices and positions open to all under conditions of fair equality of opportunity", *see* JOHN RAWLS, A THEORY OF JUSTICE 302 (Cambridge MA, Harvard Univ.Press, 1971) For a criticism on Rawls's theory of justice, *see* WAYNE MORRISON, JURISPREUDENCE FROM THE GREEKS TO POST MODERNISM 391-396 (London, Cavendish Pub, Ltd., 1997) arguing that Rawls' theory of justice has latent utilitarian creeps).
54. *See* MAHBUB UL HAQ, HUMAN DEVELOPMENT IN SOUTH ASIA, 1997 47-53 (Karachi Oxford Univ. Press 1997); *See also* NASC, NEPAL HUMAN DEVELOPMENT REPORT 1998 ii (Kathumandu, Nepal South Asia Centre, 1998).
55. Similar views are expressed about the Indian Constitution, which also through its Preamble, Part III and Part IV makes similar promises of social, economic and political justice to India people. *See* P.N. BHAGWATI, LAW AS INSTRUMENT OF CHANGE 20, 93 (Madurai, Society for Community Organization Trust, 1985).
56. *See* the second principle of Rawals, *supra* note 53.

57. *See also supra* ch 4.4.
58. Whereas 46.62 per cent of the people live in the narrow flat agricultural belt on the southern part stretching from the east to the west, 53.3 per cent live in the mountain. *See* NPC, EIGHTH PLAN REPORT 624 (1992-1997) (Kathmandu, National Planning Commission, 1992).
59. GERARD J GILL, MOUNTAINS THE GRANARY 4 (Kathmandu, Winrock International, 1996).
60. Michael Cernea, *supra* note 52, at 2152 (stating that "if all losses were compensated at their market value, the cash compensation would fall far short of the amount needed to restart the economic and productive activities of resettlers in a new setting at levels that provide equal or improved income. To improve the livelihood of resettlers above their previous levels, which is the essence of resettlement programme, additional investment is required").
61. *See e.g.* the Draft UN Guiding Principles on Internally Displaced Persons UN DOC E/CN 4 1998/53 Addz Feb 11, 1998, Principle 1(1), (providing. "internally displaced persons shall enjoy, in full equality, the same rights and freedoms under international and domestic law as do other persons in the country").
62. It is submitted that both existing and emerging norms at the national level in different countries and at the international level are guided by the concern for human rights.
63. *See also supra* ch 3.5.
64. *See* the policies *supra* ch 5.2.1.3 (India), 5.2.2. (China), 5.2.3 (Bangladesh). Besides there quite a few other countries like Laos, Thailand, Turkey in Asia and Central African Republic, Uganda and Cote de Ivor in Africa and Brazi, Columbia and Costarica in South America which have development policies and laws on RR. *See* Roli Astha, *Involuntary Resettlement: Survey of International Experience* 31 (24) EPW 1468-74 (1996); *See also* MICHAEL CERNEA, AFRICAN INVLOUNTARY POPULATION RESETTLEMENT IN GLOBAL CONTEXT (Washington DC, World Bank, 1997); NTFC, NAM THEUN 2 HYDROELECTRIC PROJECT RESETTLEMENT ACTION PLAN (Ventine, 1998).
65. Though so far there exists no case law decided by the Supreme Court with regard to resettlement and rehabilitation, the approach of the Supreme Court of Nepal on several issues on land acquisition and more specifically on the question of "public purpose" seems to be reasonably articulate. For a detailed discussion on this, *see supra* ch 3. 3.

66. NEP CONST., Preamble.
67. *Id.* Art 88.
68. *Id.* Art 84.
69. The Supreme Court of Nepal has begun to issue guidelines to give effect to the rights (including to the right to information). *See* Gopal Sivakoti v Ministry of Water Resources NKP 1994 (2051) P. 256. Issuing of guidelines of legislative nature is a practice in the Supreme Court of India. The Court in several cases has issued guidelines for the resettlement and rehabilitation of the PAPs, though the attitude of the Indian Court is also not very encouraging. A discussion on this has been made in *supra* ch 5.2.1.5 *See also* Laxmi Kant Pandey v Union of India AIR 1987 *sc* 232; Vishaka v Rajasthan (1997) 6 SCC 221; M.C. Mehata v Tamilnadu (1996) 6 SCC 756.
70. In India the process of expansion of the existing legal framework has surfaced in the form of the Land Acquisition Bill 1998. A discussion on this has been made in *supra* ch 5.2.1.4.
71. *See* Amulya K.N. Reddy, *Big Dams: a Fresh Approach* 12 THE HINDU, Bangalore, Sept 20, 1999.
72. This is based on the experience of the World Bank funded Multi-Model project in Nepal where the PAPs were totally forgotten after the land was purchased for the project. Information derived from personal interaction with Mr. Achyut Bista, Legal Officer at the Ministry of Transport at Kathmandu, April 2, 1999.
73. *See* OED, RECENT EXPERIENCE IN INVOLUNTARY RESETTLEMENT (Washington DC. World Bank, 1998).

BIBLIOGRAPHY

A.M. Honore, *ownership* in 1 OXFORD ESSAYS IN JURISPRUDENCE (AG. Guest ed.) (Oxford, Clarendon Press, 1961)

A.M.BHATTACHARJEE, EQUALITY, LIBERTY AND PROPERTY UNDER THE CONSTITUTION OF INDIA (Calcutta, Eastern Law House, 1997)

ALAN BYOLE, *The Role of International Human Rights Law in the Protection of Environment,* in HUMAN RIGHT APPROACHES TO ENVIRONMENT (Alan Byole and Michael Anderson eds. Oxford, Clarendon Press, 1996)

ANINIDDHA DEY, *A Critique of the Orissa Rehabilitation Policy,* in REHABILITATION POLICY AND LAW: A RIGHT TO LIVELIHOOD (Walter Fernandes and Vijay Paranjpye eds.) (Pune/Delhi, Econet/ Indian Social Institute 1997)

ARMIN ROSENCRANTZ ET AL, ENVIRONMENTAL LAW AND POLICY IN INDIA (Bombay, NM Mani Tripathy, 1991)

ARNE NACES *Deep Ecology* in KEY CONECPT IN CRITICAL THEORY ECOLOGY, (Carolyn Merchant ed.) (Jaipur, Rawat Publications, 1996)

ARVIND ANJUMAND MANTHAN, *A Reviw of the Policy of Coal India,* in REHABILITATION POLICY AND LAW: A RIGHT TO LIVELIHOOD (Walter Fernandes and Vijay Paranjpye eds.) (Pune/Delhi, Econet/ Indian Social Institute, 1997)

Asbjorn Eide, *Economic, Social and cultural Rights as Human Rights* in ECONOMIC SOCIAL AND CULTURAL

RIGHTS: A TEXT BOOKS (Asbjorn Eide et al. eds,) (Dordrch,Martin Nijhoff, 1995)

B. N. UPRETY, ROYAL BARDIA NATIONAL PARK (Kathmandu, HMGN/ NPC/IUCN, 1994)

B.G. VARGHESE, WATER OF HOPE: HIMALAYA GANGA DEVELOPMENT AND COOPERATION FOR A BILLION PEOPLE (Delhi, Oxford & IBH Publishing Co., 1992)

Balkumar K.C., *Physiography of Nepal*, in NEPAL, PERSPECTIVES ON CONTINUITY AND CHANGE (Kathmandu, CENAS, Tribhuvan University, 1989)

BANI POROGHAIN, HUMAN RIGTHS: SOCIAL JUSTICE AND POLITICAL CHALLENGE (New Delhi, Kaniksha, 1999)

Bill Devall, *The Deep Ecology Movement* in KEY CONECPT IN CRITICAL THEORY ECOLOGY (Carolyn Merchant ed.) (Jaipur, Rawat Publications, 1996)

BLACKS'S LAW DICTIONARY 470(5th ed St. Paul Minn, West Publishing Co., 1979)

BRAFORD MORSE AND THOMAS BERGER, SARDAR SAROVAR: REPORT OF THE INDEPENDENT REVIEW COMMISSION (Ottawa, Resource Futures International, 1992)

Catherine Redgwell, *Life, The Universe and everything: A Critique of Anthropocentric Rights* in HUMAN RIGHT APPROACHES TO ENVIRONMENTAL PROTECTION (Alan Byole and M Anderson eds.) (Oxford, Clarendon Press 1996)

CBSN, *THE STATISTICAL YEAR BOOK OF NEPAL* (Kathmandu, The Central Bureau of Statistics, 1997)

Chhatrapati Singh, *Rehabilitation and the Right to Property* in DEVELOPMENT DISPLACEMENT AND REHABILITATION (Walter Fernandes and Enakshi Ganguley Thukral eds,) (New Delhi, Indian Social Institute, 1989)

CHRISTOPHER WOOD, ENVIRONMENTAL IMPACT ASSESSMENT: A COMPARATIVE REVIEW (Harlow, Longman, 1995)

DANA CLARK AND MICHAEL HSU, A CITIZEN'S GUIDE TO THE WORLD BANK INSPECTION PANEL (Washington: Centre for International Environmental Law, 1997)

DAVID TRUBEK, *Economic Social and Cultural Rights in the Third World: Human Rights, Law and Human Needs Programmes* in HUMAN RIGHTS IN INTERNATIONAL LAW AND POLICY ISSUES (Theodor Meron ed., Oxford, Clarendon Press, 1983)

DILLI RAM DAHAL, LAND AND MIGRATION IN RAR WESTERN NEPAL (Kathmandu, INAS, TU, 1977)

DIVYA D. BHATTA AND T.K.SHRESTHA, THE ENVIRONMENT OF SUKLAPHANTA (Kathmandu, Tribhuvan University, 1977)

DOROTHY MIERO, THIRTY YEARS IN POKHARA (Kathmandu, Ratna Books, 1998)

DOS, STATISTICAL SURVEY OF NEPAL 1995 (Kathmandu, Department of Statistics 1995)

E.W. BALSON, GENERAL REPORT ON THE ROYAL SUKLAPHANTA WILDLIFE RESERVE (Kathmandu, NPWC Project/FAO/UN, 1976)

EDWARD GOLDSMITH AND NICHOLAS HILDYARD, 1 THE SOCIAL AND ENVIRONMENTAL EFFECTS OF LARGE DAMS (France/UK European Ecological Action Group (ECOROPA), 1984)

ENV, REGIONAL REMEDIAL ACTION PLANNING FOR INVOLUNTARY RESETTLEMENT IN WORLD BANK SUPPORTED PROJECTS: A REPORT ON ONE YEAR FOLLOW UP TO RESETTLEMENT AND DEVELOPMENT (Washington DC, World Bank, 1994)

FLOYD J FLOWER, SURVEY RESEARCH METHODS (London, Sage Publications, 1993)

G.W.F HEGEL, PHILOSOPHY OF RIGHTS (T.M. Knox trans. London, Oxford Univ.Press, 1971)

George Sessions, *Ecocentricism and Athropocentric Detour* in KEY CONECPT IN CRITICAL THEORY ECOLOGY (Carolyn Merchant ed.) (Jaipur, Rawat Publications, 1996)

GERARD J GILL, MOUNTAINS THE GRANARY (Kathmandu, Winrock International, 1996)

GRANVILLE AUSTIN, THE INDIAN CONSTITUTION: THE CORNERSTONE OF NATION (New Delhi, Oxford Univ Press, 1991)

GURDIP SINGH, ENVIRONMENTAL LAW (New Delhi, Lawman, 1995)

H.M.SEERVAI, 1 CONSTITUTIONAL LAW OF INDIA (4th ed Bombay, N.M. Tripathy, 1991) (1967)

HMGN/ LRMP, LAND UTILIZATION REPORT (Kathmandu, Land Resource Project, 1986)

Imre Szabo, *Historical Foundations of Human Rights and Subsequent Development* in 1 INTERNATIONAL DIMENSIONS OF HUMAN RIGHTS (Paris, UNESCO, 1982)

IVOR GENINGS, THE LAW AND THE CONSTITUTION (Kents, ELBS/Holder & Stoeghton, 1979)

J.M. Merrills, *Environmental Protection and Human Rights: Conceptual Aspects,* in HUMAN RIGHT APPROACHES TO ENVIRONMENT (Alan Byole and Michael Anderson eds. Oxford, Clarendon Press, 1996)

J.S.MILL, ON LIBERTY AND REPRESENTATIVE GOVERNMENT (London Blackswell 1948)

James Cameron and Ruth Mackenzie, *Access to Environmental Justice and Procedural Rights in International Institutions* in HUMAN RIGHT APPROACHES TO ENVIRON-

MENT (Alan Byole and Michael Anderson eds.) (Oxford, Clarendon Press 1996)

JEREMY BENTHAM, THEORY OF LEGISLATION (R. Hildreth trans.Bombay N.M. Tripathy 1986 (1876)

JOHN A DIXON ET AL, ECONOMIC ANALYSIS OF THE ENVIRONMENTAL IMPACT OF DEVELOPMENT PROJECTS (London/Manila, Earthscan/Asian Development Bank, 1989?)

JOHN GLASSON, INTRODUCTION TO ENVIRONMENTAL IMPACE ASSESSMENT (London, University College, 1994)

JOHN H. GARVEY & ALEINKOFF, MODERN CONSTITUTIONAL THEORY: A READER (2ND ed .StPaul Minn, West Publishing Co 1991)

JOHN RAWLS, A THEORY OF JUSTICE (Cambridge MA, Harvard Univ. Press, 1971)

JOSEPH RAZ, THE AUTHORITY OF LAW (Oxford, Clarendon Press, 1985)

LOUIS B. SOHN & THOMAS BURGENTHAL, INTERNATIONAL PROTECTION OF HUMAN RITHTS (New York, The Bobbs-Merril Co Inc., 1973)

LOUIS HENKIN, *Introduction* in THE INTERNATIONAL BILL OF RIGHTS (Louis Henkin ed New York, Columbia Univ. Press, 1981)

LOUS HENKIN, RIGHT OF MAN TODAY (London Steven & sons , 1978)

LSC, 9 CONSTITUENT ASSEMBLY DEBATES (Delhi, Lok Sabha Secretariat , 1950)

M C REGMI, LAND TENURE AND TAXATION IN NEPAL (Kathmandu, Ratna Pustak Bhandar, 1978)

M HIDAYATULLAH, RIGHT TO PROPERTY AND THE INDIAN CONSTITUTION (New Delhi/Calcutta, Arnold Heinemann/Calcutta University, 1983)

M.K. Ramesh and Francis Guntipally, *A Critique of the Karnataka Resettlement of the Project Displaced Persons Act 1989,* in REHABILITATION POLICY AND LAW: A RIGHT TO LIVELIHOOD (Walter Fernandes and Vijay Paranjpye eds. Pune/Delhi, Econet/ Indian Social Institute 1997)

MAHBUB UL HAQ, HUMAN DEVELOPMENT IN SOUTH ASIA, 1997 (Karachi, Oxford Univ. Press, 1997)

MARIE BJONESS, SOCIO ECONOMIC ANALYSIS OF THE EFFECTS FROM KULEKHANI HYDRO ELECTRICITY PROJECT, NEPAL (Department of Geography, University of Oslo, 1983)

Martin Lau, *Islam and Judicial Activism: Public Interest Litigation and Environmental Protection in Islamic Republic of Pakistan* in HUMAN RIGHT APPROACHES TO ENVIRONMENT in HUMAN RIGHT APPROACHES TO ENVIRONMENT (Alan Byole and Michael Anderson eds., Oxford, Clarendon Press, 1996)

Michael Anderson, *Individual Right to Environmental Protection in India* in HUMAN RIGHT APPROACHES TO ENVIRONMENT (Alan Byole and Michael Anderson eds. Oxford, Clarendon Press, 1996)

Michael Anderson, *Overview* in HUMAN RIGHTS APPROACHES TO ENVIRONMENTAL PROTECTION (Alan Byole and Michael Anderson eds.) (Oxford, Clarendon Press, 1996)

MICHAEL CERNEA, AFRICAN INVOLUNTARY POPULATION RESETTLEMENT IN GLOBAL EONTEXT (Washington DC, World Bank, 1997)

MICHAEL CERNEA, EIGHT MAIN RISKS: IMPOVERISHMENT AND SOCIAL JUSTICE IN RESETTLEMENT (Envt. Dept, The World Bank, 1996)

MICHAEL CERNEA, HYDROPOWER DAMS AND SOCIAL IMPACTS: A SOCIOLOGICAL PERSPECTIVE (Washington DC: World Bank, 1997)

Michael Cernea, *Understanding and Preventing Impoverishment-Reflections on the State of Knowledge* in UNDERSTANDING IMPOVERISHMENT: THE CONSEQUENCES OF DEVELOPMENT INDUCED DISPLACEMENT (Christopher McDowell ed.) (Oxford Berghann Books, 1996)

MRIDULA SINGH, DISPLACEMENT BY SARDAR SAROVAR AND TEHRI (Delhi, Multiple Action Research Group, 1992)

MYERS S. MCDOUGAL ET AL, HUMAN RIGHTS AND THE WORLD PUBLIC ORDER (New Haven, Yale Univ. Press, 1980)

N.E. SIMMONDS, CENTRAL ISSUES IN JURISPRUDENCE, JUSTICE AND RIGHTS (London, Sweet and Maxwell, 1986)

NARAYAN BELBASE, THE IMPLEMENTATION OF INTERNATIONAL ENVIRONMENTAL LAW IN NEPAL (Kathmandu, IUCN, 1997)

NASC, FACTS ABOUT NEPALESE ECONOMY (Kathmandu, Nepal Society for Applied Research, 1998)

National Thermal Power Corporation Ltd. (India) Rehabilitation and Resettlement Policy; reproduced in REHABILITATION POLICY AND LAW: A RIGHT TO LIVELIHOOD (Walter Fernandes and Vijay Paranjpye eds.) (Pune/Delhi, Econet/ Indian Social Institute, 1997)

Nihal Jayawikrama, *The Bill of Rights* in HUMAN RIGHTS IN HONGKONG (Hongkong, Oxford Univ. Press, 1992)

Nikhil Verma, *A Critique of the Draft Rehabilitation Policy of the Ministry of Water Resource Development*, in REHABILITATION POLICY AND LAW: A RIGHT TO LIVELIHOOD (Walter Fernandes and Vijay Paranjpye eds.) (Pune/Delhi, Econet/ Indian Social Institute, 1997)

NPC, THE EIGHTH PLAN REPORT (1992-1997) (Kathmandu, National Planning Commission, 1992)

NPC, THE FIFTH PLAN (1976-1980) (Kathmandu, National Planning Commission, 1976)

NPC, THE FOURTH PLAN (1970-75) (Kathmandu, National Planning Commission, 1970)

NSAC, NEPAL HUMAN DEVELOPMENT REPORT (Kathmandu, Nepal South Asia Centre, 1998)

NTFC, NAM THEUN 2 HYDROELECTRIC PROJECT RESETTLEMENT ACTION PLAN (Ventine, Govt. of Lao Republic, 1998)

OED, RECENT EXPERIENCE WITH INVOLUNTARY RESETTLEMENT (Washington DC, The World Bank, 1998)

P. C. RAO, INDIAN CONSTITUTION AND THE INTERNATIONAL LAW (Delhi, Taxman, 1993)

P.N. BHAGWATI, LAW AS INSTRUMENT OF CHANGE (Madurai, Society for Community Organization Trust, 1985)

PARYAVARAN KANOON THATHA NYAYA (Environmental Law and Justice) (Kathmandu, IUCN/Nepal Judges' Society, 1998) (Nepali Text)

PATRICK McCULLEY, SILENCED RIVERS: ECOLOGY AND POLITICS OF LARGE DAMS (London, Zed Books, 1996)

R.S. BHALLA, THE INSTITUTION OF PROPERTY (Lucknow, Eastern Book Company, 1984)

R.V. Bhuskute, *The Maharastra Rehabilitation Act 1989* in in REHABILITATION POLICY AND LAW: A RIGHT TO LIVELIHOOD (Walter Fernandes and Vijay Paranjpye eds.) (Pune/Delhi, Econet/ Indian Social Institute, 1997)

RAMACHANDRAN'S LAW OF ACQUISITION AND COMPENSATION (8th ed C. Mathur ed) (Lucknow, Eastern Book Co., 1996) (1960)

RAMCHANDRA GUHA, VARIETIES OF ENVIRONMENTALISM (Delhi, Oxford Univ. Press, 1998)

ROBERT NOZICK, ANARCHY, STATE ANDUTOPIA (Oxford, Basil Blackwell, 1974)

Roberta Cohen, *Recent Trends in Protection and Assistance for Internally Displaced People* in INTERNALLY DISPLACED PEOPLE (Janie Hampton ed.) (London, Earthscan1998)

Roberta Cohen, Recent Trends in Protection and Assistance for Internally Displaced People, in INTERNALLY DISPLACED PEOPLE (Janie Hampton ed.) (London, Earthscan, 1998)

RONALD DWORKIN, A MATTER OF PRINCIPLE (Oxford, Clarendon Press, 1985)

RONALD DWORKIN, TAKING RIGHTS SERIOUSLY (Cambridge MA, Harvard Univ. Press , 1977)

S. Parasuraman, *The Anti-Dam Movement and Rehabilitation Policy* in DAMS AND THE NATION: DISPLACEMENT AND RESETTLEMENT IN NARMADA VALLEY (Jean Dreze et al eds.) (Delhi, Oxford Univ. Press, 1997)

SAARC, REGIONAL STUDY ON THE CAUSES AND CONSEQUENCES OF NATURAL DISASTERS AND THE PROTECTION AND PRESERVATION OF ENVIRONMENT (Kathmandu, SAARC Secretariat, 1992)

SANJAY K NEPAL AND KARLE WEBER, STRUGGLE FOR EXISTENCE: PARK PEOPLE CONFLICT IN THE ROYAL CHITWAN NATIONAL PARK, NEPAL (Bangkok, Asian Institute of Technology, 1993)

Satyajit singh, *Introduction* in DAMS AND THE NATION: DISPLACEMENT AND RESETTLEMENT IN NARMADA VALLEY (Jean Dreze et al eds.) (Delhi, Oxford Univ. Press 1997)

SHIVA RAO, 2 FRAMING INDIA'S CONSTITUTION (Delhi, Indian Institute of Public Administration, 1968)

SOUTH COMMISSION, THE CHALLENGE TO THE SOUTH (New Delhi, Oxford Univ. Press, 1990)

STEPHEN R MUNZER, A THEORY OF PROPERTY (Cambridge, Cambridge University press, 1990)

SUKLA'S CONSTITUTION OF INDIA (M.P. Singh ed., 9th ed Lucknow, Eastern Book Co., 1994)

SURYA P.S. DHUNGEL ET AL, COMMENTARY ON THE NEPALESE CONSTITUTION (Kathmandu, Delf Publications, 1998)

T.K TOPE, CONSTITUTIONAL LAW OF INDIA (2nd ed. Lucknow, Eastern Books, 1992) (1982)

THE DEVELOPMENT DEBATE (S.P. Srivastava ed.) (Jaipur, Rewat Publications, 1998)

THE POST DEVELOPMENT READER (Majid rahema & Victoria Bawtree eds.) (London Zed Books, 1997)

UNDP, HUMAN DEVELOPMENT REPORT 1(New York, Oxford University Press 1991)

Upendra Baxi *Introduction* to K.K. MATHEW, DEMOCRACY, EQUALITY AND FREEDOM (Lucknow, Eastern Book Co., 1979)

Upendra Baxi, *Notes on Constitutional and Legal Aspects of Displacement and Rehabilitation, in* DEVELOPMENT DISPLACEMENT AND REHABILITATION,168 (Walter Fernandes and Enakshi Ganguley Thukral eds) (New Delhi, Indian Social Institute, 1989)

Upendra Baxi, *The Development of Right to Development* in HUMAN RIGHTS IN CHANGING WORLD (E.S Venkatamaramiah ed.) (Delhi, International Law Association, India Branch, 1991)

VANDANA SHIVA, ECOLOGY AND THE POLITICS OF SURVIVAL (New Delhi, Sage Publications, 1991)

Vasudha Dhagambar, *The Land Acquisition Act: High Time for Changes* in REHABILITATION POLICY AND LAW IN INDIA: A RIGHT TO LIVELIHOOD (Walter Fernandes and Vijay Paranjpye eds.) (Pune/Delhi, Econet/ Indian Social Institute, 1997)

Vijay Paranjpye and Lolita Sewarstamani, *Swamped by NTPC*

Fly Ash: A Review of the Rehabilitation Policy, in REHABILITATION POLICY AND LAW: A RIGHT TO LIVELIHOOD (Walter Fernandes and Vijay Paranjpye eds.) (Pune/Delhi, Econet/ Indian Social Institute 1997)

W FRIEDMANN, LAW IN A CHANGING SOCIETY (2d London, Sweet and Maxwell, 1972)

Walter Fernandes et al, *Displacement and Rehabilitation: An Estimate of Extent and Prospects* in DEVELOPMENT DISPLACEMENT AND REHABILITATION (Walter Fernandes and E.G. Thukral eds) (Delhi, Indian Social Institute, 1989)

Walter Fernandes, *The Draft National Policy for Rehabilitation of the Displaced Persons: Is Displacement Inevitable*? In REHABILITATION POLICY AND LAW: A RIGHT TO LIVELIHOOD (Walter Fernandes and Vijay Paranjpye eds.) (Pune/Delhi, Econet/ Indian Social Institute, 1997)

WAYNE MORRISON, JURISPRUDENCE FROM THE GREEKS TO POST MODERNISM (London, Cavendish Pub. Ltd., 1997)

WB, RESETTLEMENT AND DEVELOPMENT: BANKWIDE REVIEW OF PROJECTS INVOLVING INVOLUNTARY RESETTLEMENTS 1986-1993, (Washington DC, World Bank, 1996)

WB, TRENDS IN DEVELOPING ECONOMIES (Washington DC, The World Bank, 1994)

WECD, OUR COMMON FUTURE (Delhi, Oxford University Press, 1987)

WESLEY N. HOHFELD, FUNDAMENTAL LEGAL CONCEPTIONS (Walter Wheeler Cook ed., Green Wood Press, 1978)

WILLIAM J. GOODE & PAUL K. HATT, METHODS IN SOCIAL RESEARCH (Auckland, McGrawhill Book Company, 1981)

ENCYCLOPAEDIA

26 Am Jur 2d Eminent Domain (1966)

27 Am Jur. 2d Eminent Domain (1966)

Ernest Beaglehole, *Property* in 12 INTERNATIONAL ENCYCLOPAEDIA OF THE SOCIAL SCIENCE 589-592 (David L. Sill ed. Macmillan & Co 1968)

Walton H. Hamilton & Irene Till, *Property,* 11 ENCYCLOPAEDIA OF THE SOCIAL SCIENCE 528-538 (Edwin R.A. Seligman ed. New York, Macmillian 1933)

ARTICLES /PAPERS ETC

A.S. Anand, inaugural address on *The Domestic Application of International Human Rights Norms,* Bangalore, Dec.27, 1998

Ajaya Dixit, *Water Projects in Nepal: Lessons From Displacement and Rehabilitation* 4(1) WATER NEPAL 74 (1994)

Amulya K.N. Reddy, *Big Dams: a Fresh Approach* THE HINDU, Bangalore, Sept 20, 1999 at 12

Arthur Lenhoff, *Development of the Concept of Eminent Domain* 43 COLUM L REV 596 (1942)

Arundhaty Roy *The Greater Common Good,* FRONTLINE July 14, 1999 at 5

Asbjorn Eide, *The Human Rights Movement and the Transformation of the International Order,* ALTERNATIVES 367(1986)

Balgovind Baboo, *Big Dams and the Tribals: The Case of Hirakud Dam Oustees in Orissa,* SOCIAL ACTION 289 (1991

Buckner F Melton, Jr, *Eminent Domain, "Public Use" and the Conundrum of Original Intent,* 36 NATURAL RESOURCE JOURNAL 59 (Winter1996)

Byron J Good, *Mental Health Consequences of Displacement and Resettlement,* 31(24) EPW 1504 (1996)

Charles De Wet, *Moving Away from Apartheid: Resettlement in a Changing South Africa,* (paper presented to the Conference on Development Induced Displacement and Impoverishment, Weldam College, Oxford, Jan 3-7, 1995)

David Trubak, *Towards a Social Theory of Law: An Essay on the Study of Law and Development,* 82 YALE LAW JOURNAL 1(1972)

Dipak Gyawali and Ajaya Dixit, *Mahakali Impasse and Post 1990 Indo Nepal Water Conflict,* 34(9) EPW 553 (1999)

Edith Brown Weiss, *Our Rights and Obligations to Future Generations,* 84 AJIL 198 (1990)

Enakshy G. Thukral, *Development, Displacement and Rehabilitation: Locating Gender,* 31(24) EPW 1500 (1996)

Harka Gurung, *Review of Policy and Experiences of Project Related Resettlement in Nepal,* 1(4) WATER NEPAL 4 (1989)

Harriet Nguhene, *The Politics of Land Restitution in South Africa;* Charles De Wet, *Moving Away from Apartheid: Resettlement in a Changing South Africa,* (papers presented to the Conference on Development Induced Displacement and Impoverishment, Weldam College, Oxford, Jan 3-7, 1995)

ICIMOD, *Occasional Paper No 1,* Kathmandu, International Centre for Integrated Mountain Development, 1985

John Bizer and Tod Ragsdale, *The Development of Resettlement Policy in China: Two Case Studies in Sichuan and Hebei Provinces,* **http://www.his.com/~mesas/chinapol.htm** accessed on 22.12.1998

John O'Manique, *Human Rights and Development,* 14 HUMAN RIGHT QUARTERLY 78 (1992)

Joseph Sax, *Public Trust Doctrine in Natural Resource Law: Effective Judicial Interaction,* 68 MICHIGAN LAW REVIEW 473(1973)

Kalpana Sharma, *Dams Projects Must Take into Consideration Social Factors,* THE HINDU Dec 12, 1998 at 14 and http://www.bangladesh.web.com/news/dec/19/

Zu3n/o/.htm accessed on 6th Aug, 1999

Lawrence Berger, *The Public Use Requirement in Eminent Domain* OREGEON LAW REVIEW 203 (1978)

Luthar Gundling, *Our Responsibility to Future Generation*, 84 AMERICAN JOURNAL OF INTERNATIONAL LAW 211 (1990).

Mariauyjhmn Stavropoulau, *The Right not to Be Displaced*, 9 AMERICANUNIVERSITYJOURNAL OF INTERNATIONAL LAW AND POLICY 689 (1998)

Martin Stein, *The Three Gorges: The Unexamined Tales of Development Induced Displacement*, http://www.nrc.no/global_idp_survey/FMR/1998_1/stein.htm accessed on Aug 6, 1999

Mathew Areeparampil, *Displacement Due to Mining in Jharkhand*, 31(24) EPW 1544 (1996)

Michael Anderson, *International Environmental Law in Indian Courts*, 7RECIEL 25 (1996)

Michael Cernea *The Risk and Reconstruction Model for Resettling Displaced Populations*, (Keynote address presented at the International Conference on Reconstructing Livelihoods: Towards New Approaches to Resettlement, September 9-13, 1996 University of Oxford, RSP, Oxford)

Michael Cernea, *Public Policy Responses to Development Induced Population Displacement*, 31(24) EPW 1515 (1996)

Michael Cernea, *Understanding and Preventing Impoverishment from Displacement: Reflection on the State of Knowledge*, 8(3) JOURNAL OF REFUGEE STUDIES 245 (1995)

Michael Cernea, *Why Economic Analysis is Essential to Resettlement*, 34(31) EPW 2149 (1999)

Neera Chandhoke, *Why People Should have Rights*, 29(4), EPW 2697-2700(1994)

Niraja Gopal Jayal, *Displaced Persons and Discourse of Rights*, 33(5) EPW PE 30-36(1998)

Nita Mishra, *Tribal Resistance in the Chhechhari Valley*, 31(24) EPW 1539-1940 (1996)

P.K. Tripathy, *Right of Property After 44th Amendment-Better Protected than Before*, AIR 1980 Journal 49

Ranjit Dwivedi, *Displacement, Risk and Resistance: Local Perceptions and Actions in the Sardar Sarovar*, 30 DEVELOPMENT AND CHANGE 14 (1999)

Roli Astha, *Involuntary Resettlement: Survey of International Experience*, 31(24) EPW 1468 (1996)

S. Parasuraman, *Development Projects Displacement and Outcomes for Displaced: Two Case Studies*, 31(24) EPW 1529-31 (1996)

S.P. Sathe, *Right to Property After the 44th Amendment: Reflections on Prof. P.K. Tripathy's Observations*, AIR 1980 Journal 97-100

Shahid Alam, *A Short Paper on the Resettlement Operations of the Jamuna Multipurpose Bridge Project, Bangladesh*, (paper presented at the workshop on the Development Induced Displacement and Impoverishment, 3-7 Jan. 1995 Wadham College Oxford).

Smitu Kothari, *Whose Nation, The Displaced ad Victim*, 31(24) EPW 1478 (1996)

Tasheem Siddiqui, *Jumuna Bridge Project Policies and issues in Resettlement of the Displaced*, DAILY STAR 1(147) Jan 8, 1998, http://www.banglanet..html, accessed on Dec 23, 1998

Tyler E. Chapman, *To Save and Not Save: The Historic Preservation Implications of the Property Right Movement*, 77 BOSTON UNIV. L REV 112, 115(1997)

Usha Ramanathan, *Displacement and the Law*, 31(24) EPW 1486-1491 (1996)

Walter Fernandes, *Land Acquisition (Amenement) Bill, 1998: Rights of the Project Affected People Ignored* 33(42&43) EPW 2703-2706(1999)

William B. Sroebuck, *A General Theory of Eminent Domain*, 47 WASH. L. REV. 553-555 (1972)

Willian Michael Treanor, *The Original Understanding of the Taking Clause and the Political Process*, 95 COLUMBIA L REV 782-785 (1995)

Wu Ming, *Resettlement Problems of the Three Goreges Dam: A Field Study Report*, [International River Network, Berkeley 1998], **http://www.hrichina.org/reports/3gorges.html** accessed on 23.12.1998

Book/Statute Review

Himansu Thakkar, Book Review 478 SEMINAR 73 (1999) (reviewing PATRICK MCCULLEY, SILENCED RIVERS: THE ECOLOGY AND POLITICS OF LARGE DAMS (Hyderabad, Orient Longman, 1998)

Mukti Rijal, *Local Self Government Bill* (Statute Review), 27 ESSAYS ON CONSTITUTIONAL LAW 67 (1198)

Policy Documents

Coal India Ltd, Resettlement and Rehabilitation Policy reproduced in REHABILITATION POLICY AND LAW:A RIGHT TO LIVELIHOOD Annex Walter Fernandes and Vijay Paranjpye eds.) (Pune/Delhi, Econet/ Indian Social Institute, 1997)

HMGN, The Electricity Development Policy, 1992 (Kathmandu, Ministry of Water Resource 1992)

HMGN, The Industrial Policy 1992 (Kathmandu, Ministry of Industry 1992)

MRD/GOI, The National Policy, Package and Guidelines for Resettlement and Rehabilitation- 1998 (In the file of Ministry of Rural Development, GOI, 1998)

NTPC, Resettlement Policy, reproduced in REHABILITATION POLICY AND LAW: RIGHT TO LIVELIHOOD Annex (Walter Fernandes and Vijay Paranjpye eds.) (Pune/Delhi, Econet/ Indian Social Institute, 1997)

UNPUBLISHED DISSERTATIONS

Ananda M Bhattarai, Participatory Forest Management in the Mountain 13 (1995) (unpublished LL.M dissertation, National Law School of India University, Bangalore)

Harka Gurung. Pokhara Valley, Nepal Himalaya: A Field Study in Regional Geography, (1965) (Unpublished Ph.D thesis, Univ of Edinberg, Edinberg,)

Jagadish Pokharel, Large Scale Resource Development Projects and Problems of Displacement, Compensation and Resettlement (1989) (unpublished M.SC. dissertation, University of Hawaii).

Other Unpublished Materials

Written submission made by Counsel of the petitioner Mr Prasant Bhushan in Narmada Bachao Andolan v Union of India (Writ no 319 of 1994) at the Supreme Court on Jan 1999 in the file of the Supreme Court at 1-2)

Newspaper Reports

HMG/SMEC Talk for Power Export Near Conclusion, The KATHMANDU POST, Apr 22, 1977 at1

Jasper Berker, *Dam Cadres Steal $ 217 Million*, SOUTH CHINA MORNING POST Feb.14, 1999 at 1, in http://www.irn.org/programs/threeg/coverage99018.html accessed on Nov.18, 1999

New York Times, *see* http://www.irn.org/programs/threeg/991018art3.htms. accessed on Nov.18,1999.

The Displacees of Koshi Tappu and Koshi Bank Decide to Go for Agitation, KANTIPUR DAILY(Nepali text) Aug 1, 1999 at 3.

Web Sites

The Norwegian Refugee study Center gives the figure of refugee as 20 to 22 million refugees. *See* http://www.nrc.no/global idp survey.htm assessed on Sept. 1. 1999

OD 4.30, OD 4.20 etc of the World Bank http://www.worldbank.org/inv.res.htm accessed on Sept. 2, 1999

World Bank Country Office, Nepal, Information on Nepal's economy, http://www.worldbank.org/html/extdr/offrep/sas/no2.htm accessed on Sept. 1, 1999

ILO Convention no 169,http://www.ilolex.ch1567/script-s/convde.pl?=(169)queryo=169 accessed on June 17,1999

Involuntary Resettlement, OMS 2.33 of the World Bank) http://www.worldbank.org/inv.res.htm accessed on Sept. 2,1999

Daily Star Bangladesh, http://www.bangladesh.web.com/news/dec/19/Zu3n/o/.htm accessed on 6th Aug, 1999

Three Gorges Project China, **http://www.hrichina.org/reports/3gorges.html** accessed on 23.12.1998 and **http://www.his.com/~mesas/chinapol.htm** accessed on 22.12.1998

Bangladesh Net (for information on Bangladesh) http://www.banglanet..html, accessed on Dec 23, 1998

Global Internal Displacement, Norwegian Refugee study Center, http://www.nrc.no/global_idp_survey/FMR/1998_1/stein.htm accessed on Aug 6, 1999

Information on Pokhara/Nepal, http:/www.al/pokhara.htm, accessed on 14th Apr. 1999 and http:/www.windownep.com.pokhara.htm accessed on Apr. 14th 1999.

International Instruments and other Documents

Agenda 21, A/CONF.15/26 VOL I

Agreement Governing the Activities of States on the Moon and Other Celestial Bodies, reprinted in 18 ILM 1434 (1979)

Committee on ESCR, General Comment 7(para.4), UN/Doc. E/C. 12/1997/4(1997; http://www.umn.edu/humanrt/gencomm/econ.htm accessed on July 10, 1999)

Committee on ESCR, General Comment No 4 UN Doc. HRI/GEN/1 Rev.1, at 53 (1994) http://www.umn.edu/humanrt/gencomm/econ.htm accessed on July 10, 1999

Convention Concerning the Protection and Integration of Indigenous and Other Tribal and Semi Tribal Populations in Independent Countries, 1957 (ILO Convention No 107) 328 UNTS 247

Draft Declaration of Principles on Human Rights and the Environment UN Commission on Human Rights, Sub-Commission on Prevention of Discrimination and Protection of Minorities, Final Report of the Rapporteur, U.N.Doc.E/CN.4Sub.2/1994.9 (6 July 1994),74

EC Convention on Access to Information Public Participation in Decision-Making and Access to Justice in Environmental Matters, reprinted in 38 ILM 517 (1999)

Commmittee on ESCR, General Comment No 2 (1990) para 11, UN Doc. E/C 1992/23 Annex III

OECD Guideline for Aid Agencies on Involuntary Displacement and Resettlement in Development Projects, Doc. OECD/GD (91) 201 (1991) reprinted in REHABILITATION POLICY AND LAW IN INDIA:A RIGHT TO LIVELIHOOD (Walter Fernandes and Vijay Paranjpye eds.) (Delhi: Indian Social Institute, 1997)

The Additional Protocol to American Convention in the Area Social and Cultural Rights, Art 11OAS Treaty Series No 69(1988) Nov. 17, 1988

The African Charter on Human and Peoples' Right, June 27,1981; OAU Doc.CAB/LEG/67/3 Rev.5. reprinted in 21 ILM 58 (1982)

The Convention Concerning the Protection of Indigenous and Other Tribal Populations 1989 (ILO Convention No.169) reprinted in 28 ILM 1382 (1989)

The Convention for the Protection of the Marine Environment of the North East Atlantic, reprinted in 32 ILM 1969(1993)

The Convention on the Protection and use of Trans-boundary Water Course and International Lakes, reprinted in 31 ILM 1312(1992)

The Convention on the Right of the Child, 1989 UN/GA Doc A/RES/44/25 (Nov.20, 1989)

The Council of Europe Convention on Damage Resulting from Activities Dangerous to Environment 1993 reprinted in 32 ILM 1228 (1993)

The EC Convention on Environmental Impact Assessment 1991 reprinted in 30 ILM 802(1991)

The General Comment No 16 of the Human Right Committee, UN Doc HRI/GEN/i/Rev.1 (29 July, 1994)

The International Covenant on Civil and Political Rights G.A. Res. 2200A, 21 U.N. GAOR 21st Session, 16 Dec 1966 Supp., No 16, at 53 UN Doc. A 6316

The International Covenant on Economic, Social and Cultural Rights G.A. Res. 2200A, U.N. GOAR 21st Session, Dec 16, 1966Supp.No 16 at 49, UN/Doc A 6316

The North American Agreement on Environment and Cooperation, reprinted in 32ILM 1482(1993)

The Optional Protocol II on International Convention on the Civil and Political Rights

The Optional Protocol to the International Covenant on the Civil and Political Rights, G.A. Res. 2200 A (XXI) 21st Session, 16 Dec 1966 Supp. No 16 at UN/Doc A 6316

The UN Declaration on Human Environment UN Doc. A/CONF.48/14(1972) 1 11 ILLM 1416(1972)

The UN Declaration on Right to Development, 1986, GA/Res. 41/128, Dec. 4 1986

The UN Framework Convention on Climate Change, UN Doc. A/AC. 237/18 reprinted in 31 ILM 849(1992)

The UN Guiding Principles on Internal Displacement UN Doc. E/CN 4/1998/53 Add.2. 11 Feb, 1998)

The Vienna Convention on Law of the Treaties, 1969 reprinted at 8 ILM 679 (1969) adopted on May 22, 1969)

UN CHARTER,

UN Commission on Human Right Resolution 1993/77 para 4 (March 10, 1993)

UN Convention on Biological Diversity, reprinted in 31ILM 818(1992)

UN Declaration on Environment and Development UN Doc. A/CONF. 15/25. Vol 1 (1992) 14 June 1992, reprinted in 31 ILM 876(1992)

Universal Declaration on Human Rights UNGA res. 217(III) A, UNGAOR 3rd sess., at 71, UN Doc. A 810 (1948)

Vienna Declaration and Programme of Action 1993 UN. Doc. A/CONF. 157/23, 12 July 1993

World Bank Documents

Conclusion of the Board of Directors of the World Bank, Second Review of the Inspection Panel Apr.20, 1999, http:/www.worldbank.org/html/inspanel/htm accessed on July 10, 1999

Draft IFC Environmental and Social Policies and Procedures, Part II Corrigendum (IFC/ R 97-208/1) Nov. 26, 1997

Draft OD 4.12 Involuntary Resettlement, circulated by the Bank in CODE on Nov 21, 1997 (CODE)

13 IBRD Res. 93-10/IDA 93-06.(Resolution establishing the Inspection Panel)

BP 1755 Inspection Panel (Feb.1997)

OD 4.00 Annex B Environmental Policy for Dams and Reservoir Projects (Apr.1989)

OD 4.01 Environmental Assessment including annexure (Oct 1991)

OD 13.05 Project Supervision (March 1989)

OP 4.04 Directives on Natural Habitat (Sept. 1995)

OP4.04 Economic Evaluation of Investment Operations (Sept.1994)

UNPUBLISHED FEASIBILITY/EIA REPORTS

EIA/1997 Update for XIAOLANGDI MULTIPURPOSE DAM PROJECT STAGE II 4.40 (Prepared by Yelow River Reconnsissance, Planning Design Institute(RPPI) for Resettlement Office(RO) of Yellow River Water and Hydropower Development Corporation, Feb. 1997)

UNPUBLISHED ENGINEERING REPORTS

NEA, RAUGHAT HYDRO-POWER PROJECT (1998) 1The detailed Study Report prepared by Resource Consult/ Time Consult/Mashina Consulting Associates 1998, In the file of WECS, Kathmandu)

NEA, TAMUR-MEWA PROJECT (1997), Detail Study Report 24 (prepared by Canada Int'l Water & Energy Consultancy, Kathmandu 1997, in the file of WECS, Kathmandu)

HMGN/MWR/EDC, PANCHESWAR MULTIPURPOSE DETAILED PROJECT REPORT, (1995) report available at the WECS, Kathmandu)

HMGN/MWR/NEA, WEST SETI HYDRO ELECTRICITY PROJECT, DETAIL STUDY FINAL REPORT (prepared by SOGREAH/SUGLER, Feb 1991, the report available at the WECS, Kathmandu)

HMGN/MWR, KARNALI CHISHAPANI MULTIPURPOSE PROJECT FEASIBILITY STUDY MAIN REPORT (prepared by Himalayan Power Consultants 1989 available in WECS, Kathmandu)

HMGN/NEA/UNDP/ UN DEPARTMENT FOR TECHNICAL COOPERATION, KALI GANDAKI HYDRO POWER PROJECT (1992), (Detail Feasibility Study Final Report, prepared by Nowegian Power Consultant, Oslo, available in WECS Kathmandu)

ANNEXURES

ANNEXURE 1

THE DRAFT LAW ON ACQUISITION, REQUISITION OF PROPERTY, RESETTLEMENT AND REHABILITATION OF PROJECT AFFECTED PERSONS

An Act for Acquisition, Requisition of Property, Resettlement and Rehabilitation of Persons in the Event of Them being Displaced or Affected

Recalling the promise of the Constitution of the Kingdom of Nepal to ensure justice-economic, social and political, respect basic rights of the people, and usher a people centered, transparent, participatory and environmentally benign, sustainable development;

Acknowledging that persons affected by projects possess the right not to be arbitrarily displaced, and that projects causing displacement uproot families, society, culture and heritage and thereby cause economic, social, cultural and psychological stress to the displaced and other affected persons;

Also keeping in mind the human and social cost involved, and realizing the need to avoid and minimise displacement as far as practicable; and

Realizing that in the event of displacement occurring, His Majesty's Government holds a duty to restore the asset, earning capacity of the project affected persons by undertaking measures of resettlement and rehabilitation, and to make them partners and beneficiaries of development;

Now therefore, be it enacted by Parliament in the ... year of the Reign of HIS MAJESTY KING BIRENDRA BIKRAM SHAH DEV as follows.

1. *Short Title and Commencement:* (1) This Act may be cited as the Acquisition, Requisition of Property, Resettlement and Rehabilitation of Project Affected Persons Act, 2000

(2) This Act shall come into force at once.

1. *Definitions:* Unless the subject or context otherwise requires, in this Act,

(a) "Project" means any project in public interest either to be run by His Majesty's Government or institutions of Local Self-Government or any other persons with the consent and approval of His Majesty's Government, which directly or indirectly changes or intends to cause change in the land use or displaces a person or affects her or him by expropriation of land, pastures, spring sources, forests and other means of survival or deprives of him or her income and livelihood.

(b) "Property" means any property, movable or immovable, either under individual or common use or ownership, and includes common property resources like forest, spring sources, religious and cultural sites which have individual or communal proprietary interest, and other interests, privileges, concessions, benefits arising out of such property.

(c) "Family" includes spouse, son, daughter, grandson, grand daughter and other dependant members having a common kitchen or having a share or interest in the property under joint ownership or use.

(d) "Project Affected Persons" means i) a person whose

land under ownership or occupation or cultivation or tenancy or use in whole or in part, is acquired or requisitioned in public interest, or due to acquisition or requisition, the remaining portion is damaged, fragmented and rendered uncultivable or unprofitable for cultivation, or uninhabitable. The term also includes those persons, whose remaining land is, due to acquisition or requisition, reduced to such a size which is not sufficient to meet the food requirement of the family the year round. In case of members of a joint family, every members, male or female having a share or interest in the property shall be treated as project affected person;

(ii) landless agricultural labourer, or any other person dependent on the land or persons whose land is to be acquired or requisitioned provided that such person, for a continuous period of not less than three years immediately before the publication of the notification under sub-section (1) of section 3, has been ordinarily residing or carrying on any trade, occupation or calling in the land.

e) "Affected zone" means the area to be acquired or requisitioned for the project, and includes such other area which, on account of the project, becomes inaccessible, or is rendered uninhabitable or unprofitable for cultivation or is substantially affected in terms of value or adverse environmental effect.

f) "Benefited zone" means any area receiving direct and substantial benefits from the project declared as benefited zone under section 4.

g) "Public interest" means such interest which brings or intends to bring about benefit to the general public or a section thereof or restitutes or intends to restitute project affected persons or a section thereof or ushers or intends to usher the development process as envisaged in Part IV of the Constitution.

h) "Main source of income" means the source or sources of income that provides for at least half of the gross income of the project affected family.

i) "Planning, Implementation and Monitoring Committee" (PIMC in short) means a Committee constituted by His Majesty's Government for the detailed planning, executing, monitoring and directing the process of acquisition of property, payment of compensation, resettlement and rehabilitation operation under this Act.

j) "Replacement value" means the value which restores the asset and livelihood of person at least to the level prior to displacement or the value which, irrespective of the type of holding or the size of the holding, ensures a livelihood above the poverty level.

3. *Publication of Preliminary Notification:* (1) Where it appears to His Majesty's Government that property of a locality is needed in public interest for any project to be executed by itself or the institution of Local Self Government or any other person with prior approval and under the conditions determined by His Majesty's Government, a notification to that effect shall be published in the Nepal Gazette and at least two daily newspapers circulating in the locality. An announcement regarding the same shall be made on the Radio Nepal and the Nepal Television. Where the acquisition of requisition of property is likely to displace or seriously affect a person, an individual notification in the name of the head of the family or any adult member, where such person

is not found at home or his usual place of residence, shall be duly served.

(2) The notification shall contain the following information:

a) the objective of the project outlining in what way it serves public interest in particular through the distribution of benefits among different regions, sections and gender;

b) the alternatives studied and search made for non-displacing or least displacing projects or projects having least adverse environmental impact, and result of such studies;

c) alternatives searched with a view to save agriculture land and minimise conversion of such land to non- agricultural purpose;

d) reason for the selection of the project to the exclusion of alternatives listed in clause (b) and (c) above, along with costing of all options for achieving the objective;

e) the possible extent of displacement and serious adverse effect on people and environment that the project may entail;

f) steps intended to be taken to minimise the hardship to the project affected persons and mitigate adverse environmental impact;

g) the nature of compensation, and other transitional and post resettlement support;

h) opportunities to be made available for project affected persons to be benefited from the said project or other projects as a compensatory measure.

(3) On publication of the notification, any person likely to be affected by the project or any other person having a meaningful relation with the issue can make a written

submission and request for further clarification and ask for the copy of relevant documents based upon which the notification is issued.

4. *Declaration of Affected and Benefited Zone and Cessation of Land Transaction:* (1) His Majesty's Government, wherever it deems necessary, shall also declare the affected and the benefited zone in the notification to be published under sub-section (1) of section 3 .

(2) Notwithstanding anything contained in any law in force, no land mentioned in the notification in sub-section (1) shall, after such notification, be transferred in whole or in part, in any manner including partition or in execution of a degree of the court.

5. *Constitution of Planning, Implementation and Monitoring Committee:* (1) His Majesty's Government shall, for the purpose of carrying out of acquisition or requisition of property, and planning, execution and monitoring of the resettlement and rehabilitation operation, constitute a Planning, Implementation, and Monitoring Committee (herein after referred to as the PIMC) having the following composition:

a)	Chief District Officer or the any other Gazetted Officer appointed by His Majesty's Government	Chairman
b)	Project In-Charge	Member
c)	President of the District Development Committee or any other member nominated by him	Member
c)	Chairman (one each) of the Village Development Committee (s) or Municipality(ies) likely to be affected by acquisition or requisition	Member
e)	Chief, District Revenue Office	Member

f)	Chief, District Land Survey Office	Member
g)	Chief, District Agriculture Office	Member
h)	One Representative each of every hundred families likely to be affected by the project	Member
i)	Representative of women, and other weaker section in a ratio of one in every five hundred families	Member
j)	Representative of the non-governmental organization, if any, working among people likely to be displaced or affected	Member
k)	Any officer of the acquiring or requisitioning office	Member-Secretary

(2) The PMIC shall be responsible for acquisition or requisition of property and resettlement and rehabilitation of the Project Affected Persons.

(3) The PIMC shall have power to constitute Committee of Experts to advise it on any issue it deems necessary to be advised. It may also invite any expert or member of Non-Governmental Organization in its meeting for deliberation. But the person so invited shall have no right to vote.

(4) The PIMC shall open its office at any place in the area to be affected which will be accessible to persons likely to be displaced or affected. Depending on the size of the project and the persons likely to be affected it may open one or more branch offices to carry out its activities.

(5) If His Majesty's Government comes to the conclusion that any member of the PIMC is involved in corruption or any other activity of moral turpitude, it may, after giving such member an opportunity of hearing, remove him/her from PIMC.

6. *Meeting, Quorum and Decision of the PIMC* : (1) The PMIC may, meet as frequently as is desired by the majority. The quorum of such meeting shall be one third of the total strength.

(2) Every decision of the PIMC shall as far as possible be made with consensus of the member present. Where no such consensus could be reached, decision of the majority shall be considered as the decision of the PMIC. Any member disagreeing with the majority can write his/her dissenting opinion.

7. *Actions to be Followed and Report to be made to His Majesty's Government:* (1) After the publication of the notification under sub-section (1) of section 3, the PIMC shall carry out necessary action to determine the suitability of acquisition or requisition. The actions include the following:

a) Survey of the private, common and forest land and other types of land to be acquired or requisitioned and such other land which is likely to be seriously affected by the acquisition or requisition;
b) Updating of the existing land survey record;
c) Survey of households and persons to be affected by the acquisition and eligible to claim compensation or resettlement and rehabilitation;
d) Survey of religious and cultural sites that are likely to be demolished or seriously affected by the acquisition or requisition of property;
e) Survey of other assets, earning capacity and livelihood pattern of the persons to be displaced or seriously affected by acquisition or requisition of property;
f) Tentative determination of the cost to result from the loss of common property resources, the cost involved in the acquisition, requisition of the

property, and the cost involved in resettlement and rehabilitation of the project affected persons.

Provided that the activities mentioned in clauses (a), (c), (d) and (e) shall as far as practicable, be carried out in the presence of the persons concerned and, depending on the size and expanse of the project, the representative of the Local Self-government like the Village Development Committee, the Municipality, and the District Development Committee

(2) After the publication of the notification, any member or staff of the PIMC shall have power to enter into any land, house or other structure to take measurement and carry out other necessary actions with prior notification of a reasonable period.

(3) Any person likely to be affected from the acquisition of property may within 30 days from the last date of notification published under sub-section (1) section 3 or within 30 days of the constitution of the PIMC, whichever is latter, lodge a complaint with the PIMC stating objections and the reason therefor to any of the grounds mentioned in the said notification. Any representative of the person likely to be affected or non-governmental organization with proper authority may also submit objection on behalf of such person to the PIMC.

(4) After the actions mentioned in sub-section (1) are over, the PMIC shall publish its tentative findings on the appropriateness of the acquisition or requisition of the property and circulate the same among persons likely to be displaced or/and affected. It shall also publish its findings in at least two newspapers circulating in the area to be displaced or/ and affected. The PIMC shall, in the same notification, also mention the time and date of public hearing which shall be held on the complaints lodged to it or any questions and clarification that may arise from its findings. The PIMC shall

duly notify the same to persons who have made a complaint under sub-section (4). Any change in the time and place of public hearing shall be duly notified to persons likely to be affected.

(5) The PIMC shall, depending on the size of the project, hold public hearing in one or more places to be acquired or requisitioned at the time and place mentioned in the notification published under sub-section (4). The PIMC shall, depending on the size and effect of the project, hold a discussion at the appropriate forum of the Local Self Government.

(6) After the hearing under sub section (4) and discussion under sub-section (5) is over, the PIMC shall, within a reasonable time, report its findings and recommendation on the appropriateness of acquisition or requisition to His Majesty's government. The PIMC shall also submit the summary of the objections raised at public hearing and the discussion held at the appropriate forum of the Local Self-Government. The PIMC shall also communicate its decision to every person who had made a submission to it under sub-section (3).

8. *Declaration that the Property is Required for Public Purpose:* (1) His Majesty's Government, if after receiving the report of the PIMC, comes to the conclusion that the property mentioned in the notification under sub-section (1) of section 3 or any portion thereof is required in public interest, shall make a declaration or declarations to that effect under the signature of the concerned Secretary to His Majesty's Government. Such declaration shall be published in the Nepal Gazette and in at least two newspapers circulating in the locality to be acquired or requisitioned. Such a declaration shall also state the purpose for which it is needed, the District or Village or Municipality in which the land is situated, its plot number, approximate area, the name of the owner, holder, occupant and user. A summary announcement to that effect shall also be made through Radio Nepal and the Nepal Television.

Provided that no such notification under this section shall be made after the expiry of one year from the date of the notification under sub-section of section 3. But while computing the period, the period in which any action or proceeding to be taken has been stayed by the court order shall not be taken into account.

(2) His Majesty's Government shall, in the notification under sub-section (1), also mention the name and address of the office of His Majesty's Government or PIMC, involved in the determination and payment of compensation, planning and execution of resettlement and rehabilitation operations.

(3) After the declaration under sub-section (1) is published, His Majesty's Government shall, through PIMC, communicate its decision to the persons to be displaced or otherwise seriously affected, where it shall also mention the name of the Appellate Court in which petition may be filed against its decision.

(4) Any person not satisfied with the decision of His Majesty's Government, may within 35 days from the date of the publication of the notification in Nepal Gazette under sub-section (1) or the communication received from the PIMC, whichever is latter, file a petition to the Appellate Court against the decision of His Majesty's Government. Appeal against the decision of the Appellate Court may lie with the Supreme Court. Both the Appellate Court and the Supreme Court, while hearing the petition or the appeal, shall follow the procedure as laid down in the Summary Procedure Act, 1971.

(5) Where the Appellate Court, upon any petition submitted to it, and after hearing the other party, comes to the conclusion that acquisition or requisition of property is not in the public interest or is likely to cause serious harm to persons or to the local environment, it may issue appropriate order to remedy the harm or mitigate the adverse environmental impact or

both. Where the Court deems it necessary, it may also issue the closure of the operation and restore the original status of the property.

9. *Call for Claims to Compensation for the Property to be acquired* : (1) The PIMC, shall after the declaration made by His Majesty's Government under sub-section (1) of section 8 is published, within a month, issue a public notification making a call for claim on compensation. A notice to all persons likely to be displaced and/or affected shall also be issued. The PIMC shall also require such persons to state the name and addresses of all persons interested in the compensation.

(2) The person receiving notification issued under sub-section (1), or any person interested in compensation, may within 30 days make a claim on the compensation for the property to be acquired. The PIMC shall also make arrangements for recording oral claims.

(3) If the PIMC is convinced that, the person interested in compensation was unable to make a submission within the stipulated time, it may, before the final decision on compensation is taken, allow such person to make submission with regard to his or claim on compensation.

10. *Basis and Consideration for Compensation:* (1) The basis of compensation shall be the replacement value at the date of actual displacement.

(2) While calculating the compensation, the PIMC shall take the following into account for consideration:

(a) Cost of the land to be acquired;
(b) Cost of the house, dwelling and other permanent structures to be acquired or demolished;
(c) Cost of shifting industry, should the area to be acquired have any;

(d) Damage caused to the land not acquired due to severing of land from other lands;

(e) Cost of grown or standing trees, orchards, crops multiplied by years till the new crops, trees, orchards start yielding;

(f) The benefit that the person to be displaced or affected shall derive from the common property resource;

(g) Livelihood of those who depend on land to be acquired for employment or service;

(h) The cost involved, if as a consequence of acquisition of property, a person is compelled to change his residence or place of business;

(i) Damage, if any, bonafide resulting from diminution of the value of property due to acquisition of other land;

(j) Diminution of value of property between the notification under sub-section (1) of section 3 and the actual acquisition;

(k) Increase in the value of property in adjoining locality;

(l) Future development possibility of the property;

(m) Loss of cultural and heritage site; and

(n) Opportunity cost that the person has to forgo due to displacement or change in habitation;

(o) Where resources are communally managed, cost to be incurred by person due to the loss of such resource;

(p) Where the project is likely to affect the minor, the elderly and the weak, cost required for education, health, and social security;

(q) Cost accruing from the loss of local or customary rights;

(r) Any other reasonable amount which the person needs to spend to bear the transitional cost and to restore the pre-displacement asset and earning capacity.

(2) The PIMC shall determine the tentative amount of compensation, and fix the date for discussion on the same and duly notify the person making claims, or any other person who in its opinion, has an interest in the compensation. The PIMC, while computing compensation may take the assistance of experts on the subject.

(3) If, after the discussion with the person making claim for compensation or any other person notified by the PMIC under sub-section (3), a mutually acceptable amount for compensation is agreed upon, the PMIC shall announce the award.

(4) Where no agreement on the compensation is reached between the PIMC and the person interested, the PIMC shall refer the matter to the District Court for determination.

(5) If, on the date fixed for discussion, or any other subsequent date no discussion on the tentative amount of compensation could not be held due to absence of person making claim or any other person interested in compensation, the PMIC shall declare the compensation tentatively determined under sub-section (3) as final. The PIMC shall, thereupon, communicate to persons claiming compensation or such other person having an interest in compensation.

(6) Any person aggrieved by the decision of the PIMC may file a petition with the District Court within 35 days of receiving the notice from the PIMC.

9. *Determination of Compensation by the Court:* (1) The District Court shall follow the procedure as laid down by the Summary Procedure Act, 1971 and dispose of the reference made by the

PIMC or any other petition filed to it for the determination of compensation.

(2) The Court may either fix the compensation by itself or lay down guidelines for determination of compensation and refer the case to the PIMC for making the award. The decision of the District Court on the issue shall be final and shall be acted upon accordingly.

11.*Persons Eligible for Claiming Compensation, Resettlement and Rehabilitation:* (1) All project affected persons individually or jointly are entitled to make claim for and receive compensation. Every member of the family shall, irrespective of the age or sex, shall be considered as a separate unit for claiming compensation.

(2) Any other person, who establishes that she or he has incurred a substantial economic loss due to project for reason whatsoever, is also entitled to make claim for compensation.

(3) The following persons shall be eligible for resettlement and rehabilitation:

a) Any person, whose 25 percent or more land or other property is acquired ;
b) Any person whose less than 25 percent land or other property is acquired, but due to acquisition, the economic standard dwindles below the poverty line;
c) Any person, whose remaining land, due to acquisition is, reduced to such a size which is not sufficient to meet the food requirement of the family for the year round;
d) Any person, who either due to acquisition of his land or acquisition of land in the neighborhood, is compelled to change his dwelling;

e) Any landless agricultural labourer, or any other person dependent on the land or persons whose land is to be acquired provided that such person for a continuous period of not less than three years immediately before the publication of the notification under sub-section (1) section 3 has been ordinarily residing or carrying on any trade, occupation or calling in the area to be acquired.

(4) There shall be no discrimination on the basis of sex, age, race, caste, religion, place of habitation or avocation or legality of holding for awarding compensation and resettlement and rehabilitation. Acquisition by mutual agreement shall not be a ground for denying claim for resettlement and rehabilitation if the project affected person is otherwise eligible for the same.

12. *Payment of Compensation and Devolution of Property to His Majesty's Government:* (1) Except in case it becomes urgently necessary to acquire or requisition land as mentioned in section 19, no person shall be displaced without compensation being paid and persons likely to be displaced being or be affected eligible for resettlement under sub-section (3) of section 11 being resettled.

(2) No property shall devolve to His Majesty's Government unless compensation is paid and persons eligible for resettlement are resettled.

13. *Compensation to be Adjusted With Resettlement Cost:* (1) Where a project affected person elects to resettle in the resettlement village created by His Majesty's Government or the PIMC, the compensation amount that such person is entitled to get shall be adjusted against the cost of property he or she is entitled to hold. The surplus amount, if any, shall be paid in cash.

(2) Where the amount of compensation that the project affected person is entitled to get is not sufficient to meet the cost of resettlement, the amount such person is liable to pay shall be obtained in suitable installments to be decided on mutual agreement commencing three years after the resettlement of such person takes place.

14. *Forms of Resettlement and Power of His Majesty's Government to Decline Land Based Resettlement:* (1) His Majesty's Government through the PIMC devise, declare one more forms of resettlements. For agricultural families, land based resettlement shall be mandatory.

(2) Notwithstanding anything mentioned in sub-section (2) His Majesty's Government, may declare any or all of the following persons as ineligible for land based resettlement and rehabilitation.

a) Person not directly involved by himself or through members of his family in cultivation or not ordinarily staying in the area to be acquired;
b) Person obtaining compensation at least five times higher than the income of the person at or below the poverty line;
c) Who is left with agricultural land more than the land intended to be given to the project affected persons;
d) Whose income from non-agricultural source is at least five times higher than the income of the person deriving income from the agriculture at the poverty line.

15.*Preparation of the Resettlement Plan and its Publication*: (1) His Majesty's Government shall create resettlement villages with a land pool in the agriculture zone of all five development regions having the facility for irrigation for resettling persons to be displaced or affected by any project in the Kingdom. Every resettlement village shall have the following facilities.

a) Plots for house site with at least 2000 sq. ft plinth area,
b) Agriculture land,
c) School,
d) Health Center,
e) Water supply and sanitation,
f) Access Road,
g) Electricity,
h) Play ground,
i) Common thrashing ground for agriculture produce,
j) Pasture land,
k) Cremation ground.

(2) Where His Majesty's Government has created resettlement village as provided in sub-section (1), it shall create a permanent government of semi-government body to plan and design, resettle and rehabilitate project affected persons in tandem with the PIMC and the Project In-Charge of the project causing displacement. His Majesty's Government, while creating resettlement villages and resettling the project affected persons, shall also be guided by the provisions laid down in section 14. The cost of such resettlement and rehabilitation operation shall be born out of the project requesting resettlement and rehabiliatation.

(3) If the PMIC, after assessing the view of the persons likely to require resettlement, comes to the conclusion that, in view of the interest of the project affected persons a separate resettlement plan is required, it shall as soon as the tentative number of people requiring resettlement is determined, prepare the resettlement and rehabilitation plan with the approval of His Majesty's Government and publish the same for

consideration of the project affected persons. The PIMC shall also communicate to the project affected persons giving option and requiring the response within two months of such communication.

(4) Any person eligible for resettlement but not notified under sub-section (3) may also apply to the PIMC if he or she elects to accept the resettlement plan prepared by the PIMC or by His Majesty's Government.

(5) The PIMC shall, if the project affected person eligible for resettlement through a written submission desires to make a visit of the site before giving consent to the resettlement plan, arrange for such visit of the resettlement site at its cost. The PIMC may, in case the project affected persons eligible for resettlement so requests, extend the time limit to consent or reject any of the resettlement plan by one more month after the expiry of the time under sub-section (3).

Provided that where the installation of basic amenities to the resettlement zone is incomplete, the PIMC shall give a reasonable time to the project affected persons either to accept or reject the resettlement and rehabilitation offer after the completion of the basic amenities works.

(6) The resettlement of the project affected persons shall, as far as possible be, carried out in the benefited zone of the project for which displacement is likely to take place or any of the resettlement villages created by His Majesty's Government at the choice of the person requiring resettlement and rehabilitation. In case where resettlement and rehabilitation plan is prepared by the PIMC, the resettlement site shall have all the facilities enumerated in sub-section (1).

(7) Where the project affected person has made a choice and informed the PIMC about his choice, a reasonable time shall be given to him or her to review the choice at least once.

Provided that in case of persons belonging to indigenous or other agro-based, socially and economically weaker section without any other viable means of earning or income, the right to go for cash compensation shall be honoured only with appropriate guarantee.

16. *Major Considerations for Resettlement and Rehabilitation:* (1) His Majesty's Government or the PIMC, as the case may be, shall, while fixing compensation and carrying out resettlement and rehabilitation operations ensure that the interest of the person to be displaced or affected is given importance.

(2) His Majesty's Government shall ensure that the project affected persons get benefit from the project for which the property is acquired or requisitioned in the form of free or preferential share, employment etc. It shall also ensure that the asset and earning capacity of the project affected persons is restored higher than it was prior to eviction.

(3) In case of people falling below the poverty line, His Majesty's Government shall link the resettlement and rehabilitation operation to the poverty alleviation programs and restore the living above the poverty line.

(4) The benefits and support to project affected person shall not be denied by reason of him or her electing to opt for cash compensation.

(5) His Majesty's Government shall ensure that no person displaced or affected by the project who is eligible for resettlement and rehabilitation is left homeless and without means of income after resettlement.

(6) The project affected persons shall as far as possible be resettled in group. Care shall also be taken to minimise the distance between the original site and the resettlement village.

(7) The minimum amount of agriculture land to be provided to the project affected family in the resettlement villages created by His Majesty's Government or by the PIMC, as the case may be, shall be determined keeping in mind the availability of irrigation, productivity of the land and the price index of the region for resettlement.

(8) The Property to be devolved to the project affected persons in the resettlement village shall be free of all encumbrances. The legitimate interests of project affected persons shall be kept in mind while transferring property to the project affected families.

(9) His Majesty's Government or the PIMC, as the case may be, shall give priority to the views of the project affected person as to what kind of resettlement and rehabilitation shall be suitable for him or her and as far as possible involve persons in the planning and execution of the resettlement and rehabilitation operations.

(10) His Majesty's Government or the PMIC, as the case may be, shall ensure that resettlement and rehabilitation results in mutual benefit to both host and the project affected person. For this, His Majesty's Government or the PIMC, as the case may be, shall devise measures to involve host community in the planning and execution of the resettlement and rehabilitation programme.

(11) His Majesty's Government or the PIMC, as the case may be, shall ensure that the project affected persons get better housing facilities and sanitation and better environment in the resettlement village. The PIMC shall take special care to meet the present and future need of the project affected persons in the resettlement village.

(12) His Majesty's Government or the PIMC, as the case may be, shall take special care to relocate community, cultural

and heritage sites in the new resettlement villages. The PIMC shall also ensure that the project for which land is acquired contribute to the overall development of the community

(13) His Majesty's Government or the PIMC, as the case may be, shall encourage the involvement of the project affected persons in design and construction of their houses and other facilities limiting itself to ensure that more spacious houses are constructed and better sanitary facilities are installed in the house.

17. *Payment of Compensation for Requisition of Property:* (1)His Majesty's Government may develop appropriate yardsticks for the payment of compensation in case where property is requisitioned in public interest.

(2) The property so requisitioned in public interest shall be treated as property under lease and shall devolve to the original owner, user, holder or his successor, as the case may be, after the expiry of the said duration for which it was requisitioned.

18. *Allocation of Budget, Payment of Compensation, Resettlement and Rehabilitation:* (1) His Majesty's Government shall ensure that compensation, resettlement and rehabilitation cost is included in the total project cost. It shall also cause allocation of sufficient budget for the completion of resettlement and rehabilitation operations.

(2) His Majesty's Government shall ensure that all rehabilitation operations are carried out and completed before the completion of the main construction work.

19. *Special Powers to Acquire or Requisition Property in Special Circumstance:* (1) Notwithstanding any thing contained elsewhere in this Act, in case it becomes urgently necessary for His Majesty's Government to acquire or requisition any

property to maintain transport or communication facilities or to ensure safety of life and property against extensive damage, or to protect any other public property in the event of sudden diversion of the course of any river, or any natural disaster or any other extraordinary circumstances, it may after taking decision, make declaration to that effect and order the Chief District Officer to initiate action for the acquisition or requisition of such property.

(2) Where a declaration has been made under sub-section (1), the Chief District Officer shall issue a notice to the persons giving them reasonable time to remove their belongings, valuables, stored food and other movable property. In such event the Chief District Officer shall make immediate arrangement for food, shelter, medicine and meet other transitional requirement of the person so displaced. Other resettlement and rehabilitation measures shall immediately follow.

20. *Resettlement and Rehabilitation in the Event of Multiple Displacement:* (1) His Majesty's Government shall, as far as possible, avoid multiple displacement of persons. (2) Where acquisition of property in public interest results in multiple displacement of person within twenty years of earlier displacement, such person shall be entitled to double the benefit that a project affected person normally gets. On every succeding displacement the benefit shall be similarly increased.

21. *Transitional Support:* (1) The PIMC shall extend support to project affected persons in the form of food, shelter, grant for the construction of house, seed for agriculture, fertilizer etc.

(2) In case of non-agricultural families, the PIMC shall extend support in the form of training, and creation of chances of employment and self-employment, preference in

construction activities in the project and other involvement in income generation measures.

(3) The PIMC shall also draw plans to diversify sources of income generation like intensive agriculture, establishment of industries, development of service sector, use of local niche etc.

22. *Suspension of Claim for Recovery of Debt or other Civil Proceedings:* No claim for recovery of debt or execution of court judgement can be filed against the project affected person at least for three years after resettlement.

23. *Reddressal of Grievance:* (1) Any person aggrieved by any decision of PIMC with regard to eligibility or ineligibility for resettlement and rehabilitation or any actions or decision of the PIMC or His Majesty's Government or both in the execution of resettlement and rehabilitation operation resulting in breach of contract or violation of basic human rights may file a petition to the Appellate Court for necessary instruction.

(2) The Appellate Court, after hearing the other party, may issue necessary order including the restitution of economic loss suffered and payment of other reasonable costs incurred by the petitioner.

(3) Where the Appellate Court, upon any petition filed to it, comes to the conclusion that a dereliction of duty or breach of law has occurred because of the action or inaction of any public servant or member of the PIMC, it may impose fine on such public servant or member of PIMC. The fine thus imposed shall be personally born and paid by such public servant or the member of PIMC. Once such fine is imposed on any person, he or she shall cease functioning in any capacity in the resettlement and rehabilitation operation.

24. *Coordination:* (1) His Majesty's Government shall extend

necessary assistance, guidance and issue instructions to authorities or the PIMC, as the case may be, involved in the planning and implementing the resettlement and rehabilitation operation.

(2) It shall be the duty of every officer of His Majesty's Government to assist authorities involved in the implementation of resettlement and rehabilitation operation.

(3) In case any law and order problem arises in the acquisition or requisition of property or planning and implementation of the resettlement and rehabilitation operation, it shall be the duty of Local Administration, the Police and the Armed forces to restore peace and order and assist the authorities in smoothly carrying out the execution of the planned action.

25. *Property to be Returned to the Original Owner or User:* (1) Where a property acquired in public interest is, in whole or in substantial part, not used for the said purpose for ten years after the title is devolved to His Majesty's Government, it shall return to the property to the original holder.

(2) Any person, whose property is acquired, if such property is not used for the stated purpose, may, at the expiry of ten years, file a petition with the Appellate Court for the return of the same property.

(3) Where His Majesty's Government or the Court, as the case may be, decide to return the property, it may require the original holder or his or her successor, to repay the compensation amount back to the His Majesty's Government. After the return of the said amount, the property shall devolve back to the original owner or user or holder.

26. *Restriction on the Use of Acquired or Requisitioned Property for other Purposes.* (1) No property acquired or requisitioned

in public interest shall be used for purposes, either by transfer or sell or any other form other than what originally it was acquired or requisitioned.

(2) In case anything contained in sub-section (1) happens, the original owner or holder or his successor, as the case may be, may file a petition to the Appellate Court for regaining such property.

(3) If the Appellate Court, after hearing the other party, finds that the property is being used for purposes other than the purpose for which it was acquired, it may issue appropriate order for restoring the property to the original owner or user or holder.

27.*Creation of Resettlement and Rehabilitation Support Fund:* (1) His Majesty's Government shall create a fund called "Resettlement and Rehabilitation Support Fund" to extend support to the project affected persons after resettlement.

(2) His Majesty's Government shall make arrangements to deposit a minimum of one percent of annual revenue to be generated by projects causing displacement in the said fund created under sub-section (1).

(3) The amount so deposited in the Fund under sub-section (2) shall be used for assisting the project affected persons in restoring their income and earning capacity after resettlement by devising appropriate means and opportunities for income generation as decided by the Committee constituted under section 28.

28. *Coordination, Monitoring, Evaluation, Research etc.:* (1) His Majesty's Government shall constitute a Committee for coordination, monitoring, evaluation and research on different aspects of project induced displacement, resettlement and rehabilitation in the Kingdom of Nepal. The Composition of the Committee shall be as follows:

a)	Representative of the Ministry of Finance	Chairman
b)	Representative of the Ministry of Housing and Physical Planning	Member
c)	Representative of the Ministry of Law and Justice	Member
d)	Representative of the Ministry of Local Development	Member
e)	Representative of the Ministry of Environment	Member
f)	Representative of the Ministry of Social Welfare	Member
g)	At least two persons representing Non-Governmental Organization Working in the field of project induced displacement	Member
h)	At least five representative of the project affected persons elected by them for a period of 4 years	Member

(2) The Committee shall coordinate, monitor, evaluate the resettlement and rehabilitation activities of the PIMC and other authorities involved in resettlement and rehabilitation.

(3) The Committee shall allocate amount for post resettlement support to the project affected persons. Such support shall continue till the income and earning capacity of the project affected persons is restored to a higher level than they were before moving from the original habitat.

29. *Overriding Effect:* Notwithstanding anything contained in any law in force in the Kingdom of Nepal, this Act shall apply in the acquisition and requisition of property, resettlement and rehabilitation of persons.

30. *Power to Make Rules:* His Majesty's Government may make rules to implement the objectives of this Act.

31. *Repeal and Saving:* (1) Any activities carried out and completed under the prevailing law shall not be called into question for being against any provision laid down in this Act.

(2) With the commencement of this Act the following Acts shall stand repealed:

a) The Land Acquisition Act, 1977
b) The Immovable Property Requisition Act, 1955
c) The Compensation Act, 1962

ANNEXURE 2

LAND ACQUISITION ACT 1977

[Nepal Gazette Vol. 27. No 25 (Extraordinary), Bhadra 22, 2034 (September 7, 1977)]

The following law, enacted by His Majesty Kind Birendra Bir Bikram Shah Dev on the advice and with the approval of the National Panchayat, is published for the information of the public.

A Law Enacted to Amend and Consolidate Current Nepal Legislation Pertaining to Land Acquisition

Preamble: It is expedient to amend and consolidate, current Nepal legislation pertaining to land acquisition, now therefore, His Majesty King Birendra Bir Bikram Shah Dev has enacted this law on the advice and approval of the National Panchayat.

1. *Short Title, Extent and Commencement*

(1) This law may be called the *Land Acquisition Act, 1977*

(2) It shall be applicable throughout the Kingdom of Nepal

(3) It shall come into force at once.

2. *Definitions*

Unless otherwise meant with reference to the subject or context, in this Act:

(a) *Land* means any land belonging to any person and walls, buildings, trees etc., permanently located thereon. The term includes any object permanently installed thereon.

(b) *Public Purposes* mean functions undertaken in the interest of or for the benefit or use of the general public, or function to be undertaken by His majesty's Government. The term included the following:

(1) Project approved by His Majesty's Government.

(2) Projects undertaken by Panchayat at different levels.

(c) *Local Officer* means an officer designated by His Majesty's Government, where no such officer is designated, the Chief District Officer.

(d) *Concerned person* means the person who is entitled to the compensation payable for lands acquired under this Act.

(e) *Institution* means a company, development board, or corporation established or formed according to current law.

3. *Power of His Majesty's Government to Acquire Lands for Public Purposes*

His Majesty's Government may, if it so deems necessary acquire any land at any place for any public purpose, subject to compensation under this law.

4. *Power to Acquire Land for Any Institution*

(1) In case any institution requests His Majesty's Government for the acquisition of any land for any of the following purposes, subject to payment of compensation and all other expenses under this Act, His Majesty's Government may decide to have the land acquired for institution: -

(a) To construct residential quarters for the staff, workers or laborers of the institution, or otherwise provide for their welfare, or undertake any function in the interest of the general public.

(b) To operate a project connected with an institution fully owned by His Majesty's Government, or to construct a godown for the storage of any commodity or material connected with or manufactured by any such institution.

(2) Proceedings regarding the acquisition of land under this Act shall not be initiated unless the institution requesting for land acquisition has executed a deed in respect to the following matters:

(a) Payment to His Majesty's Government of all the expenses incurred or likely to be incurred for the acquisition of the land.

(b) If the land is meant for the construction of residential quarters for workers or technical personnel, or for any function intended for their comfort, the period required for the completion of such building, the design or type thereof, and the period for which it will be maintained.

(c) If the land is meant for any other construction purpose, the time limit for the completion thereof, and the purpose for which it will be used.

(3) Notwithstanding anything contained in sub-section (1) in case such institution is required to undertake farming for executing its project, His Majesty's Government shall not acquire land for it under this Act for farming any type other than experimental farming for research purposes.

5. *Decision on Land Acquisition and Authority Competent to Initiate Preliminary Action*

(1) After His Majesty's Government has decided to acquire land for the purposes mentioned in section 3 or section 4, an employee of at least gazetted third class rank belonging to the office for which the land is to be acquired, and, where he is not available, the chief of such office, and if the land is meant

for any project chief of such project, may initiate preliminary action to determine the area of land to be acquired at any specified place.

(2) Notwithstanding anything contained in sub-section (1), in case the concerned institution requests for the nomination of its own employees for initiating preliminary action as mentioned therein while acquiring land for itself, His Majesty's Government may issue orders empowering any employee at least of the rank of officer designated by such institution to initiate such preliminary action.

6. *Preliminary Action Regarding Land Acquisition*

(1) The officer who initiates preliminary action under section 5 shall affix one copy of a noticc at each of the following offices or places for the information of the concerned persons:

(a) At thoroughfare around the concerned land,
(b) At the appropriate village or Town Panchayat Office,
(c) At the house or compound wall, if it too is to be acquired.

(2) After three days following a notice being issued under sub-section (1), the officer may enter into the concerned land, or house or compound, along with employees or workers in the necessary number, for taking any of the following actions:

(a) Prepare a map of or survey such land,
(b) Collect sample of soil, stone, etc., dig ditches or conduct boring to determine whether or not it is suitable for acquisition.
(c) Erect pillars, etc., or otherwise determine lands considered suitable for acquisition,
(d) Install any equipment for any of the operations mentioned in Clause (a) or Clause (b).

(3) In case the concerned person is not satisfied with the amount of compensation determined under sub-section (2), he may file a complaint with the Chief District Officer within fifteen days from the date on which he receives information thereof, and in such cases the decision of the Chief District Officer shall be final.

8. *Report to be Submitted in Respect to Findings of Preliminary Action*

(1) The officer responsible for preliminary action shall complete such action within fifteen days from the date of starting it, determine whether the land is suitable for acquisition, and then submit a report containing necessary information in respect to such action to the local officer as early as possible.

(2) The report to be submitted under sub-section (1) shall also mention the amount of compensation determined under sub-section (2) of section 7, and contain full particulars of losses.

9. *Notification of Land Acquisition*

(1) After receiving a report of preliminary action submitted under section 8, the local officer shall issue a notification containing the following particulars in respect to the land:

(a) The purpose for which the land is to be acquired,
(b) Whether only the land is to be acquired, or whether it is to be acquired along with the houses and walls located thereon.
(c) The name of the Panchayat and ward number which the land is located,
(d) The plot number, if the land has already been surveyed and measured.

(e) If the land has not already been surveyed and measured, such particulars as will help to identify it, and particulars regarding the boundaries thereof,

(f) Area of land,

(g) Other necessary particulars,

(2) One copy of the notice mentioned in sub-section (1) shall be affixed at one of the following offices or places:

(a) The local office of the project for which land is to be acquired,

(b) District government office,

(c) The appropriate village or town Panchayat,

(d) The Land Administration or revenue Office,

(e) Thoroughfares located around the concerned land,

(f) Such other place as the local officer may deem appropriate.

(3) In case the local officer is satisfied that the concerned person will not be able to know (about the land acquisition) notwithstanding the publication of a notice under sub-section (1), he may, if he so deems appropriate and feasible, personally send a notice to such person. In case the amount of compensation has already been determined by the time such notice is delivered to such person, the local officer shall also indicate in such notice the period within which he should appear for receiving the compensation, and the name of the office from where he should do so.

(4) After the notice mentioned in sub-section (1) has been affixed, the appropriate Land Administration or Revenue Office shall suspend the registration of documents relinquishing title to the concerned land in any manner. The suspension shall be lifted in case the local officer directs the Land Administration or Revenue Office in writing to that effect.

10. *Particulars to be Given in Notice Relating to Land Acquisition:*

The notice to be issued under sub-section (1) of section 9 shall also indicate the following particulars for the information of the concerned person:

(a) Particulars to the effect that the concerned person shall submit an application claiming compensation within a minimum time-limit of fifteen days, along with documentary evidence of his title to the land,

(b) The time-limit within which the concerned person will be allowed to fell trees or crops grown by him on the land, and demolish houses or walls located therein, if he is permitted to do so.

11. *Right of land owner to File Complaint*

(1) Within a time-limit of seven days from the date of publication of a notice under section 9, plus the time required for the journey involved, the concerned land owner may file a complaint with the Zonal Commissioner through local officer, explaining the reasons, if he has any, why his land should not be acquired. If the tenant has built any brick-house on the land with the consent of the landowner such tenant may also file a complaint under this sub-section with respect to such house and the land occupied by it.

(2) Before taking a decision on the complaint filed under sub-section (2), the concerned Zonal Commissioner shall consult the officer responsible for preliminary action, and if necessary, the local officer as well.

(3) For the purpose of taking decisions in respect to the complaints filed under sub-section (1), the Zonal Commissioner hearing complaints under this section shall exercise the powers vested in a district court, in respect to conducting local investigations, summoning witnesses, recording statements

or procuring documents.

(4) Decision on complaints to be made under sub-section (2) shall be pronounced ordinarily within fifteen days from the date of receipt of such complaints.

12. *Power to Occupy Land:*

(1) The local officer shall take possession of the concerned land and hand it over to the office or institution for which it is acquired after a decision has been made on complaints, if any, filled under sub-section (1) of section 11 after the publication of the notice under sub-section (1) of section 9, or at any time after the expiry of the time-limit for filing complaints, if no complaint has been received, such land may then be utilized for the purpose for which it is acquired. After taking possession of the land in this manner, the local officer shall notify His Majesty's Government accordingly.

(2) Notwithstanding anything contained in sub-section (1), in case any house is to be acquired along with the land, and if it is being occupied personally by the owner thereof, it shall not be taken possession of (by the local officer) unless (the owner thereof) is paid 50 percent of the amount of compensation payable to him, if such compensation has already been determined, or reasonable expenses in advancing required to enable him to shift his residence, if the amount of compensation has not already been determined.

13. *Form of Compensation and Officer Empowered to Determine It:*

(1) Compensation payable under this Act shall be paid in cash.

(2) There shall be a Committee consisting of the following officers to determine the amount of compensation payable under sub-section (1).

(a) Chief District Officer,
(b) Land Administrator or Chief of the Revenue Office,
(c) The project-in-chief, if the land has been acquired for a project, and if it has been acquired for any other purpose, an officer designated by the Zonal Commissioner,
(d) A representative of the District Panchayat.

(3) Notwithstanding anything-contained in sub-section (1), the amount of compensation may be determined separately in the case of persons whose land is wholly acquired, and of those whose land is partially acquired.

14. *Allotment of Other Lands in Exchange*

In case any person whose land is wholly acquired under this Act wants to obtain compensation in the form of land elsewhere, His Majesty's Government may, in exchange for such land, allot him any waste land, or land belonging to itself, or any other land which it is going to allot or sell in accordance with current Nepal law, if available.

15. *Compensation for Guthi Lands:*

In the case of Guthi lands acquired under this Act, compensation shall be paid in accordance with the provisions of the 1976 Guthi Corporation Act.

16. *Criteria to be considered while Determining Compensation*

(1) The Compensation Fixation Committee shall take the following criteria into consideration while determining compensation for lands to be acquired for His Majesty's Government, Panchayats, and institutions fully owned by His Majesty's Government:

(a) The guidelines provided by His Majesty's Government from time to time in respect to the fixation of compensation and,

(b) The losses suffered by the concerned person as a result of his having been required to shift his residence or the place of his business by reason of acquisition of his land.

(2) While determining the amount of compensation for land to be acquired for institutions other than Panchayats and institutions fully owned by His Majesty's Government, the Compensation Fixation Committee shall take the following criteria into consideration:

(a) The price of the land current at the time of publication of a notice of land acquisition under section 9.

(b) The value of the crop, houses, walls, sheds, etc., if any, acquired along with the land,

(c) The losses which the concerned person will suffer as a result of his having been required to shift his residence, or the place of his business, by reason of the acquisition of his land.

17. *Determination of Compensation for Land Acquired Out of Surplus Lands*

Notwithstanding anything contained in section 16, in case the land to be acquired for His Majesty's Government, Panchayats or institutions fully owned by His Majesty's Government on being found to be in excess of the ceiling on landholding prescribed in the 1964 Land Act, the amount of compensation therefore shall not exceed the amount payable under the 1964 Lands Act.

18. *List of Persons Entitled to Compensation and Complaints Thereagainst*

(1) On the basis of the applications received within the

time-limit prescribed in the notification issued under section 9, the local officer shall prepare a lost of persons entitled to compensation, and issue a notice accordingly for the information of the concerned persons.

(2) Any person who is not satisfied with the list contained in the notification issued under sub-section (2) may file a complaint with the Zonal Commissioner within fifteen days after the publication of such notification.

(3) In case any complaint filed under sub-section (2) relates to questions other than those involving a dispute over ownership or possession, the Zonal Commissioner shall dispose of the same ordinarily within fifteen days. But in case such complaint concerns a dispute over ownership or possession, no action shall be taken thereon, and a notice stating that compensation shall be paid to the person who establishes his title through the final decision of the court shall be served on the concerned person. Such notice shall also indicate the name of the office which will hold custody of the amount of compensation.

(4) The person who establishes his claim on the basis of the final decision pronounced by the court on a case relating to dispute over ownership or possession shall receive the amount kept in custody under sub-section (3) within two years after such final decision. In case such person fails to receive the amount kept in custody after the expiry of that time-limit, it shall be credited to the Consolidated Fund.

19. *Notice to be given After Fixation of Compensation*

After the Compensation Fixation Committee has determined the amount of compensation, the Chief District Officer shall notify His Majesty's Government accordingly.

20. *Compensation to be Obtained by Tenants*

In case the land to be acquired under this Act is a tenancy holding, 25 percent or the amount of compensation payable for such land shall be obtained by the tenant. Provided that in case a house constructed by the tenant with the consent of the landowner is also acquired, the tenant shall receive the entire amount of compensation paid for such house.

21. *Arrears Due to the Government may be Deducted from Compensation*

In case any amount of land or other tax or levy is due from the concerned person at the time of payment of compensation for his land, it may be deducted from such compensation.

22. *Devaluation of Ownership*

After any land has been taken possession of (by the local officer) under section 12, the ownership thereof shall accrue to His Majesty's Government or to any institution for which the land has been acquired.

23. *Transfer of Title and Adjustment in Land Tax Assessment Register*

(1) Within fifteen days after taking possession of land ownership of which has accrued to His Majesty's Government or any institution under section 22, the local officer shall write to the office possessing records of such land to effect the transfer thereof of to His Majesty's Government, or to the concerned institution, as the case may be, after removing entries thereof in the land tax assessment records and such office shall do so, and notify the local officer and the outgoing landowner accordingly as early as possible.

(2) Adjustment in records and transfer of title to the land shall be deemed to have been effected from the date of accrual of ownership thereof, irrespective of the date on which removal or transfer has been actually been effectuated.

(3) In case the records of land acquired under Nepal Law in force immediately before the commencement of this Act do not appear to have been adjusted, these shall be deemed to have been *ip so facto* adjusted after the commencement of this ıct.

24. *No Effect on Circumstance Existing Prior to Transfer of Ownership*

(1) In case any land or other tax is due from the expropriated landowners till the day preceding the accrual of ownership of his land to His Majesty's Government or to any institution under this Act, this section shall not be deemed to have affected the power to take action to recover such arrears from him even after the transfer of ownership of his land.

(2) In case any tenancy holding is acquired, nothing contained in this section shall be deemed to have affected the right of the expropriated landowner to initiate action to recover arrears of rent due from the tenant for the period preceding the acquisition.

25. *Special Powers to Acquire Land in Special Circumstances*

(1) In case it becomes urgently necessary for His Majesty's Government to acquire any land to maintain transport or communication facilities, or to ensure safety of life and property against extensive damage, or to protect any other public property in the event of sudden diversion of the course of any river, or any natural disaster, or any other extraordinary circumstance, it may notwithstanding anything contained elsewhere in this Act, order the local officer to initiate action for the acquisition of such land after making a decision to that effect.

(2) In relation to the land to be acquired for the purposes mentioned in Clause (1), (the local officer) shall issue a notice

for the information of the concerned persons, containing such of the particulars mentioned in sub-section (1) as are available. Such notice may be issued in any form he may deem appropriate, after being satisfied that the concerned persons will be informed of it as early as possible.

(3) The local officer may occupy land at any time after the issue of a notice under sub-section (2), and the ownership of His Majesty's Government over such land shall be effective from the date of the occupation of such land.

(4) In case any crop, tree, house or wall standing on land to be acquired under this section is acquired along with the land, the concerned person shall be paid compensation therefor.

(5) Compensation for land to be acquired under this section shall be determined by the Compensation Fixation Committee formed under section 13.

(6) Except in cases relating to the amount of compensation no complaint against the acquisition of land shall be entertained.

(7) Any person who is not satisfied with the amount of compensation may file a complaint with the Zonal Commissioner within fifteen days from the date of the issue of the notice of fixation of compensation, and in such cases, the decision of the Zonal Commissioner shall be final.

(8) In regard to the removal of entries in the land tax assessment records of lands acquired under this section, the local officer shall take action on the basis of the procedure indicated in section 23. The provisions of section 24 shall also be applicable to such lands.

26. *Consent of Landowner*

In case His Majesty's Government has already used any land for any public purpose, compensation payable for such land, even if it has not been acquired in accordance with the provisions of this Act, may be determined under this Act, provided that the concerned landowner gives his consent to do so. Such land shall be deemed to have been acquired under this Act after compensation has been determined in this manner.

27. *Acquisition of Land Through Negotiation*

Notwithstanding anything contained elsewhere in this Act, His Majesty's Government may acquire any land for any purpose through negotiations with the concerned landowner. It shall not be necessary to comply with the procedure laid down in this Act while acquiring land through negotiations.

28. *Power to Acquire Lands for Diplomatic Missions and International Agencies*

(1) Lands may be acquired under this Act on behalf of diplomatic missions, including consulates, and of international agencies.

(2) Compensation for lands to be acquired under sub-section (1) shall be determined in accordance with sub section (2) of section 16.

29. *Acquisition of Land Along With Buildings etc.*

In case the concerned person submits an application requesting that all crops, trees, walls, buildings etc., located on the land which is to be acquired under this Act also be acquired, action shall be taken accordingly.

30. *Power of His Majesty's Government to Take Decision Not to Acquire Land*

(1) At any stage of the proceedings already started for the acquisition of land under this Act, His Majesty's Government

may decide not to acquire the same, and in such cases, the local officer shall affix a notice under sub-section (2) of section 9 for the information of the concerned persons.

(2) Irrespective of whether proceedings in respect to the acquisition of lands (are stated, if any losses are suffered as a result of preliminary) action initiated under section 6, the officer responsible for such action shall determine the amount of compensation under section 7, where it has not already been paid.

31 *No Tenancy Right on Land Given to Others for Cultivation*

His Majesty's Government or any institution may let any land acquired under this Act for cultivation by any person on contract until it is used for the purpose for which it has been acquired. Such cultivator shall not be entitled to tenancy rights according to current Nepal law by virtue of his cultivation of such land in this manner.

32. *Confiscation of Building Constructed or Crops Grown Without Permission*

(1) After the ownership of land acquired under this Act has been devolved on His Majesty's Government, or on any institution, no person shall construct any buildings, shed, wall etc., on such land, or cultivate it without the written approval of His Majesty's Government or the concerned institution.

(2) In case any person constructs any building, shed, wall etc., or cultivation of land in contravention of sub-section (1), His Majesty's Government or the concerned institution, may confiscate such structure, or the crop grown on the land, without paying compensation.

33. *Power to Use Land for Purpose Different from the one for Which it is Acquired*

In case the land acquired under this Act for His Majesty's Government or any institution fully owned by it is not necessary for the purpose for which it has been acquired, or in case any surplus land is left after use for such purpose, the land which is thus rendered unnecessary or surplus may be used for any other purpose, it has been acquired for His Majesty's Government, and for any of the purposes mentioned in sub-section (1) of section 4 if it has been acquired for institution.

34. *Land Found Unnecessary to be Returned to Expropriated Landowner.*

(1) If any land acquired under this Act is found unnecessary for the purpose for which it has been acquired, or in case any surplus is left after the use of any land for such purpose, it shall be restored to the expropriated land owner, unless it is otherwise utilitised by His Majesty's Government or an institution fully owned by it under section 33.

(2) In case any land acquired under this Act for any institution other than one fully owned by His Majesty's Government is not utilised under sub-section (2) of section 4, such land shall be returned to the expropriated landowner.

(3) Notwithstanding anything contained in sub-sections (1) and (2), no land shall be returned under this section unless the expropriated landowner has refunded the amount of compensation paid for such land under this Act.

(4) It shall be the responsibility of the local officer to return the land on refund of compensation and additional funds by the expropriated landowner under this Act.

(5) After land has been returned to the expropriated land owner, the local officer shall direct the appropriate officer in writing to have it determined to such landowner, and the appropriate office shall then act and notify the local officer accordingly.

35. *Power to Sell Land which Has Been Acquired*

In case the expropriated landowner refuses to get back the land to be returned under section, 34, or is not traced, it may be sold to any other person.

36. *Goods Not to be Returned if Not Lifted Within Prescribed Time-Limit*

In case the person permitted to lift the crop, tree, or building or well constructed on any land in accordance with the different provisions of this Act fails to do so within the prescribed time limit, the local officer may impound the same, and no claim by such person to such crops, trees, house, or wall shall be determined.

37. *Compensation to be Received Within Prescribed Time-Limit*

In case the concerned person fails to receive compensation within the time limit prescribed for the purpose under different provisions of this Act, or refuses to accept it , the local officer shall issue a notice prescribing a final time limit of three months for receiving such compensation. In case the concerned person fails to receive compensation even which such time limit, he shall not be entitled to any compensation.

38. *Local Officer to Provide Assistance*

Any officer who is empowered under this Act to perform any action may request the Zonal Commissioner, the Chief District Officer, or the police for assistance in the course thereof, and in that event, the Zonal Commissioner, the Chief District Officer, or the police shall provide assistance.

39. *Penalties*

(1) In case any person opposes or obstructs any action being taken under section 6, or mobs the persons who are taking such action, or assaults them, or destroys any equipment

installed or erected, or erase or damages any marker or map installed or made in the course of such action, he shall be punished with a fine not exceeding one thousand rupees, or with imprisonment for a term not exceeding one month or with both.

(2) In case any person opposes or obstructs the afixature of notices, or creates disturbances while this is being done, he shall be punished with fine not exceeding Rs 1,000.

(3) In case any person opposes or obstructs or the occupation of land or creates disturbances, while this is being done by the local officer under sub-section (3) of section 25, he shall be punished with a fine not exceeding Rs 1,000 or with imprisonment for a term not exceeding one month or with both.

40. *Authority Empowered to Hear Cases and Appeals*

(1) The original jurisdiction in respect to offenses punishable under this Act shall vest in the local Chief District Officer.

(2) Appeals filed against any decision made by the Chief District Officer under sub-section (1) shall be entertained by the Zonal court is filed within thirty-five days.

41. *His Majesty's Government to be Plaintiff*

His Majesty's Government shall be the plaintiff in all cases filed under this Act.

42. *Power to Frame Rules*

His Majesty's Government may frame rules to implement the objectives of this Act.

43. *Repeal and saving*

(1) The 1961 Land Acquisition Act has been repealed.

(2) Any action taken for the purpose of acquisition of land under the 1961 Land Acquisition Act at the time of the commence of this Act shall be deemed to have been taken under this Act after the commencement thereof and may be continued as if it was started under this Act.

Royal Seal Affixed on Bhadra 22, 2034 (September 7, 1977)

ANNEXURE 3

INTERNATIONAL CONVENTIONS ON HUMAN RIGTHS AND ENVIRONMENT TO WHICH NEPAL IS A PARTY

S.No.	*Conventions*	*Date of ratification or accession*
1	Slavery Convention 1926, amended by the Protocol 1953	Jan 7, 1963 (A)
2.	Supplementary Convention on the Abolition of Slavery, the Slave Trade and Practices Similar to Slavery 1956	Jan 7, 1963(A)
3.	Convention on the Prevention and Punishment of the Crime of Genocide 1948	Jan 17, 1969(A)
4.	International Convention on the Elimination of All Forms of Racial Discrimination 1966	June 30,1971(A)
5.	International Covenant on Civil and Political Rights 1966	May 14,1991(A)
6.	International Covenant on Economic Social and Cultural Rights 1966	May 14, 1991 (A)
7.	The Optional Protocol on International Covenant on Civil and Political Rights 1966	May 14, 1991(A)
8.	Second Optional Protocol to the ICCPR aiming at the Abolition of the Death Penalty 1989	Sept 26, 1997(A)
9.	Convention on the Elimination of All Forms of Discrimination Against Women 1979	Apr 22, 1991(R)
10.	Convention Against Torture and Other Cruel Inhuman or Degrading Treatment or Punishment 1984	May 14, 1991
11.	International Convention Against Apartheid in Sports 1985	March1,1989(R)
12	Convention on Political Rights of the Women 1953	Apr. 26 1966 (A)
13.	Convention on the Right of the Child 1989	Sept 14,1990 (R)
14.	Convention for the Suppression of the Traffic in Persons 1949	Dec 27, 1995(A)

15	International Convention on the Suppression and Punishment of the Crime of Apartheid 1973	July 1977 (A)
16	Plant Protection Agreement for the South-East Asia and Pacific Region, Rome 1956	Aug. 12,1965(A)
17.	Convention on the High Seas, Geneva 1956	Dec. 28, 1962 (R)
18.	Treaty Banning Nuclear Weapons Tests in the Atmosphere, in Outer Space and under Water, Moscow 1963	Oct. 7, 1964 (R)
19	Convention on Wetlands of International Importance Especially as Waterfowl Habitat, Ramsar 1971	Dec. 17, 1987 (A)
20	Treaty on the Prohibition of the Emplacement of Nuclear Weapons and Other Weapons of Mass Destruction on the Sea Bed and the Ocean Floor and the Subsoil Thereof, London, Moscow, Washington, 1971	July 6, 1971
21	Convention Concerning the Protection of the World Cultural and Natural Heritage, 1972	June 20, 1978
22	Convention on the Prevention of Marine Pollution by Dumping of Wastes and other matter, 1972	Jan 1, 1973(R)
23	Convention on International Trade in Endangered Species of Wild Fauna and Flora, 1973	June18, 1973
24	Vienna Convention on Protection of Ozone Layer, 1985	
25	Montreal Protocol on Substance that Deplete the Ozone Layer 1987	
26	Agreement on the Network of Aqua Culture in Asia and the Pacific 1988	Apr. 4, 1990 (R)
27	United Nation Framework Convention on Climate Change 1992	May 2 1994 (R)
28	Convention on Biological Diversity 1992	Nov. 23, 1993 (R)
29	Convention on the Control of Trans-boundary Movements of Hazardous Wastes and their Disposal, Basal 1989	Aug. 1994 (R)